PRAISE FOR WIND I

"*Wind in My Wheels* by Jan Down chronicles an amazing feat: she and her husband bicycled across all fifty states of the USA. Yes, all fifty. *Wind in My Wheels* is filled with details, humor, and the reality of biking over 20,000 miles. You feel like you're traveling alongside Jan as she describes the scenery, numerous historical sites, and the nitty-gritty aspects of long rides—traffic, flat tires, storms, exhaustion, and oh, let's not forget the hills, hill, hills. *Wind in My Wheels* is a must-read."
—Mary Jedlicka Humston, co-author, *Mary and Me: A Lasting Link Through Ink*

"*Wind In My Wheels* will appeal to all who follow their dreams, rise to a challenge and cherish friendships, old and new. Bicyclist or not, you will enjoy the way Jan Down has woven her tale of bicycling across all fifty states, alongside husband Jim. This book is written with historical content, many funny stories, stories of triumphs, mishaps and adventures. Jan's writing captures the vast diversity of people, places and geography in our USA while she pedals mile after mile with her 'can do' attitude."
—Dan Nidey, founder World of Bikes, Iowa City, Iowa

"*Wind in my Wheels* is a delightful memoir by Jan Down, a teacher who, over a period of thirty years, spent vacations with her husband, Jim, an orthodontist, and various friends bicycling border to border through all of America's fifty states. An exciting travelogue, but much more, it is filled with humor, occasional sadness, suspense, lovely descriptive language covering moments of high drama and often of contentment and joy. This is an exhilarating read from first page to last."
—Ethel Barker, author, *For the Love of Pete* and *The Andersens of Eden*

"In a beautifully written memoir, Jan Down shares in great detail the realization of her dream to bicycle across every state, border to border. She provides so much more than descriptions of bicycling terrains, ups and downs, in fifty states. She shares the people—bicyclists and locals, the history of remarkable places discovered, and the call of poetry and song that the diverse landscapes and cultures imparted. For the reader, this is a colorful journey shared in very personal terms. For a fellow cyclist on many of these trips it is a welcome reminder of a great life adventure."—Sandra Schuldt, long distance cyclist

"A word of advice. Don't be dissuaded from picking up *Wind in My Wheels* if you don't happen to be a bicycling enthusiast. That would be doing yourself a grave disservice. This book is about much more. It is a history of our country showcased with fascinating and ofttimes obscure facts to capture your imagination. It is a fresh metaphor of life wrapped in tales and adventures of an inspired journey, the goal being to bike all fifty states in the USA. Exceptional writing creates ease and a sensation of camaraderie, causes shared moments of weather in your face, satisfaction of eating when you're really hungry and the unnerving anxiety of traffic cruising by way too close for comfort. True kindness expressed genuinely by total strangers kindles a glowing ember of faith in our shared humanity. One feels they've experienced the adventure right alongside Jan Down and friends. Humor, wild situations, hardships, losses, ecstasy provided by tailwinds while spinning through God's masterful creation, stack up to provide a worthwhile read, and then some. The author's writing style is a pleasure. Engaging and inviting, it goes down easy. One feels one has accomplished the dream, right along side the dedicated and spirited team that made it all come true. The narrative is not mere fluff, these stories are filled with reverence. There are sacred moments to partake of inside the cover. Now, open it!"
—Suzee Carson Branch, author, *Under a Tie Dye Sky*

WIND IN MY WHEELS

JAN DOWN

Enjoy the ride!
Jan Down

Ice Cube Press, LLC
North Liberty, Iowa, USA

Wind In My Wheels

First Edition

ISBN 9781948509268

Library of Congress Control Number: 2021938320

Ice Cube Press, LLC (Est. 1991)
1180 Hauer Drive
North Liberty, Iowa 52317 USA
www.icecubepress.com | steve@icecubepress.com

The paper used in this publication meets the minimum
requirements of the American National Standard
for Information Sciences—Permanence of Paper for
Printed Library Materials, ANSI Z39.48-1992.

Manufactured in USA using recycled paper.

Front cover photo: Jan and Jim in Wyoming
Back cover photo: Jan on lonely road in West Virginia

Photos courtesy of: John Carlson, Mary Down,
Tania Down, Jim Down, Jan Down, Ray
Haas, Dave Schuldt, Sandra Schuldt

DEDICATION

To all those who have shared my journey,
especially my life-love Jim,
our children Mara, Tania, Jennifer, Doug, Bernd,
and our grandchildren Cameron, Ryan and Priyanka.

CONTENTS | SPOKES

Dedication	5
To the Reader	9
1. In the Beginning… And Then…	10
2. RAGBRAI Miles	14
3. Kansas-1980	24
4. New York-Vermont-Massachusetts-Connecticut-1981	35
5. Florida-1982	51
6. Mississippi-Alabama-1983	54
7. Minnesota-1983	58
8. Washington-1983	62
9. Texas Part 1-1984	68
10. Wisconsin-1984	71
11. District of Columbia-Maryland-Delaware-1985	76
12. Illinois-Indiana-1985	80
13. Ohio-1986	82
14. Pennsylvania-1986	88
15. Michigan-1987	94
16. Louisiana-1988	99
17. Virginia-1989	106
18. Colorado-North to South-1989	110
19. New Jersey-Rhode Island-1989	117
20. North Carolina-1990	120
21. Oklahoma-1991	124
22. Natchez Trace-1992	128
23. West Virginia-1992	135
24. Haleakala, Maui-1993	141
25. North Carolina-South Carolina-1993	144
26. South Carolina-Georgia-1994	149
27. Georgia-Florida-1995	153
28. Alaska-1999	158
29. Kauai-1996	181
30. Oregon-1996	192
31. Arkansas-1997	207

32. South Dakota-1997   211
33. Texas Part 2-1999   221
34. Idaho-Montana-1999   224
35. Missouri-1999   235
36. Tennessee-Kentucky-2000   239
37. Wyoming-2000   245
38. Nebraska-2001   263
39. New Hampshire-Maine-2001   276
40. Texas Part 3-2003   286
41. Montana-North Dakota-2003   289
42. California-East to West-2003   294
43. Big Island, Hawaii-2004   297
44. But What About the Van?   304
45. Arizona-New Mexico-2004   306
46. Nevada-Utah-2005   317
47. Colorado-West to East-2006   342
48. Bicycling Blues   348
49. California Coast Part 1-2008   350
50. Molokai-Maui-2009   367
51. Mystery in Maui   373
52. Borthwick the Beautiful   375
53. Woods, Porta-potties and Other Joys   378
54. California Coast Part 2-2011   380
55. In Retrospect   393
56. More Roadside Attractions   394
57. In Gratitude   402
58. About the Author   409

TO THE READER

Once upon a time someone told a little farm girl something that puzzled her, "You're just like your dad and your brother. You were born under a wandering star." She wondered what that meant but just smiled and didn't ask. She thought and thought and finally realized she was a dreamer, she liked to sit in a tree to read and think about what could happen in the future. And she always wanted to see what was on the other side of the next hill.

When her parents gave her and her brother shiny new bicycles, she stood at the top of the lane straddling hers, looking at the hill ahead of her. She had no way of knowing what vistas would open for her nor did she dream that two wheels would take her places she could never have imagined.

Decades later as I thought of that little girl—me—I recalled my physical, spiritual, mental and psychological quests during that incredible interlude. Reflecting on that time, I envisioned a crazy quilt, a montage of poignant, joy-filled, laughter-laced stories gleaned from bicycling travels across the fifty United States with my husband Jim. Anecdotes multiplied from the simple pleasures of lovely biking weather, quiet roads, camaraderie of family and good friends doing what we loved—together. Other adventures birthed a myriad of even more complex tales.

I love remembering the wonderful paths of my life that emerged on this pilgrimage, and how writing about them created its own journey. My hope is these accounts bring the reader pleasure, revelation of some delights and woes of long-distance cycling, and insight into the dreams of a long-ago little girl who wanted to see what was on the other side of the next hill.

IN THE BEGINNING...

Participants: Keith/Jan Gabel, Bruce/Sandra Atkinson. Date: 1948

When my older brother Keith announced he wanted a bicycle, I decided I wanted one too. We knew most country kids like us didn't have bikes of their own—they just had family ones and everyone rode whatever happened to be available. Being the only kids in our family, our parents bought each of us a new bicycle.

They chose a blue Shelby girl's bike for me and for Keith, a blue, red and white Schwinn. I'd heard of Schwinns, but Mother and Dad assured me a Shelby was just as good. Big brother bragged, "Mine's better. It's a boy's bike, not a sissy girl's bike like yours."

Being eleven, Keith already knew how to ride. Two years younger, I had only ridden my dad's rusty 1918 tricycle and a red and cream scooter in the driveway, an open area large enough to allow farm equipment to turn around. The dirt lanes on our farm came from both the south and north. The south one curved through the grove and zig-zagged past the straw stack where it widened between the chicken coop, windmill, garage and house. As it shrunk back to one lane, it sloped toward the cattle yard and down the hill to the barns, corncrib and hog house. That's the hill I rolled down inside a wooden buttermilk barrel, following Keith's suggestion it would be fun. After that head-rattling experience, going down that hill on anything but my two legs seemed risky. I would never face the dilemma of trying it on a bike.

I learned to balance and eventually ride my new bicycle pedaling around and around that driveway. When I mustered up enough confidence, I rode it down the rutted hilly lane toward my cousins' house. Once I crossed the county road, it became a straight downhill shot on gravel, across a bridge at the creek where we caught pollywogs, and on to Aunt Vera and Uncle Milton's always wet and stinky farmyard, thanks to poor drainage.

My younger cousins, Bruce and Sandra, got their beautiful new Schwinn bikes complete with push-button horns not long after Keith and I got our plainer bikes. Keith didn't play with us much though because he thought we were pesky little kids.

The three of us took turns riding double on a bike and just let 'er rip on the last hill of our lane, down the rough and treacherous way to their house. We took some bad spills but came up giggling and road-rashed. After one spectacular fall, I was afraid Sandra's bicycle would never be the same again. Significant new scratches marred its formerly pristine deep red paint.

Once Keith rode his bike eighteen miles to Akron where our grandparents lived. I imagined it was an exciting adventure and wondered what it would be like but never bothered to ask Mother if I could do it too. She thought girls needed protection. I didn't agree but didn't contradict her.

Even when I wanted to climb the inside of the Statue of Liberty with Dad and Keith, she grabbed onto me and said, "She won't be going." I should have but didn't protest. While we lived with our parents, Keith did all the limit-pushing and I did most of the acquiescing. As adults we shared more memories and feelings. Keith admitted, "Sometimes I just wanted to be good like you." I confessed, "And how I wanted to be rebellious like you."

When I no longer went to our one-room country school and rode the bus to the one in town, I pretty much stopped riding my bike. My parents moved to California in 1960, so I left it on the farm for the tenants' little girl to ride. The last time I remember seeing my first bike, it stood propped against the workbench in the dusty garage.

AND THEN...

Riders: Jim/Jan, Connie/John Carlson. Date: The 1970s

Ten years later Jim, our three daughters and I lived in Seattle. Mara, our oldest, decided I didn't get enough physical exercise and adamantly determined I should ride her bicycle each morning before the six two-year olds I cared for came to our house. So I did. I pedaled around our neighborhood, down to the kids' elementary school and back home while Mara cheered me on. I thought I had really accomplished something. That activity stopped when I began to work at the Mason Clinic and had to catch the bus very early in the morning, often in the dark. In winter I returned in the dark.

In 1972 Jim completed his orthodontic training and we returned to Iowa City where we had done our undergraduate work and Jim had gone to dental school. 1973 marked the year when one of Iowa's major newspapers sponsored a bicycle ride across Iowa, informally called *The Great Six-Day Bike Ride Across Iowa.* When we heard of it Jim and I smiled at each other and commented, "That sounds like fun." *The Des Moines Register* columnists John Karras and Donald Kaul both liked biking so asked a few friends to pedal with them across Iowa, just for fun. Some of their readers and bike enthusiasts joined them.

In 1974 when we heard there would be *SAGBRAI,* the *Second Annual Great Bike Ride Across Iowa,* we smiled and said, "That sounds like fun."

When we learned in 1975 that there would be a third bike ride across Iowa, now known as *Register's Annual Great Bike Ride Across Iowa,* RAGBRAI III, we graduated to, "We really need to do that."

Jim added, "You know, I've always wanted to take a long distance bike ride. When we lived in LeMars and the Prices lived across the street from us, Yuma's sister came to visit the summer I was fourteen. She and a college friend had bicycled across Canada on their three-speed bikes. I was really impressed." Later when he told the story, he noted that after our senior year in high school, he and a classmate had planned to do that same bike trip but Montie ended up in a body cast (from a back injury not related to bicycling.) Jim didn't want to go alone but a bicycle trip waiting to be ridden always lingered in the back of his mind.

Several other events occurred that hastened our biking careers. In 1966, shortly before his twenty-seventh birthday, Jim spent a month on bed rest and ultimately had back surgery. He recovered well and continued his normal life which included as much golf as he could manage. After a dental internship with the army in California, a year in Kansas, another in Vietnam, and two years at the University of Washington, we returned to Iowa City where he joined an established orthodontic practice. By mid-1973 his back made him miserable with constant flare-ups which precipitated two more back surgeries. Jim knew his golfing days had ended. He needed another active sport.

Each succeeding year Jim and I did our little "That sounds like fun," routine about RAGBRAI, but never committed to doing it. I considered myself a total non-athlete because of my erring eye-hand coordination. I tried playing golf but discovered the only time I seemed to be able to hit the ball was during pregnancy when I had a changed center of gravity. It didn't take much for me to decide it was not worth being pregnant every summer just to play golf. In my mind's eye I could play tennis but reality foiled that image. When I tried running, our youngest daughter asked, "Mom, may I walk with you?"

1978: *The Des Moines Register* published the RAGBRAI route the last Sunday in February. The paper came, Jim and I looked at the route and saw it started in Sioux City, within twenty-five miles of where we had grown up. "Let's do it!" We sent in registrations for us and our two younger daughters. We committed to RAGBRAI VI!

Despite my other athletic limitations, I believed the adage that one never forgets how to ride a bike, but the three-speed we'd bought at the Iowa City Police Bike Auction did not inspire trust. I needed a new bike.

"No problem," said Jim. I believed that too. "But it will need to be a ten-speed."

"A ten-speed? But I've never ridden a ten-speed."

"No problem. It's just like a three-speed but with more gears."

"Oh."

Spring. Off we went to the bike shop to look at ten-speeds. What would be the most crucial thing to look for? I knew it wouldn't be color although that's always important to me. Our friend Paul told us the people at a particular bike shop would help me choose just the right bike. I believed that too. So I came away the proud owner of a new metallic gold Motobecane ten-speed bike. Shiny and pretty, but I still needed to think about those ten speeds.

First ride out with Jim: "Shift!"

"I can't! It doesn't want to shift!"

"Don't stop pedaling! You have to keep pedaling while you shift!"

"I am pedaling!"

"No you aren't. You're stopping while you try to shift and the chain drops if you do that."

"I'm trying."

"Try harder! Concentrate. You can do it!"

At this rate, learning to shift the gears on my new bike might tax our marriage. I had not promised to obey Jim in our marriage vows—I wouldn't be able to if I had. I couldn't even follow his directions on how to shift gears on a bike. I decided to practice shifting on my own. I biked out to a nearby flat road to practice. I thought I had improved but soon jammed the chain again with the consequence of a quick dismount (bikespeak for I fell off.) I sprained my gear-shifting thumb and was so embarrassed I didn't tell anyone even though it hurt to use it.

Our friends Connie and John asked if we wanted to ride our bicycles with them around what we called the Little Block—from our house, across nearby Coralville Dam, onto beautiful backroads and looping back to our house—a total of nine gorgeous Iowa River Valley hill miles.

We said we'd go but I had serious reservations. John the wise said he would ride behind me and help me learn how to shift gears. He told me exactly what Jim had been telling me, but not in the Spouse Voice. Slowly but surely I learned to shift and slowly but surely I gained confidence. I was incredulous to have actually ridden those nine hilly miles circling the Little Block and still remained conscious and unscathed!

Soon every weekend included sixty mile back-to-back days of riding. I accepted the challenge—I would ride RAGBRAI!!

🚲

RAGBRAI MILES

Our gang of riders from various years: Jim/Jan/Mara/Tania/Jennifer Down, Dick/Carolyn Duncan, Robert Duncan, Dave/Les Fredrickson, Betty Oglesby, Connie/John/Phil/Cara Carlson, Dave/Jane Loynachan Bousfield, Sherrilyn Loynachan Nikkel, Deb/Allen Wiese.
Distance: Varied from year to year, generally 400-500 miles

After years of procrastination, in 1978 Jim and I stood on the brink of what would prove to be a life-long adventure with cycling. Little did we know, it would become a journey of self-discovery which affected not only our individual growth but also greatly enhanced our relationship, beginning with the sixth iteration of RAGBRAI, *The Register's Annual Great Bike Ride Across Iowa.*

One might expect we would launch this maiden voyage standing on a precipice overlooking the wide Missouri River, a favorable breeze ruffling our hair. Instead, we assembled in a nondescript parking lot just blocks from the stockyards in Sioux City, Iowa. Jim and I were thrilled to be there even if Tania and Jennifer did not share our level of enthusiasm. They came as willing-to-semi-willing participants and Mara agreed to drive the SAG wagon. I love true family affairs!

Even Jim's parents came from LeMars to see us off. Mom captured the moment with numerous photos and Dad made it possible to experience a signature RAGBRAI tradition—dipping our bikes' rear tires in the river. Well, sort of. Because the steep rocky riverbank was too unstable to drag our bikes down to it, he improvised, grabbed an empty milk jug, picked his way down the precarious slope and returned with precious fluid. With a background of a repair shop and Kentucky Fried Chicken inviting us to take home some chicken, I had the honor of baptizing our tires by dumping water on them. We could now officially begin RAGBRAI VI.

That little ceremony developed into a full-fledged ritual. We ran our back tires in whatever body of water separated Iowa from Nebraska, the Missouri River, or from South Dakota, the Big Sioux. We celebrated the end of each adventure by running our front tires into the Mississippi River, making sure we took photos to prove we had indeed biked across the entire span of the state. We did not celebrate as some riders did by pedaling straight into the muddy water, submerging both their bikes and themselves.

Tania, Jennifer, Jan and Jim. Start of RAGBRAI, 1978

I hadn't envisioned this ride as a baptism into the world of long-distance bicycling which would influence every multi-day ride we took from then on. We experienced proof positive our need to always have filled water bottles, biking gloves, helmets, comfortable clothes, sunscreen, food, extra tubes and a bike repair kit with us. Other essential lessons seeped into our psyches, sometimes learned the hard way, but often benefiting from advice and modeling of more experienced cyclists. Immediately however, we needed to learn how to ride safely among thousands of rank amateurs who possibly knew even less than we did.

We made experimental choices that first RAGBRAI, such as staying in motels, generally in another town away from other cyclists. We did have Mara driving our car, after all. We'd rethink that flawed concept before the next RAGBRAI. Why miss the color of the towns, interactions with more people, eating in churches with other riders, all for a bit of comfort?

One of our biggest reproofs? A question our daughters could have asked, Do you hear me now? Jim and I didn't always listen as carefully to them as we should have. When Jennifer told us her bike didn't work right, we thought she was mainly expressing her disdain for a bicycling vacation. I knew very little about bikes and Jim knew much more but both of us missed the parental mark here. She, teeth gritted and muttering about her parents who didn't understand, kept on keeping on. She forced her just turned thirteen year old body and new bike across the state. After we were home, Jim discovered the reason. "No wonder she complained. Her bike frame is warped and couldn't track properly." Chagrin for us and a lifelong love-hate relationship with bicycling for Jennifer.

毐

Excitement reigned for most of this first cross-state ride. Jim and I thought this could become habit-forming since so much happened and all of it within Iowa's borders. On the way out of Sioux City, a flat tire stopped Tania and punctuated our first ride with a teachable moment: *No matter how hard we try, we are not always in charge.* After Jim's expert tire change, we pedaled off to wend our way through small towns of Iowa. Among other villages unknown to me, Varina, Unique, Dahloninga and Titonka lay along our route. Residents greeted the ten thousand of us riders with enthusiasm all our way through the center of Iowa to the Mississippi River.

RAGBRAI begins on Iowa's western border so first days usually included the treat of pedaling the fabled loess hills. These rare geological wonders, comparable to deposits in Shaanxi, China plus a few smaller areas in the US, were formed by fine wind-blown silt. Some rise as much as 350 feet from the river floodplains and extend about two hundred miles from near Hawarden south to beyond Missouri's border. Jim and I grew up at the edge of them, did warm-up rides in them and knew what we were in for. But the poor RAGBRAI newbies...

NEWS FLASH: *IOWA IS NOT FLAT!* Expletives uttered by first-timers who crested one loess hill only to find another looming ahead amused locals and us. Riding alongside a weary young man as we climbed yet another hill I inquired, "Did you assume Iowa was flat?" Shoulders drooping, he shook his head in despair, "Yeah. But I don't anymore." Others muttered about the climb but suddenly beamed, "Did you see the incredible views from the top?"

Tania approached the ride matter-of-factly, with a few bits of enthusiasm mixed with occasional complaints, up to the one hundred mile day. She felt whipped and ready to quit but didn't want to flag down one of RAGBRAI's SAG wagons. She didn't even feel like eating, she just wanted to stop until—magic moment—along came two cute teenaged boys from our church. They chatted with her and voila! Her malaise vanished. "Bye! I'm going with Derek and Brent!" Re-energized, she finished the entire century with them, and for good measure they made a side trip and ended up riding one hundred thirteen miles. When she found Mara and our car, she still had a bounce in her step and flashed a happy smile, "That was fun!"

Jim, Tania, Jennifer and I were totally unprepared for what transpired as we cycled into Clinton on our way to dip our tires in The Great River. Spectators lined the street, some having waited for hours to cheer the riders in. I loved every minute of it. Who could possibly resist grinning and waving back at them?

All in all, our first RAGBRAI was great for Jim and me. We loved the ride, the people, the color, the feeling of accomplishment and sharing in this amazing festival on wheels. From those positive experiences, our desire to keep on pedaling grew, although not necessarily with all three offspring on long rides. But time would tell.

In the afterglow upon arriving home, the more Jim and I rode, the more we read articles about cycling and talked to other riders, the more we realized we needed to make safety and comfort changes in our equipment and clothing.

Something caught our eyes, a jarringly bright yellow flyer fairly yelling: *Wear a brain bucket! Save your brain!* Brain buckets? That got our attention and we soon improved the Bell helmet company's economy when we requested, "Five please." The bike store expert admonished us, "Don't wear them tipped on the back of your head. Wear them parallel to the ground so your forehead will be protected. If you fall, that's probably the direction you would fall." Got it.

Riding in the rain could never be construed as one of my favorite things to do. Although I personally may have been drip-dry, most of our clothing was not. Connie Carlson and I thought outrageously priced rain jackets were an extravagance. We sleuthed out some new-to-the-market Gore-Tex fabric to make some. We even took classes on how to create all kinds of biking gear. Both of us managed to sew rain jackets. She made four olive green ones for her family and I made three cobalt blue and two bright yellow for ours. It was harrowing to work with such expensive fabric and I feared making a mistake and jeopardizing the whole project. When I succeeded in finishing the last jacket, I lay down on the floor just to let myself breathe until I felt a smile come over my face. I'd done it! I had successfully, meaning nothing had been sewn where it wasn't supposed to be, made jackets for my family. I thought they were beautiful.

Year by year, our gear grew to encompass padded biking shorts as well as easy wash and dry biking shirts with front zippers and deep back pockets. Hard-soled biking shoes provided more power and eventually, we bought those with cleats. Jim had them long before I did—I lacked confidence in my ability to get them released from the pedals before I fell over. Soon I depended on cleats to help me bike more efficiently. Bicycling was teaching me how to push myself in so many ways.

⬲

Between the first year's motels and later years' camping, we took advantage of the programs in overnight towns which matched cyclists with local hosts. They wowed us with amazing quantities and varieties of food prepared in their best Iowa way. Overwhelming hospitality prevailed, not only in opening their homes to us for food, showers and beds, but providing transportation to places in town if we wanted it. One year we were excited to not camp but stay with Jim's aunt, Corinne Down in Odebolt. No standing in line for showers, a wonderful meal, comfy beds and, best of all, being with Corinne.

However, late one afternoon, Dave, Les, Jim and I straggled into Elkader and found our host home. Our hostess was a sweet, elderly, wary lady who didn't quite know what to expect from these strange people on bicycles. We had the feeling someone must have talked very hard and long to convince her she should do this. We thanked her and assured her all would be well. She showed us where we would sleep in the second story of her old four-square house. We climbed up steep rickety stairs and saw completely empty rooms. No beds, no chairs, nothing. Well, that's not entirely true. There were ants. A plethora of tiny ants crawled everywhere. Our hostess gave us a couple of blankets and Jim and I had a throw rug apiece. Les and Dave had their sleeping bags. She also provided us a pitcher of lemonade and four glasses. The ants loved the lemonade.

Staying in the BIC (Bicyclists of Iowa City) campground areas lived up to their reputation of being relatively quiet, off the major beaten path away from The Register's main campground. The luxury of the BIC baggage truck drivers filling all the portable shower bags with water and placing them in the sun to heat—terrific! Sometimes Ol' Sol didn't quite do its job and at others, the water became so hot, we kind of splashed it on ourselves so we didn't get burned. The shower bag held enough water for Jim and me to shower/shampoo with our clothes on, peel them off for the rinse and still have enough hot water to share with another rider. No long, luxuriating showers for us. Two little battery-operated fans affixed to our tent with magnets stirred the air providing heat and humidity mitigation during Iowa's prime corn-growing season. We lived high.

⬲

Jim and I loved watching other cyclists, and a memorable serendipity for any biker is to meet a truly inspiring role model such as Bernice Tillson. I happened upon her in western Iowa and began a conversation as we rode. A sixty-five year old, she lived in Seattle and had participated in self-contained transcontinental rides, bicycle toured Ireland, climbed Mount Rainier and returned to Iowa nearly every year to visit friends and ride RAGBRAI. We periodically saw each other throughout the ride, and eventually exchanged addresses so we could keep in touch in between. Two years later, she joined us in staying overnight in an Adel dental office whose owner hosted several of us riders.

(How about that for comfort?) A sad day filled with otherwise happy memories came when her niece informed us that Bernice had died.

One hot day in July, 1973 Clarence Pickard plopped a pith helmet on his head and declared he would join the first ride across the state. When asked if he had trained, he retorted, "I rode around a block or two," definitely in keeping with his persona. While still in his seventies, this plucky man had volunteered for the Peace Corps. His pith helmet, tan pants and long-sleeved shirt, along with a long-sleeved woolen undershirt, became hallmarks of this easily recognizable man. He claimed they kept him cool. He was cool, that's for sure. Sadly, a few years later while on a pleasure ride, Mr. Pickard was struck and killed by a vehicle. The next RAGBRAI was dedicated to him.

Teams from the United States Navy, Army, Marines and Air Force joined the parade of those taking part in this folk celebration. Fit and attractive in their special military bike clothes, they added to the spice of the event. I recall nearly falling off my bicycle with laughter when I heard a voice blasting out as most riders struggled up a hill, "Come on there! Pick it up! You can do better than that! Move it!" This Navy man created quite a stir as he raced past us to the top, zoomed back down and roared his orders as he drubbed the hill again—effortlessly.

Many families cycled together with a young child on a Tag-Along behind a parent who also pulled a Bugger/cart with a child or two in it. Another parent might pedal a tandem with an older child as the stoker, the one behind. Seeing them biking together brought smiles to lots of faces. The kids? They all seemed to be troopers and rarely complained—that we could hear anyway.

I had just topped a hill outside my birthplace town when I heard someone shout my name. Friends from childhood waved and I managed to safely pull off and go back to hug them. "Have you seen the organ grinder monkey?" I shook my head. Just then I spotted Pepper, a Capuchine monkey riding in a box on the front of a tandem. She was being taught to become a partner/helper for someone with physical disabilities. Her volunteer trainers' job was to familiarize her to the ways of human beings, so wherever the family went, so did Pepper. They had read about the ride in the *Smithsonian Magazine* and decided their unique family should join in. Pepper headed my list as the most surprising RAGBRAI participant.

🚲

Favorite snack foods for Jim and me? Cookies, brownies and lemonade sold by little kids for a quarter apiece. Inflation hit them too so prices rose considerably by the 2000s. We took along a couple of film canisters filled with quarters so we could stop at virtually every kid-operated stand along the way.

We gravitated to churches, civic groups, Scouts and other non-profits for our meals. Church food tended to spaghetti, lasagna, sloppy joes or old-fashioned chicken dinners. Mostly it tasted good and filled us up. Breakfasts by service clubs might be pancakes, waffles, scrambled eggs and bacon. During the early rides, prices per meal generally ranged from $1.50 to $2.50 but those too changed with the times. Occasionally we did buy from commercial vendors including the waffle or pancake people or Mr. Pork Chop, who hawked his food by bellowing, "Pooooork Chops!" on a rising musical scale. Pies and ice cream were afternoon favorites and Alburnett's United Methodist Church ranked number one on the most delicious pie list.

Another RAGBRAI food tradition involved cafés along the way. Somewhere on each ride, a diner would suddenly be overwhelmed with hungry bikers, and the regular personnel could not possibly take orders, prepare and serve food to all of them. In would step the super-heroes of the day—riders who would take over the operation—hand out menus, pour coffee, juice, water, take orders, bus tables, flip pancakes, scramble eggs, anything and everything to help feed the mob. Our exuberant son-in-law Bernd honed his raconteur skills by telling about being one of the diner-heroes one year, although he didn't call himself that. He described it as one of the most fun things he did the whole week.

�&

Dozens of American flags lined Belmond's Main Street and created a thrilling sight as we swooped into that stunning azure sky sight. After we left town, we glimpsed a steepled church in the distance, St. Olaf's with its green field background and rolling colors of bikers. Signs quoting the Gospel of Mark 8:3, *I shall feed them or they shall faint for some of them have come a long way* enticed us to go see what the people of St. Olaf's fed the multitudes. Not fishes and loaves but scrumptious pies—we riders did not faint despite having come a long way.

Sights from nature often indelibly imprint our minds. One crisp morning outside Carroll, shining halos around each rider's shadow mesmerized us. As we continued, sparkling gems of dewy spider webs adorned the ditches for miles. Nature's blessings.

Speaking of nature, when it called we didn't always have close access to KYBOs (Keep Your Bowels Open) or other facilities. Thoughtful Iowa farm families affixed rolls of toilet tissue to fenceposts along the corn fields, for obvious reasons, never along the hay or bean fields. Legend and practicality say the reason RAGBRAI is scheduled for late July is because the corn is tall enough for riders to take advantage of the privacy it affords those who have heard nature's call.

�&

Cooper, touting itself as the home of 151 proud people, headed our list of banner towns in 1982. Its citizens provided a carnival and circus rolled into one. We heard recorded bands playing, encountered crowds of people and saw bikes jamming the streets. A local boy-turned-successful DJ narrated the Cooper show complete with *The Iowa Corn Song*, and introduced each resident. He gave Pepsi commercials, issued invitations to check out the new industrial park south of town and to inquire about convention facilities. Good food and Disney atmosphere pervaded. A woman hawking Cooper buttons described various bikers in the crowd and called them out on her bullhorn saying she wanted to talk to them. No doubt her victims bought buttons. That much hometown schmaltz was hard to leave, but as we did, the taped Mormon Tabernacle Choir sang Woody Guthrie's classic *This Land is Your Land.*

Glenwood advertised a population of one person per every foot in a mile and tripled in size when we RAGBRAI folk overran their town. Participants in a big softball tournament, a horseshoe pitch, and a pickup pull added to the invading forces. Iowa cultural events, every one.

毶

In Jim's hometown of LeMars, we plunged into RAGBRAI XXIII crowds in 2005. After a pleasant Sunday biking through rural Sioux County, we pitched our tent in the BIC camping area near an elementary school in Sheldon. About midnight we awakened to dumping rain and rising winds. An unexpected loudspeaker announcement warned us to take cover because of a possible tornado.

We grabbed our shoes, wallets and flashlight, left our sleeping bags in the tent and raced through inches of deepening water up an incline to the school. Taking shelter in the hallway until the wind died down, we wondered if our tent still stood but refused to go outside to check. The unforgivingly numbing tile floors made rest difficult so we found a carpeted air-conditioned classroom. The AC would have been appreciated during the humid day but in our drenched condition was thoroughly chilling. We should have grabbed our sleeping bags. I remembered that elementary schools always have a Lost and Found box somewhere. I found it and grabbed sweaters, pants and anything else I thought might warm us and our shivering compatriots. The clothes would have fit only little to mid-sized kids but I tucked my frigid feet into the legs of some sweatpants and curled up into as small a ball as I could and tried to cover myself with a sweater. Eventually I fell into a restless sleep.

Good news, the rain lessened and so had the wind. Once we wakened, we discovered our tent still stood, sort of, and most of the water had drained off. With the wind had come a horrible tragedy: A young man asleep in a tent just two blocks from us had been hit and killed by a falling tree branch. What a sobering event after such a delightful first day.

毶

Spectators really made a day of it when the RAGBRAI tribe pedaled by. Many folks pulled out their lawn chairs, thermoses of coffee, ice tea or lemonade, and sat in clusters under an abundance of shade trees along the route. At times they seemed to have little interest in what happened on the road and used being together as a sort of coffee klatch or social club, just chatting away. At others they interacted with the bikers. Rural folks often offered Fresh cold water here! Cookies! Bathrooms! Occasionally, Carolyn and I preferred asking a farm wife if we could use her facilities instead of a cornfield or porta-potty. No one ever refused us and occasionally offered water, ice or pop.

My very favorite spectator, my Grandma Adams, has been a role model for me as long as I can remember. Her positive view of life, bubbly, infectious laughter, ethic of hard work and her powerful love enveloped her family and beyond, endearing her to me and to many. Her life had not been easy but her faith kept her strong.

What a thrill to learn that 1982 RAGBRAI X would start in Akron, her hometown in northwest Iowa on the South Dakota border. A stroke five years earlier had made necessary her move to the Akron Care Center, although she certainly didn't think so. When the staff there knew two of Grandma's grandchildren and their friends would be on RAGBRAI, they made sure she would be ready and waiting for every opportunity to celebrate among the cyclists.

Several of us went to rescue Grandma from the Care Center and bumped her wheelchair along the streets to the hub of activities. Her lovely round face and sparkling blue eyes reflected her delight at the sight of vividly colored tents and brightly attired people swarming the park in her beloved Akron. She waved and smiled at friends and savored the sights and sounds of this festive atmosphere.

My stepfather Harvey drove her out to the riverside park where our gang of bikers would dip of our rear tires. She marveled at this ritual baptism as only a lifelong Baptist could. Grandma's energy level didn't seem to diminish as she joined us for a lasagna dinner we had prepared for her and eighteen other people at Harvey and my mother's house. What a remarkable lady!

The following morning, some of us rode to see Grandma one last time. She'd been waiting, sitting outside watching the constant parade of riders. She expressed how annoyed she was with her fellow "inmates"who hadn't wanted to come outside either day to join the brightness and hoopla. What joy for us to share this exciting event with her. It would be one of the last times Jim and I saw her before her death the following March. We feel blessed to have had such a special person for our grandma. We miss her still.

🚲

Each year the Register's planners chose routes for the ride and towns and cities vie for the opportunity to be overnight stops. Routes change yearly and make terrain, geographical areas and lengths of rides vary for cyclists. The surging, swelling hills and flatland prairie scenes spawn more opportunities to appreciate farming, woodland and urban landscapes of Iowa, our beautiful state between two major rivers, the Missouri and the Mississippi.

🚲

As an endpoint, Burlington offered its own special gift for RAGBRAI riders, a thoroughfare called Snake Alley which owns a reputation of being a tough ride either down or up. This steep, twisty-turny street gives competition to notably crooked Lombard Street in San Francisco. Snake Alley wins. Ripley's Believe It or Not named it *The crookedest street in the world*. Built in 1894, it drops 275 feet in 439 winding feet. The engineer who masterminded it did not design it for bicycles of any generation, but that doesn't stop the biking throngs from setting their jaws and hanging white-knuckled onto their brakes to go down it. At least Mara's and my knuckles looked white.

The final day of RAGBRAI brings its own spirit which all of us share with thousands of others—we had completed a great adventure, mysterious in its own way because of how it unfolds in time and space. I started each last day thinking *I'm glad this is almost over but I'm going to miss it tomorrow. I won't miss the arduous labor of pedaling mile after mile each day, sometimes against the wind, often in dreadful heat, humidity or rain. But I'll miss the color, camaraderie of the riders, the joy of being in our own bubble away from the cacophony of the rest of the world.*

What Jim and I derived from each long-distance ride became the seed for another. Common elements exist in every trek but unique conditions impact the arc of each new adventure. We knew we'd continue to change and wondered what every new pedal-stroke would bring.

🚲

One more favorite memory, this one from 1982 RAGBRAI X: For many years and several RAGBRAIs, we had ridden hundreds and hundreds of miles with Carolyn and Dick. On the next to the last day, we stopped in Hazelton and Carolyn went down the street to check out something she'd seen. Dick watched her go, turned to us and said, "She's a wonderful woman. I'm going to ask her to marry me." With a stricken look on his face he added, "But what if she says no?"

Our instantaneous response, "Don't worry, Dick, she won't." She didn't. Three months later they married and lived happily ever after, through more RAGBRAI rides and all.

🚲

In memory of Dick Duncan and in honor of his wonderful Carolyn.
Whenever we see an orange bicycle like Dick's, we are struck with a pang of
sadness, immediately replaced by the memory of his wonderful voice, booming laughter
and mischievous twinkle in his eyes.

FIRST THERE WAS KANSAS.
"KANSAS? WHY KANSAS?"
THE SUNFLOWER STATE-1980

Riders: Connie/John/Phil, Jim/Jan. SAG (Support and Gear)
Driver: Dave Fredrickson. Distance: 450 miles

THE PLAN.

First there was Kansas.

"Kansas? Why Kansas?"

John chuckled and gave the classic adventurer's response. "Because it's there."

Jim chimed in, "And it's all downhill."

This seemingly innocuous question and answer about where to ride would change all our lives, but mostly Jim's and mine. What would require twenty-seven years worth of vacation time, one hundred seventy thousand van and airplane miles, thirty-three drivers, fifty-three family members and friends and eight bicycles? The answer lies in the tales I'm about to tell which spread out like a crazy quilt—a crazy quilt we could never have imagined one snowy night in February, 1980.

Our friends Connie and John Carlson, my husband Jim, and I had been relaxing in our cozy living room in the midst of an Iowa winter when Jim had asked, "Now that we've bicycled RAG-BRAI, where should we ride our bikes next summer?" After pondering John and Jim's responses, we agreed we should ride across Kansas. Good planning meant we'd ride from west to east in the direction of prevailing winds and ultimately go downhill from Colorado to Missouri.

We had not been thinking of capital letter BIG ADVENTURE. Little and low-key adventure would be enough. It would be fun to ride our bicycles with friends across Kansas where Jim and I had once lived, and we could visit old friends.

🚲

24

Four months later, we stood on the border near Towner, Colorado straddling our bikes, ready to ride across Kansas.

The day before, a sweltering 106-degree day, Connie, John, their son Phil, Jim and I left Iowa City to head to Eskridge, Kansas to pick up Dave Fredrickson, our sixteen-year old friend and now SAG driver.

Jim remarked, "This southwest wind is really strong. I feel like I'm wrestling the van through it."

"Wrestle away, Down. That'll make for a great tailwind tomorrow."

After our night in Scott City we drove to Tribune near the Colorado border where we'd begin our ride. We spied a restaurant surrounded by lots of pickups sporting Kansas license plates. Locals should know the best places to eat so we parked the car, went in and sat at a well-worn table for six. Jim's face lit up as he checked the menu. He ordered a stack of three buckwheat pancakes. The server's eyes widened and demonstrated with her hands how big they were. Jim grinned, "I want three. I'm really hungry."

Moments later the cook appeared asking to see the person who had ordered three—a message to some but not all of us. Jim replied, "I am," insisting he wanted three pancakes. The cook shook his head, muttered, "OK," and returned to the kitchen. I glanced around. All the other patrons, local farmers and ranchers smirked knowingly.

When the server placed three thick hang-over-the-edge-of-the-platter buckwheat pancakes in front of Jim, it was worth biking into thirty-five miles per hour winds all day just to see his face. He gamely ate all he could and managed to consume only one-third of them. Lesson learned: When the cook checks to make sure you really want what you ordered, pay attention. Five of us walked, Jim waddled back to the car to drive the remaining eighteen miles to the border.

We unloaded and checked our bikes and Phil's needed an adjustment. John switched the brake levers on Phil's bike to accommodate his broken right wrist. Eventually he was ready to bike a few miles at a time. Otherwise, he'd ride in the car, Dave would drive ten or so miles down the road where they'd play backgammon and wait for us.

We cyclists stood a few moments on the border near Towner, Colorado relishing the excitement of another long distance bicycle ride. We waved to Dave and headed east into the wind.

Into the wind? I moaned, "But ...the prevailing winds in Kansas are supposed to be from the west!" We'd planned our trip from west to east based on that theory. The wind relentlessly slammed us in the face and we progressed slowly. I felt like *All we are is Dust in the Wind* by the band Kansas had been written for us.

Game faces on, we steadfastly pedaled back to Tribune, home of prodigious pancakes, for lunch at the same restaurant where we hoped no one would recognize us. After consuming simple sandwiches we left the café. A muster of old men approached and one asked, "Where ya headin'?"

"Missouri."

With a short snort and sly smile he retorted, "Well, ya won't get there afore mornin'."

Along the way, Frank Chudy, a young Coloradan we'd met on the road, joined us. He was biking solo from his home in Aspen to Massachusetts, so we invited him to stay with us at our motel. He appreciated the luxury of indoor plumbing after his days of camping.

Mom and Dad Down, Jim's parents, fascinated by our penchant for bicycling, had seen us off on our first RAGBRAI. Now they also wanted to be part of this biking adventure and drove from Northwest Iowa to Scott City to join us after our first day on the road. They found some tuckered out, wind-whipped people. I could barely keep my head up and my eyes open during supper.

John wears his reason for biking Kansas

The following morning, Down family photographer Mom took photos of The Bikers. Frank rode much faster than we did so we wished him winds at his back as he cycled off. With the admonishment to stay safe, Mom and Dad headed west to Denver. We followed in Frank's wake.

High daily mileage, dramatic weather changes, temperature fluctuations from 40 to 106 degrees, varying wind direction and velocity and flat tires escalated the rigor of this trip. We adhered to the cyclists' adage *Bike to eat, eat to bike* but still felt weary at the end of each day.

As we traveled the mostly rural byways, we absorbed a great deal of information about the state, its people, its history. Straight roads in western Kansas are as commonplace as sunflowers, so when the road curved even slightly to the left or right, it energized us. Although the terrain appeared to be flat, each day we lost altitude. Nothing precipitous, mind you, but at day's end, we always slept at a lower altitude than we had the night before. Unless we stayed on the second floor of an old hotel.

Biking along the wheat fields, we experienced what I called the *mystery of the grain elevators.* Prairies produce a phenomenon in which distant tall structures seem much closer than they really are. I don't know if that relates to the forced perspective concept used by filmmakers to make some things appear larger, or if it is something in the quality or haziness of the air. Repeatedly, we'd see towering white sentinels of Kansas' wheat fields, grain elevators on the horizon. How many times did I think, *I can wait until we get to that town to use a real restroom.* That is *real* as opposed to using a ditch, culvert, rare bridge, or rarer still in Western Kansas, a tree or bush close to the road. Fifteen miles and an hour or so later, we'd finally pull into a town with convenience store, café or park where I'd race into the aforementioned facilities. Sweet relief.

Another lesson learned from biking Kansas provoked changes. For example, sticker-flickers are dry country cyclists' friends. These simple wire devices, designed to skim above bike tires, flick off thorns and road debris so riders have fewer flat tires. Because of his repeated flats the whole way across Kansas, John bought sticker-flickers when he returned to Iowa City. We garnered some wisdom from every trip.

Often people only hear about Kansas plains, wheat, dry weather, Dust Bowl and university sports teams. The number of rivers we encountered surprised John. Among others during our journey, we crossed or rode along the Smoky Hill, Arkansas, Saline and Neosho Rivers, and the White Woman, Cow and Dragoon Creeks. We ended the trip at the majestic waterway that inspired the song *Shenandoah,* the Missouri River. As we rode we reflected on where these names might have come from. Obviously the Saline referenced salt as in the salt mines of Kansas. Had there been fires near the Smoky Hill River or where local Indian tribes had sent smoke signals? Had a cavalry been stationed on the banks of Dragoon Creek? We had no answers but we had fun conjuring up scenarios that might explain the names.

On our third day of biking, Great Bend's grain elevators, visible from miles away, reminded us of its role as an agricultural center. The town's name derived from its location on the great bend of the Arkansas River (pronounced ar-KAN-zus in this region.) Here we intersected the historic Santa Fe Trail, and our imaginations stirred recalling tales of pioneers rolling over desolate prairies in their often overloaded covered wagons. We could almost hear the creaks and groans of these bone-rattling prairie schooners pitching through the rutted plains, accompanying the trials these stalwart people faced in their westward migration. We pampered twentieth century bicyclists rode paved roads sixty-to-ninety miles a day. They had slogged along clay tracks traversing ten miles on a good day. Wet and soggy? We'd still make our sixty or more miles. The wagon train might cover only one mile, and we thought we had been moving slowly.

We shared supper and reminisced with our friend and Jim's first grade love, Sharon Eyres Trost, and her husband, making the town a perfect spot to overnight. Before we left, they presented us with a Kansas sunflower commemorative brick which we kept on our fireplace hearth, a vivid reminder of our Kansas friends and bike ride. Fortunately, we could put it in our SAG wagon. Jim had no desire to tote a brick in his panniers the rest of the way across the state.

We left Great Bend and angled toward Salina. Hot, humid weather wilted us but we kept pedaling to the half-way point of the day's ride, Ellsworth. Once called *The Wickedest Cattletown in Kansas*, Ellsworth's cattle trade diminished after drovers established newer routes through Dodge City. With that change fewer gambling houses, saloons, and brothels existed, fewer shootouts and murders, and less violence in general.

To us the town looked quiet, no cattle, no outlaws, just a few bicylists taking a gamble by riding our bikes on country roads. On our way to Salina, a fast moving car careened way too close to us, a passenger aimed a soda can at me and hit my rear wheel. It didn't break a spoke and I didn't lose my balance but I became very wary of passing vehicles. Such incidents reinforced our realization that not everyone thinks cyclists should be allowed on highways, despite what the law says.

For me bicycling is not only the physical act of journeying through a landscape. I move through an intellectual, psychological, and spiritual landscape as well. I interact not only to what is going on around me but also to my personal history. Sometimes it becomes a time of reflection, contemplation, looking at an old experience with new eyes or at a new experience with eyes that have been there before. So it was when Jim and I returned to Schilling Manor in Salina for the first time since we had left in June, 1970.

This place marked life changes I had never contemplated earlier in my life. I grew up and took risks in becoming who I was meant to be, no longer just Cloyde and Janet's daughter, or Jim's wife or Mara, Tania and Jennifer's mother. I was me. It had taken me thirty years to get to that point. I now knew I was capable of going farther.

From 1968-1970 our family lived in Salina, the first year all five of us and the second, only four of us. The army assigned Jim as dental chief at Schilling Manor, formerly Schilling Air Force Base. This occurred at the height of the Vietnam War when many military dependents needed housing while their husbands deployed to Vietnam, Thailand, Alaska or Greenland. The powers that be decided to open the housing to those women and children and renamed the post *Schilling Manor, Home for Waiting Wives*. I became one of them when Jim went to Vietnam. The women numbered 700, the children 2500. Twenty-eight men, including the commander of the post, physicians, dentists, medical and dental assistants, and military police also lived there, most with their own families. Five of the women's husbands were among Vietnam's MIAs, Missing in Action. We all felt the loss.

When we biked into Salina, the first thing we wanted to do after checking into the motel—go see our house at Schilling. Everything looked different. The post had been closed and housing, no longer painted army beige, opened to civilians to own or rent. Public buildings became part of a junior college campus. Sunflower and Schilling Elementary Schools Mara and Tania attended remained open. Seeing them brought a flurry of memories about a favorite teacher Helen Kalb, who with her husband Paul, dear friends who adopted our family. We remembered how Mara, Tania and Jennifer loved to go to their farm to ride horses and pet the foals.

We drove to the airfield, now Salina Airport, where we had wept when Jim left for Vietnam and rejoiced when he returned. At the time of President Dwight D. Eisenhower's funeral, in March of 1969, I brought our daughters there to impress on them the historic importance of his life and death. Although his body had arrived in Abilene by train, dignitaries attending his funeral flew to Salina. We saw Air Force One arrive, the stairs being lowered, and the feet of President Richard Nixon, Mrs. Nixon and their daughter, Tricia as they deplaned and boarded a helicopter to fly to Abilene. Later we witnessed a similar event with the arrival of former President Lyndon B. Johnson and Lady Bird Johnson.

Another bit of history, this one aeronautical, occurred here at the airfield. The four of us came out to watch the new, huge 747s as they would touch and go, land and take off without coming to a stop. Major airlines knew this runway, four feet deep and designed for heavy military aircraft, stood strong enough for 747s to land, and long enough, four miles, for their pilots to train here.

Jim and I did not go to nearby Smoky Hill bombing range where the concussion of bombs had prompted then four-year old Jennifer to ask, "Mommy, are bombing rangers bad people? Do they kill children?"

Salina, specifically Schilling Manor, had forever engrained in us the importance of family, the understanding of the futility of war and necessity for peace. Best of all, we were so grateful Jim had lived through Vietnam and now, ten years later we remembered together.

In Brookville, a tiny burg we'd biked through earlier in the day, we introduced Connie, John and Phil to the Brookville Hotel. Salina born and bred Dave grew up loving the food there so needed no introduction. Since 1915, the famous family-style chicken dinner featuring juicy pan-fried chicken plus trimmings of cream-style corn, mashed potatoes, coleslaw and hot biscuits have been stars of the hotel's dining room menu. The meal we enjoyed lived up to our memories. Eat, bike, eat.

🚲

The following day, we pedaled fewer than thirty miles to another favorite spot in Kansas, former cow-town Abilene, terminus of the famed Chisholm Cattle Trail. Texas ranchers used the trail to drive their cattle to railheads, such as the Kansas Pacific Railway in Abilene, where they would be sold and shipped eastward. Much of our route paralleled that same track, now the Union Pacific Railroad, providing a perfect opportunity for Jim to race a slow-moving train. Cycling slightly uphill, urged on by Connie and me and heckled by John, he managed to stay in the twenty miles per hour range. The engineer spotted Jim, blew his whistle and waved, encouraging him to keep it up. He did for nearly three miles. The train pulled slowly away and eventually disappeared. We saw no cattle on the Trail.

After lunch in Abilene, the six of us headed to the Dwight D. Eisenhower Presidential Library and Museum. All the buildings at the center and museum had been constructed of ubiquitous native Kansas stone, limestone. Not unexpectedly, limestone is the building block of many historic buildings as well as natural landmarks because eons ago, the state had been an inland ocean. Limestone strata, bedrock, underlies much of the shallow soil there.

Although jewels, crystal, gold, silver and bronze pieces had been presented to General/President Eisenhower by heads of state and other world leaders, they were not my favorite exhibits. I preferred the modest if sparse comfort of the four-square home where David and Ida Eisenhower reared the surviving six of their seven sons. It speaks to me of their quiet Mennonite faith and their commitment to raise their sons well despite living on what was reputed to be "the wrong side of the tracks" of Abilene. That meant they lived on the south or cattle industry side of town. One year after D-Day General Eisenhower said, "The proudest thing I can claim is that I am from Abilene."

🚲

We spent the night in Abilene and hit the road early the next day in preparation for a long day of riding to Eskridge, Dave's home. Weather predictions showed temperatures and humidity rising to the 80s. We headed south then turned east onto another low traffic farm-to-market road, into the famed Flint Hills.

For those who believe Kansas is flat, we invite them to ride with us into the stunning Flint Hills, a ten-thousand square mile landscape of folded ridges and valleys in the eastern third of Kansas. In the early 1800s, as explorer Zebulon Pike rode through this land, he noted a sharp silica rock, chert, poking through the tallgrass prairie. Pike thought it looked like flint so named the rolling terrain Flint Hills.

Early settlers told stories of horseback riders having to stand up in the saddle to get their bearings amidst the big bluestem and buffalo grass. One hundred plus years later, we cyclists did not have to stand up. We enjoyed the luxury of riding paved roads, twisting and dipping through the seemingly endless hills covered with wind-rippled prairie grass.

I fell in love with the vistas. Scarce trees sometimes congregated in early-June-green ribbons in the swales, and the curve of grass matched the curve of the rumpled hills. Magical. We indulged ourselves in the brilliant tallgrass landscape, knowing it represents the largest remnant of prairie grass that once extended from Canada to Texas. Early farmers plowed much of it under, but once they discovered they couldn't plow a furrow through the limestone just below the soil, those in the Flint Hills wisely became ranchers. Now crops include wheat, sorghum, corn and hay.

The green, purple, gold and brown beauty of the land did not keep us from feeling twinges of exertion from bicycling steep country highways in Kansas heat. This became very clear to me by the time Ann, Jim, Les and Ken Fredrickson, Dave's parents and brothers, met us on the road. Ken had driven his new freshly refurbished metallic blue GTO. In my exhaustion, I stopped my bike and put my feet down, and with my fatigued reflexes, it rolled into Ken's car and marred the once immaculate finish. I felt sickened by my carelessness but kind Ken forgave me. I've never forgotten the horrifying feeling of knowing I had ruined the pristine treasure he had been so proud of. I regret it still.

Soon after, the Fredricksons left to go home and we trailed them, much more slowly, across the wrinkled terrain.

Seeing Lake Wabaunsee in the distance invigorated us, knowing we'd have only a few more miles to ride before we arrived in Eskridge. In the 1930s, this spring-fed crystal clear lake, had been formed by building an earthen dam, after progressive thinking locals had seen the need for an additional source of water and recreation area. A state agency using transient Great Depression labor ineffectually made little progress on the dam, so the Works Projects Administration (WPA) took over. They successfully built the dam using that labor as well as CCC (Civilian Conservation Corps) members. Housing built for all the workers eventually became a camp for WWII German POWs captured in Africa. They worked for local farmers, industries in Topeka, and did construction in Eskridge.

We continued pedaling to the Fredrickson's home, the Eskridge United Methodist parsonage. What a relief to get off the bikes and into air conditioned comfort!

Ann prepared the Down and Fredrickson families' traditional meal together, lasagna. We spent the evening relating our Kansas biking tales as well as revisiting the past twelve years since we first met them when everyone except the Carlsons lived in Salina. Once we stopped laughing, drowsy and then sleeping people soon filled the Fredricksons' home.

🚲

In the morning, we explored quintessential small-town America, Eskridge, *The Gateway to the Flint Hills*. We all thought the most fascinating aspect of many commercial buildings had to be the use of native Kansas limestone in their construction, both for walls and as carved trim. Pioneers had discovered that despite the paucity of trees for lumber, Kansas didn't lack building materials. Native stone fence posts (my favorite), walls, churches, homes, barns, jails and community buildings still dot the countryside and towns, especially in the Flint Hills. I had fun discovering fossils embedded in the walls.

After lunch we headed, not by bicycle but by car, to Ann and Jim's cottage on the shore of Lake Wabaunsee. A relaxing afternoon off the bikes made a perfect layover day, especially one beside a quiet lake with good friends. Jim Fredrickson recalled sunrise services, weddings, and other ceremonies he had performed on the remaining concrete bases of the CCC camp and POW buildings.

🚲

We left Eskridge having no expectation of the delights awaiting us on our morning ride. We aimed for Topeka on a scenic highway, past another native Kansas stone barn near Dover. Then we thrilled to the experience of eight miles of a zephyr at our backs, surely akin to the one in *Home on the Range—Where the air is so pure, and the zephyrs so free...* That breeze pushed us along, adding to the joy of seeing the gorgeous rolling hill landscape. When we turned east Jim grinned and whooped, "I want to go back and do that again! This is why we ride!" Those exhilarating miles zipped by too quickly. They'd been just plain fun.

Our route took us into the southwest part of Topeka, Kansas' capital city. We seemed to skim through the city, trying to make the miles we needed to complete our ride and drive home the next day so Jim and John could go back to work. Suddenly Jim hit a pothole which resulted in a broken spoke. Inconvenient, but he happened to break it in front of a bike shop. Did any other cynic wonder if that pothole hadn't been repaired so the shop could increase its business?

Two hours later, the bike was ready and we faced a dilemma: Should we try to finish the ride that day or return another year to complete this cross-state ride? Or should we ride the next day and get home later in the day than we wanted? Historic Leavenworth on the Missouri River, where we had planned to end our biking trip, lay more than fifty miles away.

We opted to drive the car to Leavenworth where we had reservations for three rooms that night, rooms too late to cancel. Ann and Jim would join us and take Dave home with them on Sunday.

We had another great time with the Fredricksons and went to bed early so we would be up at dawn to return to Topeka to complete the last leg of the route. Ann and Jim would await our return and spend the day in historic Leavenworth, once a key supply base for settlement of the Old West.

�🚲

In bike trips, as in life, things do not always go as we intend. We slept soundly until we heard urgent rapping at our door. When Jim opened it there stood a white-faced John. "Our bikes are gone!" As if we couldn't fathom what he had said, we raced outside and looked down at the car. Empty spots loomed where Jim and John's bikes had been. In the excitement of the previous evening, we had foolishly forgotten to lock them on the bike rack.

John moaned, "This is the first time in my life since I was seven years old that I've been without a bicycle!"

We reported the theft to the police and for good measure decided to go to the local newspaper to tell someone else about the stolen bikes. A reporter snapped a photo and interviewed us. Jim and John described their bicycles in their statements. Because John's bicycle was big, white and of French make at that, we hoped it would be found, as it eventually was, albeit in a local ditch. Jim's more common size never reappeared. The stolen bicycles meant the final miles of our ride across Kansas had to be postponed.

🚲

The story doesn't end there, however. That July I joined Ann Fredrickson at a *School of Missions* in Kansas. At lunchtime one day, I chatted with some women from Leavenworth. Upon learning where they were from, I mentioned the stolen bicycle story. Two responded, "I remember reading about you in the paper. Did you ever get the bicycles back?"

I told them of John's happy recovery of his bicycle but that Jim's had not been found. One of the women said that she thought she could find a copy of the news story to send to us. That clipping is among others that we have had written about us during our biking adventures.

🚲

Did we ever complete our ride across Kansas? In 1982 we bicyclists mustered our gear and returned to Topeka to bike those elusive miles to Leavenworth. We had considered riding a shorter more easterly route to the Missouri border, but discovered one of the pass-through towns was to host a motorcycle rally for the day we planned to be there. Back to our original plan.

Once again a snafu (Situation Normal All Fouled Up) changed our plan of action. Jim had securely locked the bicycles to the top rack but had forgotten to remove the key from the padlock. The key fell out somewhere between Iowa City and Topeka. An auto repair shop in Topeka made short work of cutting the padlock. We were back in the business of finishing the ride we had begun two years earlier.

Now that the bikes had been freed from their bonds, Jim rode his replacement bike, a shiny Fuji America and John the smiling had his no-worse-for-the-Leavenworth-ditch-experience Gitane. Connie and I rode the ones we had when we began this adventure.

Mild May weather should have made the trip pleasant, but it wasn't for me. I suffered repeated leg cramps and frequently had to get off my bike to rest. John diagnosed it as lactic acid buildup and suggested I eat bananas in case my potassium was low. I wondered if I had hydrated properly. Despite remembering the delayed sense of completion of riding across Kansas, mostly I recalled leg cramps for this final day. Lesson learned: No matter how long or how short the ride, prepare adequately for early season biking forays.

We had another venture to look forward to that summer—RAGBRAI X. We'd only just begun.

ADDENDUM:

In 1990, ten years after our bicycle ride across Kansas, we received a letter with unfamiliar handwriting. The name and return address surprised and pleased us.

Frank Chudy, Aspen Colorado 6-17-90
Dear Jim and Jan,
I hope this note finds your family in good health and well being. I met you 10 yrs ago this month while bike touring through Kansas. You let me stay with you at a motel and I often recall your kindness and generosity. You and many others that summer made my bike trip very pleasurable and successful. I haven't done any more long distance touring. Most of my riding is around Aspen and now there is a great deal of mountain biking. A lot steeper hills but a lot lower gears!
Take care and good riding,
Frank Chudy

WE'RE DOING WHAT?
HOW MANY MILES IS THAT?
1981 NEW YORK-VERMONT-
MASSACHUSETTS-CONNECTICUT

Riders; Mara, Tania, Jennifer, Jim/Jan. Distance: 803 miles

Wintertime for Iowa bicyclists is something like wintertime for Iowa gardeners. We plan, not our gardens, but our next junket on enticing blue highways, the backroads of our land. The winter of 1981, Jim and I decided we would like a family cycling vacation. Our daughters Mara, Tania and Jennifer were nineteen, seventeen, and sixteen years old and in generally fit condition. Surely they would love the opportunity to bike with their family.

Where to go? "How about New England?" Jim ventured. "Warren and Roz live in Pomona, New York. We could leave our car with them and make a circle-loop back again." *Yeah, one of Jim's famous circle-loops.* But what a terrific idea. It could be a trip of just about any length in the New York-New England area. We could even bike up the Hudson River to Canada and return through Vermont, Massachusetts and Connecticut if there was enough time. So Jim arranged it and our friends the Newmans consented. They lived close to New Jersey so we planned to bike from their house to that border and back as a trial run.

Over the course of winter, Jim developed a dictum which would affect every cross-state bicycle journey we would ever attempt. In order for it to be an official ride, if geographically possible, the state must be biked from border to opposite border. But there could be no biking, for example, across the thumb of Georgia. That would not fulfill the basic criterion. The Dictum also states the opposite borders do not have to be the most distant borders, opening up the opportunity to go across the panhandles of Idaho, Oklahoma, Texas and Florida. It also does not matter whether the routes are east-west, north-south or diagonal. It was a great relief, at least to one of us, to get these details writ in stone.

About the personnel: Mara and Tania, agreeable and eager, said they wanted to have this biking experience. Jennifer, however, exclaimed, "We're doing what? How many miles is that?" Once she heard the answer, her response was, "I don't see any reason to bike all those miles when what I had in mind was going to a resort. Besides that, a bike is a mode of transportation, not a vacation."

She became somewhat placated by our compromise offer to let her take her Walkman along to keep her company. In her own inimitable drama queen fashion she sighed, "Oh, all right. I'll go." It appeared that, in her mind, her compromise included making sure most photos taken of her conveyed the enormous sacrifice she was making for her family. As a tiny child, she used to sigh, "Woes is me." This trip had the potential of becoming one of her woes.

Our plan included an overnight stay with Jim's welcoming cousin, Carolyn Cox, in Akron, Ohio. We then drove to New York City for a quick visit with Marge and Antonio, Jim's sister and brother-in-law. And quick it was: one day in Manhattan, in and out and boom! We were in southern New York State at the Newmans' home.

Before we left on the trip, Mara had told Jim, "Something is wrong with my bike." He responded, or at least what she heard, "It's all in your head." The shakedown ride to the New Jersey border and back to discover potential glitches went just as planned. We found some. Throughout the day, Mara complained loudly about her bicycle. "It just won't shift like it's supposed to."

Her father proclaimed, "The bike is fine. You just aren't doing it right." *Clearly he hadn't learned a primary lesson from our first RAGBRAI.*

She was not convinced. By the time we returned to Warren and Roz's, Mara announced, "This bicycle does not work! It's going to be a disaster to try to ride it seven hundred miles." This time it was my turn to sigh. More drama.

In fact, Jim and I were still novices, not only about long distance touring, but about bikes. We had talked with experienced cyclists and read books and articles about bicycles and biking. One major drawback? We lacked extensive on-the-road experience.

After our 1978 RAGBRAI warped frame fiasco, we had to purchase Jennifer a new bicycle. Although that bike, purchased from a supposedly reputable dealer, did not track, she had managed to muscle her way across the whole width of Iowa, sometimes attempting to keep up with racers. We originally thought her complaints, "Stupid bike!" were just those of a typical thirteen year old. Wrong! We were furious with the bicycle dealers for their deceptive behavior in duping us and with ourselves for allowing ourselves to be duped—another time we wished we had a do-over in

Mara waiting for Tania and Jan on Bear Mountain climb

parenting. No wonder Jennifer had not been enthusiastic about participating in this even longer bicycle trip.

Jim and I didn't want to make the same error twice so our family scoured Pomona to find a bike that would fit Mara, perform well, and at a price we could afford. A beautiful $350 silver Soma was the choice. Mara was happy and the rest of us were not only happy but relieved. We could leave the following day to resume our first long-distance totally unsupported bicycle trip.

We had fitted each of our bikes with a handlebar bag, a rear rack, sleeping bag atop, and panniers on each side which held all our clothing and necessities, including extra food. Jim carried the bike tools, inner tubes, as well as motel information. The sleeping bags came as a fallback measure in case we needed to sleep in a church or outdoor location. We chose not to bring a tent, in retrospect, a good choice. We had no idea ahead of time how far we could travel each day so we made reservations at motels in upcoming towns by late morning or early afternoon of each day. It became a habit to check for pay phones in towns and villages we passed through to make those calls. (Yes, it was the pre-cell phone era.)

🚲

The Big Day arrived. With butterflies in our stomachs we took the mandatory beginning-of-the-adventure photos. After our goodbyes to Warren, Roz, Wendy and Evan, we pedaled off to conquer the challenging Hudson River Valley hills. We quickly learned this first day of fully loaded bicycling would become another shakedown ride. While crossing Bear Mountain Bridge, Mara felt her new bike's front tire suddenly go flat. Jim, our chief mechanic and flat fixer, displayed his customary philosophy regarding bike-related problems, "That's the way it goes sometimes."

We rode on the west bank of the Hudson River, named after Henry Hudson who, with his crew, were the first Europeans known to have explored it, and now the Down crew was doing the same. Hudson sailed up the river until it became too shallow, nearly 140 miles before he decided to return to the mouth of the river. In the mid-1800s, artist Thomas Cole, considered to be the founder of the Hudson River School, painted landscapes of the area, thereby familiarizing Americans with the rugged wilderness of the Hudson Highlands.

I heard a few moans when we saw how steeply the roads rose, but we were all determined not to walk our bikes. Jim easily passed the other four of us as we climbed the hills and, as he went around Mara informed her, "In that gear, with each rotation of your pedal, your bike will go forward twenty-seven inches." Through gritted teeth, she answered, "Thanks Dad." That after I had counseled her, "Once you've ridden about ten miles, you'll be totally warmed up and feel fine." Later on she revealed that after the fourth or fifth day, she thought she could easily ride fifty to sixty miles even though she had ridden very little before the trip because she had been focused on training for hunter-jumper horse shows.

I thought our family of five was privileged to bicycle amidst this landscape and ride up the challenging 7 percent grade of Bear Mountain. I learned I was in the minority. We stopped to catch our breath and basked in the grandeur of this incredible river valley. Sharp greens of foliage, ancient rocky outcrops dropping steeply to swirling brown water, crisp blue sky as a backdrop—the other kind of breathtaking.

🚲

We hoped to spend time visiting historic sites along our route. Early in the trip, Franklin Delano Roosevelt's birthplace, lifelong home and burial place, the Springwood Estate in Hyde Park, topped the list. The house, owned by his mother Sarah, rests on a high bluff overlooking the Hudson River. As we approached it, we saw a circular portico, an addition by FDR. We entered and, despite the dark interior of the house, we recognized its simplicity in contrast to the Vanderbilt Estate which we had visited several years earlier. Books lay everywhere and they, along with displays of family china, and photos, created fascinating windows into the lives of the Roosevelt family. I found it sad that Eleanor Roosevelt never felt at home there. She always considered it to be her mother-in-law's home. Eventually, after FDR's death, Eleanor was relegated to a small corner room. Sarah Roosevelt did not win my heart.

At one point in his storied life, FDR wrote, "All that is within me cries out to go back to my home on the Hudson River." He got his wish. He is buried in his mother's rose garden.

🚲

Vulnerability is one of the hallmarks of bicycling on highways with other vehicles. Nearly everything else is bigger than bikes and their riders who can become easy targets for angry drivers or their passengers. On an otherwise lovely day, we enjoyed our single file ride from picturesque village to village in the Catskills. Suddenly a dark green Ford pickup approached us from behind and slowed down. A teenaged boy leaned out and spat first on me, Mara, Tania, and then on Jennifer. He did not spit on Jim. Stunned and livid with rage, we screamed at him and pedaled as fast as we could to the next town. We looked everywhere for that green pickup. I don't know what I would have done had we found the culprits, but during that ride to town I stored up a lot of harsh words to hurl at them.

A short time after the spitting incident, Jim had a verbal altercation with a motorist who didn't stop at a stop sign and cut in front of us as he turned onto the highway. Jim yelled at him and pointed at the sign, "That is a stop sign!" The driver pulled over, stopped and, despite his passenger's attempt to quiet him, threatened Jim. "If you know what's good for you, you'll get off this road!" As a counter to this despicable behavior, a motorist behind us also stopped, told us he'd seen everything and if there were problems, he'd vouch for us.

Many drivers don't understand, or choose not to understand the fact that bicyclists are allowed on most highways as well as some portions of interstates. They have all the rights, privileges and responsibilities of drivers of other vehicles. They also seem to forget that cyclists are taxpayers and help pay for the roads. They are especially unaware of cyclists' major role in the late 1800s and early 1900s' development of roadways in general, and eventually paved roads in the United States.

There were other frights but one of the scariest occurred when we again had to cycle on a highway that was more heavily trafficked than we like to ride. A bread truck driver pulled out to pass us but swerved back in too soon. He missed Jim but clipped Jennifer's left elbow with his right mirror. She managed to remain upright and had only a mark on her arm. I worried, *What kind of danger are Jim and I exposing our children to?* Even though we had utilized traffic count information, we knew that sometimes there were no good routes to travel to get from one town to another. That limited our choices.

🚲

Weather. As always on a bike trip, we had to decide whether the weather was weatherable or not. We had rain. We had wind. We had wind and rain. We bicycled twelve days and eleven and a half of them featured headwinds. The half-day we didn't was the day we turned around in Canada and biked south. Ergo, headwinds became tailwinds.

Rain and more rain marked the day we pedaled to Lake George, not into the lake, although it felt like it. Our upper bodies kept relatively dry but, as cars and trucks splashed by, the rest got drenched. Although we'd made a point of wrapping our sleeping bags in plastic and our extra clothing and gear in zippered plastic bags, we had not been as proficient in waterproofing everything as we had thought.

Completely sodden, we arrived at our motel in the late afternoon. Penny-wise but pound foolish, we had only rented one room for the five of us and our bicycles. That meant five adult-sized people, five mud-splattered bikes, five damp sleeping bags, ten wet panniers, ten soaked shoes, and a multitude of plastic bags which had held all our clothing and gear draped everywhere in one small motel room—drying. Well, we hoped they would dry. It was not a pretty sight as we jostled each other for space. It didn't smell so great either.

Since there were no more rooms to rent we appealed to the motel manager to let us use her clothes dryer to help manage the moisture. She did and things began to look cheerier. Unfortunately, the only food source several blocks away meant we would have to slosh there and back.

Tania recalls thinking about the sleeping bags. We only used them when one daughter had to sleep on the floor instead of a folding cot. At the time, she silently lamented, "Why did we bring all of them?" She also wondered about the strategically placed laminated maps cut to the size of our rear racks to help keep mud spatter off our sleeping bags. She deemed them marginally effective—little mud but lots of moisture. I, however, thought these little spatter guards were quite clever. After all, I'd conceived the idea after considering how cruddy anything riding on the back racks could get. They were cheap, just old maps and laminate. And I love maps.

🚲

Jim and I savor our time with our daughters and this trip gave us that opportunity. Mara would be a junior at Knox College in the fall. Tania had been accepted at Macalester College in St. Paul and Jennifer would be a junior at Iowa City's West High School. We had no idea when we would have the opportunity to travel with the three of them again. Unfortunately, they did not always share the joy of togetherness. Sisterly jibes, sometimes heartfelt and sometimes just because it seemed like the thing to do, peppered our days. "Pick up your own mess." "Don't get your stinky socks on my clean shirt." "Don't take up so much of the bed." And, in their sultriest Greta Garbo tones, "I vant to be alone." Being alone was a luxury. Parental as well as sisterly weariness occasionally set in.

About Jennifer and her Walkman: Jim and I requested that she bicycle a short distance in front of us so we could see her but wouldn't have to hear the music she loved so much. We thought the system generally worked quite well. Mara and Tania did not always share our perspective. She undoubtedly thought Journey's *Don't Stop Believin'* inspired her to survive our trip but her sisters shuddered whenever they heard the title over and over. I guess their hearing was better than ours. Years later, Tania admitted that sometimes she really wanted to be near Jennifer and her music, especially grinding uphill. "The music helped blot out what I was doing."

Another issue arose with her Walkman. Combined with the batteries it created quite a weight in her handlebar bar. And it zipped through batteries. We heard her grousing, "This handlebar bag is so heavy!"

"What's in it?"

She opened the bag and showed us. We groaned at the jumble. "Are those new or used?"

"Both."

"Both?" We were incredulous at this otherwise bright child of ours.

"I didn't know what to do with them. I knew it wasn't right to just throw them in the trash." Obviously, she had been reared in a family that believes in re-using and recycling, not just throwing things away. She learned the lesson well, too well. That evening in the motel, she and Jim checked all the batteries. Unbeknownst to Jennifer, her prescient dad had brought along a little battery tester. They discarded the dead ones. In the trash.

🚲

Long distance bicycle trips take both physical and mental tolls on riders. Jim and I like to take layovers every seven or eight days. Because of frequent rain and constant headwinds, we decided to take an early one once we arrived in Glens Falls. *What a great place for a rest day. Lovely town, lots of*

41

historic and natural attractions, including the falls. The kids can sleep in, help with laundry and then we can all bike in a leisurely fashion around town to see the sights.

I dreamed. The motel had a swimming pool which appealed to the kids and the washer and dryer appealed to me. We decided to extend our stay but met with resistance from the managers who seemed skeptical. Did they think we were going to trash the place with our bikes? To our relief, they finally consented.

After a relaxing evening with everyone doing their own thing—reading neglected books, watching TV, catching up on the Glens Falls news in the *Post-Star*, we went to bed and savored not having to get up early. That didn't prevent me from my usual crack-of-dawn awakening but no one had to hurry to do anything. Jim and I ate before the lie-a-beds, then I gathered the laundry. Although they had wakened, the girls preferred relaxing in bed to getting up to eat. They also had no interest in sightseeing. They wanted to do nothing all day long except whatever required the least energy. Jim wanted to watch television in peace.

"Humph!" I made a snarky face and felt quite sorry for myself. I really didn't want to spend my time finishing the laundry for these ingrates. None of my best glares or harumphs budged them. I flounced out and stomped to the laundry room. No one paid any attention to my futile attempt at drama. It's difficult for me to stay mad for long, especially on a clear sunny day. I finished the laundry, returned to my happy family who were doing whatever they wanted. They thanked me, took their now clean clothes, squashed them into plastic bags which they slid into their panniers.

Mara, Tania, and Jennifer decided to go swimming. I rolled my bicycle out to the street to go discover the town. I quickly tired and realized I missed being with my family. I didn't feel refreshed yet but I knew I didn't need a bike ride that day. I needed quiet time. I grabbed my book, sat in the shade near the swimming pool, and let my mind and body relax. *I don't have to see everything, experience everything. I can just be.*

⚛

New York's Adirondack Mountains are separated from Vermont's Green Mountains by 125-mile long Lake Champlain which eventually drains northward into Canada and the great St. Lawrence River. Why do we remember it? Because we searched for Champs, the Lake Champlain monster. Darn! We didn't see him and pedaled on.

⚛

As a special treat, Jim and I decided to book a night at the Holiday Inn in Plattsburgh, New York. As we always do, we requested ground floor accommodations so we could easily wheel the bikes directly into our rooms. The reservationist assured us it wouldn't make any difference what floor we stayed on because the motel had an elevator. Great, we thought.

Prematurely, we discovered.

We arrived at the motel in high spirits, knowing we'd have a good place to stay. The desk clerk apologized and told us the bad news. "The elevators are not working. And your room is on the fourth floor. "

"What? But we were promised. Are there any vacancies on the first floor? Even just one?"

"I'm sorry but there aren't. We can put your bicycles in a storage room where they'd be safe." We've learned from past experiences that putting bikes in a storage area at a hotel or motel, even if it is on the first floor, is not ideal. Everything needs to be taken off the bikes, sometimes a difficult feat. Putting things back on often isn't any easier. The panniers won't pop off or go back on as they are supposed to. Things shift so the weight isn't evenly distributed. Faced with two unhappy choices, we chose to haul those loaded *muffertygobblin'* (a cycling friend's fake curse word that seemed appropriate) bikes up seemingly endless stairs. Two people toted each bicycle up one flight, paused for breath and continued on until all the people and equipment made it to the room. We tried not to think about having to lug them back downstairs the next day.

We had a pleasant and uneventful dinner that evening, planned our route for the following day. All five of us slept well in a bigger room than we've ever had before. Jim, Mara, Jennifer and I didn't mind rising early and going. Tania required enormous amounts of sleep and didn't really like anything that began before 8 AM. Unfortunately for her, we had an early breakfast.

We each attempted to bring our own bicycles down the flights of stairs, putting on the brakes then releasing them with every bump-bump-bump of the steps. We helped each other as best we could, risked being run over, and finally reached the safety of the lobby. By then we had exerted more energy just getting the bikes to the street than we sometimes do in an entire morning. After a short breather, we were, if not rarin' to go, at least ready to go.

Surprise, surprise! We faced a headwind the day we reached Canada. The hope the wind brought was, when we headed south to enter the United States, it would stay the course. A tailwind blessed us for a half day as we cycled into Vermont. We cherished this wonderful feeling and hoped we would have another before the trip ended. Tania recollects one hill took us an hour to climb and only ten minutes to descend. "It was really steep and winding. I didn't want to brake but there were lots of curves too, so I had to." Nothing is sure on a cycling trip except pedaling.

Many people think of Vermont as a postcard with picture perfect autumn kaleidoscopes of glowing vermillion, amber, russet, saffron trees. Winter scenes included snowbound villages, steepled churches piercing the brilliant sky, woodsmoke curling from chimneys, horse-drawn sleighs emerging from rustic covered bridges, rolling pastures dotted with red barns and white houses. Vermont means sugaring time with pungent scents of maple syrup boiling down, the Vermont Country

Jennifer and Tania near a Quebec cornfield

Store, taciturn old men quick with quips, Ethan Allen and the Green Mountain Boys. The list goes on and on. When I think of Vermont, I think of this bike trip and *Flying*. Yes, flying. It happened one day during our family's ride.

Turning south from Canada to return to our car in New York included biking Highway 7 the length of the state of Vermont. We loved rambling through the farmland, immersing ourselves in the hamlets along the way, breathing the fresh clean air. Suddenly, or perhaps not so suddenly, the road tumbled downward alongside a valley, seeming to dance, curving right, left, sweeping us with it. I felt as free as I had ever felt in my life. I began to sing at the top of my voice, praising God, creation, life, breath, family, love, hope, peace, freedom. All the good things I so often take for granted.

All these years later, I remember that day, the moment I was struck with a clarity I don't remember experiencing before. I was flying and I felt free.

🚲

Although headwinds usually make bicycling more difficult, they helped make each member of our family stronger. This was never more evident to us than the day we met two fit young men on their first day biking. We asked the questions cyclists who meet on the road ask of each other: *Where are you coming from? Where are you heading? How long have you been on the road?*

With obvious pride, they told us they lived in Northampton, Massachusetts and planned to bike all the way to Canada. Jennifer gave them a triumphant look and informed them, "We biked all the way from New Jersey to Canada and are on our way back!" Jim and I caught each other's eyes. At last she felt a sense of accomplishment.

Long afterwards, Tania confessed she hadn't realized how special the trip had been until she began her first year in college. When she told her new friends what she and her family had done during the summer, they stood gape-mouthed. "You did what?" Then she understood.

🚲

One of the many joys of bicycling is to have time to see and revel in details, like some signs we might have missed had we been in a car. We were tootling along in a town in Vermont when Jim pointed out the *Sunset Nursing Home*. Next door the *Ready Funeral Home* displayed driveway signs directing *In* and *Out*. We nearly laughed ourselves off our bikes when it struck us that these signs came as close to fast funeral service as one could get. I guess people in that town, like the proverbial Boy Scout, knew how to always be prepared.

🚲

Midway through Vermont, a remarkable group of twelve cyclists crossed our paths. They traveled on six tandem bikes, each captained by a sighted rider with a blind stoker in back. They had begun riding in New York City and would soon finish, as soon as they rode a few miles in Ontario. What an impressive feat, amazing camaraderie and memories for all of them. We felt humbled.

BIKING ON EMPTY

Our family's routine included checking our money supply each evening and if necessary planning banking stops for the following day. Through experience we had learned that not every New England village had a bank. Long before debit cards existed and ATM machines graced most towns, travelers' cheques had been the safest way to carry funds.

Late in the Vermont leg of our trip we needed another infusion of money. This time we planned to cash some of my travelers' cheques. Just before signing into our motel Jim asked me to get them for him. I rummaged through my handlebar bag and searched its pockets, "I can't find them."

"What do you mean you can't find them?"

"I've looked. I'm positive I put them in my handlebar bag but now I can't find them." Before we had left our friends' house ten days ago, I had carefully secured my zip-locked cheques in the innermost part of my handlebar bag. Now I nearly pulled it apart in the search. I could not find them. *Had I really put them in the bag? Had I unwittingly left them at the Newmans? Could I have accidentally pulled them out when I retrieved something else and lost them?*

It was Saturday. Vermont banks were not open on Saturdays. We had enough money to pay the motel fee that night but not enough to provide adequate food all day Sunday and through Monday morning until we could get to a bank.

Fortunately, we spotted a McDonalds nearby. We have never been so happy to see those golden arches. And they had one of their scratch card promotions going on, games that often resulted in food as prizes.

Separately, each member of our family placed one order, paid for it, and received a scratch card with a history question on it. If we answered correctly, we'd get another item of food, for example, french fries or a beverage and another scratch card. We collectively and carefully weighed the answer to each question. Correct answers became proverbial gold mines for our bicyclists' appetites. One at a time, scratch card by scratch card, we increased our bounty, mostly French fries. It became the slowest fast food experience we'd ever had. Eating it, quite quick.

We felt anything but sated when we returned to our motel and settled into our classic 1960s room. We checked out the knotty pine paneling and forest green ribbed bed spreads. We studied framed magazine prints of flaming maple trees alongside a placid stream and sawmill. We recognized the durable but worn maple bed and nightstand with a brown floral printed shade on the colonial style lamp from other tired-looking motels. There were no amenities we take for granted today—like telephone, microwave, extra pillows or small refrigerator for our snacks—this motel simply provided a place to shower and sleep.

Jim and I saw Jennifer raiding the gorp and told her to stop. Mean parents, we salvaged the rest of it and stored it with the apples in our panniers for the proverbial rainy day. That might be tomorrow. Stomach growls accompanied our tossing and turning as we each tried to go to sleep. Eventually everyone did.

⚲

Sunday morning after a disappointing light breakfast of muffins and juice, Jim and I assured our offspring we would find restaurants and a motel that took Master Card. We would eat and we would sleep. Despite our promises, it proved difficult to find small town businesses that accepted Master Card in the early 1980s.

Biking long distances on empty stomachs is never pleasant, especially for those of us who seem chronically hungry. Throughout the morning one or another of our daughters reminded Jim and me, as if we could possibly forget, "I'm really hungry."

"It's sure hard climbing these hills on an empty stomach."

"It's been a long time since breakfast."

"How much gorp do we have left?" Pause. "Just checking."

We survived the day, made easier by the pastoral scenes that would make any former farm girl happy. Clear skies, lush woodlands, verdant pastureland, red barns and silos, black and white cows chewing their cuds, occasional cornfields. The only cloud—I couldn't find the travelers' cheques.

⚲

Monday after breakfast, Jim vowed, "We will reach a town with an open bank by late morning. I will get a two hundred dollar cash advance with our Master Card. It will all be OK." After seeing our daughters' faces he queried, "Why are you looking at me that way? Don't be so skeptical. You're not going to starve."

Jim and I heard a mumbled chorus, "Right, Dad."

New England smiled on us with another perfect blue-sky day, temperatures in the 70s, undulating emerald hills dotted with red-barned farms. Our family arrived in Bennington, Vermont by 11 AM and stopped on the sidewalk across the street from a bank. Jim removed his helmet, pulled his comb out of his back pocket, carefully combed his hair, straightened his biking clothes and strode into the bank.

As if on cue, Mara, Tania and Jennifer sang out, "Good luck, Dad."

We assumed this solemn occasion would not last more than a few minutes. The four of us relaxed, enjoyed the warm sun and colorful streetscape lined with trees, accented by flowering shrubs and bright blue and red July blooms. We waited. And waited. And waited.

We glanced at our watches and wondered *How difficult could it be to get a Master Card cash advance?* We wandered up and down the street, peering in windows of antique shops, clothing and shoe stores. We took turns watching our bikes. But who would want them, fully laden with everything but food? An hour had passed and Jim still had not emerged from the bank. What in the world was going on?

Finally, Jim appeared with a slightly wild look on his face. He signaled for me to come in. I fluffed my helmet-hair, smoothed my clothes, and walked across the street to join him. Jim, the steady and calm, was neither. He quickly explained what had been happening. He had tried to get cash from our credit card but Mara's new bicycle plus other expenses had put us over our limit.

He had inquired if the bank would cash a personal check for two hundred dollars. For security reasons, the teller had asked if he knew the name of the bank president. All he could think of was his nickname, Bud. That's when he summoned me.

"Clark Houghton."

The teller called our Iowa City bank and turned to us with a strange look on her face. "I'm sorry sir. But you have insufficient funds to cover that amount of money."

Jim was flummoxed. "How large of a check can I write?"

The teller continued, "I'm sorry sir, but we are not allowed to reveal how much money you have in your account." What now? In a last-ditch effort to provide for his family, an embarrassed Jim suggested calling his orthodontic office. His office manager Petra could transfer funds from his office account to his personal one. He muttered to me, "I feel like I'm trying to con these people out of their money."

The long-suffering teller put Iowa City's First National Bank on hold while she dialed Jim's office. Thank goodness Petra answered. On a three-way conference call she agreed to transfer funds to Jim's account. As this transaction took place, a thought floated into my stressed out brain. *My monthly salary from the Iowa City School District had been automatically deposited into my checking account a few days earlier. I could have written a check that wouldn't bounce.*

Later when I apologized to my family for not remembering that fact earlier, one of them responded with a classic family line, "We forgive you, Mom. But if you ever do that again…"

So it came to pass that with calls between bank officers, Jim's office and The Bank of Bennington, we eventually had enough money for the rest of the trip. Our incredulity showed when Jim tried to pay for the phone calls and service charges required to make these transactions. No one would take our money. Could this be their usual bank policy? Was it out of the goodness of their hearts they didn't want to take money from this family who obviously had not planned well, and were out roaming the countryside with little food and nothing but bicycles for transportation? Or was it because they had already been paid in humor? We don't know but will always recall their help with gratitude.

At last our daughters would be well-fed and safely housed. They suffered no long-term ill effects from the deprivations inflicted on them by their seemingly clueless parents. They didn't even begin to hoard food. I did surreptitiously check their panniers though, just in case.

About the travelers' cheques—their whereabouts remained a mystery.

We felt flush with success at finally having funds to finish the Hudson River bike trip. We didn't anticipate the next bump in the road.

On the outskirts of town a speeding car veered too close to Mara. To avoid being clipped, she swerved, her pedal grazed the curb. She hit loose gravel and fell, slicing her leg on the guard rail. We all dropped our bikes and ran to her. From where she lay on the ground, she surveyed her cuts and abrasions and fumed, "That stupid jerk could have killed me!"

Other motorists stopped to check on her, among them a doctor carrying his black bag medical kit. "I'm an obstetrician." This Good Samaritan cleaned her wounds, bandaged her leg and, after receiving our thanks, disappeared. Mara, still furious but not yet stiff simmered, "Some people shouldn't be allowed to drive! Bozo!" She limped to her bike, grimaced, mounted it and rode away. The rest of us followed, grateful she had not been more seriously injured and that so many people had stopped to help. Once I got over my initial fright, I was furious but tried not to show it. Mara expressed herself well and didn't need me to add fuel to the flame.

Our day's destination, Pittsfield, Massachusetts, had been home to Oliver Wendell Holmes, the famed jurist. Despite the trauma of the accident making all of us a bit skittish, we rode the 38 miles, straggled in and settled into our classier-than-yesterday's motel. It didn't take Justice Holmes' great legal mind to detect our offsprings' thoughts. The prospect of witnessing Prince Charles and Lady Diana's *Wedding of the Century* the following day totally eclipsed the excitement promised by long hours on a bicycle with all its dirt, grime and hard work. Frankly, I was relieved.

"Would you three like to stay here tomorrow while your dad and I finish the ride and get the car from the Newman's house?"

Sheer joy exploded from them. "Yes! We can sleep in and then watch the Royal Wedding!" Jim and I would be happy too.

⚲

Just after dawn the next day, the two of us left the motel, our sleeping beauties sprawled all over the beds. We planned to ride 130 miles, more than we've ever ridden in one day. I wondered *Can we really ride that far before dark?* In our original itinerary, the distance was to have been split into two days. Now we needed that second day to return to Pittsfield with the station wagon to retrieve Mara, Tania, and Jennifer, get our gear and start toward home.

The July sky reflected the sparkle of the day. Jim and I swept up and down the rolling hills on curling roads. Cobalt lakes nestled in the oak, beech, and maple woods. We passed old New England farms shimmering with freshly painted barns and ringed by mossy rock walls.

At a roadside inn built in George Washington's era, a cinnamony scent enticed us to stop. Scrumptious hot apple pie fed our tiring bodies and raised our spirits.

Then came the second Bear Mountain Bridge crossing. Everything seemed different from crossing it early in the trip. Now when I recall the combination of wind and high bridge, it still causes my stomach to clench. Usually I am not fearful of heights, but perched on my bicycle, higher than the guard rail, made me terrified of being blown over it.

On the approach I had seen signs for the Appalachian Trail route. I have always been in awe and a bit envious of the courage, determination and will of the through-trail hikers to undertake such a bold endeavor. *I would love to meet some hikers today. Maybe a little of their resolve would rub off on me and I wouldn't be so jittery about this bridge.*

Jim passed over the 2,332 foot span with seeming aplomb. I quaked in my tennies just thinking about the possibility of toppling nearly 150 feet into the Hudson River below. Amid my wild apocalyptic thoughts, I managed to half-ride, half-scoot my bike until I found myself safely on the other side. We didn't meet any hikers.

Although we pedaled through the landscape of a Washington Irving tale, the day became a cluttered collage of hills, mountains, streams, and miles and miles of road needing to be ridden. Meanwhile, my mind blurred with memories of the past two weeks. Riding in the rain, facing headwinds every day but one, too-crowded motel rooms with five people, five bikes, five different ideas of how this trip should be conducted. My mind and weariness spawned a very long day on a skinny bicycle saddle. *At least we don't have to be concerned about our daughters today. All we have to do is make it back to the car.*

In the fading sunlight, I paused and drooped over my handlebars to catch my breath. I heard a vexing voice, "We're never going to make it to the Newmans' before dark if you keep stopping."

An irritation-induced surge of adrenaline hit me. I hopped back on my bike and just rode. All. The. Rest. Of. The. Way.

And I rode a victory lap around the cul-de-sac.

At the Newmans' house I marveled at the number I saw on Jim's odometer: 132.9 miles for the day and 802.6 miles for our twelve-day trip. I had enough zip left to unzip my handlebar bag and dump the contents out on a bed. I still hoped to find our wayward travelers' cheques. Nothing. I probed the pockets and brushed the fabric with my fingers. What's that? Between the fabric and a flat metal panel, I detected a barely perceptible bulge.

The quest for the errant cheques was over, as was our longest day. So was our bicycle trip, except for the memories and the tales we would tell—like this one of crossing states numbered three, four, five and six.

FLORIDA, THE SUNSHINE STATE-1982

Riders: John/Connie/Phil/Cara. Jim/Jan. Drop off: Tania/Jennifer and Jennifer's best friend, Dana Heath. Along for the Ride: Three of Tania's Macalester College friends. Distance: 110 miles

1982 marked another progressive step in our bicycling path. Wanting an early start to our biking season and sick of Iowa's winters, we craved mild temperatures where we wouldn't have to shovel anything. We realized we had an opportunity we should capitalize on—Spring Break! Why should college kids have all the fun?

Utilizing this simple plan, we could go south to warmer climes, get some fun cycling miles in and have a unique vacation. Thus we set the template, naturally subject to variations, for Spring Break cycling adventures to follow:

1. Choose a warm, generally southern state. Warm is anything warmer than Iowa.

2. Study possible routes, points of interest and traffic counts.

3. Plan the route.

4. Find accommodations between fifty to seventy miles apart along the route.

5. Contact any relative or friends who live near the route. Maybe we could see them.

6. See if any of our kids or friends could drive the van for drop off and pick up duties.

The Iowa City Schools' March spring break was perfect to travel to the Sunshine State—Florida. Fortunately, our daughters, Tania and Jennifer plus friend Dana's breaks coincided, so they handled the drop-offs. When Tania's Macalester College friends heard what she got to do, three of them volunteered to keep her company.

We organized three cars and twelve people, Carlsons in their car, Jim and I in our little brown Datsun, plus Tania, Jennifer, Dana and crew in our station wagon. We all headed southeast through snow to sun and sand.

A Crystal River park along the Gulf of Mexico became our launching point where we symbolically dipped our bikes' rear tires once the kids unloaded us and our gear. They hightailed it with the vehicles to a seaside motel in Ormond Beach. We would not see or hear from them until we biked to meet them four days later. We were on our own.

We had chosen a route with low traffic count and we hoped few retirees with unpredictable driving styles and skills. We understood our endpoint, just north of Daytona, was a hopping place for college kids to have fun. Everyone should be happy.

Blue sky and temperate days soothed our Iowa winter-frazzled souls. What a joy to observe the quiet stealth of herons wading in roadside swamps, pedal along orchards of orange and grapefruit trees through this rural north-of-Orlando territory with its cattle and farms. Phil kept the cattle on edge as he rode by, yelling to make them run. My farm kid history prodded me to tell him to stop, but I didn't. As a teenager riding bikes with his parents, their friends and his kid sister, he probably needed the outlet, and the cattle would recover moments after we passed.

Cara's strong attack of teenage angst made her feel understandably confused and upset. Among other things, when any of us called out the time-honored bicyclist warning, "Car up!" she heard "Cara!" and stopped. She repeatedly expressed her frustration. She opined later that she did very well considering biking wasn't exactly the thing she wanted to do on spring break— in Florida, no less. Phil remembered the austere conditions of our pit stops with sand, crabgrass and ants. It's a wonder he and Cara ever chose to continue to ride more trips. But, hardy souls that they were, they did.

It's hard to determine how our sore bodies will tolerate the first trip of a season. Some of us grew uncomfortable and weary, as we biked through DeLand and seemingly on and on to the interstate motel where our beds awaited us. Not only that, but our roads had been consistently narrow. We had to be hyper-alert for traffic and, oddly enough, for slippery and smelly citrus fruit smashed on the road near the processing plants.

Nevertheless, we riders felt a sense of accomplishment as we dipped our front wheels in the Atlantic Ocean.

When we arrived in Ormond Beach to meet our offspring and their friends, Tania suffered from mononucleosis, Derek had sliced his thumb opening a can of oysters while trying to impress Dana. He had refused stitches in the ER because of the cost. The unscathed others loved lolling on the beach and catching rays and tried to get us to join them. I hadn't recovered from the appalling condition of their motel room—dirty, probably wet, clothes everywhere, hardly a place to stand or sit. And it smelled damp and musty. Yuck.

Instead, several of us zipped to the Space Coast to Cape Canaveral to see what had been happening at the Kennedy Space Center. We were treated to the sight of huge sections of a rocket being transported to another part of the facility. Little did we know that a few years later, from Connie and John's new Orlando home, we would watch rockets launch live in the distance.

As we mused on the highs and not-quite-so-highs of this excursion, we agreed it had been clock and calendar driven. Nothing and no one had really relaxed except for those who had a beach vacation. As the years went on, we learned that Spring Break bike rides would never be relaxed, primarily because of the distance from home to many of the warmer areas. We would accommodate and accept that as part of the occasional craziness of this overall adventure.

MISSISSIPPI-ALABAMA -1983

Riders: Connie/John/Phil/Cara, Jim/Jan. Drivers of two vehicles: Jennifer, Dana, Jennifer's boyfriend Bernd Knorr and his brother Uli. Distance: 190 miles

Our vehicle crew dropped us riders off just east of Bogalusa, Louisiana at a very unassuming bridge over the Pearl River, one that would figure prominently on another ride. We pedaled east on State Highway 26 as they drove away to explore the beaches and sights of the Gulf Coast on their own.

On some bicycling trips, it can seem as though what traffic was like and where and what we ate overshadowed nearly everything else. Our Mississippi-Alabama ride confirmed that. Mississippi memories focused on feeling threatened by lumber trucks barreling along the flat rural backroads. We frequently checked our rearview mirrors especially when we heard trucks approaching from the rear. Within the first hours of cycling, we learned that few lumber truck drivers would pull over for us even when there was no oncoming traffic. They steadfastly remained in the right lane, as far right as they wanted to go. It became automatic for us to pull over to the rarely present shoulder or completely off the road to let them pass. None of us felt safe. Mississippi soon earned and then maintained its reputation among us as the state with the least considerate and most hostile acting truck drivers.

Our fear of pickup trucks, especially those with gun racks, added to our unease in biking through Mississippi. They too spelled danger. As with lumber trucks, we'd pull to the roadside and pray they didn't veer toward us. We began to feel as though we had targets on our backs. *What kind of mentality brings out this menacing behavior?* I guess they hated bicyclists on principle. However, the people we encountered in the towns treated us well and we felt comfortable with them and their friendliness.

While cycling in these two states, everyone in our group noticed something that made us very grateful to live in Iowa. Everywhere we looked, we saw plastic bags, newspapers, candy wrappers, pop and beer bottles and other trash. We shook our heads. "Look at that mess—it's everywhere. We are so lucky to have a bottle law in Iowa!" Because of this law, we have become accustomed to clean roadsides, parks, and other public spaces. What could have been attractive in Mississippi became eyesores because of the trash.

Whenever the Carlsons and Downs reminisce about biking together, we rehash some favorite stories. One reprises what alliteration-loving John calls "wild, wonderful Wiggins." We had over-nighted in Wiggins, Mississippi and needed breakfast. We found a café surrounded by pickups and cars with local license plates—that had to be a good sign. We sat down, ordered our food and waited. We heard periodic loud laughter from a nearby table where seven or eight men sat drinking their morning coffee. The scene and sounds reminded us of early morning coffee groups we'd observed and heard all over the country.

As we eavesdropped, we determined from the latest conversation that the guys were about to leave and would play a game which decided who would pay the bill. A number was silently chosen by the person who paid the bill last time, then the others around the table chose a number. After the first number had been chosen, the man in the know would indicate whether it was too high or too low. The next person picked a number and learned whether it was too high or too low. That continued until the ultimate lucky guy had only one number left to choose, the winning one. Another burst of laughter while they looked at us and laughed some more. Why? The chosen number 47 was the number Phil was wearing on his West High football jersey.

Cool weather, gentle hills and more logging trucks marked the morning ride with piney woods lessening the impact of the beige and brown landscape. Along the way, we gave extra credit to the problem-solving homeowner whose driveway mud puddles needed amelioration. They cleverly covered them with jeans, jackets, overalls, everything blue denim, thereby sopping up the muck. They definitely one-upped Sir Walter Raleigh and his cloak.

One of our great discoveries of the trip was in Lucedale. We ordered something none of us had ever heard of before—muffulettas. We became hooked by the sesame seed crusted eight-inch wheels of bread layered with cured meats, cheese and giardiniera—pickled vegetable and olive salad. They had been called a *two-fisted workman's lunch, portable and hearty*. Our later recipe search told us muffulettas had been perfected in New Orleans and reflected part of the city's diverse culinary heritage, in this case, Sicilian working class, butchers, farmers, dockworkers, fishermen, laborers during the early twentieth century. The taste blew us away.

We sat on the front step of the café to eat our muffulettas and noticed a sign—*Lingerie Factory and Outlet Store*. Connie, Cara and I went in to check out the nightgowns and undies and Connie bought a couple of things that she tucked into her bike bag. The number of garment factories in the state surprised us.

Once we left Lucedale, we altered our easterly course and headed southeast across the Alabama border and on toward the edge of Mobile where we spent the night.

⚲

Connie and John suggested we visit Bellingrath Gardens, just south of Mobile, so we skimmed along the west and south sides of the city to get there. The original owner Walter Bellingrath was one of the first Coca-Cola bottlers in Southeast United States. He must have done quite well in that business considering how many signs of Coca-Cola products we'd seen. Now about the beverage containers in the ditches, Mr. Bellingrath…

We wondered what we should do with our bicycles while we strolled through the gardens. The Bellingrath Gardens Pet Hotel answered that question. We locked our bikes in the cages designed for animals which were absent that day. Despite the chilly and overcast spring day, we appreciated the layout of the sixty-five cultivated acres of sprawling lawns punctuated by Mirror Lake, bubbling Little Mermaid Fountain, live oaks, just-beginning-to-bud-and-bloom purple, yellow and gold flowers, trees, and shrubs. Touches of pink, rose and lavender on green, together with azaleas, and pink hydrangeas encircled by white ones enhanced the designs. Most dramatic were the deep rose and red tulips backed by the Bellingrath's brick mansion. After ambling down flagstone paths, we huddled together for our let's-remember-this-day photo on the bowed Japanese bridge. We hoped to return some summer day to see the gardens in another season.

After leaving the Gardens, we continued riding south where suddenly we looked ahead and saw an arched bridge resembling a highway to nowhere except the sky. It went somewhere, to Dauphin Island. We pedaled the three-mile bridge over the Gulf Intracoastal Waterway to the island and 1821 era Fort Gaines. There we met Jennifer, Dana, Bernd and Uli who clambered around the fortress and its Civil War cannons just a few feet from the Gulf of Mexico.

Although there is periodic ferry service from Dauphin Island to Fort Morgan, we opted to pop our bikes onto the van and drive it and the Carlsons' car north along Mobile Bay. We then traveled south along the Bay to Gulf Shores where we overnighted.

⚲

In the morning light we drove the ten miles out to the tip of the peninsula where historic Fort Morgan faces west to Fort Gaines. Fort Morgan is a masonry pentagonal bastion fort at the mouth of Mobile Bay. Protecting Mobile Bay, the two forts were deeply involved in the Civil War providing defensive fire for blockade runners which brought food and arms to their troops and civilians. From there, we grabbed our bikes and left our drivers to meet us at the Florida border. We finished this trip by cycling about thirty miles along the Gulf of Mexico, through Gulf Shores, Orange Beach and all the other tourist meccas that line the coast, the ones that lure so many Iowans in winter.

With no fanfare at all, we completed our ride in Gulf Beach Heights on the Florida Panhandle border. My mind said, *Another one (state) bites the dust.* Actually, two bit the dust since we had bicycled across both Mississippi and Alabama and Jim and I had racked up states number eight and nine in our bicycling quest.

From spring back to winter as we traveled north. From Missouri on, we drove home in a snowstorm. At least we weren't biking in one.

MINNESOTA -LAND OF SKY BLUE WATER -1983

Riders: Connie/John/Phil, Deb Rogiers (John's niece), Jim/Jan. Driver: Tania. Distance: 240 miles

Bike trip beginnings are filled with hope and a bit of nervous excitement. We hope we've trained enough, biked enough miles, and climbed enough hills to meet our expectations of the ride. On a comfortably warm day we began our across Minnesota ride at the South Dakota border.

Because of the gentle terrain and slight tailwind, we biked far and fast that morning. We decided we had plenty of time to relax and nap after lunch. Where do six people find places to lie down? In a cemetery of course. This suited me perfectly. I could I get my cemetery fix since I love roaming cemeteries, particularly old ones.

First I investigated the oldest grave markers, noting the birth and death dates, wondering what caused so many young people to die—cholera, influenza, measles, scarlet fever, farm accidents? The overwhelming number of babies dying, many close in time to the death of a sibling, compounded the tragedy. I searched for the always poignant Civil War and Spanish-American War veterans' grave sites. Often they edged the graveyard with weather-worn, moss covered and hard to read limestone markers. Cemeteries are great places for remembering our country's as well as our own family histories. And for napping.

Each of us found a place, some secluded, some closer to each other, used our jackets or bike helmets for pillows and settled in for a snooze. Eventually, insects or birds or a tiny tickle from a piece of grass wielded by a friend roused us. We yawned, stretched, and tried to convince ourselves it was time to move on toward our destination on this idyllic day.

At first Tania tried to keep track of us riders every few hours—unless she was in a central Minnesota town visiting classmates from St. Paul's Macalester College. We stayed in Alexandria that first night and Tania stayed out late with her friends and slept in the next day. She didn't have to keep bikers' hours. She'd find us down the road later in the day after she'd tried her hand at water-skiing—being pulled by a slow-moving fishing boat and with bruises to prove it.

However, one day she circled repeatedly trying to find us. We didn't have cell phones so the only way she could locate us was to do what she already was. Exasperation and bewilderment fought within her. *Where did I miss them? Have they already been here? Did they change routes? Are they going faster than they thought they would? Should I just go to tonight's motel and wait for them? What if they need me?* At last she spotted us, waved as she passed us and stopped at a pull-off on the top of the next rise. She greeted us with a smile and slight consternation: "I've been all over the place looking for you! Where have you been?"

"Uh, on our bikes, wondering if we'd missed you." That scenario and others of the younger generation feeling like they needed to parent the parents became reasons we preferred not having a SAG driver with us during most of our bike trips. The SAG might worry and spend a lot of time conscientiously searching for us when they could have been sight-seeing, going to museums, dallying at the beach or reading books. The trade-off? We appreciated not having to tote our panniers every day.

Now that we'd found each other, we went on and Tania headed to our day's destination. She dropped our panniers off at the motel and headed to the Twin Cities to be with friends and go tubing the next day. We had our own excitement—John spotted and pointed out thirty to forty sky-divers in formation, parachutes deployed. A heavenly sight.

Summer in rural Minnesota teems with bucolic settings. Gently rolling hills graced with green corn fields, white farmhouses, silos and barns, dairy cattle, pigs, occasional sheep, fragrance of freshly mown alfalfa, putt-putt of the John Deere tractors, few of my favorite Farmalls, tire swings gently blowing in the breeze—mid-America farm country.

We have discovered biking long distances requires not just endurance but the ability to entertain oneself and each other. The landscape provides joy, distraction, or weariness, but what goes on in our bodies and minds helps make or break a trip. Good humor and the ability to be flexible in expectations, and reality itself add to the camaraderie of sharing experiences. This trip had all those qualities.

We six bicyclists rolled down the blacktop and without warning, Jim and John's shoulders began to shake and their bicycles lurched. I heard faint guffaws and wondered what was going on, then glimpsed the cause of this mirth. I was not amused which was why they were. In the midst of this pastoral scene was a lodestar, a hallmark of the culture I grew up in, a farm sign labeled: *Karl Hanson, wife and kids.* Jim and John slowed down enough for me to look them directly in the eyes. Before I could sputter anything, John howled, "See! I told you what she'd do!"

I grew up on a farm and by the time I was ten I knew I did not want to marry a farmer. I didn't want to have to work as hard as my mother and all the other work-worn farm women I knew. Just the idea, let alone the reality, of fixing three meals a day for twenty-two men in a threshing crew made me refuse to date farm boys for fear of falling in love with one of them. I treasured my life as a farm child but had other ideas about my grown-up life. One of them included women getting credit for who they were and what they did.

In many respects, things have improved in our culture. But all these years later, my predictable reaction to that Minnesota farm sign continued to be fodder for chortles and chuckles by my non-farmer orthodontist husband and his biking buddy John, architect of buildings and mischief. A bicycle trip worth its name requires laughter and we had plenty of it.

The following day, a huge splotch of white in a field ahead surprised us. Then we heard the sound, gobbling. Phil moved quickly to take advantage of this opportunity. He wanted to master the language of critters which he'd begun on the Florida ride. He made a guttural, chortling sound. The non-confined turkeys gobbled back. He did it again and curiosity quelled fear in a few of them. They not only gobbled but came closer to check him out. Most gobbled louder and moved toward their shelters. Turkey humor.

⚴

Stormy weather however, is never a laughing matter. As the afternoon's ominously dark clouds approached, we knew we needed to be watchful. When I heard thunder, I yelled to Jim, "Take shelter!" Connie and Deb agreed. Jim, John and Phil scoffed at us saying we were overreacting. The thought that went through my brain besides *Don't be stupid* was *Machismo.* When we saw lightning, we scampered under the deck of a nearby brick farm home. That's not particularly safe either but there was nowhere else to escape. We huddled there until the lightning and thunder ceased and only a steady downpour remained.

We knew Princeton lay four or five miles ahead so biked hard and fast to get there. A thoughtful mailman stopped to check on us and said a town seventeen miles away had received seven inches of rain within a few hours. We could imagine it because by the time we got to town, the rain had developed into a slicing sideways drenching, despite our being in a so-called shelter in the town square. Water filled the street gutters and began to flood the flat park. No place else looked more appealing so we bunched up there with our bicycles and tried not to think *Noah,* a name that comes up repeatedly when a gully-washer hits while we are biking.

We stayed under the shelter until it was safe to go to a café to warm up. We eventually made it to our toasty accommodations, reveled in the hot shower and dry clothes. And we didn't have to dry out our panniers because they had been in the van with Tania. Our raingear, shoes, and socks needed to drip dry.

🚲

When our trip ended at the St. Croix River, we celebrated our ride across state number ten, not by dipping our tires in the inaccessible river, but by offering a double dip ice cream toast from a former creamery. We deemed it perfect.

🚲

THE EVERGREEN STATE-WASHINGTON-1983

Riders: Jim/Jan/Tania. Drop off: Tania. Pick up: Dave Ashby. Distance: 310 miles

I had just been home a few days from three-weeks of backpacking in Europe with Mara and Jennifer when it was time for Tania and me to pack the van with bicycles, panniers and gear for our cross-Washington State ride. I loved spending such great times with our daughters and was happy I no longer needed the crutches I had used in Europe because I'd badly sprained my ankle before I left.

On the way, we stopped in Utah to stay overnight with my cousin Sylvia Hulce and her family. I awakened in the middle of the night wondering. *Where are we? Has the train stopped? Is it time to get off?* I got up, looked out the bedroom window and realized we were not moving nor was I on a train somewhere in Europe. *Oh. We're in Utah.* Back to bed.

Tania and I continued on to Seattle to see dear friend Kendra Smith and her young sons Toby and Alexander. We packed a lot of fun into our brief time with them, including zipping up the elevator at ten miles per hour to the Observation Deck of the Space Needle, the most well-known symbol of Seattle since the 1962 World's Fair. From 520 feet over the city, we oohed and aahed at the sight of the downtown skyline, the wharf, Puget Sound, Lake Washington, as well as the Cascade and Olympic Mountains.

After our too-short visit, Tania and I drove to Sea-Tac Airport to pick up Jim. Then the three of us pressed on to Longview on the Columbia River where Jim and I would begin riding and Tania would sightsee and drive the van. She hadn't been to Mount St. Helens or Mount Rainier—tops on her Must See list, pun intended.

The rank smell of lumber mills permeated Longview where we had once considered living. We decided against it because of air pollutants and pervasive odors, and other towns because of too few opportunities for orthodontists.

Jim and I meandered north along back roads going toward our one-time home, Seattle. We spent our first night in Chehalis hoping for clear enough weather to see iconic mountains St. Helens, Rainier, or Adams from the hills near town. Washington, especially the western part, is rich in such stunning views and with luck, one of them might be majestic Mount Rainier.

I love perusing maps and discovering unusual geographic names—Washington has a slew of them. Often they were from a tribal language such as Puyallup, part of the Puget Sound Salish languages which included Snohomish, Muckleshoot, Snoqualmie and Skagit. The towns named Sequim, Tulalip, Klickatat, Tumwater or Twisp all sounded more interesting than those dubbed Monroe or Dayton.

When we arrived in the town Rainier, we knew how it had been named—a great view of a glorious mountain through the hyaline sky! The snowcap lay low on Rainier's slopes but we couldn't make out the yellow and white daisies Tania described to us that evening. When our family lived in Seattle I rode the bus to work at a large medical clinic downtown. I could never understand why other riders, whom I supposed were native Seattleites, kept their noses in their newspapers when we could see Rainier! I squelched the urge to shout, "Wake up! Look at that! The Mountain is out!" We didn't get to see it every day. How could those folks take that stunning, sparkling, lofty sight for granted? Looking back, I shouldn't have squelched that urge. Maybe people would be happier after seeing, really seeing something beautiful at the beginning of the day.

The Puyallup River, fed by the waters of Mount Rainier, ran through the city. Puyallup, meaning generous and welcoming to all people, was perhaps best known as the home of the Washington State Fair. During World War II, the fairgrounds had been used as an internment camp for citizens and residents of Japanese descent at, in my opinion, ill-conceived and oxymoronic name, Camp Harmony. What a travesty. Eventually all the internees were moved to another camp in Idaho, a continuation the tragedy.

The shimmering green of the Pacific Northwest's forests and fields beckoned us. We loved returning to Washington, especially Seattle, where Jim had done his orthodontic graduate training. A Perry Como song described the city as having the bluest skies and the greenest green winged its way into my mind, made me pedal in rhythm to it, reminding me of six-year-old Tania singing it as our family motored into Seattle in 1970. In real time, August of 1983, Tania met us each night and we each shared the wonders we'd experienced during the day including the greenest greens.

63

Grateful for Seattle's foresight in establishing the Burke-Gilman Trail along the west side of Lake Washington, Jim and I found it a super way to bypass downtown. We planned to meet Tania at our friends' the Ashbys where we would leave our van. This was the first of a series of the far-flung Ashby family hosting us on our bicycle journeys. After a brief but fun reunion with three Ashby generations—Jeanette, Vernon, Dave, Jeanne, Bob and Ben—we three Downs gathered our gear and pointed our bikes north.

But first we had to take a detour in the neighborhood to see our old house and Decatur School which our daughters had attended. Both places had contributed to my biking. This was where Mara insisted I ride her bike each day to the school and home again before my baby-sitting charges arrived.

Next stop, Everett, a short distance from Seattle and, aside from being where my brother Keith was stationed in 1957-58, was notable for being the western terminus of US Highway 2. Although it meant little to us in 1983, over the ensuing years this road would become a primary biking route for us, stretching from the eastern border of Washington through Idaho's Panhandle, across Montana and North Dakota, and then crossing Michigan's Upper Peninsula. We also rode the eastern portion of this highway from the Vermont border, traversing New Hampshire and most of Maine.

☙🚲❧

Within a half-mile of our motel, we faced an early morning monster climb—not even time to warm up. Tania had wrapped one knee before she began riding and later had wrapped both of them to ease the discomfort. Fortunately, we soon arrived at the terminal where we would catch the Mukilteo-Clinton Ferry to Whidbey Island. We've always loved the respite and adventure of taking ferries, especially on our biking forays.

After smooth sailing, an immediate steep hill made me stifle a groan. The island, a mixture of evergreen-clad rolling hills, plus some roaring downhills, also possesses flat land farms where flowers, produce, eggs and other locally raised products are sold. Farm stands along the roads reflected small-scale agriculture's role while tourism also played an important part in the economy of the island. Through the years, artists such as painters, writers, sculptors, wood and metal workers and actors had found a home on welcoming Whidbey.

🚲

The following day we cycled across Deception Pass Bridge, partly built by the CCC, Civilian Conservation Corps, during the Depression era. It connects Whidbey Island to Fidalgo Island on the way back to the mainland. The name Deception came about because explorer George Vancouver had thought Whidbey Island was a peninsula. His chief navigator Joseph Whidbey later discovered that the body of water was a channel, not a bay as originally believed. Another historical tidbit: A

Peace Arch Monument where the US meets Canada

small island in these waters later gained infamy as a location used in smuggling Chinese people to become local laborers.

Our backroad route took us along ripening fruit orchards. Where there is ripening fruit, we just knew fruit pies would burst forth from ovens like dandelions in spring, making our noses twitch out of sheer pleasure and anticipation. We followed them until we spotted a tiny café advertising in sign and scent *Fresh Peach Pies!* Luscious, delectable, unforgettable peach pie perfection! A single bite of it caused Jim to fall into memories of his mother's peach pies made with succulent freshly picked Colorado Palisades peaches. We crawled back on our bikes and slowly pedaled on.

We repeatedly checked to see if 10,781 foot Mount Baker, one of five volcanic mountains in Washington's Cascades, was within our view as it had been from various spots on Whidbey. Good fortune for us, it was. Tania recalled crawling out of our Seattle home's upstairs window onto the garage roof to catch a glimpse of it. Her sisters and I had done the same thing.

Unfortunately, we followed a maintenance crew spraying chemicals on weeds along the road-sides. We could not escape the fumes and couldn't bike fast enough to pass by and stay ahead. We stopped, let the crew go on, waited, hoped the spray would settle, and then continued. Not a healthy situation for bicyclists.

Friends from our Seattle days, Mary and Gary Nordquist, visited us in our Bellingham motel. What a fun time recollecting memories from orthodontic school days eleven years earlier. Although Jim attempted to collect what he said was a long overdue bet from Gary, a Big Mac, Gary insisted that he had beaten Jim in paddleball so Jim owed him. A Big Mac has yet to exchange hands.

🚲

Canada, oh Canada became our mantra after we left Bellingham. Blaine, home of the lovely International Peace Park, symbol of the long-standing peace between Canada and the United States, exuded a feeling of peace and serenity. Along with being two contiguous parks in two countries, the most striking feature was the Peace Arch Monument sited exactly on the 49th parallel, the international boundary. Engraved on the monument—*Children of a Common Mother* on the American side and *Brethren dwelling together in unity* on the Canadian. Inscribed on an iron gate—*May these gates never be closed.* A wish worth working for.

After our idyllic time in the Peace Park, Tania, Jim and I crossed into Canada, no passports needed, and biked along Boundary Bay to Tsawwassen where a ninety minute ferry ride would convey us to Vancouver Island. Once again we relaxed in the shade and ate our picnic lunch as we waited for our transport.

The ferry skimmed across Haro Strait among the archipelago Gulf Islands, allowing us time in the sun, no exertion required. We hoped to see orcas and dolphins but only spotted seagulls which amused us as they landed on and took off from the ship.

66

Our ferry landed at Swartz Bay on the neck of a tiny peninsula north of the city of Victoria. We immediately checked our maps which directed us to what we think of as the star of Vancouver Island, Butchart Gardens.

We immersed ourselves in stately evergreens, conical cypress, Japanese maples, weeping willows, and broad expanses of lawn. Splotches of gold, fuschia, peach and purple encircled the bases of trees, and red zinnias, pink geraniums and lavender rimmed the winding paths. Countless hues of green, huge troughs of blossoms, a rose garden, wedding cars adorned with chrysanthemum pom-poms and sail boats rocking in a cove formed an indelible picture in our minds.

Our senses could assimilate little more but we had to feed our hungry bodies. Too late for afternoon tea and crumpets, we savored soup, salads and cheesecake as we mellowed out in the floral atmosphere of the Greenhouse Restaurant.

Unfortunately, we had to bid farewell to this paradise in order to reach our motel and left, even though we knew we were too far north to run out of daylight.

�🚲

After a good night's rest, more of Victoria's delights awaited us—stately parliament building, vine-covered Empress Hotel, red double-decker buses, a Tall Ship, colorful Chinatown, intriguing Totem poles in the provincial park. We happened upon a naval ceremony where sailors in their whites, backed by others in blue participated in a moving flag-raising, complete with cannon fire. Above them the vivid flags of Canada and her provinces rippled in the wind.

We boarded the ferry to Seattle and watched as Victoria faded into the distance. We moved to the bow, better to see where we were going, and to marvel at the mountains in the distance. Passengers squealed when they saw orcas chasing the ferry and dolphins diving into the wake of the bow. In the distance we spotted a US Navy submarine. An island lighthouse and swooping seagulls silhouetted against the sunset sky thrilled us with brilliant orange, yellow, gold, bronze with dark blue and grey piled-up clouds. The waters of the Sound reflected gold but then morphed to red, maroon, blood, and black—our bodies tingled with the glory of this scene. Tania wondered a loud, "Can we possibly absorb any more beauty?"

As we waited to dock in Seattle, Jim and I were reminded of seven-year old Tania, huge smile on her face, bouncing up the ramp, duffel with her sleeping bag and hiking boots dangling from it, returning from Blueberry Hill Campfire Girl Camp on Vashon Island. The following day, her photo appeared on the front page of *The Seattle Times*.

No newspaper photographer awaited us this time, but Jeanette, Vernon and Dave Ashby did, with our van. They took us to their loving home to relax and relive the adventure in spirit and motion that Tania, Jim and I had shared as we crossed state number eleven.

🚲

TEXAS THE LONE STAR STATE PART 1-LAREDO TO CORPUS CHRISTI-1984

Riders: Connie/Cara/Phil, Jim/Jan. SAG: Deb Rogiers. Distance: 163 miles

Our Texas Part 1 crew strapped and bungeed our bikes to racks on the front and top of the van and bundled ourselves and gear into it. We set off with high expectations of another cross-state bike ride—such is the hope of new beginnings.

It's a long way from Iowa City to Laredo, Texas—an especially long way when we had only spring break week bookended by two weekends for our vacation. We planned to travel there, bicycle from Laredo to Corpus Christi and return home in time to resume our real lives. We drove and drove and drove some more and finally, after 1265 miles, arrived in Laredo, a city distinguished by the fact it has flown seven flags. We are most familiar with the Six Flags legacy, Spain, France, Mexico, Republic of Texas, Confederate States of America, and the United States of America. The seventh flag is the little known Flag of the Republic of the Rio Grande.

An unusual facet of this trip included designated driver Deb who would not only drive the van but, in a few cities and towns along the way, apply for elementary teaching jobs. She also managed to bike some Texas miles. Teenager Cara suffered from a strained calf muscle which limited her riding, so she acted as Deb's co-pilot. The rest of us pedaled the whole way.

We knew early springtime meant Texas bluebonnets would be blooming, but were totally unprepared for dazzling field after field of these delicately tinted lupines. Seeing such gorgeous meadows evoked Tomie de Paola's book, *The Legend of the Bluebonnet*. This tender story tells the tale of a small orphaned Comanche girl. In the time of great drought she sacrificed what she loved most to the fire and the Great Spirit. It was her buckskin clad doll wearing brilliant blue feathers on his head. She threw the doll's ashes to the wind and the next morning bluebonnets clad the hills. The drought ceased and the little girl would be forever remembered for her sacrifice for her people. The eternal reminder of it, like rainbows—bluebonnets in the spring.

Even though we were surrounded by gorgeous flowers, it was difficult to be totally at ease given our harrowing experiences in Mississippi and Alabama. Certain scenarios, especially those involving trucks and gunracks, made us wary. Given our heightened awareness, we were unprepared for an act of courtesy and kindness.

So there in a quiet corner of southern Texas with few vehicles and fewer towns, a sheriff's patrol car pulled up in front of us and stopped. Our startled reaction, "What did we do?" Imagine our surprise when a young officer stepped out of the car and introduced himself. He asked, "Has anyone been bothering or harassing you?"

"Why no."

He asked where we were from and where we were going that day, then handed us his card with the no-nonsense command, "If anyone bothers you, I want you to call me and let me know." With that and a smile, he was gone and we were left open-mouthed. I smiled in recollection of one of my favorite childhood radio programs, *The Lone Ranger.* Had we just met his contemporary who, instead of giving us a silver bullet, gave us his card? We continue to be grateful to him. After all the thousands of miles we have bicycled, he is the *only* officer ever who stopped and asked how we were doing and offered his assistance *before* we needed it.

A highlight of any biking trip has to be visiting relatives and friends, in this instance, cousins Jan and Mitch Nielsen, former Iowans-turned-true-Texans, who have lived in Kingsville for decades. After welcoming us, they took us to neighboring King Ranch, one of the largest ranches in the world, larger than the state of Rhode Island. They make certain it is on every visitor's itinerary.

Once a young boy who ran away to sea, river man Richard King eventually founded the ranch. He worked on steamboats and as an adult, tried to make a living hauling merchandise. On a four-day horseback trip, he saw the land where the Santa Gertrudis Creek flowed. He decided to buy the property which he developed into the King Ranch. The early ranch, along with horses, goats and sheep, grazed cattle, hardy Texas Longhorns, some hot-climate-thriving Brahman bulls, Shorthorns and Herefords. King, his partners and their hired hands bred Brahmans with the Shorthorns thereby producing the ranch's trademark stock, the Santa Gertrudis, the first American breed of cattle.

For supper, instead of steaks, Jan and Mitch took us to a shrimp and catfish restaurant where we more than ate our fill. In the morning, she prepared a south Texas delight with huevos rancho as the star, not the Lone Star at that.

🚲

Teaxas Bluebonnets

We hated leaving such warm and loving hospitality but we had a deadline to meet. Our next stops were Falfurrias and Corpus Christi. After the traditional dipping of our tires in the Gulf of Mexico in Corpus Christi, we played on the waterfront and made a major scientific discovery. Seagulls don't like M&Ms. We tossed M&M-laced gorp into the air. Those raucous gulls ate the raisins, peanuts and sunflower seeds but not a single M&M. They squawked as if starving but refused to eat what some human beings deem to be manna. Perhaps they know something about M&Ms that we don't.

Too soon, part one of our three-part bicycle route across Texas was over. Our 163 miles from Laredo to Corpus Christi had been a happy and memorable experience—bluebonnets, sheriff's deputy, relatives, Texas hospitality and M&Ms.

Years later, SAG driver Deb recalled the tiny, clean and quaint motels Jim had managed to find for us. She added that she wondered about one school with outside corridors where she had applied for a teaching position. Always a Midwesterner, she thought how cold it would be in the winter snow, then laughed at herself—there wouldn't be any snow there at all. Deb didn't get a teaching position in Texas but she did in Illinois. There she met her future husband, proving once again that Shakespeare was right. *All's well that ends well, y'all.*

橲

ARE WE ALLOWED TO HAVE THIS MUCH FUN? WISCONSIN-1984

Riders: Connie/John/Cara, Betty, Jim/Jan. Drop off: Tania. Pick up: Tania and friend.
Distance: 251 miles

Whenever someone asks us which was our favorite cross-state ride, Jim and I have to stop to think. More than likely, one of our choices will be Wisconsin.

An early June misty moisty morning at Taylor's Falls, we commenced our ride on the west bank of the St. Croix River where we had finished our Minnesota ride the previous year. Connie commented, "The fog feels like a cooling spa treatment for our faces." Our smiles turned to gasps as we saw the impossibly steep hill we needed to climb to get out of the river valley. Neither our bodies nor our minds were warmed up or ready, even for a moderate climb.

Cara declared, "I can't climb that thing!" I felt that way too. So much for the rejuvenating effects of nature's spa. But climb it we did, muttering about what a poor plan it was, what torment on the first day. After the trial by mist and incline, we topped the hill and followed our inclination to ride rollers and flattish terrain, not muscle-rending uphills.

The landscape featured expansive Wisconsin fields, dairy cattle, meadows and woods, stippled with red barns and silos huddling alongside white houses, tucked into vales. This matched our expectations. We bobbed and floated along the nearly deserted tree-lined backroads and took time to respond to the call of a lake, "Wadin' water…wadin' water…" The whir of a fisherman casting his line caught our attention. When we wanted a break, we'd find a peaceful cemetery or lake, lie on our helmet-pillows, relax and watch the clouds form and morph into familiar or grotesque shapes.

"I see a turtle." "There's a sailboat skimming along." "Look! A dragon." The clouds shifted, our eyes closed and we drifted off in refreshing naps.

One spectacular azure afternoon, we came upon a reed-bordered lake the exact color of the sky. Enticed by a wooden dock stretching twenty-five feet over the water, we propped our bikes against trees, sauntered onto the dock, and took off our shoes and socks. We dangled our feet in the cool water and lay back to do some serious sky-dreaming. We not only felt but smelled the warmth of the sun. An eagle soared on the currents above us. We heard the splash of breaching fish, the murmuring splish-splosh of water lapping the shoreline. Iridescent emerald and cobalt dragonflies flashed among the reeds. Eventually, we knew we had to go on. We dried our feet and took reluctant steps back to our bikes and the waiting road.

Relaxing in Wisconsin

Those are the pictures I most often see in my head when I think of this Wisconsin ride. Naturally, there were less tranquil scenes. An eight-foot fir tree, fully decorated as if for Christmas, stood on the verge of the highway, an excellent place for a summer photo of some Iowa cyclists. So we thought. We lay our bikes down in the grass and gathered to pose for the photographer. *Zzzzz. Zzzzzz. Zzzzzz!* Full attack by a horde of blood-thirsty mosquitoes. We yanked our hoods up over our heads, succeeding in trapping some of them. Swiping wildly at the predators, we simultaneously shook our jackets and raced to our bikes with a trail of Wisconsin skeeters in pursuit. Fortunately, the flight speed of mosquitoes did not exceed that of bikers escaping them, at least once they were riding. Jim still managed to get a photo before we bolted.

State and county parks pepper the countryside in northern Wisconsin, and we depended on them for picnic tables, rest stops and potty breaks. Generally, their condition was good but one outhouse wins the trophy for being the filthiest, most disgusting of any on our bike trips. Had there been a feces fight inside? The stench—well, horrific doesn't quite describe it. We didn't linger. Unfortunately, the sight and smell memories do.

Winter, Wisconsin also wins a prize. This one for a café with the most unusual style of service. We overnighted in the town and hoped to find a pleasant place to eat supper. The first restaurant had a *Closed* sign on its door so we continued on down Winter's main street. The only other option—Winter Café.

Cindy, a perky, pony-tailed waitress, greeted us. "Hi! Sit wherever you want." We chose two back-to-back booths and slid in. She brought us menus reminiscent of many small-town diners. The guys ordered chicken sandwiches, dinner salad and baked potatoes. For some reason, Connie, Betty, and I didn't feel very hungry so ordered dinner salads and baked potatoes. Cara wanted a hamburger with all the trimmings.

With only two other patrons, we thought we wouldn't have to wait long for such a simple order. As Cindy brought water to us, an older couple walked in and sat down. She called out to them, went over and plopped into the booth beside them, chattering the whole time. Obviously, they were regulars and placed their order without looking at a menu.

Meanwhile, we reviewed the day, the route and what we could expect tomorrow. Cindy headed to the kitchen, so we assumed she'd put in our orders. After nearly ten minutes, she returned with a salad in each hand which she delivered to Jim and John. We heard them chuckle. When we turned to see what amused them, we saw the dinner salad—a slab of iceberg lettuce. No tomato, no orange color sticking out that could be construed as a carrot, nothing but iceberg lettuce.

Another several minutes passed and Cindy returned with two more salads. Politely, the people at our table waited for the last one to be delivered. Eventually, it came. Then came the procession of baked potatoes, produced and conveyed one at a time with lots of friendly Cindy chitchat in between. Cara stared hungrily at our food and wondered aloud when she would get hers. Finally, it was shipped out of the kitchen and brought singly to our table. Then came the long wait for Jim and John's chicken sandwiches. The rest of our meal had nearly digested when they arrived. This definitely had to be slow food before it became popular. But it was slow food served with a smile, sparkling eyes and a warm home-town welcome in Winter, Wisconsin.

＊

Somewhere between Winter and Park Falls, John mentioned to Jim, "I need a haircut." Betty, mother of four sons and a daughter, overheard him and volunteered, "I'll cut it at the motel tonight. I cut my kids' hair all the time." Someone had a small scissors to loan to the cause. After his shower, John pulled a lawn chair into the parking space in front of their door, flung a towel around his shoulders, and submitted to Betty's expert barbering skills. We told him he cleaned up pretty well and added it was probably the least expensive haircut he'd had since he was a kid.

Our relaxed pace across the next-to-upper tier of counties in Wisconsin continued. We'd had some off and on rain showers but considered ourselves fortunate. Betty's T-shirt said it all: *Are we allowed to have this much fun?*

But one day I made a terrible and potentially dangerous mistake as we climbed another hill. I thought the road ahead was clear, so signaled to a semi-driver creeping up behind us that he could safely pass. Suddenly another truck appeared in front of us. Fortunately, both drivers saw the situation and the semi backed off. As he drove by, the driver had some harsh words and gestures for me. I felt awful. I had jeopardized him and all of us. I'd also made him use extra fuel by having to back off. John emphasized, "The driver was right." I agreed. Another valuable lesson of the road had been drilled into my head that day: Be very sure of the traffic before signaling it is safe to pass.

＊

Although this twelfth cross-state bicycling trip ended north of Eagle River, at the border of Michigan's Upper Peninsula, we decided to enjoy the town that afternoon. We browsed in the shops and, on the spur of the moment, decided to visit *Fruit of the Woods Wine Cellar*. They offered apple, cranberry, blackberry, loganberry and red raspberry wines. At first, seeing cranberry wine surprised us but then we remembered cranberries grow in the Eagle River-Three Lakes vicinity. We also learned these wines do not age well like grape wines do, and should be used within months instead of years.

We toured the wine production area where cranberries fermented in tanks, then participated in some wine tasting. We thought we might buy a bottle to take home. The tour and tasting guide provided a singular experience. She poured wine in each of the glasses, which we sipped as she spoke. Jim noticed, nudged me, and soon we all observed whenever we finished tasting one wine, the guide would quickly grab our glasses and swallow the dregs, no matter how much or how little remained. I began to feel guilty that we were aiding and abetting this woman by not drinking everything in our glasses, wine she obviously wanted but should not be drinking.

After exchanging knowing glances, we thanked her and said we'd tasted enough and wanted to buy some. Jim and I bought a bottle of apple wine while others purchased different varieties. Back at our White Eagle Motel, we shared a bottle of newly purchased wine to celebrate completing our Wisconsin bike trip. There were no dregs.

WASHINGTON D.C., MARYLAND, DELAWARE-1985

Riders: Jim/Jan Pick up: Tania. Distance: 98 miles

BRRR! Washington, D.C. in early spring. We bundled up and struck out from Tania's Georgetown apartment and moved easily and quickly to the Mall to see the Washington Monument back-dropped by the Capitol building. We paused at the poignant Lincoln Memorial, grateful to the man he had been and searched the Vietnam Memorial Wall to find my cousin's name, Corbin Tindall. His name a sobering reminder of the lives lost there mixed with gratefulness that Jim made it safely home. We pedaled on to admire the cherry blossoms at the White House.

Jim and I moved quite swiftly through this city where we had anticipated more traffic and congestion. The next hurdle didn't surprise us, the bicycles-prohibited Chesapeake Bay Bridge. To cross, we knew we'd have to stand at the side of the road, look eager and positive, or possibly pathetic, and hope someone would stop to pick us up. Within minutes, a Good Neighbor Sam did just that. We loaded our bikes in the back of a brown Chevy pickup, squeezed into the front seat and easily sailed across the big water. We hadn't wanted to ride across any bridge with a reputation as one of the scariest bridges in the world. Low guardrails and frequent high winds created hazards we could face safely in a pickup cab.

Our driver dropped us off in wooded surroundings. With our thanks and an offer to pay him, he refused our money, accepted our gratitude and drove off. We stood on Kent Island, the largest of the Bay's islands, where in 1631 the first English settlement in the present state of Maryland sprouted, the third oldest permanent English settlement in the US, after Jamestown, Virginia and

Plymouth, Massachusetts. We crossed Kent Narrows, which separated it from the 170-mile long peninsula called Delmarva—Delaware, Maryland and Virginia.

Obstacle: hindrance or obstruction in doing something, blockade, hurdle, roadblock, impediment

Scofflaw: one who flouts the law, especially those difficult to enforce, particularly traffic laws

Circumvent: get round, overcome a problem or difficulty, typically in a clever and surreptitious way

Sometimes we just can't do what we want to or go the way we want to because of obstacles. Depending on the circumstances, we might become scofflaws trying to circumvent the problem. That's what was afoot with weary Jim and me as we tried to reach our overnight accommodations on US Highway 50. The directions we'd received from the motel people sounded straightforward until we began to follow them. From the frontage road across the highway, we could see the motel but couldn't see an access.

"How can we get there?"

"I dunno. The map shows that it's about ten miles if we go the route we are supposed to use. It's only two or three if we can get on the four-lane."

"Didn't I just see a sign that said bikes are prohibited?"

"Yeah. But it's getting near dark and I don't know if we can make it the other way." Conundrum. "Let's just take the four-lane. It shouldn't take us long." Ordinarily we would just cross the highway when it was safe. But we couldn't get to the highway because of a six-foot fence. We biked a couple of miles until we could use the crossover above the highway, then took the entrance.

We'd gone about a mile and a half when I heard Jim. "Uh-oh." I glanced in my rearview mirror and spotted a patrol car. We had been caught. But had we? The officer just passed us and we cautiously hoped would ignore us. He didn't. He stopped a hundred yards farther, parked and stepped out of his vehicle under a lighted sign that read, *NO BICYCLES ALLOWED.*

We tried to explain our predicament. The officer nodded and said, "Get off the highway!" All our pleas about it being only a half-mile farther to the exit and then we would be OK did not convince him. "Get off the highway!" We both looked at the six-foot chain link fence and grimly moved in its direction, the trooper watching. We dragged the bikes through the weeds in the deep ditch, pulled them up to the base of the fence, and yanked our panniers off. We decided I should climb the fence first so I could get the panniers and bikes as Jim pushed them over. It looked like an impossible task to me. The cop stood unmoving, unwilling to help these scofflaws, then drove off.

I'm too old to be doing this kind of stuff. How can Jim possibly get the bikes up high enough to get them over without hurting his back? How can I catch the bikes without damaging them or myself? How can... Just do it, Jan.

I struggled to get toeholds and wished ever so much for a simple barbed-wire fence or even a high board fence. By the time I reached the top, I was grateful to find no barbed wire. I, oh so gracefully—NOT—dropped the last four feet and waited for the panniers. Jim tossed them one by one and I sorta caught them, well, I kinda let them bounce off me, grimacing and ducking. Then came the bikes. He, much more athletic and taller than I, managed somehow to get them on the top, tip them down toward me, and didn't release them until I had a firm grip on a spinning wheel. *Firm grip on a spinning wheel? You have got to be kidding!* It toppled on me but I managed to break its fall. We did the same thing with his bike which wasn't much heavier.

Both bikes made it and so did Jim. The Officious One had gone by the time we finished. Maybe he really didn't want to see a pile of people, panniers and bikes and think he might have to help.

In the gloaming, we jammed the panniers back on, struggled to the gravel frontage road, climbed on the bikes and warily pedaled the rest of the way to the elusive motel. After a few years we finally saw the whole episode as rather amusing.

Jan at the Atlantic

Psyched up to complete our goal of reaching Delaware's Atlantic Coast, we pedaled all back roads through rolling hills, flatlands, past brick silos, barns, cedar saltbox homes. The sight of the Bridge-town Methodist Church, a charming brick chapel rebuilt in the late nineteenth century, and called a *tiny but significant sentinel of Methodist history* delighted us. It featured simple eighteenth century lines adorned by Victorian decorative additions of fancy brickwork and a Gothic window. It stands alone in open fields and as the site in longest service as a house of worship in the Wesleyan/Methodist denominations. The sign in front reads: *1640 Log Chapel of Ease. 1773 New Chapel completed.*

Ten miles later we left *Maryland Drive Gently* and entered *Welcome to Delaware Small Wonder The First State*. The weather warmed and off came the jackets. Our next trip down Methodist history lane came as we arrived at Barratt's Chapel, the *Cradle of Methodism* in America. A simple two-story built of brick in 1780, this chapel looks austere and almost barnlike in contrast to the Bridgetown Chapel. Philip Barratt, a newly-minted Methodist and prominent political figure in the county, deeded the land for the chapel. Thomas Coke, a representative of John Wesley, founder of Methodism, administered the sacrament of holy communion here for the first time by a Methodist in America in 1784. We appreciated seeing two historic sites of our denomination.

Within minutes, we leaned on a gigantic driftwood log on Bowers Beach, recalling the pleasures and challenges of the past two days as we waited for Tania to retrieve us with our van. States number thirteen and fourteen completed.

ILLINOIS-INDIANA 1985

Riders: Connie/John/Cara, Betty, Jim/Jan. Drop off/pick up and first day rider Deb. Distance: 385 miles

Launching this ride at Jim's orthodontic office in Muscatine seemed fitting since in preparation, several of us had biked to Iowa City from there. We pedaled past some of the town's lovely Victorian mansions to the bridge over the river. From high above it, how awing to see the grandeur of the Mighty Mississippi River from a bicycle seat. Imagine the stories this grand river could tell.

Typical Midwest summer heat and rural scenes accompanied us throughout Illinois and Indiana—corn fields on each side labeled with DeKalb or other seed corn signs, wildflowers gracing the roadsides and ditches. Those scenes soothed me. I had hoped this ride would be just that, cycling through new but familiar landscapes, rolling hills and manicured farm lawns.

Without warning, we saw a dreaded *Road Closed 500 Feet Bridge Construction* sign. A blip this soon? How could we find a way to get through without having to bike extra miles? From a hilltop, we looked down to the bridge, clogged with equipment. Our former Boy Scouts assured us we would manage to get to the other side. Somehow. First-in-line-John scrounged around the site and found a plank long enough to stretch across the creek bed. He positioned it, tested its strength, balanced himself and carried his bike across. With Jim's help, the rest of us maneuvered our bikes to John and gingerly walked the plank. No landing in the drink for this bunch.

A few more miles into Illinois, we met a truck coming from the opposite direction. When the truck turned a corner, an 8"x8"x4' piece of lumber slipped off and bounced in middle of road toward us. We swerved and braked to avoid the hazard. Whew! Another adrenaline pumper!

᠅

A sign configuration we all love came into view: signs on tall poles with dozens of arrows pointing in all directions except up, to places throughout the United States or world: Los Angeles 2035, New York

80

828, Miami 1,346, Chicago 73, Tapineau 3, Watseka 15, Kankakee 12. Smiles all around as everyone but our official photographer continued on our merry way, following the arrow toward Kankakee.

However, merriment turned to alarm in minutes. We were about fifty yards ahead of Jim who saw something we didn't, an enraged dog making a beeline for John at the head of our pack. When John spotted it, he was able to out sprint his potential attacker. So the snarling canine turned on the rest of us, charged and snapped at each one as we veered all over the road, trying to stay upright and avoid its teeth. Like a one-man cavalry, Jim pedaled faster, grabbed his bike pump off the frame and brandished it. He bellowed as loud as he could. The dog whipped around, saw the tire pump, and streaked away cross-country, tail between his legs, emitting terrified yelps, anywhere to get away from that madman. Jim thinks it may be running still.

As we passed through various towns and cities on our route such as Cambridge, LaSalle, Ottawa, Resselaer, Peru, most were pleasant but didn't have a particular impact on us. Two did, however. We especially liked seeing the house where Connie and John had once lived in Kankakee, where Cara now left the ride to stay with a friend.

Princeton had particular meaning for Jim. As a twelve-year old in 1951, he played on the first Little League Baseball team in Iowa. The LeMars All-Stars endured four hundred miles of bouncing in a school bus at forty-five mph on two-lane highways to get there. Jim played center field in game one losing to Kankakee 7-6. He pitched the last four innings in game two against Kewanee. After thirteen innings, the score was tied 1-1. Jim was selected to call the coin flip determining who would receive the third place trophy. His team did and Joliet went on to the Little League World Series.

Rivers, lots of rivers lay beyond the Mississippi and its locks: Illinois, Vermillion, Kankakee, Iroquois, Tippecanoe, Eel, Mississinewa, Salamonie, Wabash. I love the sounds and rhythms of the Native American names, the names that reflect the first people who called this area home. The Tippecanoe River in Indiana made me think of the historic presidential race between William Henry Harrison versus incumbent president Martin Van Buren. Harrison, known as hero of the Battle of Tippecanoe, fought against Chief Tecumseh and his confederation of tribes who objected to the westward settlement of whites. That battle helped precipitate the War of 1812 when, understandably, many tribes sided with the British against the Americans.

Most of us relegate these facts to eighth-grade history memory. But when we encounter those places in person, the past comes to life as it would so often on this and future cycling trips.

All too soon, we reached the Ohio border where Deb waited for us, and our cross-two-states ride, numbers fifteen and sixteen, was history too. It had a happy ending.

RAMBLING ACROSS OHIO-1986

*Riders: Sandy Matthes, Dave Schuldt, Vicki Burketta, Betty, Loren Ellerson, Jim/
Jan. Drop off: Michelle Matthes, Sandy's daughter. Pick up: Jennifer, Bernd.
Distance across Ohio: 325 miles*

Our cadre of people planning to bike across Ohio welcomed a new member, Loren, who had just begun biking seriously and had never biked a long distance. Long ago, the rest of us had passed through our own novicedom, and knew some of the issues he might face. We attempted to forewarn him: *Buying huge panniers and packing them full of those things you think you might need will force you to unload, sort your belongings, scrounge a box, and pack it with stuff you can no longer carry. Then you will need to stop at a post office to send the box home.*

His bulging bags indicated he hadn't gotten the message. After a day of struggling to balance the weight in his panniers and cycle with extra pounds, he understood. The second day we stopped at a post office to mail his box—relief for him and us who had felt his pain when he grimaced over fatigue and lack of control.

⚲

The ride commenced in southern Michigan at Hillsdale where Jane and Bill Nash, Sandy's generous sister and brother-in-law opened their home to us. They also fed us as though these were to be our last meals on earth. We cycled twenty miles from their town to Ohio's border then jogged a bit into Indiana to make this a true west-to-east route across the state. After all, we had to stick to The Dictim about cycling border to opposite border.

Light Sunday morning traffic on the farm-to-market route allowed us to ride side by side. After we passed two buggies filled with Amish men, women and children, Sandy and I heard whoops of laughter coming from our husbands at the head of our pack. Between guffaws, Dave explained, "We're riding like the Amish! The men are in front and the women are in back."

Sandy and I cheered ourselves knowing Amish women drove their own buggies just like we rode our own bikes. I've wondered how much that experience influenced my opposition to riding behind Jim on a tandem.

To celebrate our ride in her home state, Betty and her artistic son Dave had designed a gold T-shirt with black trim, the University of Iowa colors. The back featured a black outline of Ohio with the logo *Outstanding Hawkeyes Investigating Ohio O.H.I.O.* Jim puffed up a bit when he saw the letters *JDBC* under the map and Betty told him that stood for Jim Down Bike Club. *Would his helmet still fit his head?*

Although he was an experienced cyclist, Jim had neglected a crucial step in preparing for this ride—checking the tread on his tires. Dave noticed them early on, "Down! Didn't you check your tires before this trip?"

"Nope."

"Well, they're bald, you dummy!" There is nothing like respect between friends.

"Guess we'd better do something about it then." *Oh yes, we'd better.* Now where in the Northwest corner of rural Ohio would we find a pair of bike tires on Sunday? At Zachrich Trading Post in Napoleon, that's where. This small spot on the road advertised their expertise in *Bicycle Sales and Service* as well as *Fur Buyers.* We didn't have any pelts to sell but we did buy two tires with deep, unsullied tread that fit Jim's rims. Alleluia!

We overnighted in the town of Clyde. That pleased me because *Winesburg, Ohio,* a group of short stories written by Sherwood Anderson, was purported to have been set in this town. A puzzlement since the actual Winesburg, Ohio lies in another part of the state. Before supper, we relaxed on the swings and lounge chairs, then headed off to an excellent chicken dinner at the Winesburg Inn, where the owners at least recognized that Anderson had grown up in the town. We'd heard that for many years, if you wanted to check out the book, a taciturn, tsk-tsk-ing librarian would reluctantly bring it out for you, conveying her disapproval with a scathing look.

🚲

SMILE, YOU'RE ON CANNED (NOT CANDID) CAMERA

I love flipping through our bike trip photo albums or looking at slides, my memories tweaked by images of those exhilarating and occasionally mundane times. Though all of us riders snap candid shots along the way, a highlight for Chief Bike Trip Photographer Jim involves photos of individual riders on the move.

Sometimes his zeal created tension. Riders became a bit cranky, pun intended. They didn't want to slow down, move over, turn around, come back and pass again until he got the shots he wanted. Later on, they appreciated the results, but occasionally were compelled to express a few caustic or tongue-in-cheek, "Well, it took you long enough" type comments.

Somewhere in Ohio, the usual instruction poured from Jim's mouth. "OK. I'm going to bike a ways down the road, so wait until you see me stop and set up the camera. Then ride slowly one by one. Make sure you leave enough distance between you so I can get good pictures. If you go too fast, they'll be blurry and you'll have to do it again."

Our eyes rolled. We'd heard it all before, "Yes Jim. Yes Jim. We get it. We'll do it." He happily pedaled off to find the perfect spot for his perfect photographs.

The rest of us waited silently for a moment, watching our taskmaster ride away. I don't remember how it happened but soon we set about scheming our own *Mutiny on the Bountiful Hills of Ohio.* In order to confuse Jim, we decided to switch bikes so each of us would ride someone else's. Ordinarily he would identify us by our distinctive riding styles on our bikes. Betty, Sandy and I grabbed the biggest bikes while taller Vicki, Dave and Loren snagged the ones too small for them. They scrunched their bodies over the Lilliputian frames, knees to their chests, like clowns in a circus. I felt like a little kid straining to touch the nearly unreachable pedals on my big brother's bike. Puckish grins flitted across faces at the prospect of flummoxing Jim.

Meanwhile, he settled into the grassy ditch with his Minolta ready for his classic low pictures. The rest of us rode sedately toward him, remembering the spacing required for excellently executed images. We chortled as the pace mutated into a Keystone Kops routine, jiggling and bobbing along like Weebles wobbling but not falling down. Only those at the head of the line heard the sputtering, "Hey, you guys! What're you doin'? Now we have to do it all over again!"

Jim refused to consider "Posing for pictures," as an acceptable answer to his question. Our mission had not been totally successful because he hadn't clicked the photos, but we had managed to pull his chain. His grumbling, "I don't get any respect," was met with snickers from the mutineer wannabes. Back at the original scene of the crime, we chucked a u-ey on our own steel steeds, pasted smiles on our faces and relished our symbolic victory as we pedaled back to Jim. We heard the clicking camera and he seemed content. For a while.

Once we returned home, he had the film developed. All the hullabaloo was for naught. In his effort to squeeze out one more photo from a thirty-six frame film, it had not caught the spindle and the film had not advanced at all when he wound it. No exposures, no photos. Just memories.

Most of our group had bicycled together at least several times, so rarely did we have any personnel problems. Occasionally, someone might be irritated about someone or something but it would be short-lived. We understood that, as a team, we try to ensure that everyone is doing OK and we support and encourage each other. Unfortunately, although a very nice person, our newbie shared a room with others and didn't appear to comprehend time limits in the bathroom while readying for the day. He looked great, but this was a bike trip when cleanliness in the morning and after showers in the afternoon were expected, but no one primped. In between, it depended on the day.

Adding to that, Vicki felt left out, specifically by the person who had gotten her into cycling and had ridden a lot with her. Maybe while all of us had tried to make our newbie feel comfortable and enjoy the ride, we'd neglected Vicki. She didn't like her feelings but she owned them. After I heard her tale of woe, I thought she required understanding, encouragement and distraction. What does one do with youngsters to distract them? Same thing one does with adults. After the situation has been aired and discussed, play games. First we quizzed each other about our middle names. "What's your middle initial?"

"L. Bet you will never guess what it stands for."

"Ummm." *C'mon Jan. What's an unusual name beginning with L?* "Lucretia."

"How'd you know? Did someone tell you?"

"Nope. But we had a cousin named Lucretia." Pause. "My middle initial is C. Bet you'll never guess what it stands for." She didn't.

Then we launched into a series of the game, "What do you call a person who…" for miles and miles down the road. What do you call the man who lies in front of the door? "Matt." What do you call the Roto-Rooter man? "Dwayne." What do you call a man who hangs on the wall? "Art." The silliness helped pass time and a potential emotional crisis averted—at least for now.

Another dilemma developed when we arrived at our motel on the edge of Oberlin. We were stunned to see the unkempt grounds, buildings needing paint, rooms not ready. Everything was exactly opposite of what we expected for an overnight stay. We spoke to the proprietor and told him the accommodations were in no way acceptable. He assured us the rooms would be ready soon, but we doubted that. We canceled our reservations, which had not been paid for, and grumpily cycled into town not knowing if we'd find a place to stay or not.

Lucky us, the Holiday Inn had three rooms available so we wheeled our bikes into our rooms. We cleaned up quickly so we could stroll the streets of this historic town. In our wandering, we came upon an irresistible bike shop. We filed in to check out its wares. Jim declared, "I need some new biking shorts." Translation: He wanted to spend more time there. The rest of us told him we'd see him later and continued perusing the shops and meandering by the campus of famed Oberlin College.

Jim popped out of the bike shop with a happy face, opened a bag and pulled out his purchase—a pair of biking shorts with the thickest padding I'd ever seen. Dave roared, "Down! Those look like marshmallow shorts." Jim grinned and declared he'd never have a sore bottom while wearing them. Despite Dave's marshmallow description, the rest of us called them Jim's cushy-bottoms. He wore them for years, until they were threadbare. Just as he had predicted, he never had a sore derriere.

☗

All of us eagerly anticipated wading in Lake Erie hoping the cool water on our sweaty skin would feel as delicious as it did. We didn't swim in our biking clothes, but Vicki dipped and splashed until she was soaked. Love those refreshing interludes.

Our next highlight would be staying with relatives in the city of Akron, Betty's parents, Mr. and Mrs. Butts, and Jim's oldest cousins, Carolyn and Dave Cox. On the edge of the city, Vicki had a flat which she wanted to change by herself with guidance from our traveling tool men, Dave and Jim. We gathered around and cheered her when she succeeded. What a delightful evening sharing biking tales, family memories and dinner with these dear people. Afterward, Cousin Carolyn frequently visited Betty's mom as well as becoming Betty's good friend.

☗

Eastern Ohio's terrain changes considerably from the flatter central area. On especially hot and sticky days, as the heat and hills exhausted us, we sought out a cemetery or city park with cut grass and lots of shade. Quietly sprawled out, as we frequently do, we relaxed and sometimes caught some Zzzs.

Deep into eastern Ohio near the village of Hiram lived a couple none of us had ever met, Kathy and Don Havener. They, like Jim and I, had signed up in a bicycling home stay directory to host cyclists. Jim found their names there and they consented to host the seven of us. They greeted us like old friends with hugs and a sign, Welcome Iowa Cyclists. What amazing hosts! They loved to bike too so knew what we needed to eat and what would make us feel at home— hot showers, a washer and dryer, filling food, and an opportunity to hear their stories and tell ours too. They had built their home two years earlier and had seemingly thought of everything—including Kathy's huge closet fitted out as a gift-wrapping center.

🚲

When we departed in the morning and wheeled our bikes along their rocky lane, we felt like we were leaving old, dear friends. Jim and I communicated with them for many years at Christmas time and have always cherished their gifts of hospitality and friendship.

One more day of beautiful Ohio hills and we'd reach the Pennsylvania border, a day of serious hill-climbing including one memorable downhill. We had crested The Hill and saw a freshly blacktopped highway plunging down and away from us. Each of us knew this would be the best downhill of the entire trip, and who knew how far and fast we could coast?

Jim and Dave had to rein in their bikes, a Fuji America and a Fuji Royale, which seemed ready to bolt out of an imaginary starting gate. They both wanted this opportunity to set new personal speed records. Dave zoomed away first. For safety reasons, Jim waited a few seconds and blasted out after him. Halfway down the hill, a gasoline transport pulled onto the road and blocked Jim's lane. He had to brake so lost his golden opportunity to set his new record. He felt crushed. Dave hit fifty-four miles per hour and triumphantly set his. The rest of us sailed down, caring more about health preservation than personal bests. Speed, breeze, super smooth surface, and the pleasure of nearing the Pennsylvania border were our rewards.

But even rewards can have a sad side. Soon, Jim and I would have to leave our biking buddies and strike out on our own across Pennsylvania.

🚲

I'm named after my dad Cloyde. C stands for Cloydean.

🚲

PENNSYLVANIA PASSAGE—1986

Riders: Jim/Jan. Pick up: Jennifer/Bernd. Distance: 518 miles.
Total for Ohio and Pennsylvania: 843 miles

With tears in their eyes our friends waved goodbye to Jim and me at the Pennsylvania border. Bereft, forlorn and with tears in my eyes, we pedaled away. What had we been thinking when we decided to leave them at the Ohio border and cross Pennsylvania by ourselves? Even the otherwise inspirational sign written in large letters on the nearby metal building didn't help: *Life. Be in it.* The joy of bicycling drained from us as Sandy, Dave, Vicki, Betty and Loren disappeared from sight.

The only explanation? "It seemed like a good idea at the time…" Not only that, Jennifer and Bernd had been traveling in the east while Bernd interviewed for jobs, and they planned to pick us up at the end of our biking trip to return to Iowa. Logic told us to continue riding across another state, but why did it feel so awful? We'd had so much fun with the others and now they were gone and just the two of us were going it alone.

Jim and I heaved huge sighs and kept our legs moving round and round. The day grew hotter and hotter as the hills grew longer and steeper. The chatter of friends had kept us going when we hit the tough ascents of eastern Ohio. Now we silently climbed without their encouragement. Fortunately, we had only thirty more miles to go before our night's stop on this seventy-eight mile day. Up and down. Up and down. The hills seemed endless.

Our last downhill into Franklin, Pennsylvania brought us almost immediately to our motel. We checked in, took our bikes to our room and looked wearily at each other. "Jim, I don't want to clean up before we eat. I just want to eat, come back, shower and go to bed."

"You'd feel better if you showered first."

I fought back tears, "But if I showered first, I wouldn't eat. I'm beat. Let's go. Please." Supper was unremarkable except for our sticky skin clinging to the plastic seats of our booth. We were relieved to return to our room, shower, wash our clothes and fall into bed. I prayed we'd have more emotional and physical strength the next day.

Information overload

Rest had refreshed and energized us. We no longer felt mournful but ready for adventure. The Pennsylvania hills and mountains, still as unending and arduous as they had been the day before somehow seemed more beautiful.

Usually we revel in downhills but that day and in the ensuing days, we sometimes grumbled softly when we had a long one. We knew there would be a concomitant uphill to try our bodies and spirits. During one particularly challenging climb, a fly accompanied me. That's precisely what I didn't want or need. I swatted at it and knocked the rearview mirror off my glasses. "Dang!"

I shot off my bike, stomped back to where my mirror lay in the middle of the steaming asphalt, snatched it and reattached it to my glasses. Then I had to figure out how to gain enough momentum to go forward. After looking at what looked like an impossibly steep incline, my brain kicked in. I rode perpendicularly across the road and then angled upward trying again and again to get my left foot into my toeclip. Futilely. Finally I pedaled up the hill with only my right foot clipped in, not the most efficient way to climb a hill. The good news, the fly did not return to harass me. Jim waited at the top wondering what had become of me. He shook his head as I explained I had been beset by a besotted bug.

The highway continued to curve around itself in scary but exhilarating descents. I decided the next climb would not be made easier by descending slowly, so I let gravity do its thing. Gravel-filled chuckholes stretched across the road. It was all I could do to apply the brakes just enough, but not too much, steer around the holes and avoid slipping or crashing. I managed to stay upright, no road rash for me today, just a rush of adrenaline and gratitude for safe passage. I promised myself not to take such a chance again, but knew I would be tempted on winding roads.

We've heard cross-country cyclists say that going over the Rockies seemed to be nothing compared to Iowa's loess hills, Arkansas' Ozarks and Pennsylvania and West Virginia's Appalachians. We agree, but persistence and willingness to work very hard are key.

Near Willow Hill we spied Pennsylvania Turnpike traffic heading into the Kitatinny Tunnel. Pennsylvania law prohibits cyclists from riding the turnpike and we had no desire to. Our scenic route took us through valleys and over and around mountains while the tunnel took the cars and trucks a mile through the mountain. We viewed grassy meadows, orchards with fruit just beginning to pop, and lightly traveled farm-to-market roads and experienced quiet. Turnpike drivers saw rock and concrete walls and heard the staggering din in the tunnel.

The days became a blur of hills and valleys until a spectacular *My Lord, What a Morning,* when dawn kissed the mist in the vales. Jim and I seemed to be transported to a silver and emerald Never-Never Land. The sparkle of dew on grasses and filigreed spider webs created intricate delights.

Beyond being entertained by the luscious scenery, we amused ourselves by spotting place names such as Seldom Seen Valley Mine. Does that mean the valley is seldom seen or is it the mine? Speaking of seen, we did not see the groundhog Punxsutawney Phil as we passed through his home town. We did read his historical marker:

GROUND HOG DAY As early as 1886, German immigrants here observed Groundhog Day and established the Punxsutawney Groundhog Day Club in 1899. According to folklore, if the hibernating groundhog...leaves its burrow on February 2 and sees its shadow, there will be six more weeks of winter.

We had no idea if Phil saw his shadow on last Candlemas/Groundhog Day or not.

Jim and I had read about hiking the Appalachian Hiking Trail. As we crossed the Trail, the concept of hiking 2180 miles from Springer Mountain, Georgia to Mount Katahdin, Maine awestruck us. What an amazing venture that would be. Besides the obvious potential problems of sunburn, blisters, poison ivy, oak or sumac, we knew black bears, lightning, giardiasis, cuts, scrapes, venomous snakes, and all manner of insects and spiders exist. I would think more than twice about walking very far on it, but my gypsy spirit loves the idea. Being on bikes, we didn't have to contemplate anything but the romance of hiking the Trail. That might have vanished at first sign of a hot-spot on my foot or spying a snake.

Our thirty-three mile ride from Shippensburg to Gettysburg took us through the last of the character-building Appalachians and into more of the character-building history of our country. What a somber look back at the Civil War, even though peacefulness surrounded us 120 years later. Reading the inscriptions on some of the fourteen hundred markers and monuments created a reality check moment: 165,000 people fought here; 51,000 casualties—killed, wounded, captured and missing in a three day carnage-filled battle.

Many say that Gettysburg, a place of courage, sacrifice and conflict in 1863, has become a symbol of reconciliation. On an anniversary of the battle, veterans from the North and South met and shook hands over walls they had fought over fifty years before. We remembered Lincoln's words at the dedication of the Soldiers' National Cemetery for the Union dead: *"…we here highly resolve that these dead shall not have died in vain; that this nation shall have a new birth of freedom; and this government of the people, by the people, for the people shall not perish from the earth."*

Within the borough of Gettysburg we were surprised to see restored timbered homes and taverns dating back to the 1770s. We learned that James Gettys, land owner and entrepreneur, settled at the crossroads of two major trade and military routes and by the 1780s he began selling town lots to what would become Gettysburg. The 1776 Dobbin House became the first stop on the Underground Railroad north of the Mason-Dixon Line after it had been a temporary field hospital during the Civil War.

☠

Our special mission the day we left Gettysburg? To reach The Mennonite Central Committee Store in rural Akron, Pennsylvania. Backstory: One of Jim's adult orthodontic patients had moved from Kalona, Iowa to Akron to work at the store. Jim does routine post-brace checkups and had promised Ruth he would make a house call to see how she was doing. He told her to expect us on July 30. "By the way, we'll be riding our bikes."

But first we had to get through Lancaster. Founded in 1718 it is known as the oldest inland city in the United States and better known as the center of the Pennsylvania Dutch-Amish country. We enjoyed sightseeing as we biked among the brick buildings and row houses. We stopped briefly for our picnic lunch, mindful that we had a couple of important goals to reach that afternoon.

Although we knew the number of the highway that would take us to the MCC Store we had no specific map of Lancaster to help us find it. It shouldn't be difficult. We carefully watched for signs all the way through town. Nothing. We retraced part of our route to no avail. We stopped and asked motorists, questioned people walking along the sidewalks. No one knew. We repeatedly checked our watches knowing we had about thirty miles to go to our motel. Bur first we had to escape from Lancaster and get to Akron. In desperation, we asked a mail carrier. Surely he would be familiar enough with Lancaster to direct us. His puzzled expression and shrug of his shoulders clearly told us he had no clue. All the time we had been biking we didn't pass any gas stations where we would usually stop for directions or maps. Persistently we kept cycling sure we would come upon the highway soon. Eventually we just headed in a northerly direction and, as we often admit, we dumbed into it.

All that day, Ruth told her co-workers that her orthodontist and his wife would come to see her that afternoon as they biked across Pennsylvania. No one really believed her until we showed up. We parked our bikes, Jim retrieved pliers from his bicycle tool kit, we left our helmets on and strolled into the store. Amidst the laughter of her co-workers, Jim asked for Ruth. He checked her teeth, posed for photos with her, brandished his handy-dandy pliers and quipped, "It's not every patient whose orthodontist bikes eight hundred miles to check her teeth." We bought a small token of our trip, a jar of jam, waved, smiled at Ruth and continued on to our motel.

I waited outside as I usually did as Jim checked in. I waited and waited and wondered what took him so long. No matter where we are we don't like to leave our loaded bikes unattended. So I waited some more. When Jim came out he had a strange look on his face and my heart flip-flopped. *What was wrong? Had something happened to someone in our family?*

When he arrived at the reception desk he received a message for him to call Jennifer. We thought she and Bernd had been traveling in Connecticut. They had. Unfortunately, while stopped behind a car at a rural intersection, waiting to turn left, they had been rear-ended. No one was injured but the van sustained a smashed rear end and seats had sprung. They had done all the appropriate things, got the name of the man who had hit them, contacted the police and their insurance company. Later they called to say they had been at a service station vacuuming broken glass from the van when a nearby transformer blew and the whole quadrant of the city they were in had been left in darkness. They would meet us in a few days to head home.

🚲

The uneventful bike ride from Denver, PA to Blue Bell, a suburb of Philadelphia, proved to be a true pleasure. There we visited friends Claire and Walt Gerber who had once lived and bicycled with us in Iowa City. Other friends, Carol Ashby and Rob Kuhlman, joined the Gerbers and us for dinner making this celebration even better. A telegram for us had arrived at the Gerbers. We were stunned. Who would send us a telegram, especially an acrostic? Our Ohio bicycling friends, that's who.

PEDDLING (sic)
EASTWARD
NEARING
NEW JERSEY
SPEARING
YOUR
LOAD
VICTOURIOUSLY(sic)
ACROSS NINETEENTH*
INCREDIBLE
ACCOMPLISHMENTS

LOVE JDBC FANS

*We had inadvertently counted Texas as a state crossed, one more than we had actually done. But *nineteenth* worked to spell PENNSYLVANIA.

⚲

The following day, our way to visit Carol and Rob in Norristown consisted of more city biking than we had been used to. We love that various members of three generations of the Ashby family crop up in four of our bike rides. It's always a treat to see any of them.

Jennifer and Bernd drove the slightly rattling van to Norristown to retrieve us so we could all return to Iowa City. The front passenger seat had been roped into a mostly stable sitting position. Other seats had been stuck in upright positions so that worked well. The smashed rear door of the van had been roped shut too. Off we went to conquer Interstate 80 and get home. We made it! We had crossed states number seventeen and eighteen and had a banged up van. Bernd had a new job in Pennsylvania.

⚲

MICHIGAN HONEYMOON-1987

Riders: Sandy/Dave, Connie/John, Betty, Vicki, Jim/Jan. Drop-off Drivers: Tania and Lisa, Sandy's daughter. Pick up Drivers: Jennifer/Bernd. Distance: 620 miles

"Where did you go for your honeymoon?"

"Michigan. We rode our bikes across Michigan—with six of our closest biking friends."

"You what? You're kidding! Why in the world would you do that?"

Dave Schuldt elaborated, "Well, Jim Down was planning a ride across Michigan since he and Jan had already biked Wisconsin, and Sandra and I had joined them in Ohio the year before. He asked if we'd like to come too. We said sure. This could be our honeymoon." The nonplussed questioner, not a dyed-in-the-wool bicyclist, walked away shaking his head.

At first, Jim and I wondered if they really wanted to spend their honeymoon with a bunch of other people. Sandy and Dave's response, "Why not?" Frankly, we thought, "What a super idea!" That set the plans in motion.

🚲

The Menomonie River forms part of the border of Michigan's Upper Peninsula so the bride, groom and attendants cycled to the Wisconsin side of it, returned and felt welcomed by a sign saying, *YES! M!CH!GAN WELCOME.* Jim and I had informed the others we would have shirts made especially for this trek. Each of us had a single letter of MICHIGAN on it, except for Sandy and Dave who had additional letters on the backs of their shirts. This made for a hit anagram game. For example, when the right people lined up, they spelled our motto for the trip, *I CAN.* Sandy wore an *M* on the front of her shirt and *MARRIED* on the back. Dave had *I* and *JUST* so when they stood together they spelled *I M JUST MARRIED.* We not only had matching pink shirts, the bridal couple trailed silver mylar balloons from their bicycles until the helium leaked out—of the balloons, not of the marriage. Did we make a statement or what?

Too soon the sun hid behind clouds, the air turned chill and rain fell. Out came our rain jackets and pants. Seven people in cheery yellow, two trailing dipping and bobbing balloons, pedaled down a wet undulating road lined with tall, straight evergreens. What a neat photo. John wasn't in it because he was still working but would join us in a few days.

Along the way, we saw the *FOSTER CITY POST OFFICE AND MARKET.* Despite the *CLOSED* sign in the window, we ordered sandwiches and pop there and plunked ourselves down on the steps to eat. We declared it satisfactory, not a word we'd use to describe the old, sprawling B&B where we'd soon stay in Escanaba. Although it had several bathrooms, only one person could shower at a time because of low water pressure. The beds had seen better days too.

♾

Vicki, Connie, Betty, Sandy, Jan and Dave in the rain

The hostess left our breakfast on the counter—a four-ounce glass of watery juice and a small hard Danish, one for each of us. Astonished and irritated, we'd never been treated in such a way at the many B&Bs we'd stayed in. This chintzy woman was nowhere in sight at the time and we understood why. Although we'd had a teeny, tiny so-called breakfast, the hills we'd ride that day would not be. We ate again before we left town.

Immediately, we skirted a bay along the upper part of Lake Michigan, where at break time we sat on the soft sand, breathed fresh air and contemplated our surroundings. As we had in Wisconsin, we picked up US Highway 2— I'm not very good at remembering highway numbers, but US 2 sticks with me as do memories of pedaling it.

Evergreens crowded the narrow highway as we spun our way down the road, tickling the shore and then veering away from it. We eventually joined the lineup of people and cars to take the ferry to Mackinac Island, in Lake Huron between Michigan's Upper and Lower Peninsulas. What a treat! Speaking of treats, the tiny island was filled with them, sweeping lawns outlined by white fences, brilliantly blooming flowerbeds, stately evergreens, an eight-mile bike trail around it. No motorized vehicles were allowed there but horses were. We watched for them, pedestrians and other cyclists lucky enough to be there.

Perhaps most memorable for some of us, besides being chased off the front porch of the Grand Hotel because we weren't dressed appropriately, had to be the acclaimed fudge. Sandy, Dave, Jim and I bought four pounds to share, which we thought would last us a few days. We underestimated our quenchless chocolate gluttony, settled down on a park bench and ate it all. At one sitting. Connie, Betty and Vicki were more moderate and only ate gigantic ice cream cones.

We wobbled our way back to our bikes and riding compatriots to head to the ferry and then to our motel. A perfect landmark event for the bridal couple, they had their very own yellow honeymoon cabin with white scalloped trim, black shutters and trailing red geraniums in the flowerboxes. Appropriately, the groom carried his bride across the threshold.

The day we'd all been waiting for came—John would join us! Mid-morning we heard a plane and waved wildly, tears forming in our eyes when it buzzed us! We could hardly wait for the pilot to land. Soon we saw a tiny figure in the distance grow larger and larger. Enormous smile on his face, he zipped by us and greeted Connie with a big kiss. At last we numbered eight, enough to spell MICHIGAN!

Geographically, the Lower Peninsula, shaped like a mitten and more level than the Upper Peninsula, was broken by conical hills and glacial moraines usually not more than a few hundred feet tall. Divided by a low water divide running north and south, the landscape contains more deciduous trees instead of the preponderance of evergreen. We reveled in the woods, wildflowers, rocky lakeshore, wading water. Picnic tables became places to lie on, write postcards, or share a no-longer-secret-stash of chocolates. Connie wore her gold *People do this for a vacation?* shirt. Our response? "Yes we do." Mother Nature's? *Turn up the heat.*

🚲

On an extraordinarily hot Sunday, we opted to eat lunch inside a restaurant. Dressed in shorts and our pink shirts, we trooped in and sat down. We thought we looked pretty good, our clothes had been clean that morning and maybe felt a bit sticky but didn't seem too sweaty. We still got "the look" from other patrons—looks that said they knew we hadn't been to church that morning. If only they had known we traveled with a preacherman—we hadn't been quick enough to address him as Pastor Dave, loud enough for them to hear. The looks could have been curiosity or slight disdain. Whatever, they amused us. Lunchtime was delightful and cheery. Afterward we meandered outside to chat and also, by chance, eavesdrop. Two ladies, in their Sunday-go-to-meetin' dresses, stood nearby and surreptitiously glanced at us. One sniffed, "Well, at least they don't have tattoos!" It was really hard to muffle our snickering!

A possible mutiny, triggered by oppressive, overwhelming heat, humidity and some long biking days, took form in the minds and words of two normally calm and moderately spoken members of our group. Usually we take a layover day every seven to eight days. This trip differed and we didn't. The pair didn't like it very much and muttered to the rest of us. As it turns out, they did not strike and refuse to go on, nor did they speak to the one who had arranged the route and timing. He didn't find out about it until after we returned to Iowa City. Time spent wading in a lake, and relaxing on the shoreline helped. What is it about the heat of the moment? We didn't laugh about it then, but we do now.

Math teacher Vicki had just had knee surgery six weeks before the ride. Her surgeon okayed her riding but told her he doubted she'd be able to complete the trek on her bike. Every night she iced and elevated The Knee. Every one hundred miles we had a minor celebration, checking her odometer and taking photos of it with Vicki holding up the number of completed hundreds of miles with her fingers. Competitive and goal-oriented, she was determined to do it. After all, Jim had promised he would kiss her knee if she did.

For too many years, Jim and I hadn't seen Vivian and Bob LeVier, our good neighbors from our life in married student housing barracks at the University of Iowa. We planned our route so we could be with them, and shared a laugh when Vivian brought out snacks for us. She had carefully arranged crackers and dip on a yellow plastic salad plate we recognized. My parents had given us the set when we were married, after Mother received it free from Mormon Feeds. The LeViers had custody of it since 1967 when Jim graduated from dental school and we moved away. Vivian figured twenty years of use or non-use, was enough and we should have it back. We still have it, just for smiles and memories.

Whenever one of the riders recollects this trip, besides Mackinac chocolate, "Ice cream," pops out. That is followed by, "Remember the man and his son who had that gargantuan dish of ice cream? It had to be at least eight inches tall."

"And Betty asked if she could take their picture." We each relished our own ice cream—but of more controlled proportions. We patted ourselves on our backs for being so constrained.

How quickly the time passed. We reminisced about how we draped all our wet laundry on a paint-peeled, two-wheeled homemade trailer, dumped Pringle remnants into each other's open mouths, composed artistic photos of ruined rock walls, cooled our hot swollen feet in a lake, admired a placid stream along our backroad, searched antique stores where Vicki was certain a "Mickey" (as in Mouse) waited for her. But more memories would be made before we left for home.

Vicki exulted, "I did it!" She had, through grit, determination and a supportive cheering squad, cycled the length of Michigan. The kissing of the knee ceremony awaited. Jim, on his knees beside Vicki's left one, her hand on his shoulder, dutifully kissed the once wounded but now nearly healed knee. Anagram time followed with our lettered MICHIGAN shirts. We composed words of joy: *I can, I gain, I am, Hi, him, ham*. We ended the trip across state nineteen with the laughter of friends ringing in our ears and in anticipation of our next venture together.

LOUISIANA-*LAISSEZ LE BON TEMPS ROULER CAJUN*-LET THE GOOD TIMES ROLL-1988

Riders: Betty, Vicki, Jim/Jan. Drop off/Pick up: Tania and her best friend, Darcy Blossfeld.
Distance: 303 miles

Spring break again and time for three teachers and a wire-bender to enjoy a vacation on bicycles. For a long time, Jim and I had our eyes on Louisiana—close enough to get to during the week allowed from school and warm enough to not have to bundle up in our wintery best.

Betty and Vicki volunteered to join us. Tania and Darcy chipped in, "We'll drive the SAG wagon. Then we can go to New Orleans!" So off we went to Leesville, Louisiana, home of Fort Polk, a US Army post. I'd never heard of it until Jim joined the army after dental school. He said then, "I hope I won't be assigned there. It's hot and humid and the mosquitoes are terrible. People who have been there have told me how much they hated it." That was enough of a deterrent for me.

But twenty-one years later, it seemed like a good place, at least to start a bike ride, only a few miles from the Texas border. Immediately, we drove to the border and four of us biked back to Leesville where Tania and Darcy waited. Then we headed out to discover the location of the Huckleberry Inn B&B. What a great name! A gorgeous home complete with a wrap-around veranda and a swing hanging from a tree in the front yard! Furnished with handsome walnut Victorian furniture, we would sleep in beds that required stairs to get into. Remembering the height of the bed didn't come easily in the middle of the night, but none of us broke any bones getting out of, well, off the bed. We poked into all the public rooms admiring the museum quality decor. All of us had been to enough antique stores and auctions to appreciate how fortunate we were to be staying here. Once again, Jim had found a gem.

✤

Too soon we had to leave this cocoon to hit the road, only to find our least favorite road sign: *ROAD CLOSED AHEAD*. What to do? What we usually do—bike on and check it to see if we can possibly cross the construction zone somewhere safely. Well, mostly safely, but not necessarily to OSHA standards. Next sign: *ROAD CLOSED TO THRU TRAFFIC.* Surely that wouldn't mean us, would it? The gap in the bridge was twelve to fifteen feet wide. Astute Tania and Darcy found, rescued and circuitously drove us to the other side of the construction. Delivery complete, they left on their vacation.

Along the way we delighted in early morning fog; bikers' respite in local cemeteries; examining above-ground tombs; pine logs tumbling down the banks of the Mississippi like pickup sticks waiting to be loaded by crane onto a barge; equilateral triangles forming a cantilevered truss bridge over Atchafalaya River at Simmesport; cycling along the levee, amazed at how much effort it must have taken to build it so high, and wondering if it did its job of flood control.

✤

One day a sign appeared directing us to cross the Mississippi on the *New Roads/St. Francisville Ferry Free Ferry 24 hours.* A rusty, well-worn small auto and passenger ferry, like other ferries we've ridden on bicycle trips, was a good place to strike up conversations with people interested in our venture. We had the good fortune to be plying the Big River's waters at the same time as a paddle-wheeler whose size overwhelmed our ferry.

Another reprieve from highways came as we biked down rural lanes stretched out between evergreen trees leading to Rosedown Plantation. We strolled among blooming lavender azaleas and pink magnolias and toured the great house. I posed in my best Grecian water carrier's form using my plastic water bottle. Somehow the effect wasn't the same—yellow rain jacket and black biking shorts did not measure up to the graciously swathed body of the water carrier statue. I reflected on the lives of the slaves who made such luxury possible. What a travesty.

A memorable overnight at the triple gabled St. Francisville Inn charmed us. Painted grey with white bric-a-brac and arched windows with green shutters, its broad front porch invited us to sit and stay. So we did. We remember St. Francisville for another reason: a restaurant that served the most beautiful and definitely the most delicious baked potatoes we have ever eaten. They raised the bar for all potatoes thereafter.

On the road, we loved homey little cafés and stopped at them whenever we could. Bonhomie and scrumptious food combined with rural folksiness, just like I remembered from my growing up years.

✤

LOUISIANA PURCHASE

"Isn't it lunchtime?" called Vicki as we rolled down a bumpy Louisiana highway.

Betty responded, "Maybe there's somewhere we can get something to make sandwiches." Sure enough, the highway markers indicated a crossroads was coming up. A shabby collection of houses appeared, among them a country store labeled *Groceries-Sandwiches*. Sounded good to us. The nearly bare siding dripped with curly paint peels. If anyone took a mind to painting it, the old building would have digested gallons and gallons of it.

We parked our bikes next to a tree that nudged the broken concrete foundation. Sagging double screen doors banged satisfactorily behind us as we walked in, recalling our childhood experiences with wooden screen doors. This time, however, there was no parental "Don't slam the door!" reminder except in our memories.

We hoped to find bread, peanut butter or jam and maybe some fruit for our usual picnic lunch on the road. As we spread out in the aisles to scan the nearly empty shelves, I found the bread shelf—two loaves of white sandwich bread and three packages of hamburger buns, all a brand I'd never heard of. Jim reported, "No peanut butter. No jam." Vicki searched for her favorite *nanners* but there was no yellow fruit, no fruit at all. Betty didn't find cookies but discovered chips.

Then we saw her—a shriveled little lady of indeterminate age with a dentured smile, wearing a stained, formerly white dress partially covered by a faded blue print apron trimmed with red rick-rack. Her name was Iris and her shoulders barely reached above the scarred wooden counter. Her eyes sparkled as she eagerly greeted us, "What kin Ah do for ya?" Seeing no cars in the parking lot we presumed we were her only customers.

Assuming our newly acquired southern vocabulary, we allowed as how we were hungry. "Could you make us some sandwiches?"

Yes she could, but first she wanted to know what we were doing. We loved telling people, "We're biking across Louisiana."

Iris was incredulous, probably thinking about her Avoyelles County store halfway across the upper part of the boot of Louisiana. "Where'd ya start?"

"On the Texas-Louisiana border just west of Leesville. We're heading to Bogalusa."

Still wide-eyed at the audacity, perhaps stupidity of bicycling that far, she got back to our lunch. Her choices included sliced ham on white bread with mustard. Oh yes, she had some cheese too, a Velveeta look-and-taste-alike.

As Iris bustled to the back we inquired, "Could we fill up our water bottles?" She seemed surprised by the request but told us to follow her. Betty and I did, passing through a set of louvered swinging half-doors into what we guessed would be the kitchen. She pointed to the rust stained long shallow sink to our right and disappeared through an adjacent door.

We stared at the sink, our four water bottles in hand. We looked at each other, grimaced, shrugged and turned on the faucet. What sputtered out was the most gosh-awful spout of we guessed-it-was-water, the color of Crayola's burnt sienna. The smell? Sulphur. We opted not to fill the bottles. We'd take our chances and hope there was water somewhere down the road. Fanta orange or Pepsi would have to do for now. We returned to the main store to wait with Vicki and Jim. We waited. And waited.

Fifteen minutes later there was still no sign of our sandwich lady. "Do you think something happened to her? Should we go back and check?"

We were contemplating doing just that when we heard a car pull up in the hard-packed dirt parking lot. We looked out the smudged front window and saw an elderly, to us at least, lady climbing out of her rusty early 1970s Chevy. We watched her approach but before we could return to our sandwich predicament, another older car rolled in. The driver and passenger, two more white-haired ladies, joined the first woman and chattered away as they came into the timeworn grocery.

They greeted us with brief smiles and unabashedly appraised us and our tight shiny black biking shorts. *What must they be thinking about us and our pannier-laden bicycles?* We would never know, but we could guess. Betty, Vicki, Jim and I quickly understood why it was taking Iris so long to make our sandwiches. She had obeyed the adage *First things first* and called her friends to inform them she had four foreign bicyclists in her store. She had invited them to come on down for the viewing of these weirdly attired, curious creatures.

Iris proudly brought our white bread, ham, cheese and mustard sandwiches. We paid and thanked her, nodded our goodbyes to her friends and went outside. We ate our lunch sitting in the sand and dried grass of the dusty parking lot, tree branches shading us from the hot Louisiana noon-day sun.

Iris made our lunch but we agreed we'd probably made the ladies' day, maybe even their week.

PANCAKE BIRTHDAY

"What are we going to do for Vicki's birthday tomorrow?" Betty's question was one I'd wondered about too. In 1988 in wee burgs on Louisiana backroads, we found no bakeries or stores that had anything but Twinkies. No way would we pop some candles in a Twinkie for her thirty-fourth birthday. We kept riding and pondering. And whenever Vicki wasn't riding close to us, we talked about it.

All of us chatted about the joy of bicycling in such a beautiful state. We recalled all the warnings we'd had from Louisianans: "Be careful out there! These Louisiana drivers are terrible! They'll drive you right off the road!" So we'd been careful and we'd been surprised. No one tried to run us off the road. No one threw anything at us. No one played chicken with us. No one shouted or spit at us.

Everyone was courteous. We felt happy and safe. Even the weather had cooperated so far. But we still had this dilemma. What do we do about Vicki's birthday? We had to come up with something.

That night our motel had a restaurant attached to it. Or the restaurant had a motel attached to it, I don't know which. That was convenient since the rest of Amite had few amenities for a bicycle traveler, or anyone else for that matter. By supper time Betty and I had a plan which, if executed properly, should delight Vicki and us.

Usually we went to breakfast at quarter to seven but Jim and I arrived early to deliver a clearly written note and some candles to the server: *A young woman will be joining us for breakfast. No matter what she orders, bring her pancakes. Three large pancakes in one stack and four small ones in another stack. Please put the three big candles in the large pancakes and four little candles in the small ones and light them. It's her birthday. Give us the bill. Thank you.*

Then we waited for Betty and Vicki to arrive. We gave Vicki birthday hugs and the server took our orders. Vicki wanted eggs over easy, hash-browns, and whole wheat toast. Our fellow-conspirator cast a knowing glance our way. Vicki missed it. We just smiled and placed our orders.

Breakfast talk always included what we might expect on the day's route—what the mileage might be, how many towns we will pass through, how far apart they are, particularly good to know for nature breaks. If we were aware of any notable topographical changes, hills, for instance, that would be mentioned. Jim thought today was going to be slightly rolling hills, flattening out as we came to the Pearl River. Our total mileage would be about fifty-four miles with towns ten to fifteen miles apart. If they have facilities, that distance between breaks is good. Otherwise, it's into the woods. Or the field. Or wherever there's a modicum of privacy.

In came the pancakes with candles flaming. With a flourish, the server set them in front of the Birthday Girl who responded, "You guys!" We burst into our best rendition of the *Happy Birthday Song*, Vicki closed her eyes, made a wish and blew out all the candles. We hoped her wish would come true.

Why two sizes of pancakes? Vicki was a math teacher extraordinaire. In math-speak, three tens, the big pancakes, and four ones, the little pancakes, equal thirty-four.

We've delighted in recalling this birthday story for many years and with every telling, Vicki smiles and her face shines.

🚲

Happiness, sadness, delight, reluctance for the trip to end, dismay at the thought of returning to the mundane instead of the open road—such feelings surface on the last day of a multi-day bicycle tour. Sometimes our minds flip forward to the moment of accomplishment. "We did it! Another state down!" That kind of mental celebration can be a bit premature.

Cloudy sky, mild temperatures, light wind and high spirits reigned as we left our motel in Arcola, Louisiana on the final day of our spring break ride. The miles flowed by for us, at least until eleven o'clock, an hour short of our projected meeting time with Tania and Darcy at McDonald's in Bogalusa. We already contemplated the joy of an unfettered ride to the Pearl River.

We've heard people talk about skies opening up—precisely our experience that day. It dumped on and instantly soaked us before we could even get rain gear out of our panniers. This was not a brief mid-western style gully-washer. This was an *Ah really mean business* drencher which fortunately, did not conjure up lightning and thunder.

Unbeknownst to us, in her eagerness to get to what she called *Mickey D's*, her favorite eating place on earth, Vicki missed a turn and went right instead of left. Betty and I had followed our leader Jim as he continued on the planned route. One-half mile later, Vicki was nowhere in sight. Jim turned around to go find her. He'd figured out where she'd gone astray. Later on she reported that when he finally caught up to her he yelled through the storm, "Whaddaya doin'? You shoulda turned left!"

"It was raining so hard I couldn't see which way to go!"

"Then you shoulda waited for us to find out!"

Meanwhile, Betty and I stood water-logged along the roadside as we waited for the shepherd and the lamb. They sloshed by without greeting us and we fell into line behind them.

Water-covered roads and streets greeted us on Bogalusa's outskirts, moments later the gutters ran full. As traffic increased, so did our apprehension. Rain, cars, trucks, and bikes don't make a good mix but luckily, no one drove too close to us. They splashed us but what was a little more water?

Soon the water lapped at the hubs of our bike wheels. Our already chilly feet were submerged at the bottom of each pedal stroke. Fearful of dropping into unseen potholes we managed to emerge intact from the still-forming street ponds.

Vicki's victorious voice sounded, "Arches! I see golden arches!"

We slogged into the parking lot. *At least we didn't have to tread water.* We clambered off our bikes, leaned them against the building and squished our way to the doors. After a few puppy shakes, we entered. Tania and Darcy hadn't come yet but the store was dry, at least until we arrived. We stood away from other patrons, well aware of the puddles forming at our feet as we discussed what to do, wait or eat. "Let's eat!"

We dribbled back to the door, took off our jackets and shook them again, found a table and settled our bedraggled selves in and savored the moment. Hot chocolate, French fries and a burger sounded really good. Just as we placed our orders Tania and Darcy pulled into the parking lot—our dry ride back to Iowa.

The rain stopped while we ate. We still hadn't reached the end point, the Pearl River which forms the southern section of the border between Louisiana and Mississippi, lay six miles away. Naturally we planned to ride across the bridge to make it an official border-to-opposite-border ride, Jim's and my twentieth.

To one local, the old iron-framed bridge spanning the Pearl was "…a thing of beauty, making an 'S' curve across the river and through the swamp." He added, "When the creek rises, it isn't much good at being a bridge." The Pearl was rising and its swirling cocoa brown water ran only eight to ten feet below the bridge. We wondered how much it would rise with today's downpour. We didn't intend to stay to find out.

As we rode across the bridge, I kept looking down at the water and singing to myself, *Michael, row the boat ashore*…all the while hoping nobody had to row anybody to shore. Instead of singing *The Jordan is deep and wide*…I substituted *The Pearl is deep and wide…And getting wider…*

Tania and Darcy met us with the van on the State of Mississippi side of the river. What a relief to load the bikes, climb in the van next to our sodden panniers and collapse on those wonderfully soft, cushy and not-the-slightest-bit-damp seats, that is, until we got there. The cross-Louisiana ride was over and the time had come to return to Iowa.

We toured historic Vicksburg and four days later in our warm dry home, watched the evening news and saw film clips of floods in the south. The newscaster reported, "The Pearl River has crested at thirteen feet above flood stage just east of Bogalusa, Louisiana…"

And we'd thought we'd been wet.

On Saturday, February 4, 2012, six weeks short of her five big and eight small pancakes birthday, Vicki died. Two days before, I had gone to see her, to pray with her, and tell her I love her. She thanked God for her journey and said she was ready to go home. I asked if she remembered her pancake birthday. She smiled and nodded and her face shone. As I left her, we both knew she would celebrate her next birthday in a place that is heavenly, even if it doesn't have pancakes. And her face will shine.

VIRGINIA-*GIVE US A SIGN*-1989

Riders: Betty, Jim/Jan. Drop off/ pick up: Tania, Darcy. Distance: 175 miles

Our canary yellow rain suits contrasted brightly with the facade of the Lincoln Memorial on a pearl gray March day. We three riders eagerly posed for the start-of-the-bike-trip photos, taken by our loyal van drivers, Tania and Darcy. They planned to explore museums and historic spots in Washington, D.C. before wandering south to Williamsburg and Virginia Beach to meet us in Franklin, Virginia, the terminus of our spring break ride.

Jim, Jan and Betty at the Lincoln Memorial

We had already paid our respects to Mr. Jefferson, felt solemn in the presence of Mr. Lincoln and thrilled to start this trip in such an auspicious location. But, as we often quote on bicycle trips, with apologies to Robert Frost, we had miles to go before we could sleep.

Although bleak and bare trees did not reflect our optimistic anticipation of clearing skies, we headed for the Mt. Vernon Bicycle Trail. This wide paved path with long, picturesque wooden bridges led from Arlington to Mt. Vernon. To our chagrin rain soon pounded us.

Despite our early morning breakfast, hunger pangs set in. We spotted a restaurant near the trail and I stopped, ready to enter. Jim and Betty looked at our dripping selves and deemed the restaurant too fancy for us in our condition. I convinced them since there seemed to be no other options we should go in anyway. If the management didn't want to serve us they would tell us and no ominous sign reminded potential patrons *We reserve the right to refuse service to anyone.* Obviously they hadn't anticipated serving people in what has been called our drowned rat condition.

With feet slopping in soaked shoes, we shook ourselves off outside and went in. The hostess greeted us pleasantly even as we created puddles. A warming meal and beginning-to-be not-quite-so-wet clothes humored us. A curious fellow diner approached and asked if we belonged to a bowling team. After our initial startled reaction we realized she thought our rain gear comprised uniforms. We assured her we were not a bowling team. Another person queried, "Firefighters?" Did we disappoint them by saying no?

A light mist accompanied us as we arrived at elegant Mt. Vernon. Unfortunately, we had started later than we had anticipated so couldn't spend much time there. We still felt the history of the place and relished the fact of being there on our bikes. Traversing hilly, wooded, rural Virginia inspired us to stop to admire the beauty but we couldn't linger, ever mindful that dusk comes early in mid-March. We had to arrive by five at the Fredericksburg B&B where Jim had arranged an overnight.

Expert route maker and chief navigator Jim generally used the reliable Bike-centennial and East Coast Bikeway maps to plan our route. About three thirty he, who also has an excellent sense of direction, stopped at an intersection. He pulled over to the side of the road, looked around in consternation, "This just doesn't seem right. I think we should go straight but the maps say we should turn left."

As drivers paused at the stop sign, we asked them, "Which way is Route 27?" None of them had a clue. The intermittent rain turned to snow and our concerns grew about being stranded in the middle of unknown territory at nightfall. After another moment of hesitation, Jim decided, "All right. Let's follow the map." We turned left and rode twenty yards. He stopped at a bridge and shook his head. "This still doesn't feel right." The light began to fade.

In desperation I raised my arms and pleaded, "OK God, give us a sign." Before we could take another breath, Jim's back tire went "Sssss." Betty and I glanced at each other, stifled giggles and all three of us returned to the stop sign, a better spot to change a tire. With Betty's and my expert assistance Jim changed the tube, replaced the wheel, spun it to make sure the brakes worked, put the panniers on, smiled slightly, looked up and said firmly, "OK, God. The next time my wife asks for a sign, give it to her."

As we mounted our bicycles again, a driver of whom we had previously asked directions returned from picking up her child. She assured us we should go straight, just as Jim had thought. We pedaled as fast as we could until we reached the state highway. There we rode on the potholed, water-filled shoulder, praying to be safe as snow evolved to pelting sleet and frigid, grimy spray from passing trucks made us even more miserable. I was getting worried when in the darkness, we saw the welcoming neon light of a motel. What relief when we learned there was room for us in that inn. Jim called the B&B several miles farther into town, spoke to the owner and explained our predicament. He graciously told Jim he understood and said he wouldn't charge us for the night. That, hot showers, dry clothes and food went a long way to soothe us.

While one person showered, the other two checked the gear to make sure that nothing had gotten wet. Even though we put individual pieces of clothing in ziplock plastic bags they sometimes get damp. We emptied and dried the inside of the panniers. We also washed the clothes we had worn that day and hung them up to dry in the room. We hoped our shoes would dry next to the motel room's heater. We appreciated the occasional B&B hosts who allowed us to wash and dry our clothes in their laundry machines, or infrequent motels with guest washers and dryers. Most importantly, we wiped grit and grime off our bicycle frames and chains, lightly oiled the chains so the gears would change smoothly the following day.

Fredericksburg sparkled in the morning sun as we pondered the monuments and historic sights. Being wet and anxious—already a memory. However, other solemn thoughts enveloped us as we came upon reminders of the War Between the States, markers describing battles, buildings, the wounded, all part of the unfortunate landscape of war.

When Jim got his sign-from-God flat tire, that had been his first flat tire in thousands of miles of riding his bike but not the last one on this trip. He looked stunned when he had another even before we got to Richmond. Lesson of the road: No one is immune to little perils of long distance cycling.

As we biked through rainy Virginia, we discussed our driving conditions from Iowa to Virginia. Traveling through Pennsylvania had been an education in Muck. A combination of snow, gravel, salt and sand splattered up on the van and solidified. Mounted on a front rack on the van, Jim and Betty's bikes bore the brunt of road gunk, while mine rested securely in what our family calls "the back-back" inside the van. When we arrived in D.C., we went directly to a car wash to chip off the hard-as-concrete globs and scrub the van and two bicycles. What a mess!

Betty, Jim and I recall Virginia as the state where we wore all the clothes we had all the time we were on the road: long-sleeved shirts, tights, raingear, gloves and warm socks. Even though the weather brought us cold and drizzling rain, we had a great time. People stopped to ask about riding in such inclement weather. We told them honestly we were having a good time. Why didn't they believe us? Red dripping noses? Sopping gloves? Soggy rainsuits? Sloppy puddles marking wherever we went? Hot soup became du jour and a hand dryer in a restroom a joy, not just for hands but for wet rain suits. Bliss.

As we toured the James River Plantation late in the trip, an elderly woman hesitantly queried, "Are you from outer space?" We think she saw our yellow rain gear and thought we were astronauts. We told her we were not from outer space, but silently considered what we were doing crossing state number twenty-one might make a lot of people think we were out of our minds.

BIKING COLORADO NORTH TO SOUTH-1989

Riders: Sandy/Dave, Vicki, Betty, Connie/John, Jim/Jan. Drop off: Connie/
John. Pick up: Sami Balestri, Mara. Distance: 340 miles

Every valley shall be lifted up, and every mountain and hill be made low; the
uneven ground shall become level and the rough places a plain. Isaiah 4:9

Colorado! Always an important state in our lives, Jim spent several weeks of his newborn life there
with his family in Greeley. The destination for our honeymoon? The Rocky Mountains in Colorado.
Where we checked out locations for Jim to practice dentistry? Boulder, Loveland and Fort Collins.
Two of our daughters, Mara and Tania, lived in Boulder and, since Jennifer was a senior in high
school, she had loved to ski in the high country. Additionally, our friends Connie and John own a
condo in Summit County's Keystone and had invited us to visit them again in the summer of 1989.
What more impetus would we need to ride across the state? None. The eight of us who had biked
across Michigan in 1988 made it a done deal.

ڸ

To celebrate our adventure, Betty and her talented son Dave designed white with blue Colorado-spe-
cific T-shirts, *Iowans Cycling High in Colorado* arched over a high-wheeled bicycle and underlined
with *Switzerland of America 1989.* The small back wheel of the high-wheeler depicted the final O in
Colorado. We wore them proudly.

We picked Connie and John up from Keystone to drive to the Wyoming border where our trip
would officially begin. She volunteered to drive our van to our first Colorado overnight, Walden, so
he could cycle that day. Connie joined us on her bike at other times.

Something we all noticed—the northern Colorado countryside, mostly short scrubby shrubs backed by mesas, seemed very green for late July. The transition to pines and aspens came gradually along our route.

Meeting solo rider Kathy on the road added to the fun of the day. We talked with her and invited her to ride with us as long as she'd like, and to stay the night with us if she wanted. She gladly accepted the offer of companionship, and throughout the day we learned more about her and her journey. Originally from Pennsylvania, she had become a traveling nurse after twenty-five years of nursing in more conventional scenarios. Kathy had been married that long too, and during that time, her husband had felt free to travel and do whatever he wanted to in addition to his addiction to bowling. She said most of the child-rearing of their three had been her responsibility.

At that magic quarter century point, Kathy told her husband her life goals included a long-distance bike ride. She welcomed him to come with her if he wanted but she planned to cycle and work her way across the United States. He declined her offer, so after more serious planning, she flew to Seattle, where she launched her quest. We asked how she felt being a woman traveling alone. She responded she generally felt quite safe and, after requesting permission, usually camped adjacent to the sheriff or police department. Their always positive response added to her security and heartened her.

She camped, as was her wont, instead of staying in a motel with us, then pedaled toward Granby and Rocky Mountain National Park. We continued going south toward Kremmling and Summit County. Spending time with her made us ponder solo cycling and how lonely it must sometimes be to not be able to share experiences and encouragement with a companion.

Although the terrain provided both ups and downs, generally we climbed in altitude and would continue to do so until we crested the Rockies at Fremont Pass, several days hence. Meanwhile nature treated us to more mountains, lakes and summer flowers. Green Mountain Reservoir, created from the Blue River whose path we paralleled, reflected the landscape against the beryl sky. I loved the undulations as we pedaled along this spun-out lake.

As we approached Silverthorne, we spotted an osprey nest constructed high on a pole by this bird with an innate architectural bent. By this time the valley of the Blue had widened, opening itself to denser human habitation, some of whom imitated the osprey by positioning their homes high on the mountainsides. Our Keystone destination lay a few miles beyond, a long climb and a modified roller coaster along Lake Dillon. Tucked into pine trees, Connie and John's condo welcomed us. So did they.

On our layover day the guys decided to tackle riding part of the way up challenging Loveland Pass while the rest of us did mundane things like laundry. We shared lunch beside Keystone Lake and relaxed and strolled along the tumbling Snake River. An added highlight, the visit of our Iowa City friends, Betty and Dick Mitchell and their daughter Beth who taught school in Silverthorne.

We bikers "dressed for dinner" by wearing our crisp, and so far, clean and sparkling white Colorado bike trip t-shirts. I was totally surprised when they plopped me down on a high stool and told me to sit there. Obediently, I did. Out came a white birthday cake decorated with a female cyclist riding under a blue sky, mountains and pines in the background with the caption *Keep on pedaling*. What a treat! What a way to end the first and begin the second half-century of my life with a slightly early surprise birthday party.

⚲

After that excitement, a daunting challenge confronted us—one we approached with eagerness and angst. Betty, Vicki, Dave, Jim and I, flatlanders all, challenged ourselves to bicycle Colorado's 11,318 foot Fremont Pass. We'd spent the previous four biking days climbing the Blue River Valley from the Wyoming border to Keystone's 9,300 foot altitude, gradually acclimating ourselves to the thinner air. None of us had any symptoms of altitude sickness— dizziness, headache, nausea, vomiting, fatigue—except for sleep disturbances which we attributed to our pre-climb jitters. There was, however, the throbbing question: *Can we do this?* We had facetiously told each other the only way to train in Iowa for a high altitude ride was to pedal and hold your breath at the same time.

Early the following day we mounted our trusty bikes fitted with granny gears to allow us to climb steep hills without compromising our knees. At least that's the theory. Connie, John and Sandy lingered at the condo and planned to join us for our overnight in Leadville.

The mostly gentle bike path to Dillon had one puffer hill stuck in to remind cyclists they were in Colorado. With our minds being what they were at the thought of even thinner air, we opted for the not very busy highway the first few miles.

Lake Dillon shimmered below the Tenmile Range we'd be skirting. This azure lake, formed by the damming of the Little Blue River, is owned by Denver which uses this mountain water to sustain its ever growing thirst for development. The white wings of the sailboats scudding across the lake created a wonderful picture. The bike trail across the dam and on, with short, quick climbs, drops and curves all the way to Frisco made bicycling akin to flying—absolutely delightful!

Frisco's Main Street still had a mining town ambiance with only a few shops and no upscale *I'm a mountain tourist town* feeling to it. A few hundred pedal strokes got us through it to begin a slow climb on the paved trail to Copper Mountain and our second breakfast of the day.

Tenmile Creek rippled and gurgled down the high valley. Creekside willows and birches created a welcome green barrier between the paved bike path and Interstate 70, isolating us from the sight and sound of it. As we felt the incline increase, we downshifted and kept pedaling up toward the Pass.

Betty was in the lead when she suddenly toppled over. Jim and Dave, close behind, stopped to help her. As Vicki and I approached, we prepared to stop but Jim signaled to go on, so we continued for another one hundred feet and dismounted to pensively wait for the others. We were relieved to see them appear on the trail and resume riding. In her trepidation about the Fremont Pass ascent, Betty had begun to hyperventilate. Recovery came quickly.

Hunger pangs hit us and Copper offered the only place to buy food until we neared Leadville. Disappointed to discover that only one open restaurant existed in Copper we, as cyclists, took what we could get. Most selections on the menu included meat but we rarely eat meat for breakfast. The others ordered pancakes, I ordered French toast but we all told the waiter that we didn't want any sausage, bacon or ham. He replied, "But it comes with meat." Dave patiently explained, "We know it does but we just want the pancakes and the French toast. No meat."

The puzzled waiter tried again, "But it has to come with the meat." Jim, hoping to clarify our wishes, repeated the litany, "We know it comes with meat but we don't want meat. We won't eat it and we don't want it to be wasted. We just want the pancakes and French toast."

"But..." sputtered the waiter. Jim interrupted him, "We'll pay the full price but just don't bring us the meat."

In disbelief or confusion, I don't know which, the waiter shook his head and tried one last time, "But the meat..."

"Could we please speak to the cook?"

In a few moments a glum looking cook approached and rasped, "What's the problem?" The whole scenario was run through again with the emphasis on "We don't want meat, we don't want it to be wasted so please don't serve it." He nodded, we thought with understanding, left and began making kitchen noises.

We spent what seemed to be a longer than necessary interlude checking our watches. When the waiter finally brought our food, we gaped in astonishment. There, nestled in with the pancakes and French toast were—slices of ham. As we had promised, we didn't eat it. And as we had promised, we paid for it, all the while shaking our heads and rolling our eyes in bewilderment. What part of "We don't want meat," did these people not understand? Or maybe they enjoyed the meat once we'd left.

After our meaty but meatless meal, we zipped out of Copper and back to Highway 91 which we'd ride to Leadville. Our lovely bicycle path had ended.

I had chosen a Bible verse for this ride: "*Every valley shall be lifted up, and every mountain and hill be made low... Isaiah 40:4.* I must have hoped that would give us courage and promise. That would remain to be seen. Then Isaiah 40:9 goes on to say *Get you up to a high mountain...*

Our first few days biking in the state helped us acclimate at least a bit but I felt very apprehensive and sensed that others did too. I planned to stop any time I needed to catch my breath and/or calm my nerves on the way to the Fremont Pass Summit. We pedaled and pedaled, really enjoyed the views from the scenic over-looks, but always in the back of my mind reigned the question, *Can I do this at this altitude?* I had no doubt Jim and Dave could but they seemed tense too.

That question came to the forefront at a view over a canyon. A granite pedestal informed us that the Kokomo Masonic Temple, the highest in Colorado, had been located at 10,000 plus feet. We knew the Continental Divide at Fremont Pass measured 11,318 feet and we had only a mile or so to get there. Nearly one thousand foot climb in a mile? Panic. The first thing I thought of—*I need more energy.* So I peeled a banana and stuffed it into my mouth. *Would that be enough?* I dug around in my handlebar bag until I found an errant Snickers bar. I lay down on the gravel next to my bike and ate the bar. *Would that do it?* We all wondered about our capabilities in those few minutes so everyone ate whatever they hoped would give them stamina. Finally, I got up and said, "I'm going." Determinedly, I slung my leg over my bike, head down and put all my effort into making that mountain into what I hoped would be a molehill. Two switchbacks later I saw the Fremont Pass Summit sign. We were there. Huh? Stunned, I looked around, "This is it?" We had exerted ourselves very little after our stop. How disappointing.

Strange what fear and nervousness can create in our minds. We all interpreted the sign to read that we were only at 10,000 feet instead of us actually being at over 11,000. Rewriting the sign in this way would have helped us: *Look down into the valley to see where the Kokomo Masonic Temple once stood at 10,000 feet.*

Vicki, Betty, Dave, Jan and JIm celebrating the summit

The immediate downhill made us oh-so-happy we had biked from the north. I hated to think of the pains and mental agony we might have had on the last ascent coming from the Leadville direction. What joy to swoop down past the Climax Mine, an open-pit molybdenum mine, on one of the quickest thirteen mile rides I've ever done. We did pause to learn that molybdenum, highly resistant to corrosion, is used primarily in making steel alloys. It can withstand extreme temperatures without softening or expanding so is especially useful in aircraft parts, industrial motors and military armor or weaponry, such as the howitzer Big Bertha in World War I.

Then I wondered if the *moly* in *chromoly* used in our bikes, had molybdenum in them. It sounds like it should and it does, about 1 percent for strength. But we were having too much fun to focus long on mines and molybdenum. We kept swooshing down the mountain toward Leadville, then we were there, in a town obviously named after the lead ore found in the area.

A pamphlet from the Leadville Chamber of Commerce embellished the basic gold and silver strikes of the town in this way: *Not even Monte Carlo ever developed millionaires or paupers with the pace set by Leadville during the first year of its existence (1878-79.) Many a fortune made in a day was squandered at night in the gambling dives. But millions of dollars spread to other parts of the world and in many cities today stand buildings which sprang, so to speak, from some lucky strike in Leadville.*

Much of Leadville's history is entangled with the name Tabor, as one might assume after seeing the Tabor Opera House and the Tabor Grand Hotel, both on Harrison Avenue, the main street. Horace and Augusta Tabor, originally from Maine moved to Kansas, then joined the gold rush in Colorado. For eighteen years Augusta did everything in the mining camps to keep them solvent, from cooking and laundering for boarders, nursing, being a postmistress, transporting gold dust in her skirts while riding horseback to transport it to Denver. She was an entrepreneur and established and successfully ran a general store. To the people of Leadville, she was always their much loved "first lady" despite being married to a first class cad who flaunted the money from a surprising silver discovery. He had expected gold would be their fortune. They became fabulously wealthy but he wanted to spend it and she wanted to save it causing much marital strife. From various accounts, Horace, now known as the Silver King, traveled throughout the country with a variety of women whom he called Mrs. Tabor. He eventually deserted Augusta and their expensive Denver home, and moved close to his last mistress known as Baby Doe.

Augusta and Horace divorced and he married Baby Doe, much to public consternation. They moved to Leadville. Augusta remained in Denver but frequently visited her sister who lived there too.

Leadville's fascinating history plus 10,152 foot altitude and surrounding mountains amazed us. But for all its appeal, we really needed to relax and breathe, thin though the air was, to prepare for the next day. We would leave these breathtaking surroundings to focus on completing our ride. Connie and John would return to Keystone and Sandy would hop on her bicycle again.

After leaving Leadville, we could see Mount Elbert, at 14,433 feet, the tallest fourteener in Colorado. Snowmelt from another part of the Sawatch Range gives rise to the Arkansas River which eventually confluents into the Mississippi River. The river runs alongside Highway 24, our route, until it turns east at Salida toward Canon City and Pueblo. None of us had any inkling what an impact that stretch of river would make on our family in the future.

Bicycling over 9,010 foot Poncha Pass presented another learning opportunity. After we made the not too rigorous climb, the sign at the top showed me a geographic concept I wasn't familiar with. It labeled the *Rio Grande River Watershed* with an arrow pointing south, the one pointing north indicated the *Arkansas River Watershed*. I only knew of the markers indicating water flows to the Pacific or to the Mississippi or Atlantic.

The magnificent Great Sand Dunes National Park teased us with a tiny glimpse in the distance, but we had to pacify ourselves with a pile of white sand along the side of the road. Tire tracks ran through it, but none were from our bikes.

Despite the sign on Poncha Pass, I was still surprised when we crossed the Rio Grande River at Alamosa. It flows out of the San Juan Mountains of southwest Colorado, dissects New Mexico on its way to the Texas-Mexico border until dropping from high elevation and emptying into the Gulf of Mexico. Jim and I had only crossed the Rio Grande twice before, driving our little green 1954 Plymouth in and out of Mexico one day on our honeymoon. I need geography lessons regarding the routes of rivers of North America.

But I knew enough of the lay of the land to know once we went through San Antonito we had but a mile or so to ride until we had crossed state number twenty-two at the New Mexico border.

TWO STATES, TWO DAYS-NEW JERSEY-RHODE ISLAND-1989

Riders: Jim/Jan. Drop off: Carol/Rob/Nathan/Colin Ashby-Kuhlman. Distance:
New Jersey 103 miles Rhode Island 57 miles, double-crossed

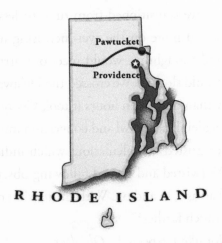

"Eighty miles is all we have to ride? Great!" I exulted. This trip had become a celebration of sorts. Even though I hadn't felt burned out, I had just retired from a job I'd loved, teaching third and fourth graders. Jim and I had decided we wanted to simplify our lives so I could travel with him during the school year and not just at spring break. Summers, Jim's busiest time as an orthodontist, meant lots of college kids come home for required check-ups and adjustments.

Our reward: A September bicycle ride across New Jersey and Rhode Island. On this brief trip, we planned a day of biking for each state.

For two nights we stayed with the Ashby-Kuhlman family in Norristown, Pennsylvania, a suburb of Philadelphia. We'd known Carol and her family since her teenage years in early 1970s Seattle. With good reason, Jim and I believed that she and her older sister Nancy had been the world's best and most creative kid sitters. Our daughters thrived under their care and artistic talents, Carol and Nancy harnessed the energy of all the neighborhood kids who flocked to our front yard to help build an extensive cardboard box village, learned how to crochet and do other crafts and just have fun. So many years later, we felt sheer joy at spending time with Carol, Rob, and their young sons.

Early the next morning all of us piled into our van to drive to the New Jersey coast. As we traversed the incredibly narrow old ironwork Washington Crossing Bridge and met another vehicle, our van's right outside mirror clipped the crossbeams without damage. Obviously, the bridge had been built for horses, wagons and carriages, not wide-bodied vehicles.

Once we arrived at Point Pleasant Beach, Jim and I retrieved our bikes from the back of the van, waved our goodbyes and called, "See you this afternoon!" as the others drove off. We began to pedal back toward their house.

We felt confident we could bike eighty miles in the allotted time, so we rode easily, enjoyed the scenery and gazed at the ornate Orthodox churches and cemeteries we passed—so many clustered into such a few miles. Their gold three-bar crosses gleamed against the cerulean sky and the back roads lulled us into an easy pace.

Soon we transitioned from rural to less rural to small towns to urban zones. We relaxed less and focused more on the ever-increasing number of vehicles. By noon we had ridden over fifty miles and thought we would meet our arrival goal of four o'clock, even though we realized city traffic would slow us. We crossed the Delaware River, New Jersey's border with Pennsylvania, more quickly than the eleven hours it took George Washington and his compatriots.

Philadelphia's sprawl and congestion impeded us, but Jim, a skilled, patient and thorough route designer trusted his calculations which indicated we had fewer than thirty miles to go. I believed him. We twisted and turned following obscure roads and streets through industrial and then residential areas. On and on. With the tension of city riding, my energy began to flag by three o'clock. "How much farther?"

"Not like I expected." *Oh, dear.*

"Do you have any idea where we are?"

"Pretty much." *Pretty much?*

We continued wending our way and I prayed we were truly heading toward Norristown. We stopped frequently to try to get our bearings. Each time ever-positive Jim vowed, "I know where we are," and continued on. I tagged along. *What else was there to do?*

"Do you see any landmarks?"

"Not like I expected." *Sigh.*

Four o'clock. Four fifteen. "Don't you think we should find a payphone and call Carol and Rob to let them know we'll be a little late?"

"We should be there soon."

Four thirty. "I think we should call them. They might be getting worried."

"We're fine."

I asked myself *Is Jim doing the Moses thing and not stopping to ask directions?*

Four forty-five. "I see a pay phone. I want to call to tell them we are OK but will be late." Rob told us we were still quite a distance from their house and it'd be city riding. He gave Jim directions we clearly needed.

At last we straggled onto Linwood Street. What a relief to see lovely familiar faces of Carol, Rob, Nathan and Colin cheering us in. It had taken us longer to get through Philadelphia than it did to cross the whole state of New Jersey. Our odometers read one hundred three miles. We had done a century ride without planning to.

Shortly before seven o'clock, we were seated at the dinner table, thanking God for safety, strength, and wonderful friends who warmed our hearts and souls. Homemade broccoli soup spiced with eye-watering curry followed by Jim's favorite bread pudding did the rest.

Later on, as he tried to determine why we had ridden so much farther than expected, Jim said there was a misprint on the Philadelphia and environs map we used.

Obviously Ben Franklin had not been in charge of the maps.

🚲

DISTANCE: 57 MILES, DOUBLE-CROSSED, ON TO RHODE ISLAND

We allowed ourselves an overnight to recover and then headed north to Rhode Island. We had no one to visit there so rented a motel room for one night. Jim portrayed this portion of the trip as all business. Park the van in the middle of the state, ride west to the Connecticut border, return to the van to eat lunch. After that we'd head to the Massachusetts state line and return to the center of the state where the van awaited us.

Unlike our New Jersey foray, bicycling in Rhode Island went exactly as planned—no glitches. The perfect weather made the day even better. The route we had chosen seemed to ripple and didn't feature precipitous hills. The minimal to non-existent shoulders on the two-lane road meant we had to be alert for traffic coming from both east and west. But this time we really had no cause to hurry, so we didn't.

Although it stood at an unassuming 812 feet, Jerimoth Hill's fame came from its recognition as the highest point in the state. Hence, it became the high point of our ride, at least two of the word's many meanings.

Oak and pine forests lined much of the highway so our color memory proclaimed *Green!* A low traffic count made for pleasant riding. Because the terrain and scenery varied little in this short span of highway we took only one photograph at the Connecticut border. We rode a total of fifty-seven miles that day, a pleasant reprieve from New Jersey's one hundred three.

True to what Jim had envisioned, this ride had been a matter of accomplishing a goal: Crossing states number twenty-three and twenty-four as well as visiting friends. We had come nearly half-way to our ultimate goal of biking across all fifty states border to opposite border. At fifty years of age we deemed that *Good.* The year—1989.

🚲

NO WONDER THE WRIGHT BROTHERS CAME HERE NORTH CAROLINA-1990

Riders: Betty, Jim/Jan. Drop off, pick up: Tania, Darcy. Distance: 205 miles

Jim and I had already decided we wanted to continue our route down the east coast for our next spring break ride. North Carolina made the most sense since we had ridden Virginia the year before. Next question: "Where in the state do we want to ride?"

"Well, it would be fun to ride the Outer Banks since they are flattest part. Besides that, going to Kitty Hawk would be a blast." Betty agreed.

The Outer Banks consist of a string of barrier islands running two hundred miles along the North Carolina and southeastern Virginia coasts. These islands, made entirely of sand, are not anchored to offshore coral reefs like some barrier islands, and violent storms sometimes close older inlets in the sand and open new ones.

One more important question: "Should we ride north to south or south to north?"

Out came the bicycling magazines we depended on for reliable bike touring information. Everything we read about the Outer Banks indicated cycling south to north to take advantage of the prevailing winds would be wise. Another easy decision.

We knew we shouldn't bite off more than we could chew because of our limited time and the distance we had to drive. We picked Jacksonville, where Camp LeJeune is located, to be our launching point and headed east toward the ocean riding forty-four perfect weather miles to Morehead City/Beaufort. With the most coastal of all the US national forests, Croatan National Forest on our left and Bogue Sound and Emerald Isle to our right, we began our singular experience riding the Outer Banks.

Beaufort, lying on the Intracoastal Waterway, maintained its Old Burying Ground, one of the oldest cemeteries in the state. The information on gravestones demonstrated the role the town played in the Revolutionary War and War of 1812—many deaths. Equally as interesting to me, this port attracted famed pirate Edward Teach, AKA Blackbeard, and a young Irish woman Anne Bonny, one of the first named female pirates.

Someone described the Outer Banks as solitude of ocean, beach and sky. Everywhere we looked, we saw water and dollops of land that resembled flooded and flattened lumps of soil. Brown pelicans floated placidly among the buoys as sea grass, scrub plants and palmetto added texture and color. And always, water, water everywhere.

Where water and land meet, often there are bridges, and we traversed some of them on this junket. Until the 1930s when bridges were first built here, the barrier islands remained isolated and reachable only by boat. Now beautiful swooping ones outline some of the string of barrier islands. Marking the land-and-skyscape, local lighthouses keep vigil over centuries of shipwrecks caused by treacherous seas, violent storms and sandbars, a calm or wild place, dependent on the times.

Betty, Jim and I had eagerly anticipated our ferry ride from Cedar Island to Ocracoke Island but the 57 degree temperature, headwinds and cloud cover that whole day created misery! At least it felt a tiny bit warmer when we docked on Ocracoke where Carolina coast plunderer Blackbeard met his demise in 1718.

North Carolina's oldest lighthouse and second oldest in the United States, the still-functioning 1823 Ocracoke Lighthouse doesn't look very imposing. However, its beacon can be seen up to fourteen miles in the sound and the Atlantic Ocean, exactly why it's there. A quirky fact: Ocracoke Lighthouse's exterior, covered with a mixture of salt, lime, whiting (calcium carbonate-chalk sometimes added to paint to improve opacity,) ground rice and clear glue mixed with boiling water became—Ta-da!—the only totally white lighthouse on the Outer Banks.

But like many tourists, we focused on the commanding 280 foot tall Cape Hatteras Lighthouse, which stands on the seventy miles of open beach of the same named National Seashore. Built in 1870 and still the tallest brick lighthouse in America, the massive black and white barber-pole-striped structure needed to be relocated in 1999 due to encroaching sea levels. Lifted from its foundation and transferred to a transport system, it was placed on another foundation twenty-nine hundred feet away. What a feat! For nearly 150 years, this beacon has transmitted light to illuminate perilous Diamond Shoals—definitely a light to help people find their way.

Jan and Betty dwarfed by the Cape Hatteras Lighthouse

As some pundit has phrased it, most people come to the Outer Banks for the beaches but Orville and Wilbur Wright came for the wind and sand. When I thought of that first flight, I had always linked it with the wind, but the soft sandy surfaces for cushioning the landing made perfect sense. So did the massive dunes they needed to glide from. Once we arrived in the Kitty Hawk/Kill Devil Hills locale, I thought *With those winds, it's no wonder the Wright Brothers got their flying machines to fly!*

After doing their research, the brothers started their flying experimentation in 1900 at Kitty Hawk, a tiny coastal village. Their determination bore fruit on December 17, 1903 when they achieved the world's first powered flight there. The soaring machine, as they called it, weighed 750 pounds and used a twelve horsepower motor, enabling that flight to last twelve seconds and cover 120 feet. By the end of the day on the fourth flight, it flew 852 feet in fifty-nine seconds.

I think the lines of the Wright Brothers National Memorial lack the grace I associate with flight. The design resulted from a competition and used an art Deco motif, a triangular shaft of masonry embellished with relief carvings of stylized sculpted wings on the west and east sides. Later on, after we'd ridden Oregon's Coast Highway and crossed Art Deco inspired bridges designed by Conde McCullough, I saw the similarities between his bridges and the Wright Memorial. Who knew we'd have lessons in architecture while riding opposite sides of the continent?

The day we left the Outer Banks, we rode across the almost three miles long Wright Memorial Bridge II over Currituck Sound to a finger of peninsula on the mainland. We could hardly believe the weather—sunny with mostly a tailwind. The negative was bad traffic on a narrow highway. After days of riding with water on both sides, it seemed strange to suddenly be back to roads edged by tall trees.

This had not been an easy ride because of the capricious wind. Betty's severe fatigue led Jim and me to alter our pannier arrangement. I put her large panniers on my bike and Jim took mine and put them on his front rack. We hoped she would be able to continue pedaling when unencumbered by that weight. It helped and she was able to complete the trip.

Our backroads route took us through the woods and the tail of the Great Dismal Swamp with its black water and leafless trees. Finally we spotted some azaleas in bloom and rejoiced that spring was on its way, despite the crosswinds that plagued us throughout the day. Then on to Franklin, Virginia where we'd ended our biking last year and where we joined Tania and Darcy.

Our trek home was made happier by our visit with Jennifer and Bernd in their new home in Pittsburgh. Rested and cheery after that respite, the rest of the way to Iowa City Betty and I mellowed out while Jim drove. He says he always relaxes more when he is driving.

OKLAHOMA, WHERE THE WIND...1991

Riders: Sandy/Dave, Jim/Jan. Drop off, pick up: Betty. Distance: 350 miles

Oklahoma lived up to its beyond-breezy promise as the wind swept down the plain, strong and constant. Fortunately, it blew mostly from the south, a good omen since we rode our bikes almost entirely in a northerly direction from the Texas border to Kansas.

Betty had a disadvantage—she'd broken her right wrist in January so wasn't ready to bike during March spring break. Instead, after dropping the rest of us off at the border she drove to Dallas to visit her oldest son and daughter-in-law. She would pick us up at the end of the ride. We bikers eagerly headed north from the Red River which separated Oklahoma and Texas, the plan—to catch the wind.

The four riders' memories ranged from weather, art, traffic, logistics, signage, accommodations to people. A most vivid recollection: The courtesy of the Oklahoma truck drivers really impressed us (blew us away?) They did not attempt to drive us into the ditches or otherwise threaten us, and pulled over to the other lane when passing. They even waved and smiled when we waved at them. They showed no impatience when they couldn't immediately go around us due to limited sight range. Years later, after many thousands of bicycling miles, they remain crowned as Kings of Courtesy. The Pennsylvania Road Warriors came in second. Alas, we saw no women driving trucks then so we had no queens.

Our simple goals for these five short days of riding included reaching Kansas safely and seeing Jim's and my high school friend Kay Parker. We didn't plan to go to any museums or monuments unless directly on our route. We would avoid the traffic of Oklahoma City and Tulsa and, in order to experience low traffic counts, Jim mapped the route on blue highways. We would enjoy the freedom of propelling ourselves across one more state, number twenty-five for Jim and me and number six for Sandy and Dave.

Gently rolling hills, just beginning to spring green, greeted us daily. Our constant companion the wind kept us from aspiring to any speed records, not our ambition anyway. We expressed gratitude each day and felt safe and content with our progress. As a spring break ride, our daily mileage, except for twenty-five miles the first day, ranged from a comfortable fifty to sixty miles, perfect after a winter off our bikes.

Our first overnight, Coalgate, originated as a mining camp in the Choctaw Nation, unsurprisingly, in the heart of coal country. The mines closed due to strikes in the 1920s and agriculture now forms the core of the present economy. The names of the streams in Coalgate? Clear Boggy and Muddy Boggy Creeks.

武

After we left, we learned a tornado had just ripped through the town. Six people were injured but there were no fatalities. A close call for bicyclists.

Holdenville, birthplace of Boone Pickens, billionaire oil and gas businessman, featured not oil but Southern crops of cotton, peanuts, and pecans. Farmers also raised sweet and Irish potatoes and what we Iowans grew up seeing, corn, hay and oats. Our friend Kay met us for dinner in Bristow. We hadn't seen her in fourteen years so we quickly caught up on families, jobs, bike trips and her master's degree program at Oral Roberts University. A delightful interlude.

We eased on down the road to our next overnight, Pawnee, named after the Native American tribe who had been forcibly relocated here from eastern United States in the mid-1800s. Estimates vary, but at least ninety-thousand Cherokee, Pawnee, Delaware, Sauk, Fox, Seminole, Shawnee and others were moved by the US government to Indian Territory which would become the state of Oklahoma. Records state up to four thousand of them died along the route, the tragic *Trail of Tears*.

This history affects our family directly. My Great-grandfather Edward Cobb and his siblings bought farmland in far western Oklahoma Territory in the early 1900s, after the Great Land Rush of 1889, but before statehood in 1907. The land had been part of our heritage. Oklahoma's history as a territory and how poorly the Native Americans have been treated remains something our family must remember.

Chester Gould, creator of the comic strip *Dick Tracy*, was born and grew up in Pawnee. To honor him a huge mural of Dick Tracy has been painted on a late 1800s brick building in the downtown. Chisel-faced Tracy is depicted as saying, "Crime does not pay." Junior Tracy, Dick's red-haired adopted son, added, "Little crimes lead to big crimes." This crime-stopper motif created a distinct contrast to the reality we faced that night in 1991 Pawnee.

When Jim designs our bike trips, he chooses possible beginning and ending points depending on who we want to visit or what we want to see. Then he searches for towns with motels, hotels or B&Bs that are between fifty and eighty miles apart, with our routes generally avoiding large cities such as Tulsa and Oklahoma City. Hence we had reservations at the motel in Pawnee. Looking back on it, we should have had another kind of reservation, one that would have made us wonder if we should stay there. Had we had another mode of transportation, we wouldn't have.

We turned our bicycles into the graveled parking lot of a white wooden building. It didn't look like a motel to us. We searched for the office and were surprised we had to stand outside the building to register with the check-in clerk who, ominously, sat behind a barred window. We checked in and took our bikes and panniers into our two rooms. We were not surprised at the condition of the furniture and carpeting—old, battered, tattered and dirty looking. We had no other choice so we shrugged, "We'll survive one night here."

As we strolled about downtown Pawnee Jim spotted a men's store. He always looks for knit pullovers with a left chest pocket for his pen, so we had to check it out. He found exactly what he wanted in an attractive pale blue. The town looked better to us. After an undistinguished supper of meat, potatoes and green beans in an equally undistinguished café we headed back to the motel.

A few minutes later we went next door to Sandy and Dave's room to see how they were faring—nearly speechless was how. When they pulled back the blankets to get ready for bed, they found blood on the sheets. With crinkled noses they stripped the bed, took the sheets to the attendant behind the barred windows and requested clean sheets. They got them.

We thought that would be the end of the motel tale. However the following morning when we met to check out and go for breakfast, Dave told us what had transpired after the bloody sheets episode. They had remade the bed and were settling down when they heard a rap at the door. Dave went to see who was there. A dramatically made up woman, wearing a skimpy dress, stood there. She asked, "Is there anything I can do for you?" Quick-thinking Dave replied, "I'll ask my wife." The lady of the night vanished. Lesson learned: If there are bars on the check-in windows of a motel, it probably is not the most reputable in town.

⅗

Oklahoma had already won the prizes for most considerate truck drivers, best continuous tailwind, and worst motel. It was about to win another accolade: One of the most giggle-producing signs. As we cycled along a quiet county road we spotted a log arch spanning the driveway of a modest home. Dangling from the arch hung a sign with these carved words: *El Rancho Not So Grande*. We loved it. To us those words represented the incredible spirit and sense of humor of the American people.

⅗

Our fifth and last day of spring break cycling brought winds we could not fathom. Lucky for us, mostly tailwinds. The wind whisked us right along and we arrived earlier than expected at the Kansas-Oklahoma border. We intended to turn around and ride about one hundred feet to greet Betty who waited in the van. We couldn't pedal a single stroke. The wind buffeted and nearly bowled us over. By putting our heads down and scrunching over our bikes, we painstakingly wheeled them to the van. We couldn't stand up long enough to attach them to the rear bike rack. Instead, we torqued and squeezed them into the van and clambered in out of the wind. Sandy and I felt cramped and compacted sitting on the rear bench seat with our legs up on the seat and two bikes snugged in. Betty fit in the middle seat with two of the bikes beside her. Jim and Dave assumed their usual front seat positions. We managed to untangle ourselves and stretch when we arrived at our motel in Wichita, Kansas nearly eighty miles farther north.

When we got out of the van, we looked around at each other in surprise. No wind. Other joys were in store for us. The riders got to share dinner with my best friend from Macalester College, Judy Conners. Betty's great pleasure was to be with her wonderful new grandson, David Propp, and his parents. We all felt blessed.

NATCHEZ TRACE-MISSISSIPPI MEANDERINGS-1992

Riders: Betty, Sandy/Dave, Jim. SAG driver: Jan. Distance: 310 miles

"No," said the orthopedist.

My hopes shattered. His negative response meant I couldn't bike with the others as they traversed the legendary Natchez Trace. Two months earlier I had broken my ankle badly when my bike hit a patch of black ice. I hadn't healed enough to ride and I still used crutches.

That meant I would be the SAG driver for this spring break's trip. How I disliked it! Driving SAG meant I couldn't be on my bike, I'd miss the camaraderie of the riders even though I would meet them occasionally during the day. I'd also miss the big and little things along the way. On the positive side, it also meant there would be no van-rental car switch and we'd have an extra day for them to ride or for us to play. I tried to console myself that I would be able to take some side trips too far away for the bikers. Yes, but...

Many years ago ancient peoples carved a path with their feet into what eventually would become a vital route from Natchez to Nashville. A sign informed us *Here is a portion of the Old Natchez Trace—a wilderness road that grew from wild animal and Indian trails. Traders, soldiers, "Kaintucks," post riders, circuit riding preachers, outlaws, settlers and adventurers trampled a national road...a bond that held the Southwest to the rest of the nation...* Boatmen traversed it on their way to and from the Gulf of Mexico. Settlers came too, their wheels digging deeper into this soil of the Natchez Trace. Trading posts and wayside inns cropped up.

Old Trace Exhibits, the original shaded sunken route with patches of grass pushing through the once hard-tamped earth, enlightened us. Walking brief portions of it made me feel the history of the place, one where people such as depressed Meriwether Lewis trudged, after the enormity of his expedition with William Clark and their entourage.

Jim and Dave on the old Natchez Trace

No commercial traffic, stoplights or billboards marred the landscape. Nature's beauty, wildlife and the opportunity to visit fascinating historic sites that highlight the Natchez Trace Parkway would be our reward. The bicycling portion began, fittingly enough, in the Mississippi River town of Natchez where antebellum mansions set the tone. We definitely were not in Iowa anymore.

Surprise, surprise! Despite what we had always been taught, we came upon a loess bluff, edging the Trace. As I mentioned in the RAGBRAI chapter, out the window went the tried but obviously not true maxim that western Iowa's loess hills and those in the Xian, China area were the only two places a loess landscape could be found. Where the loess dust had blown to a depth of thirty to ninety feet from Baton Rouge into Tennessee and the Trace route passed over it, it formed sunken roads up to twenty feet deep. We walked in this Sunken Trace.

Near Port Gibson the impressive ruin Windsor, once one of the most magnificent homes in the antebellum South, remained only as twenty-three complete and five partial columns. Each column, constructed of brick covered by stucco, was about three-and-a half feet in diameter and stood forty feet tall. The house had been enormous, seventeen-thousand square feet, and even had two indoor bathrooms with rainwater supplied from a tank in the attic.

Nearby, a rusty metal-roofed slave cabin, wooden siding hanging off, made the vivid contrast between the lives of those who lived here even sadder. Lavender wisteria draping the trees added to its forlorn appearance.

We were delighted to stay in the stunning town of Port Gibson, a town that General Ulysses Grant reportedly declared was, "too beautiful to burn." That's now part of their motto. Our accommodation, Oak Square Plantation, was filled, well, jam-packed with antique walnut and cherry furniture from the mid-1800s. Although many were lovely, there was not enough room to show them to advantage and we had to sidle between some of them.

Our B&B host Mr. Lum, proud of his home, his family and town, urged us to see his latest project, the twenty thousand dollar purchase and renovation of the Jewish synagogue in town. Because he had funds of his own, he did not require associates to assist with the renovation. He spent ten thousand dollars to buy brilliant chandeliers, then went to great lengths to find wall sconces because the originals had been removed and placed in a Jewish museum in northern Mississippi.

In the late nineteenth and early twentieth centuries, a lively Jewish population lived in Port Gibson and built this synagogue. *The architects of Temple Gemilith Chassad, which means gift of the righteous, combined Moorish, Byzantine and Romanesque styles to produce a building unique in Mississippi.* It definitely was, with its Russian style cupola and keyhole doorframe and accents continuing in its interior.

While I was in the synagogue admiring the workmanship, a gentleman came in and began talking to me. He said he owned the Exxon station next door and for years had maintained the grass around the synagogue. He wanted to purchase the building for restoration but needed assistance and was going to receive it from Exxon. However, he was outbid by "him," meaning Mr. Lum whom he pointed his head at. I imagined the relationship was a bit rancorous. I didn't know what to say except, "I'm sorry."

Continuing our tour, we came upon children practicing for a May Day Maypole dance in front of a large, columned white house, our B&B. Like every Maypole dance I've ever seen, tangled ribbons prevailed. No doubt more practice followed. As we wandered, we found an enticing cemetery. True to my appreciation of old ones, we stopped to examine the unique headstones and monuments. Some were of styles I had never seen before with lots of carved children, angels, crowns and flowers. The oldest, least well-kept section's stones were simple marble, many moss-covered and stained. The cemetery's boundaries seemed to wander up and down slopes, around and about old trees, looking as though they had been haphazardly placed.

We did a double-take when we saw the 1859 First Presbyterian Church. Its steeple is adorned with a giant hand pointing to the heavens, not just any hand but one covered with thin gold leaf, multiple times thinner than a sheet of paper. A local craftsman carved the original one from wood. Time and weather destroyed it so a second was commissioned and placed on the steeple about 1901. The replacement hand, fabricated of steel and weighing two hundred pounds, measures over ten feet tall with a four foot index finger. We could have found more treasures in Port Gibson, but had to move on.

⏚

The number of Woodlands Native American mounds along the Natchez Trace Parkway intrigued us. The Boyd Site, Emerald, Byrnum and Pharr Mounds are parts of twenty such interpretive sites dating from as early as the first century CE. Copper ornaments and other artifacts have helped anthropologists and archaeologists understand the cultures of people who once lived here. Some groups built their graves on the tops of the older ones. A reproduced Chickasaw Village vividly showed the daily life and early history of one such settlement.

Mount Locust's history provided a glimpse of frontier style hospitality. Even before 1820, dozens of stands or inns had been built to host weary, thirsty travelers. I found it fascinating that Rocky Springs was the point where travelers at one time knowingly said farewell to civilization before they entered the wilderness. An old church and cemetery still invite exploration. In 1860, the population had been twenty-six hundred compared to the current zero.

⏚

Before we left Iowa City, friend Harry Weber asked Sandy to go to the Madison County Courthouse in Canton to look up his Gwinner family's records and, if possible, go to the grave sites. One day she chose not to bike so she and I could go to the county seat to do some sleuthing.

Harry's father's uncle Henry Gwinner, wife Clara, and cousins had lived in the town for many years. The imposing Georgian courthouse is part of the extensive collection of buildings and homes listed on The National Register of Historic Places. But inside, it felt like old courthouses do, kind of fusty, musty and ancient. The very dusty gold with red label record books pulled from the shelves yielded information about the family, where their property had been and where they had been interred. That happened to be in what is called the new cemetery, new, a relative term, in this case meaning it had been established in 1853, considerably after the old one from the 1700s. The next logical step was to locate it and search for the gravestones.

After discussing what we needed with a local historian who had a map of the site, we wandered up and down the rows and eventually found the family burial plot. We checked the names and dates to ascertain whether this could be the right family. It was. We set about taking photos of the area, then focused on individual stones. Henry Gwinner's gravesite, part of the larger family plot, edged close to the tall smooth Tuscan-appearing column that marked their area. We found he had died July 2, 1911.

Then it happened. We found the gravestone of Clara, the wife/mother of the family. We both exploded with righteous indignation. "Look at that! Can you imagine anyone carving that on a headstone? She gave birth to all those children and undoubtedly worked herself to the bone and this is the thanks she gets. Henry probably chose it! How infuriating!"

As we stared incredulously at the offending stone, we read the epitaph again. *She did what she could.* Still sputtering, we took more photos, wrote down as much information as we thought pertinent, and prepared to drive to the motel where we would meet Betty, Dave and Jim. "Just wait until we get home and tell Harry what we found!"

Back at the motel, our husbands waited for us. Their first innocent question, "Did you find anything?"

Instead of a simple yes or no and an explanation, we bombarded them with, "YOU are not going to choose our epitaphs! No way!" Their mouths dropped open to speak but neither Jim nor Dave knew what to say that wouldn't further this verbal rampage. Sandy and I calmed a bit and explained what we had found. "Imagine! After all she had undoubtedly done, being labeled for eternity with *She did what she could.*" In my outrage, I could feel myself starting to sizzle again.

Eventually, our emotions spent, we had the grace to ask how their biking day had gone. They answered with an inoffensive, "Fine," and a shrug of their shoulders.

That started to ignite my fire again, "Fine? That's all? Fine? Did you find anything of interest, were there any sights…" My voice tapered off as I realized I should just take what they gave us and let it be. I was still too riled inside by the epitaph and frustration from not being able to ride my bike. I would be placated by morning.

Long after we were home, I was studying the Gospel of Mark when I came upon this, chapter 14:8. *She did what she could.* This time my mouth dropped open. The episode took place at the Last Supper when a woman (some think she was Mary Magdalene, not the other Mary of the Mary and Martha stories) had come in to where Jesus and the disciples ate and had anointed Jesus's head. The disciples rebuked the woman about this waste of expensive perfume when it could have been sold and the money given to the poor. In the rest of Mark 14:8 Jesus says, *She poured perfume on my body beforehand to prepare for my burial.* He defended the woman against the rebukes of some of his disciples by admonishing them that she had done a good thing for him.

A very late lightbulb popped on over my head. *Oh.* I had wasted a lot of emotional energy misunderstanding the verse on the gravestone without context. *She did what she could* was a positive statement about how the woman had treated Jesus.

Once again, I had jumped to conclusions without all the facts. I still don't know all the facts but one thing I do know. This story has been a fun one to tell people over the years, and I learned another lesson. Do I always remember the lesson? History will tell.

Two other quite different but similar sad reminders of our tragic history exist on the Trace. One, Pigeon Roost commemorates the spot where millions of hunted-to-extinction passenger pigeons once roosted. The other, the unspeakable *Trail of Tears* as noted in the Oklahoma chapter occurred. In the 1830s, Andrew Jackson's Indian Removal Policy, in an act we now know as ethnic cleansing, many Indian Nations were forced to leave their ancestral homelands in southeastern United States and move to Indian Territory, eventually known as Oklahoma. This *Trail of Tears* devastated families and left thousands dead of disease, hunger and cold along the way. As on several of our cross-state rides, we saw signs, sobering reminders that the victims crossed the areas where we bicycled. How white people have treated other human beings and creatures throughout time, continuing after our ancestors arrived in North America. Heartrending!

Memorable French Camp imprinted itself on our minds. The five of us gathered to eat soup and, best of all, each of us had our own quart canning jar filled with refreshing iced tea, refills available. The camp had once been a stand/inn, then in 1822 became a still-existing school. Among the crafts-people there, a white-haired woman, thimble on her finger, made tiny even stitches on a nearly completed flower basket quilt, amazed us with her skill. French Camp proved to be a relaxing interlude.

But who could forget our visit to Tupelo? Yes, the Tupelo Battle site sits on Main Street, but anyone who knows an Elvis Presley-enthralled family member or friend, Sandy's sister Jane, for instance, knows her/his assignment: Go see Elvis's birth home. So we did, taking photos of course.

Forty-five miles to the Tennessee border went quickly. Spring blossoms sprang from trees and shrubs and softened the landscape making us yearn for an early Iowa spring. By this time, I was mostly off my crutches and ever so eager to be back on my bike which sat in loneliness in our dining room at home. But here at the border, Betty let me sit on hers, my short legs stretching to reach the pedals.

Jim and Dave kept guard so I didn't do anything stupid and break something else. (That would come years later.) I could hardly wait to be back in the saddle again. Summer would bring a biking trip to Prince Edward Island with Connie and John. To quote a woman I know, "Yahoo! Yippee!"

ALMOST HEAVEN, WEST VIRGINIA–1992

Riders: Jim/Jan. Drop off, pick up: Jennifer/Bernd. Distance: 175 miles

In 1992 Jennifer and Bernd lived in Pittsburgh, Pennsylvania which we thought was convenient for our prospective bicycle ride across West Virginia. We worked with their schedules until they were available to drop us, our bikes and gear off at the Ohio-West Virginia border.

The State of Ohio sign near the point where we officially dipped our rear wheels in the Ohio River said the Iroquois called it the *Ohio—Beautiful River*. The next sign welcomed us to Parkersburg, West Virginia, with the invitation *Let's Be Friends*. We accepted the offer and cycled off to meet this state.

🚲

Our early morning start meant we had the whole day to adjust to the lay of the hilly and panoramic land. What a treat to be there in mid-September when leaves change colors. Jim and I remembered cycling back roads of Pennsylvania so expected a similar if not more difficult challenge in this Appalachian Mountains-graced state. We set shorter daily mileage goals than we often had, giving us all the more opportunity to savor our surroundings, especially the hills.

Morning mist rose in the valleys and tumbled tombstones marked small roadside cemeteries. Autumn hues touched the trees, dusty red blossoms with yellow centers edged the vivid green of the cut alfalfa and golden ripening grain waiting for balers. Brooks burbled with water from hillside springs and fuchsia fireweed marked our way.

A billboard announced *Jesus is Lord. The Way of the Cross Leads Home*. I recalled John Denver singing about country roads taking him home. I wondered if the *Way of the Cross* sign creators had his song in mind.

Jim's voice rang out, "There! There's the bike trail!" West Virginia was working on their Rails to Trails program and this one, North Bend, paralleled Highway 50 part of the time. That was the same highway we would travel as we crossed Nevada years later. We totally supported former railroad tracks becoming multipurpose trails and appreciated being able to use them. Although North Bend Trail was not officially open because of improvements being made, we rode a short distance between Toll Gate and Greenwood just to experience it. Rocks and loose gravel made us wish for mountain bikes. We saw a familiar name on the map—Philippi. We pronounced it like in the Bible, FIL-i-pie. When we got to town we mentioned something about the town name, mispronouncing it in the process. The man told us the name was fil-UP-pea. We didn't do so well with another New Testament name either, Canaan. We said it with a long *a* in the first syllable. "You mean ka-NANE?" a man in the know asked. He pronounced it with a long *a* in the second syllable. Another "Oh." What did we know about geographical names in West Virginia? Obviously not enough, but we were learning.

Until we biked through Philippi, we'd had no idea this was where a battle of the Civil War took place in 1862. It was considered a skirmish because the ill-equipped, ill-trained Confederate soldiers left after little resistance. Although the battle was minor, it became one of the precipitating factors for the northwestern counties of the Commonwealth of Virginia to form their own state in the Union, West Virginia, in June of 1863.

The name cropped up again at the Philippi Development, Inc. Sentinel Mine. Here underground mining was used to extract coal lying deep beneath the surface. Nearby we saw coal processing equipment, a preparation plant where coal is cleaned, sorted and crushed to different sizes for delivery. Historically, many West Virginians rely on coal mining as their economic base so whatever the coal industry does, the communities are affected positively or negatively. And when the industry thrived, connected environmental and health issues arose. A terrible conundrum for people to face.

We continued down narrow one-lane roads paved many years ago or never, pedaling picturesque valleys with weathered red barns and white houses tucked in beside them. Nearby, remains of other houses made me ponder what happened to the farmers who once lived there. We laughed when we read the sign *Dairy Farm: Dewdrop Farm Melvin and Vernon Howdershelt. All we own—we owe to udders.* Our route paralleled rock-strewn shallow creeks moving swiftly or sometimes forming quiet eddies. Trees met each other across the byways. We ate lunch on a boulder beside a quiet pocket of water. Peace.

The farther we biked into the center of the state, the steeper the hills became as they grew into the Appalachian Mountains. Jim and I had purchased bicycling altimeters before this ride. By the end of it, our altimeters recorded that we had climbed over thirty-two thousand feet in six days of cycling. That meant just up, not down so that distance in feet made for a lot ups, downs and back up again. As I thought about these hills, I remembered my brother Keith when he first married West Virginian Glenda, saying, "She calls it a hill by their house. That's not a hill, it's a mountain."

The potential dangers of the rivers we'd been seeing became clear with pamphlets advertising *Swiftwater Rescue Training Information Flood Rescue Seminar 1992*. We didn't see anything telling truck drivers to watch out for roaming cyclists, but they appeared to have received that message anyway. They earned our respect as the most considerate lumber truck drivers of our bicycle trips. Take that Mississippi! They had earned the most dangerous lumber truck drivers award from us.

We repeatedly pulled out our cameras to attempt to capture the atmosphere. Picturesque ramshackle barns with weather-beaten shades of gray wood, slats falling from cupolas, sagging windows and doors, boards missing around windows, vines seeming to pull the buildings down as they inexorably climb over the openings and onto roofs. When the barns leaned to the side, looking ready to collapse, Jim reminded me of his hex sign story. As we traveled with our family through Pennsylvania in 1972, our young daughters noticed all the hex signs on barns and asked, "What are they for?" Jim the quick came up with this explanation: *You've noticed that all the barns that have them are in good condition. That's because the hex signs help keep them that way. Look over there at that collapsing barn. If it had one, it wouldn't be in such bad shape.* Well, no wonder these buildings were in such terrible straits. Not a single hex sign in sight.

Jim and I raved about what we could see from our route, often high above the misty valleys and tannin-stained rivers meandering through the wilderness. But our hearts clutched when we saw a sign warning of 10 percent grade for five miles. That was the longest consistently steep hill or mountain we had ever bicycled. Jim and I set our minds and bodies and did it. Crushed rock and dirt lanes tamped solid by trucks became our own nearly private bicycle highway except for the infrequent trucks passing by. Every one of the drivers encouraged us with honks and waves.

Once we reached the top, I lay down on some soft sand alongside the road to recover. The sign over my head was not an epitaph but a hand-painted wooden board saying *Danger Blasting Area—Fairfax Sand and Crushed Stone Company*. I briefly contemplated it but decided irresistible soft sand conquered any qualms I might have about blasting. When both of us felt refreshed, we pedaled on in search of more wonderful sights. Tucked into an idyllic wooded glen, we found another natural gem, dark Blackwater Falls tumbling over sandstone walls.

Eventually we wended our way back to a more major highway with smooth curves going up the hills. Our reward: Vistas of five mountains beyond mountains, each a shade of blue lighter than the previous one. We returned to a narrow paved road where few vehicles passed us going either way. Over and over, uphill, downhill, all through stunning deciduous forests, up on a ridge, trees began to bronze, wood and barbed wire fenced pastures lined the road. Unexpectedly, up cropped a corn field. And beyond that, a blue Harvestore stood in line with three silos, fronted by an alfalfa field, golden mustard blooming by the road. Old rounded Appalachian Mountains emerged in the hazy distance. Beauty fed our bodies and souls.

Made it!

We were mostly alone but never lonely. We cherished the solitude, the sounds of nature and absence of traffic. A white sign emblazoned with a red and white striped barn and silo with a blue and white starred roof caught our attention. We had never seen a National Bicentennial Farm sign before. Beginning with the USA's bicentennial year, 1976, certificates from the Agriculture Department were presented to families whose farms had been in their family for two centuries. The certificates read: *In this, the 200th anniversary year of the US Constitution, the US Department of Agriculture is pleased to acknowledge the vital contribution of farm families to the growth and strength of this great nation.* Imagine a family owning land in the United States for that long. In contrast, our family has owned our century farm in Northwest Iowa since 1902.

When we saw Maryland's greeting with its coat of arms saying, *Maryland Welcomes You Please Drive Gently,* we did. We crossed the Potomac River bridge into Maryland and Allegany County. Jennifer and Bernd retrieved us from the border and swept us away in the van. We'd just finished riding state number twenty-six.

🚲

They took us to nearby Rowlesburg, West Virginia to visit my sister-in-law Glenda's Sanders family. Glenda had come from her California home that week so it was quite a reunion with her, her mother Daisy, sister Joy, and brothers Sam, Jack and their families. Except for Daisy, I hadn't seen them since Keith and Glenda's wedding in 1957. Jim had never met any of her West Virginia family.

Gifted quilter Joy showed us some of her exquisitely crafted creations. Sam and Jack took us to their lumber mill, the one started by Glenda's dad Ray many years ago. It is now called Sanders Brothers Lumber, Inc.

Bernd's excitement at learning how a sawmill with computerized sawyering operated, energized us. Sam and Jack gave a descriptive tour of their sawmill and Bernd peppered them with insightful questions about the saws, how automation had increased their productivity and generally whatever made a sawmill work. What an education for us!

Glenda shared a story about her dad being the owner of this sawmill in the 1950s. Some of the locals began to complain about the noise from it and the dust and traffic Ray's logging trucks made in the hills. He was not only a smart man but a wise one. The next payday, he paid all his truck drivers and other employees with two-dollar bills. Soon those two-dollar bills began appearing at the grocery store, the hardware store, in church collection plates, at local doctor and dentist offices, all throughout the community. When the people saw how the Sanders Sawmill affected the economy of the small mountain town of Rowlesburg, the complaints stopped.

We said goodbye to our West Virginia friends and family and headed to Jennifer and Bernd's Pittsburgh home for a day of recuperation. Our drive back to Iowa gave Jim and me time for reflection about the ride and for self-satisfied sighs. We agreed. That had been a wonderful reprieve. We were so glad we got to bicycle in mountain home West Virginia.

I remember West Virginia for another reason, one that countered all the positive experiences we had there. Jim often rode ahead of me, enjoying the rhythm of his pace. Most of the time we could see each other so didn't worry about not being together. Suddenly, in the rearview mirror attached to my glasses, I became aware of a fast-approaching pickup. I instinctively believed I was about to be targeted on this lonely road. I thought, at least I hoped, the driver would not run over me but I expected he would use scare tactics. I determined I would not flinch or react in any outward way to whatever the occupants of the pickup did. I could see at least two people in the cab. Jim had disappeared over a hill.

I could hear the pickup close in on me. I breathed a prayer of *Help me get through this God* as the vehicle loomed larger and larger. The driver slammed on the brakes just behind me but nothing touched me. I could see laughing faces of the teenagers. When I didn't react like they assumed I would, they backed off and gave it another run. Again I managed not to respond but guessed, *They probably think I'm deaf and don't know they are behind me. They'll try something else. I hope they don't force me off the road.* Once again they tried to startle me but failed.

Their next tactic was to blast around me so they'd be sure I'd see them, then stop abruptly in front of me. I kept pedaling. I refused to make eye contact with them or change my expression which I hoped was placid even though I felt anything but. They repeated the brake-ramming two more times and then screeched away. *Thank you, God.*

When I crested the hill, Jim waited at the bottom. He, suspecting what might have happened, got out of the way and stopped as the pickup careened by. Though my heart still raged at the young hot bloods, I knew I was okay and would not let this episode make me fearful; watchful but not fearful. I imagined these kids cackling at this episode and regaling their friends with their feat of "showing that woman on a bike who was boss of the road."

Later, when less adrenaline poured through me, I realized my experience in motherhood had helped me get through this. How many times had our kids acted in such an annoying way that I just decided to ignore them. *Thank you, my dear daughters, for giving me practice in a skill I would need at this most crucial time.*

DOWNHILL HALEAKALA, MAUI—1993

Riders: Tania, Jim/Jan. Distance: 27 miles

Haleakala—The House of the Sun: Just the rippling sound of that word excited my imagination. Legend says Haleakala's crater was home to the demigod Maui's grandmother who convinced him to capture the sun and force it to slow its journey across the sky in order to lengthen the day. Modern geology indicates that two volcanoes developed on the ocean floor near a weak area in the middle of the Pacific Plate, part of the earth's crust. After millennia of lava, windblown ash and alluvium, these shield volcanoes joined to form Maui, 75 percent of it Haleakala.

Inspiring and exhilarating 10,023 foot tall Haleakala is considered the world's largest dormant volcano. The massive crater, seven and-a-half miles across, over two miles wide and nearly three-thousand feet deep, features a barren appearing landscape smattered with cinder cones. When Mark Twain came to the Hawaiian Islands, he thought of Haleakala as the highlight of his trip. "It was the sublimest spectacle I ever witnessed, and I think the memory of it will remain with me always."

Jim, Tania and I had the opportunity to not only go to Maui but to bicycle down that magnificent mauna. Downhill means all thirty-nine miles from the top of Haleakala to its land base, not its sea base, although it does rise from the sea. We'd read about it, seen photos and now we'd take this fabled ride, but stop in Paia at twenty-seven miles where our van would pick us up.

The day after Jim and I arrived on Maui, we perused the brochures we'd found at the airport. We wanted a good company, an experienced guide and most of all reliable bikes with mega-brakes. No namby-pamby brakes like we had on our road bikes, great for touring in the contiguous United States but this was Halaeakala, the unforgiving.

Maui Downhill topped them all. We visited their business to check out the bicycles and ask questions: *How fast do we go on the descent?* Not too fast. *How many people per group?* Enough to fill up a fourteen-passenger van. *How do the brakes work?* Very well. *Are there ever accidents?* Sometimes through stupidity. *How much does it cost?* Seventy-nine dollars per person. *What time do we meet?* 4:30 AM. *How long is the van ride to the top?* An hour. We made reservations for the day after Tania joined us.

🚲

We rose very early to drive to the pick-up spot. The van towed a flatbed trailer with clamps to hold a full complement of bicycles. The guide fitted us, well, fitted might be an exaggeration, with yellow rain pants and jackets. They came in several sizes, voluminous for some of us and a bit snug for the potbellied lot. Then came helmets—gosh-awful heavy duty modified motorcycle styled drag-your-head-down-with-the-weight helmets. We gathered our gear, prayed the persons who wore the helmets earlier had not been lice-infested, and bundled ourselves into the van for the ride to the top.

Dawn had already broken as we ascended Haleakala; some of us drowsed. We had chosen to not get up at 2 AM to be at the summit before daybreak. We settled for watching the sun rise over Haleakala from our condo on another day. The orange, gold, rose, coral colors were magical even from there.

Our guide, Kelly Kelly, told us a story about the lei of Haleakala, the ring of clouds that rolls in and out over the mountains. A few years earlier, as he guided a group down the mountain, one of the women suddenly braked just before she entered the clouds. Kelly, thinking something was wrong with her bike, rode back to check on her. "I'm not riding through that." He attempted to convince her she should.

She gave her reason. "When we flew into Maui there was a lot of turbulence when the plane went through the clouds. I'm not riding a bike through that." No amount of explanation would persuade her to ride. She would have none of it. So the woman climbed into the van. The driver, having been apprised of the circumstances, made the van and trailer shimmy and shake as he drove through the clouds, then let her out once they came back into the sunshine. The grateful woman thanked him and said, "I'm never coming back to this place. There is too much turbulence."

Kelly told our group that as we coasted down the mountain we'd have to use our mega-brakes a lot. With that in mind, we hopped on our bikes and began the long glide down. Well, some of us did. I had no glide with my bike. It felt like a clunker. I gave a few strong pedal strokes expecting to catch up with the other riders. I traveled a short distance, stopped pedaling and slowed to a near stop. *What was going on?* No one else pedaled. They rapidly scooted away from me. *Don't be a laggard, Jan!* I pedaled harder and got some momentum going. Again the heavy bike slowed to a near stop. I couldn't understand what caused this problem, so decided to just keep pedaling and hoped I could catch up. I felt like I was riding my old one-speed uphill and wondered if I'd have to ride the entire way pumping like crazy.

Jim turned around to see where I was. "What's the matter? C'mon!"

"It won't coast. I have to keep pedaling."

"Whaddaya mean it won't coast?" Then a lightbulb went off in his brain. "Your center of gravity isn't heavy enough to keep you going. You'll have to pedal until we get to a steeper part." Terrific.

I didn't have to pedal far, around a few curves. At last I hit a stretch that allowed me to coast. Fear of Haleakala's lei didn't deter me but another of nature's wonders did. Gravity. Frustrating for her, Tania rode behind a woman who braked so much she could never get to a full coast.

Our ride provided us wonderful opportunities to see the official bird of Hawaii, Nene/Hawaiian geese, rare and unique to Maui Haleakala ahinahina/silversword, and exotic protea flowers which thrive because of the volcanic soil plus weather conditions here. As we cruised the series of switchbacks in upcountry Kula, we passed papaya trees and orange groves, sugar cane and pineapple fields. The landscape of scrubby-bush open country, past grazing horses, two rattling metal cattle guards stretching across the road near pasturelands whizzed by.

An average grade of 5 percent made it possible to sail down the mountain while switchbacks eliminated what could have been impossible steepness. Our guide cautioned us to take it easy as we descended because a spill could have landed us into one of the many patches of volcanic rock that line the highway. We were also warned to beware of rotting mangoes on the road—a cause for slip-sliding messes. We loved the variety of our downhill, from the miles of volcanic not-quite-wasteland to low-cloud Maui lei to sunny coastal areas. There was no cloud turbulence.

We had biked exotic Haleakala and its slopes all the way to Paia. I thought arriving there felt anti-climactic, but on reflection I realized I wanted more. I wanted to sail all the way to the sea.

"UNLESS YOU ARE THE LEAD DOG..." NORTH CAROLINA-SOUTH CAROLINA-1993

Riders: Betty, Sandy/Dave, Jim/Jan. SAG: Michelle. Distance: 252 miles.

A spring break bicycle ride in South Carolina sounded great. But first we needed to finish riding ninety miles in North Carolina, our twenty-seventh state. All of us would get away from the snows of Iowa, we'd have a week off from our jobs, we'd be together and on our bikes. We'd heed the call of Dean Martin's lyrics: "Nothing could be finer than to be in Carolina in the morning..."

Because of our five-days biking time constraints, we decided our route should not be in the mountains of western Carolina but in the flatlands. The mountainous route would have to wait. Our illustrious driver Michelle mischievously grinned, "I'm glad I'm at the wheel of the van and not on a skinny-seated two-wheeler."

We had no trouble finding the exact spot for our official start—a bold red and gold sign welcoming us to *Marine Corps Base Camp LeJeune, NC.* This camp, established in the fall of 1941, is the home of *Expeditionary Forces in Readiness.* We hoped we would be as ready. It seemed a bit odd to be taxpayer-tourists riding bicycles through the base, especially one with Camp LeJeune's reputation as a hard-nosed training facility. Additionally, reports stemming from the 1980s reported industrial waste and chemicals had contaminated the water. Lawsuits had ensued. None of us chose to drink the water.

During the first days of the trip, our proximity to the Atlantic Ocean provided us with views of hillocks of seagrass growing on tiny isles in the estuaries and rivers. When we arrived at the beach we celebrated with photos and toe-dipping for being truly at the Atlantic! Well, at least at the Intracoastal Waterway. We didn't celebrate it, but after our first day ride of seventy miles, some people iced and elevated their sore knees. So much for being slothful during the winter.

After an overnight in Wilmington, we pedaled down long and skinny Pleasure Island to the toll ferry across blackwater Cape Fear River which empties into the Atlantic. Although *blackwater* sounds ominous and looks dramatic, it refers to rivers flowing through forested swamps becoming darkly stained as tannins from decaying vegetation leach into it. The river, named Cape Fear after the headland, not the movie, has been called that since the 1580s when two ships nearly wrecked there. Many sailors feared the Frying Pan Shoals which extend nearly thirty miles from the mouth of the Cape Fear River into the ocean. Littered with shipwrecks, these long and shifting sandbars still pose a hazard to navigation.

Even though we dressed in our foul weather gear, the brisk wind chilled us. After Michelle met us we stoked up on food and warmed up in the van to wait for the ferry. Once we boarded, we had to leave our bicycles unprotected in the hold where the cars and trucks were parked. But ferry rides are usually fun and often, as in this one, a reprieve from the wind.

Periodically sights along our biking routes trigger memories of random songs or poems. A pelican perched on a ferry beam reminded me of this limerick:

A wonderful bird is the pelican;
His beak can hold more than his belican.
He can hold in his beak
Enough food for a week,
Though I'm darned if I know how the helican!
  -Unknown but misattributed to Dixon Lanier Merritt and Ogden Nash

Back on land, we laughed at the sight of over one hundred seagulls all facing the same direction, into the wind. We wondered why and none our hypotheses—waiting for a parade to start, listening to a boring lecture, acting like members of a stand-offish family—answered that question. We continued on to Calabash, named after the gourd. The name amused us as we remembered comedian Jimmy Durante's sign-off, "Good night Mrs. Calabash, wherever you are." It seems Durante had met a woman in a local restaurant whom he told he would make famous. Instead of calling her Mrs. Coleman as he left, he addressed her as Mrs. Calabash, and the rest became entertainment history. Now the town's fame comes from Calabash-style buffets common to the area: seafood dipped in milk, breaded lightly with corn meal and flour and fried quickly.

Along the way to the North and South Carolina border, hunger pangs led us to stop at yet another dusty, musty, mildewed, weatherworn store, this one called *Doc Grieps*. We stop when we can for bathroom breaks, food and a chance to get off the bikes and stretch. Sometimes we eat something we otherwise wouldn't, like a candy bar. We tell ourselves, "We'll bike it off." Right.

Jim and I had never been to South Carolina so once our wheels crossed its border, we at last realized our goal of spending time in all fifty of the United States. We couldn't know it then but we were thirteen years shy of accomplishing our next goal of bicycling across all of them.

Traffic really picked up on the highway toward Conway so we happily turned off onto a quiet byway, this one even quieter than usual. A *Road Closed* sign meant exactly that. In years past, we occasional scofflaws have been known to ignore such signs hoping we could find a way around the destruction or construction. As a result, we've had to walk on planks to carry our bikes across streams or walked our bikes along railroad tracks. We've no doubt made construction workers clench their teeth when we ask if we can go through because it's ten miles more if we follow the detour route.

We couldn't do any of those things now and had to remain law-abiding citizens. Grumpily, we returned to the bustling highway and rode sixteen extra miles to our overnight.

橋

We shortened our final day of biking by twenty miles when Mother Nature blessed us with rain and dropping temperatures. Someone said, "Enough!" The rest of us agreed and flagged Michelle down. She had watched the declining weather conditions and realized we probably had experienced all the vicissitudes we wanted to, and decided to check on her erring adult charges. Amidst swarming insect attacks, we loaded up the bikes and headed to Charleston to sightsee.

橋

In the late 1950s Keith, a photographer in the Navy, had been stationed on the famous *Flying Lady of WWII*, the aircraft carrier *USS Yorktown*. Now a museum and dry-docked at Patriots' Point just across the bay from Charleston, we wanted to visit it. Keith had been killed in a mid-air plane crash in 1971, so I thought of this as a kind of pilgrimage, being where we knew he had lived an important time of his life. We couldn't find the photography lab but Jim and I thought he might have taken some of the photographs on display. I discovered being on the *Yorktown* was even more emotional than I had expected, and realized again how much I missed my brother. Later, we learned that a seat in the on-board movie theater had been dedicated in his memory. We wished we had known earlier so we could have searched for it.

As we wandered on the various decks, the maze of pipes, valves and gauges had us shaking our heads in wonder. What are they for? I noted in our photo album: *What a confusing place. Apparently someone knew what to do since the ship stayed afloat for a long time!* We chuckled at the attitude the Machine Shop workers displayed on their sign: *The difficult we do right away. The impossible takes a little longer.*

The Bakery: Astonished at the sizes of the mixers and mixing bowls, we had to copy the recipe for Chocolate Chip Cookies:

112 pounds chocolate chips
12 pounds butter
165 pounds flour
75 pounds brown sugar
500 eggs
1 quart water
100 pounds sugar
1-1/2 pounds baking soda
87 pounds of shortening
3 pounds salt

In case you wondered, you could make one batch of these cookies to treat ten thousand of your closest friends.

From the absurdity of imagining Navy bakers baking that many cookies, we moved to the reality of boarding the diesel-powered submarine, *USS Clagamore*, docked next to the *Yorktown*. I knew my tendency to claustrophobia would be tested by the too-confining feeling. *Aboard* hardly seems to be the appropriate word, I felt like we crawled inside this pencil-shaped beast. I attempted to convince myself, *Submariners had to live in these minuscule quarters for months at a time. If they could do it, surely you can last the few minutes it will take to walk through.*

I focused on continuing to breathe as normally as possible, held my breath when I thought I needed to, chatted with my companions to get my mind off how tiny the bunks seemed, how closely stacked they were, how even at my height of five feet two inches I felt the need to scrunch down so my head wouldn't hit the ceiling. The boldfaced sign didn't console me,

WATCH YOUR HEAD AND SHINS AS YOU GO THROUGH! Head AND shins?!

What do I remember? The feeling of cramped confinement. The wonder that more than seventy people could live in these conditions and remain mentally stable. The metallic harshness, smell of stale air, clanging sounds. I found no mollifying factors.

Despite the gray dripping sky, I was ecstatic when I burst into the brisk sea air of Charleston Harbor. Fresh air! Freedom! I staggered at the thought of anyone being confined to a submarine for months and months and felt thankful for the stalwart submariners.

We had just a few hours to see all we could in Charleston. We opted for a trolley tour advertised as having *unrestricted views of Charleston's most historic and beautiful areas.* We enjoyed the cobblestone streets, Old Citadel, nineteenth century houses, churches, theatres. Then we wanted to roam on our own, especially down the renowned King Street. This beautiful city demanded we return. When we came again, we'd plan to have enough time to immerse ourselves in Fort Sumter history.

One remarkable culture we did not want to miss learning about—the Gullahs. The geographically isolated and distinctive group of Black Americans lived along the Atlantic coastal plains and on the chain of Sea Islands. Their long history spans back to the west coast of Africa where European slave traders came to buy people.

Enslaved and transported to America, the Gullahs had been brought to the Low Country of South Carolina and preserved their African cultural heritage in many ways: telling African folk tales, using African names, and speaking a creole language known as Gullah. Historians attribute the prosperity of this waterlogged place to the slaves' expertise cultivating rice. Their descendants continue to make African-style baskets, quilts, fish nets and walking sticks, and sell them at the City Market which has become a magnet for those who love baskets. Low Country Coil or Gullah basketry remains one of the oldest crafts of African origin in the United States. African baskets had been coiled, woven, twined and beaded, but the Low Country coil is what remains. Although the baskets were utilitarian, after The War Between the States, a cottage industry developed with sweet grass basket art. Mesmerized by the sheer beauty and individual expression of the baskets and by the fresh fragrance of the sweet grass, I succumbed and bought a coiled ten-inch basket with a handle, crafted and sold by the Gullah artist, Linda Huger.

Although the African aspect predominates, the Gullah culture blends West African, European and Native American cultures. Some people believe the word *Gullah* could be a corruption of *Gola* or Angola, the point of origin of many of these enslaved people.

With our treasures in hand, we continued strolling through The Market and back to King Street. Its funky glitzy stores intermingled with Woolworth's and art galleries made browsing fun. The Victorian facades, palm trees, trolleys and horse-drawn carriages, cobblestone and brick streets glistened in the rain, making an eye-pleasing experience.

Sandy and Dave joined us and said they'd met someone we knew in a gallery. Sharon Burns-Knutson, our friend and favorite art teacher of our daughter Jennifer, had an exhibit opening at Nina Liu and Friends Gallery. Her whimsical Santas, ballerinas and royalty dancing amidst stars, butterflies and hearts, make it easy to believe her when she says she loves to play with paints and clay like a child. Nina, whose son pet-sat for us, once lived near us. Surprising small world.

After we left the gallery we continued wandering down King Street. Betty and I walked together, glanced in store windows and tried to dodge the rain. As we passed East Bay Gallery we took a couple more steps, simultaneously backed up and laughed. The same thought crossed our minds and popped out of our mouths: "That would be perfect for Jim." A calligraphed sign *Unless you are the lead dog, the view never changes* had caught our fancy. We purchased it, a gift from all of us to Jim, who considers himself the lead dog of our bicycle trips.

The time to leave came, so following the now officially designated lead dog, we wended our way out of lovely Charleston and returned to Iowa City and winter.

SOUTH CAROLINA-GEORGIA-1994

Riders: Betty, Jim/Jan. Drop-off, pick up: Lynn/Tom Rundle. Distance: 221 miles

Georgia had been on our minds since we left Charleston after last year's 1993 ride. But first we had to complete our South Carolina miles, this time without Sandy and Dave. Betty's children and ours had obligations other than toting parents to their spring break fun, so we needed new drivers. One of Jim's orthodontic assistants, Lynn, and her husband Tom, had heard enough bicycling tales to know they wanted to volunteer.

We returned to Charleston, took another quick tour around the city, asked ourselves if we would ever get to Fort Sumter, then ate a wonderful and filling seafood dinner at JJ Hook's. As map lovers, we especially appreciated the seaport maps from all over the world wallpapering a hallway. We drove to Summerville where we riders would stay for two nights. What a pleasure that would be! We wouldn't have to tote our panniers the first day of cycling.

The following morning, Lynn and Tom drove Betty, Jim and me to our drop-off point, Jamestown, South Carolina, population ninety-seven. We had unceremoniously stopped last year's ride there when the never-ending rain and constant road repair had become too much. Lynn and Tom observed us as we unloaded the bikes from the van roof and assembled our gear, all the while with *Do they know what they are doing?* expressions on their faces. They didn't stick around to find out but returned to Charleston to visit the elusive, at least to the bikers, Fort Sumter and head to Hilton Head for their mini-vacation.

All along our route, the overwhelmingly fragrant lilac wisteria burgeoned as rampantly as the fecund kudzu. The scenes reminded me of some southern novelists' depictions of time-worn plantation homes with equally timeworn and creaky individuals living in them. Perfect setting for high drama if your imaginations run that way.

As we ride long distances, we often play word games to amuse ourselves and each other. This trip engendered: *What do you call a plethora of wisteria? Wisteria hysteria. Or wisteria ubiquita. What do you call a wisteria-covered haunted house? Wisteria mysteria.*

After our close encounters of the wisteria kind, we came upon the devastation of Hurricane Hugo from September 22, 1989. Hit by 135 miles per hour winds, once verdant Francis Marion National Forest's old trees snapped in two; only young ones survived. Someone said the whole area was under construction. The contractor? Mother Nature.

Signs told us the forest *covers 250,000 acres of low flatlands, coastal sand areas, black water swamps, moss-hung oaks, pines and little lakes.* These lakes, called Carolina Bays, are thought to have been caused by meteors with their craters filling with water. The forest's name comes from Revolutionary War general Francis Marion who engaged British troops in many skirmishes and battles in this region. He took refuge in the deep swamps thereby earning the nickname Swamp Fox.

Biggin Church, a gutted brick building, included evocative blackened marble grave markers. Historic markers told us: *Parish Church of St. John's Berkeley, founded by act of Assembly November 30, 1706. Church erected in 1712, burned by forest fire in 1775 and restored. Burned by Col. Coates of the British Army in 1781 and again restored. Burned again by forest fire about 1896.* No wonder it remains a ruin.

Because it was Lent, the days between Ash Wednesday and Easter, many of the rural churches placed three crosses in their churchyards, the center cross draped in purple, Lent's liturgical color. We looked forward to seeing these little churches, not only to be reminded of this holy season, but also for rest and respite. Just getting off the road and into their yards or relaxing on front steps for a snack or lunch became a welcome part of our day. Often many miles extended between towns or country stores, but churches dotted the roadside in between.

ڶ

After some cool mornings, warm days provided welcome relief from our Iowa winter. We cycled along swampland, eerie and beautiful in its own way and spied an alligator lurking in a pond that reflected the forest's image. We looked up and saw turkey buzzards.

Many villages we biked through had been torched by General Sherman and his troops in their march to the sea during the Civil War. We began to comprehend more clearly the vastness of the area laid waste as well as the fear and hatred he provoked among the people.

We crossed the rhythmically named Salkehatchie and Coosawatchie rivers before we came to the Savannah River. Finally Georgia was not only on our minds but under our feet. The welcome sign said, *"We're glad Georgia's on your mind."* So were we after completing the crossing of our twenty-eighth state.

Our ride wasn't over yet. Another historic marker indicated where Early Baptists of Tuckasee King worshiped. After the first minister died, a second one came and preached there for eight years. The reason he had to leave? He was forced to flee Georgia because by then he was a fugitive from the Tories, American colonists who supported the British during the American Revolution. Our history lessons continued.

🚲

Dogwood blossoms piled on branches like new fallen snow. We didn't need rose-colored glasses because the azaleas added their wonderland of rose-tinted blossoms wherever we looked. And the fragrance! We didn't want to leave this glory to return to Iowa's March weather. When lunchtime arrived, we chose to eat in the piney woods where our panniers served as food prep tables with nearby azaleas adding brightness. Not far away lay Glennville, the heart of Vidalia onion country. From the visual treat to the treat for the palate.

🚲

Contrary to our original plans, we terminated our spring break ride by a day. I had a cold all week and thundershowers the last morning made us decide not to continue biking. We called Lynn and Tom and asked them to come to the rescue. We met them in front of El Cheapo's, a local convenience store.

The five of us hustled to Savannah to take an Old Town Trolley Tour. Our first guide was awful so we hopped off and picked up another one, a smart move. Adding to the charm of the city, its historic waterfront has been restored and the river cleaned. The poignant statue of young Florence Marus, known as The Waving Girl, depicted her as her fiancée went to sea. She promised him she would greet every ship until his return. He never came home, and despite other offers of marriage, she waited and waved for forty years.

Savannah, known for its beauty, had been laid out in a series of wards where both commercial and residential buildings centered on a public square. Twenty of the original twenty-four squares remain attractively landscaped. During the War Between the States, General Sherman, on his quest to destroy all he could of the South, arrived at the city's doorstep. He ordered the city evacuated, entered on Christmas Day and proffered it as a gift to President Lincoln. Our trolley guide explained the stones comprising the attractive cobbled streets near the waterfront came as ballast from trading ships. What a great use of them. Another piece of trivia: When Savannah was founded, lawyers were not allowed to live within the city limits.

With a backward glance at the city we hoped to return to, we left for Fripp Island, a small island just north of Hilton Head, where my Uncle John and Aunt June Adams lived in retirement. What fun to be with them after too many years. We had one more *must do* before we left for Iowa. We had to find an alligator for Tom since he hadn't seen one the entire trip. Fortunately, two rested on the edge of the golf course Uncle John played so he was satisfied he had indeed been to the South.

Mild weather greeted us at home. How great to be able to prolong our spring as long as we could until real spring had sprung.

I GOT THE OKEFENOKEE SWAMP BICYCLING BLUES POGO LAND-GEORGIA-FLORIDA-1995

Riders: Connie, Sue/Lee Wakefield, Sandy/Dave, Jim/Jan. Drop off, pick up: Lynn and Tom. Connie, Sue and Lee came from Orlando in their van. Distance: 301 miles

After three trips back to our house to get wayward items and one to retrieve Sandy's "biking earrings" we finally left Iowa City for our spring break bicycle trip. Due to unfinished business in Georgia, the Florida aspect of this vacation would have to wait its turn. We met the rest of the contingent at El Cheapo's Convenience Store in Glennville, Georgia. Sadly, neither Betty nor John could come, experienced cyclists but new to touring Sue and Lee Wakefield joined us.

Jim and I were really excited about this trip because of the connection it would make with other bike routes. In 1982 the Carlsons, Jim and I cycled from Crystal River, Florida to Ormond Beach. In 1985, Jim and I biked from Delaware's Atlantic coast, across Maryland, Washington, D.C., and in subsequent years Virginia, North and South Carolina and into Georgia. At the end of this trip, our Delaware Shore to Florida Gulf coast route would be complete.

The group decided to pop into Savannah to explore more of it and also to seek out restaurants with more varied menus than Huddle House in Glennville. The Irish were among the first settlers, so Savannah has one of the country's largest St. Patrick's Day Parades, and the ornate city fountains spout green water during that season—we had to see that. United Methodist pastor Dave needed to have his photo taken alongside a statue of his hero and founder of Methodism, John Wesley. He had come to America in 1736 and had preached and lived in Savannah. Lack of time meant another too-brief glimpse into this city, but we managed a Fisherman's Wharf meal with hushpuppies, a weakness of mine.

⚄

Sunshine graced us for our first day biking—after our Huddle House breakfast. The seven of us enjoyed the scenery, including fields of our favorite sweet Vidalia onions. Two puppies began to follow us, happily trotting behind us for miles. Fearing they would be run over, we conferred about what we should do. Cycling back while carrying a wiggly puppy was not an option. Eventually, they tired and loped back, we hoped to where they had joined us. We met a man biking solo from Houston to D.C.. He'd had three flats that day so Good Neighbor Sam Dave gave him a tube and a patch kit. We wished him wind at his back.

We had been told by locals that the Chicken Shack in Odum was *The Place* to have lunch. An excellent tip, we arrived shortly before the rush of cars and trucks. The food—hearty, plentiful and inexpensive—that big hamburger tasted good. A flat road stringing between pines and green deciduous trees helped make our fifty-six mile first day of cycling easier than we expected.

⚄

Throughout our low-key ride, we often saw signs of deforestation, cut trees piled in the middle of stripped forest lands, and reforestation, tiny tree-lets poking their heads above stumps and rumpled soil. A sign delineated the time line for one property: Harvested-1994 Site Prepared-1995   Planted-1996 Future Harvest-2019. That's pretty quick.

Greeted in Folkston by water pouring out of two motel units made us think we would have no hot water. Much to our relief, the managers insisted they would have it fixed and hot water would be in all the units in thirty minutes They did and we loved the hot showers. Dozens of railroad tracks funneled through town and made it a kind of rail-fan mecca. However, we remained true to our passion and stayed the course on bicycles.

⚄

Connie, Sue and Lee decided not to take a nine mile detour into Okefenokee National Wildlife Refuge and to meet us in St. George. The rest of us wished we had a full day to bicycle the entire loop drive and then canoe into the swamp. The Visitor Center diorama of the swamp poacher's camp with his ill-gotten booty and a walk on the Canal Diggers Trail into the swamp gave us just a taste of the place. The late nineteenth century plan for draining the swamp seemed ill-conceived and, after years and a great deal of money, the powers that be abandoned the project. Although the ditch and canals had been started, the diggers kept finding small springs which created a flow of water that ran back into the swamp instead of draining it away. The investors, including a Mr. Jackson, had expected to make millions of dollars from the supposed fertile crop lands once the water was gone. Not to be, instead it became *Jackson's Folly.*

Our mental connection with this area had begun with the cartoonist Walt Kelly's creation of the comic strip *Pogo* whose home was the Okefenokee Swamp. The hundreds of characters, mostly animals, reflected the characteristics of human beings, philosophical, egotistical, harebrained, prickly, greedy, caring. I think Pogo the possum's most famous line had to be *We have met the enemy and it is us.* We looked for him and his buddies in the swamp but didn't spot them. But what we have found in our environment throughout our years of cycling and in our off-bike lives is—Pogo was right.

On the way to St. George to meet the others, we stopped to visit with a couple, John and Jane Butters from Edinburgh, Scotland who were biking from Florida to Canada. They had no helmets, gloves or comfy padded shorts, and mentioned they wanted to buy some nice American clothes. They recommended biking in New Zealand, France and Corsica. We wished we'd all been going the same direction so we could have ridden together. They would have made fun and fascinating biking companions.

After an ice tea break, the group's next goal was the Georgia-Florida border, that's state number twenty-nine. Shortly after that, we came to Jacksonville and The First Coast, quantified by local Chambers of Commerce as *first in history, first in geography and first in quality of life, welcome to First Coast.*

We skirted Jacksonville and headed toward the Atlantic Ocean across the St. John's River at fifty cents per bike and body. Blackbeard, the man, had joined the list of pirates who pillaged this region.

Highway A1A parallels Florida's Atlantic coast all the way to Miami, so we mostly followed it to our ultimate destination, Ormond Beach. At times we veered as close to the ocean and its white sand beaches as possible. Some streets had series of signs indicating *DEAD END* but we kept cycling. Then we saw a sign *FINAL DEAD END.* Sure enough, it was the last dead end sign we saw on that stretch of road. Sawgrass, palmetto and places to buy ice cream punctuated the route, especially appealing to ice-cream lover, Sandy.

Suddenly someone called out, "Is that a castle? It looks like a Crusaders' castle!" Yes, a castle of sorts but actually a sculpture named CASTLE OTTTIS. The three Ts were to remind viewers of the three crosses of the crucifixion. The explanatory sign read: *CASTLE OTTTIS WAS CREATED AS AN ORIGINAL SCULPTURE IN REMEMBRANCE OF JESUS CHRIST.* The last line explained, *Pronounced AH'TIS.* We wondered who the sculptor was and what event precipitated the idea and building of the castle.

History tells us when Juan Ponce de Leon first came to search for the fabled Fountain of Youth in 1513, he reached what is now known as First Coast. America's Spanish heritage was established in historic St. Augustine which became the first permanent European settlement begun a half-century before Jamestown and Plymouth. Disease, pirate attacks, food shortages beset the settlers.

Spain, disappointed by no silver, gold, or precious stones and poor soil, called on Mexico to help. Eventually Florida was ceded to England, then to Spain and then the United States in 1819. The three hundred year domination of Spain in Florida ended. It's easy to think of Florida in terms of sunshine, entertainment, family and friends who live there and neglect the fascinating history. St. Augustine was in-your-face history.

We wandered about the town, relishing the relaxed atmosphere. Turreted Castillo de San Marcos, begun in 1672, was built of coquina stone quarried on nearby Anastasia Island. Coquina, formed of lovely, soft whitish limestone comprised from broken shells and corals, has been used to construct many buildings here. The Spanish formed a regional defense system to help preserve their dominion, this one, their principal fort. The turrets reminded Jim and me of the fortified Crusader-built walls of the old city on the island of Rhodes, Greece. Nearby Juan Ponce de Leon's statue shows him one hand on hip, the other stretching to point, while wearing his rakish Three Musketeers hat.

Dating from the celebration of its first mass in 1565, The parish of St. Augustine, now part of the same-named Cathedral, is the oldest Roman Catholic parish in the present United States. Its coquina façade, erected in 1797 and severely damaged by fire nearly a century later, survived and was preserved by cathedral restorations.

🚲

The evening before our final biking day, someone mentioned that our group had been flat-free for four whole days. Others countered, "Don't say that! That's a bad omen!" Then Connie had a flat tire. We all biked back to lend moral, physical and camera support. Bicycle touring is definitely a cooperative effort—one of the many things I love about it.

In addition to being encompassed by water on three sides, St. Augustine commanded an entrance to the ocean, except for one problem, the Matanzas Inlet. Being hyper-aware of the possibility of an enemy attack, the Spanish decided to build cleverly named Fort Matanzas to provide the needed control. The French, particularly the Huguenots, encroached on what Spain considered their territory throughout the centuries, but England also entered the fray in 1740. Remember the guy who created the colony of Georgia, James Oglethorpe? That same Savannah-founder attacked St. Augustine. When he and his troops couldn't defeat the city, they laid siege to it. That didn't work either. So the British eventually left. Despite the fact they never could conquer the city, within twenty-one years they gained all of Florida by treaty. Huh? What a mess countries bring upon others and themselves.

What about us bikers? Sue joined the flat-tire club. Once again we responded and offered physical, moral, camera again, and this time, Mounds Bar support—practically a cure. We picnicked on the site of an old plantation that had been burned in the early 1800s. Later on while we lazed by the beach, we hydrated, gave each other backrubs and delighted in the soaring pelicans. As a lone bird circled us, someone quipped, "Is that The Pelican Brief?" then added, "Or is that briefly, the pelican?" as it quickly glided away. Because we move slowly enough to spot opportunities and make discoveries, we can stop to appreciate them, another gift of traveling slowly.

Ormond Beach seemed clogged with cars, some maneuvered by scary drivers. Jim escaped injury when he was cut off by one and, within moments, Sandy was nearly hit by a man coming into a parking lot. I went and spoke to him about the rights of bicyclists. He approached us on foot in a few moments and apologized and said he was wrong. He was right. He WAS wrong. Apology accepted and we silently thanked his passenger, who looked like she really chewed him out once they had stopped.

Jim appeared to have begun a new tradition when he kissed Vicki's surgically repaired knee at the end of our Michigan ride. He perpetuated it with a similar ceremony at the end of this trail. Sandy had seriously injured her knee in December. To inspire her, Jim told her he would kiss her ailing knee when she finished the ride. She did and he did.

Usually I don't call our bicycle trips vacations because there is so much hard work involved. But this one had the bonuses of more time to poke around some places we wanted to explore and time to unwind, have lots of laughs, then wish we could go on and on.

NORTH STAR COUNTRY ALASKA-1995

Riders: Sandy/Dave, Jim/Jan. Distance: 386 miles

"Alaska! We should bike Alaska!" Our imaginations conjured visions of wild animals, scenery beyond compare and challenging terrain—an adventure in the making as we biked this remote state.

Jim researched flights and accommodations, a tedious task. Before the Internet simplified the searches, everything had to be accomplished by phone and letters. Jim diligently checked every flight we could possibly take from Cedar Rapids, Moline, Des Moines, Omaha and the Twin Cities. To our amazement, it cost one hundred dollars less per person to fly from Omaha to the Twin Cities, Seattle and Anchorage, than to simply begin in the Twin Cities. For us, Omaha worked well because cousins Ivanie and Dick Joslin lived there, fed us, took us to the airport, van-sat for three weeks, and picked us up at the end of our trip. Perfect!

As always, we worried about what happens to our bikes on long flights despite packing them with foam padding in hard-shelled bike cases. In Omaha we anxiously watched the loading of the bicycle boxes, undoubtedly leaving nose prints on the window at the gate. We held our breaths as airline personnel unloaded and reloaded our precious cargo in Minneapolis. I watched, horrified, as my bike box fell off the conveyor belt in Seattle. Baggage handlers made no attempt to grab it. I fumed.

The Anchorage International Airport baggage claim system spit out our bags but no bike boxes. We comforted ourselves knowing oversize luggage is often unloaded last so, while Jim and Dave impatiently waited for the missing bicycles, Sandy and I commandeered the rest of our gear, carefully stacked it on a luggage cart and giggled as it tumbled whenever driver Sandy changed direction or hit a bump. Amused onlookers grinned as the two of us, in our best Keystone Kops style, gathered the bags again and restacked them. Periodically, I raced outside to check if our Ramada Inn transportation had arrived, then back into the terminal to help my friend pick up the scattered luggage after she had moved the cart again. We never got it right. We eventually managed to wrestle the cart and bags onto the median where we were to flag down the motel van. I turned and saw gravity had won again. We picked our gear up one last time.

The grim-faced guys emerged without the bikes, but with the airport baggage masters assurance they would come by morning. Jim was not consoled by that promise, but consented to leave the airport, check into our motel and get food.

The motel clerk told us, "Go to Harry's! You'll love the food!" I noted in my journal: *The food was excellent and the portions were more than generous.* Harry's had been named for Harry R. Truman who became a folk hero of sorts when Mount St. Helens erupted; he refused evacuation orders and died in his home. Many Alaskans thought he personified the frontier do-it-your-own-way spirit of Alaskans. Ironically, they honored Harry with a type of restaurant he probably never would have ventured into during his lifetime.

We had known food prices were high in Alaska so we'd brought our own staples. We unpacked boxes of apple juice, cans of tuna, jars of peanut butter, jam and mustard from Jim's checked baggage. Never would we be caught on the road without food, at least as long as Jim was nearby.

Three of us slept quite well while Jim took charge of worrying about the fate of the bikes, concocting alternative scenarios in case they didn't arrive in time for us to cycle to Palmer the following day. Unbeknownst to the ditherer and the sleepers, our bicycles were middle-of-the-night deliveries.

🚲

After breakfast, we reassembled the bicycles and took the bike boxes to the hotel storage where they'd be stored for two plus weeks.

We accosted an interested passerby to take our beginning-of-the-journey photos. We asked him what kinds of activities and sports he and his family participated in. "Oh, hiking, biking, climbing, skiing, windsurfing. I'm Alaskan." That seemed to say it all as far as he was concerned. He added that challenging and dangerous windsurfing for the real experts could be found at Turnagain Arm. Jim and I shared the same thought, *Bernd, our adrenaline junkie son-in-law, would love to test his skills there.*

We biked directly to a food store where we pondered the produce. As we looked, a woman confided she'd just been *outside*, meaning *not in Alaska*, often the lower 48 states. "After I got home, I saw the prices on groceries and got sticker shock." Frankly, we were pleasantly surprised by some of the prices, although Jim noted we would have paid almost a dollar more per can for our precious tuna.

Since we had a late start, we were just leaving the outskirts of Anchorage when Jim announced, "It's tummy time." The Anchorage bicycle paths had ended and no truly wide place in the road had appeared except at the Anchorage Regional Landfill. Boulders flanking the entrance gave us a flat place to make our sandwiches, and daisies brightened the spot. Blooming daisies or not, hordes of mosquitoes attacked and made our lunch a quick but unforgettable stop. We still ask each other, "Remember the Anchorage Landfill lunch?"

As we made our way toward Eagle River, three simple things made our smiles broad: a bike path, great highway shoulders and a bit of tailwind. Just before we reached the first check-point of the Iditarod, the famed dogsled race, our grins turned to grimaces as we hit treacherous gravel but we got lucky, no falls, so no road rash.

Banners of eagles, Dall sheep, moose, bears, beluga whales and wildflowers decorated the city's light poles. What we anticipated most soon appeared—the iconic Alaska Highway 1 road sign with its Big Dipper and North Star symbols. Anything that reminded us *This is Alaska!* thrilled us. This section of the highway, the Glenn Highway, was named after Captain Edwin Glenn who led a US Army expedition charged with finding a route through Alaska to the Klondike gold fields in 1898. And there we were, ninety-seven years later, benefactors of their expedition.

Jan and Jim on the much-anticipated Alaska Highway 1

160

Enormous, bloodthirsty mosquitoes inhabited the forests along this highway. Slap! Swat! Slap! No towns or facilities, nor any RAGBRAI-tall corn fields for long stretches meant we made necessary nature stops elsewhere. As a result, we had itches in places our mothers told us should never be scratched in public.

Speaking of enormous, the Matanuska-Setsina River Valleys yield huge vegetables in the intense but short Alaska growing season—such as eighty pound cabbages. We arrived July 1, just before the height of that season, so the already large veggies had yet to become gigantic. We stopped at a roadside market to buy produce, particularly radishes for Jim to top off his hallmark tuna, peanut butter, and jam sandwiches. Although the red radishes did, the gorgeous white radishes didn't make it to the sandwiches. We sampled them right away.

Apparently, the long hours of summer sun not only enhance vegetables but the wit of the market owners. We chuckled at the signs: *Buy Alaskan. Buy American. Buy Something; Boiling Hot Pepsi $9.99 Plus Tax; Free U-Pick Weeds; Bring More Money; Crime Doesn't Pay. Neither Does Farming.*

Our destination for the day, Sally Pollen's Bed and Breakfast in Palmer, featured a two-story rock fireplace and a room with a history. The blue room, where Sandy and Dave slept, saw brand new life come into the world when women from neighboring communities gave birth there. Sally related that midwives prefer having pregnant women come to a town with a good medical facility, such as Palmer, in case of delivery problems. She added, "Midwifery is very big in Alaska."

Our evening discussion included the merits of *The Milepost*, a publication advertising itself as the best travel guide to all travel in Alaska, Yukon Territory, Northwest Territory, British Columbia and Alberta. It contains *mile-by-mile logs of all Northern highways, complete with food, gas, camping, lodging, what to see and do on every road and in every town*. Locations were designated by their mileage marker, such as Mile 102.5 Glenn Highway or Mile 56 Richardson Highway. The voluminous *Spring '94-Spring '95 Milepost* published 688 pages of information and ads. Despite this plethora of data, between the time the material had been gathered, written, and published, vast changes may have transpired. Jim discovered that when he attempted to make reservations at a listed lodge which had burned down several years before. Later, we would fall victim to some of *The Milepost's* no-longer-accurate recommendations.

The following morning, Sally and her husband served us a perfect bikers' breakfast of scrambled eggs, French toast and fruit, then mentioned, "It's raining." Knowing how to dress for a day of bicycling is an art. We knew the temperature was warm but it was hard to know what to wear to not overheat but still stay dry. *Dry* being a relative term. We concluded we would spend the day stripping clothes off for uphills and donning them for the downs as well as for expected intermittent precipitation.

Our first stop of the day, Palmer Information Center, featured dazzling Alaskan summer blooms. A plastic model of the aforementioned eighty pound cabbage "grew" in the garden too. Jim and Sandy wondered how much sauerkraut such a jumbo cabbage could make.

My journal entry: *Up and down and up and up—rain, drizzle, hot going up, cool going down... not pleasant drivers.* A highway sign indicated 244 miles to Valdez, one of our stops. Sometimes it's reassuring, other times sobering to know how many miles we have yet to ride. Leaden skies drooped and occasional oppressive fog lay heavily on our shoulders. Across the broad valley, we caught glimpses of tops of dark mountains stippled with snow. The braided Matanuska River, sandbars and glacier-fed water entwining, rippled through the grey on grey landscape. When we came close enough to the river to distinguish its powdery aqua color, we saw the land not just as shades of grey but of varying intensities of black and white plus hues of green.

Suddenly, a double-trailer gasoline truck appeared in our rear-view mirrors. It passed frighteningly close to me, Jim, and then Sandy. It seemed to take aim at Dave who was riding on the white line since there was no paved shoulder. We heard a sharp "Yeow!" and the crunch of soft sand as Dave came to an abrupt stop the at the edge of a slight drop-off. As we rushed to him, fear morphed into anger and finally relief when we realized that, except for a disabled bike seat harming a vulnerable part of his body, he was not seriously hurt, but seething. Jim and Dave managed a jerry-rigged repair to the seat post with a wrench wrapped to it with lots of black plastic tape. Despite the unstable, semi-supported seat, strong, competent cyclist Dave kept pedaling.

Long Rifle Lodge, fifty-five miles from Palmer, had the address of Mile 102.2, Glenn Highway, Palmer, Alaska. At the lodge, a huge carved wooden bear, the official shield of the United States of America, and a sign stating *Right to bear arms* greeted us. A misty view of twenty-seven mile long, four mile wide Matanuska Glacier confirmed, *This is truly Alaska!*

The simmering frustrations and exertions of the day exploded as we attempted to get our gear off the bikes. I tried unsuccessfully to remove my wet panniers so asked Jim to help. He struggled too. My normally calm husband jerked so hard the bag came flying off, the spring clipping the pannier to the bike rack stretched to twice its usual length. Fortunately, his valuable orthodontic skill with pliers and wire made it usable again. Later, now calm Jim and moving-a-bit-gingerly Dave, made more adjustments and repairs to the seat post, at least temporarily retiring the black tape.

We ate dinner among stuffed musk ox, heads of buffalo, elk, moose, a ragged looking, full-sized grizzly, a wolverine pelt and lots of human guests.

When we returned to our rooms, its dank smell meant our clothes might not dry overnight. Jim and I had a small heater which aided the process somewhat. Sandy and Dave had one that didn't heat but had a tiny fan. It looked like we would wear cold, clammy clothes the next morning. Journal entry: *Tough day.*

Another day, another Alaska discovery: It's not just the land that is massive, so are the meal portions—heaping bowls of oatmeal and six-inch square cinnamon rolls. Someone murmured, "That should get us down the road a piece."

RAIN. Surpassing an expected misty morning scene, we experienced drizzle and fog. We couldn't begin to see what we had imagined as a stunning mountain landscape. Courteous drivers highlighted our day by waving at us and giving us wide berth as they passed us. Our lives did not even appear to be in jeopardy!

Wonder of wonder, the rain stopped. Then it started again. I sighed. But we came upon The Sheep Mountain Lodge, reputed to have good food. After we ate hot fortifying vegetable soup, we hated to leave the warm dry lodge, but forged on. Immediately Sandy and Dave encountered a moose wandering on the highway. "Straight out of the *Northern Exposure*," she declared, referring to the then-current TV series.

Through breaks between curtains of low-hanging clouds and those that tipped the tops of the mountains, we immersed ourselves in the vastness of this country, snow-studded peaks etched by patchy evergreen valleys, sprawling marshes, and fast-moving rivers. We climbed arduous heights and ripped down the other side, unendingly astonished by phenomenal views made more perfect by vanishing clouds and crystalline skies, wide-shouldered roads, and eagles riding the air currents.

Many people had warned us, "Watch out for the construction! It is really rough going."

A sign reading *Pavement Break* meant broken road, chopped up and tumbled, nearly impassable. We needed a break too so continued on and rode the first half-mile of the eight miles of roadwork, to Eureka Lodge.

Local residents puzzled and amused us by the casual and seemingly disinterested way they treat geologic summits, unlike the Lower 48 where every summit, especially a watershed, is carefully marked with a sign indicating the name and elevation. In response to our question about where the summit was, a ranger we met at the lodge said he thought Eureka Summit might be "a little way down the road." We later discovered the lodge hunkered on the summit.

We still needed to address the road construction situation. At lunch we spoke with a young man who helped us find Mike, a pickup owner who would haul us and our bikes the seven and a half remaining miles to the end of the construction. We found him happily imbibing in the bar but sober enough to accept the twenty dollars we offered him for a ride. Soon we knew his Wisconsin family history and Iowa roots. Mike had emigrated to Alaska twenty-six years ago to work at the Red Dog Mine in Kotzebue, three weeks on, three weeks off. He drove a truck from the mine fifty-six miles to the sea where the zinc was loaded for shipping, primarily to Japan for use in the automotive industry. He added, "After I finish my three weeks off, I fly to work on a 737 from

Anchorage where I have a home." Alaskan commute. We loaded our bikes into the pickup bed with Jim and Dave. Sandy and I climbed into the front seat and hung on while we jounced from one muddy rut to another. We thanked Mike for the ride and stepped out into sticky mud, then drier road. Neither we nor other vehicle drivers would have appreciated us riding on this hacked up road.

Glad to be out of the construction, we continued cycling on Glenn Highway. The mountains were enchanting, but sometimes I felt disenchanted by the climbs—true lung blaster hills.

Sandy, Jim and I marveled at Dave's persistence, strength and cycling skills to ride on his tippy saddle. In contrast to his ability, we were incredulous at the number of inept RV drivers we'd encountered here. We'd heard the estimate that one of every five vehicles on the road in this state was an RV. We observed that many, if not most of them, were driven by people who shouldn't. They drove too fast, too close, showed little awareness of bicyclists, and appeared to have no idea that bicycles are moving objects. Some left their steps down, right at a cyclist's ankle height, putting us at risk. Many also pull too long of a load and had no idea of how poorly they managed an RV while towing both an enclosed trailer and a boat on a trailer.

In spite of clueless RV drivers, our excitement grew as we neared Tazlina Lodge, our home for the night. Its brochure painted a glowing portrait of hand decorated ceiling fans, old fashioned dining and service, all tucked into an all-inclusive oasis wilderness log lodge. Reality? No fans, no dining, no espresso bar, no food, and virtually no service. But we got something not included in the brochure.

Tazlina's owners, Lonny and Bart, moved to Alaska in 1986, and Bart did welding on the Trans-Alaska Pipeline. He'd go to Prudhoe Bay to work until he had earned enough money to return to continue renovating their purchase—the lodge, cabins and a fly-in fishing camp. When money ran short, he'd resume welding on The Slope, the Alaska North Slope meaning the National Petroleum Reserve, the Prudhoe Bay Oil Field and the Arctic National Wildlife Refuge (ANWR.) More about The Slope later.

Located at Mile 156 Glenn Highway, the 1940s Tazlina Lodge was the oldest on the highway still in its original building. The cabins were, if one stretches one's imagination, quaint, although the word adds a new dimension to the definition. Rustic comes closer. Eight cabins and one main bath house comprised the compound beyond the Lodge. To reach the bath house from the cabins required walking the plank over a trench or wading through wild rhubarb-type plants on the other. Nocturnal visits could be hazardous, not only because of the route, but because of wild critters in the area.

To enter our cabin, we stepped up, hunched over, ducked our heads to get through the three by five foot door opening. We watched our shins, then our heads and shins again as we wended our way from room to room. If we walked in the center of the first room, we could walk upright. Canvas-covered ceilings comforted us knowing that nothing from the roof could fall on us. With every step, we bounced about three inches on the old wooden floor. I wondered out loud, "Is this floor going to hold just one more time?" The cabin had been scrubbed clean and matched towel sets added a welcoming touch. The owners had put in a lot of hard work and had plenty more ahead.

To protect our shins, we put chairs at the corners of Jim's and my bed because the bedposts had been cut off. Bedspreads hid this little problem from the eyes but not from the shins. We hung a washcloth in the squat front door so we wouldn't bump our heads every time we entered or exited. A plus, the cabin had electricity. To dry our clothes, first we used an outdoor clothesline and finished the drying in front of our indoor heat source, a tall, ancient heater.

When we asked Lonny about supper, she replied, "We don't have food at the Lodge but there is a place to eat about three miles back." We reminded her the brochure she sent had advertised food. "We are on bicycles and do not want to ride three miles back down a road we just came up on."

She surmised, "I imagine you don't want to ride back up Three Mile Hill again either." Her face brightened when she solved the problem: "You can drive Old Blue!" a tail-finned Mercury Marquis which she explained she had bought for $250.

Jim, Jan and Dave ready to roll in "Old Blue"

Having made those decisions, we allowed Dave, taking all our lives into his hands, to drive shimmying mufflerless Old Blue to supper, down the hill to KROA, Kamping Resorts of Alaska Campground and Café. Dave ordered pancakes—three Alaska-sized pancakes. Sandy had beef and mashed potatoes with the most potent-looking gravy I've ever seen. Jim and I had unremarkable veggie pizza, but at least we didn't have to eat any of our precious store of tuna.

With just the right amount of breath holding, prayer and psychological pedaling, Old Blue wheezed back up Three-Mile Hill. When we returned it to Lonny, our *What do you mean you have no food here?* mood resumed. We quizzed her further, "What do you expect us to do for breakfast?" Her straight-faced reply, "There's another lodge a few miles down the road toward Glennallen, You can eat there."

Once we settled in our cabin, we checked *The Milepost* to confirm the existence of that lodge a few miles down the road. It was listed.

⚲

The next day, we raided our panniers for a pre-breakfast snack near the bathhouse. Our choices included apples, bananas, oranges, juice, now-hard rolls, jam and brownies from our stash. We thought that would fortify us for our seven-mile journey to the next lodge and a real breakfast.

Our rancor over being misled about the culinary accommodations dissipated. The day glimmered too brightly to waste energy being upset. Huge smiles reflected anticipation and joy as we cycled on. A crystal-clear day with stunning views to the angular and surprisingly unnamed mountains provided more visual proof, *This is Alaska!* Amazing vistas in North Star Country repeatedly reinforced that hard-for-us-to-fathom fact. And, important to the two coffee drinkers among us, coffee perked just seven miles away.

Those few miles later, dismay and irritation replaced our cheery moods. The café had burned down several years before and what remained of the lodge was for sale. Groans and slight gnashing of teeth ensued. We'd been had again.

Back to *The Milepost* for guidance. It indicated Tolsona Lake Resort lay seven or eight more miles ahead. It had a restaurant. Off we rolled in pursuit of the elusive caffeine and calories. The non-coffee drinkers just wanted restrooms and food but, to cries of "Oh no!" we saw the *Closed* sign on the Lodge door. Jim, the dentist in our midst, felt alarm at hearing more teeth gnashing.

We scattered to find our own quiet places along the Tolsona River. We snacked on our last pieces of fruit and hard rolls, muttered dark and drear thoughts. A chipmunk scrabbled onto my panniers sniffing out goodies, but Jim chased him away and saved the brownies.

Nearby bushes and trees accommodated another of our needs but an extravagance of mosquitoes, all of them hungry, sullied the environs. Our morning plans did not include lingering until we finally had food and coffee. We lumbered onto our bikes in search of a few of the finer things in life. We refused to consult *The Milepost*.

As we pedaled, Jim and I glimpsed two owls and wondered aloud, "How do they manage as night hunters in summer's all-light-all-night atmosphere." But here we were, just like them, hunting for food. Nature displays her wonders in many ways and often mystifies us in the process.

On the long glide toward Glennallen, an apparition startled Jim and me. He exclaimed, "That looks like Haleakala!" I agreed. Eventually, we realized a cloud formation resembling Maui's most famous mountain loomed ahead of us. This doppelganger even had a ring of clouds forming a lei around its crown. The drone of wheels blunted Jim's voice, "Those aren't clouds! They have to be the Wrangells!" Our first glimpse of Mount Drum, a majestic volcanic mountain in this eastern Alaska range.

Many people consider these mountains, named after the one-time Governor of Russian America, to be one of the wildest ranges in the world. As part of the Wrangell-St. Elias National Park, America's largest, their territory measures greater than the whole country of Switzerland. Additionally, the volcanoes of the Wrangells, part of the *Ring of Fire* encircling the Pacific Ocean, rank among the highest mountains in North America and among the most massive by volume in the world. Their splendor beckoned to us, mountain lovers all.

According to information signs, the Wrangells *contain the most extensive array of glaciers and ice fields found outside the polar regions.* They, as well as Canada's adjacent Kluane National Park, have been designated by the United Nations as a World Heritage Site.

A sundry of little lakes, including lily-padded ones where moose should be, plus tiny ponds for tiny moose, littered the countryside. Unfortunately, we saw no moose even as we crossed Moose Creek at the outskirts of Glennallen, the easternmost town we would visit.

Named for Copper River explorers Edwin Glenn and Henry Allen, the town, a highway construction camp in the 1940s, had a 1995 population of five hundred fifty people. Sitting near the junction of two of Alaska's major roads, the Glenn and Richardson Highways ultimately connect with the Alcan Highway.

We ate breakfast, a real breakfast, not at the Moose but the Caribou Restaurant. Recalling his Kansas pancake experience, Jim ordered just two pancakes. The coffee drinkers finally drank their wake-up cups four hours late.

Replenishing our food stock had become a priority. But first we savored a sample of Alaskan art at the Old Post Office Gallery, tempting works that would not fit into our panniers. The artist-owner, Jean Rene's obvious affinity to the Wrangell Mountains, Copper River Delta and the Alaskan people, moved me. The grocery store was a letdown after the aesthetic spirit of the gallery. My journal notes: *The groceries were dismal.* No bananas, nor any other fresh produce except oranges. We also realized what an astonishing number of places all over this state have an espresso bar, drive-in ones at that, and how difficult it would be to live somewhere that didn't have easy access to the types of food we depend on, especially fresh fruit.

With oranges, tuna, peanut butter and cookies tucked safely in our panniers, we said goodbye to Glennallen, a town with views to three imposing mountain ranges: the Chugach to the south; the

Wrangells to the north; and the St. Elias extending to the Gulf of Alaska. Imagine being surrounded by such grandeur every day—it would definitely help make up for the lack of favorite foods.

As we left town, we saw Glennallen Community Church, the first church we had seen since we left Palmer's environs. This scarcity helped us understand more about distances here. We were spoiled by having little towns every ten to fifteen miles, often with churches, as we do in Iowa.

Just beyond Glennallen, on our way to the Richardson Highway, Dave's bike had a flat tire. He and Jim thought they had repaired it but soon discovered the new tube had been damaged. By the time the tire fixing finished, all of us steamed in the intense heat of the day. Sandy and I often act as sous chefs/surgical assistants when the guys are in their mechanics mode. Sometimes however, it is a good idea to just take a little walk, away from the discourse regarding those *Blarsted tubes.*

Bicyclists become avid watchers, garnering information about wind, terrain, mileage, food, weather, and points of interest. That made the next highway sign a very welcome sight: *Cordova Whittier Anchorage Via Alaska Marine Highway.* To us landlocked outsiders, the Marine Highway meant taking a ferry. Officially, we now rode Alaska Highway 4, the Richardson Highway, which extends from Fairbanks to Valdez.

We culled but didn't always follow suggestions from *Alaska Bicycle Touring Guide.* For example, the guide says, *Much of the Richardson Highway from its junction with the Glenn Highway south is windy...generally blowing from south to north. We recommend cyclists...consider riding north from Valdez.* We did consider it but that didn't work with our travel plans. We chose to defy the odds and face the wind. Face it we did.

The altitude changes along the Richardson made eye-popping panoramic views possible along the Tazlina, Klutina, Totsina and Copper rivers as we traveled toward the Wrangell-St. Elias Mountains and National Park. We never tired of the green to black landscape of the mountains or the rush of mountain streams.

At the second church of the day, the Copper Valley Community Church, Dave, who grew up in the wooden Iowa variety, wanted to photograph what he labeled "the parsonage," a plain old-fashioned canvas tent. The nearby cemetery featured fenced-in graves with brightly painted pickets. Wooden crosses displayed names, dates and plaques in dedication, memory and thanks. A particularly touching message for *Grandmother:*

For adding a warm touch of caring to every day helping so much in your quiet, unselfish way...For putting your heart into all the nice things you do showing your family how special they are to you— You're loved and always will be.

Our overnight destination, the Copper Center Roadhouse, took us back in time. According to *Alaska Bicycle Touring Guide,* like many other roadhouses on the Richardson Highway, it had been built *by private enterprise to meet the needs of the miners, freighters, mail contractors and other travelers.*

They were built approximately 10 miles apart, or roughly as far as one could travel in a single day. Some were only tent shelters, while others were lavish hotels.

The George Ashby Museum at the Center displayed a myriad of Alaskiana as well as Midwestern artifacts, a product of so many Midwesterners emigrating to Alaska. In addition to an antique Polaris snowmobile, a traditional Yu'pik basket like one our family has, thrilled me. Constructed in the same tightly woven, coiled way, with a slightly conical snugly-fitted lid, my Aunt Inez bought ours as a gift to her sister, my grandmother, when she traveled to Alaska in the early 1930s.

An information sheet related this: *The history of the Copper Center Lodge is rooted in the Gold Rush of 1897-1898 when 4000 men crossed the Valdez and Klutina Glaciers on their way to the Klondike.* Many died of scurvy due to a lack of citrus and vitamin C, and were buried near the Copper River. Other discouraged stampeders returned to the coast, leaving their supplies. The proceeds from resale of those supplies provided funds to build the Holman Hotel, predecessor of the present lodge.

Another brochure described the Lodge accommodations as homey and charmingly rustic. Umhmm. It didn't mention Jim's and my unique bathroom layout which made us think of sit and spit. When we brushed our teeth, we could sit on the toilet and without leaning, spit into the sink, but we were grateful for indoor plumbing.

One of the present owners, Lisa Ashby, added color to the Lodge story. It was open from May 15 to October 1 although she and her husband had kept it open through the first winter after their marriage. Her mother-in-law, Katherine Ashby, spent from 1948-1991 behind the grill. After Katherine's husband George died in 1980, she was supposed to be in charge of the establishment. It had become so overwhelming to her that for years she refused to even go upstairs. When her family told her about the needed repairs, she refused to believe them. Eventually, her son and Lisa took over the business, debt and all. Now they are renovating and sprucing it up.

While we were there, he finished building flower boxes and she filled them with soil and planted flowers, supporting her theory of having projects that can be completed in one day along with the big projects, such as redoing the rooms. Lisa added that *Backroads*, a familiar-to-us bicycle touring group, stops there every ten days or so during the season. That has to help their bottom line. The Ashbys overwinter at Big Lake near Palmer. These families make enormous sacrifices trying to make a living and share it with others in this beautiful but harsh, all-consuming place.

After a night of being serenaded by the Roadhouse musicians we awoke to a new day of high clouds, cool weather and another flat for Dave. The final intact spare tube enabled the guys to change the tire again. They kept busy patching the tubes and, fortunately, the patches held.

Our maps indicated we would have some terrific downhills. Small glitch, they faced the wind funneling through the canyon. But there was a bonus. The wind-challenged downhill gradually gave way to long stretches of what passes for flatlands in Alaska, giving us time to ponder the grandeur of this vast land, mountains rising sharply in the distance, and the mesmerizing effect of the landscape.

Sandy, Dave, Jim and I didn't know it at the time but we were *bearfooting*. That means we were really having a great time and what we were doing, our journey, was more important than our destination. We lost track of what day it was and we really didn't care. We were bicycling in Alaska! We didn't forget we would eventually be back in Anchorage, but we lived in the moment, seized each day and garnered a whole assemblage of glorious and some not-quite-so-glorious Alaska experiences.

More quickly than I had imagined, we reached the mountains that had seemed so distant in the morning. I love it when that happens, especially since we had faced merciless wind. Besides the wind, we had another companion, a quiet one, the whole distance from Glennallen, the Alyeska Pipeline, also known as the The Trans-Alaska Pipeline, TAPS. It wends its way eight hundred miles through Alaska from Prudhoe Bay on the Arctic Ocean to its terminus in Valdez, the northernmost ice-free port in North America. A sign explained where heat from the pipeline might thaw unstable soils such as permafrost, permanently frozen soil, the line had been insulated and elevated. The zig-zag design *provided flexibility to accommodate movements due to temperature changes or other causes.* Think earthquakes.

I also thought about the graceless manmade pipeline violating the natural beauty and health of the area. Although we knew of the terrible *Exxon Valdez* oil spill off the coast in 1989, as we biked alongside it we understood anew the potential perils of any breach of the pipeline.

Neither an earthquake nor an oil spill caused our heart-stopping experience. What happened next involved a four-legged angel. After we spotted a young moose swimming across Willow Lake, Sandy, Dave, Jim and I veered off to a scenic viewpoint. We watched and worried as the youngster appeared to weaken. He managed to get past the middle of the lake but turned to go back. We futilely chorused, "No! No! Don't go back!"

BOOM! We whirled around to find out what had exploded and saw a logging truck driver attempt to pull onto the right shoulder of the highway. One of its back tires had blown completely off the rim, caromed from the ditch to the road, skipped back into the ditch, and boomeranged out again. Over and over for nearly a quarter of a mile the tire bounded exactly where we would have been riding had we not stopped to watch the moose. It bounced for so long, we got our cameras out and photographed the action. We shuddered to think about the potential disaster had we or another vehicle been in its path.

Minutes passed as we shook our heads and tried to quiet our hearts. The young moose had disappeared from our sight. We never knew his fate, but he had changed ours. When I reflected on

Horrified, Jan watches the errant logging truck tire

the whole episode, I silently asked the question: *Was the little moose natural or was he our guardian angel who protected us from certain tragedy?*

We remained quiet as we pushed on toward Tiekel River Lodge. A few miles down the road we saw *The Alaska House* sign, pedaled past it but quickly turned around. Our aesthetic appetites had been whetted by our visit to the Old Post Office Gallery in Glennallen, so we stopped at this shop in the middle of a sweeping pine forest.

After searching and pondering, Jim purchased a simply scrimshawed fossilized ivory walrus tusk cribbage board. The owner/artist explained only people deemed Native Alaskan— Inuit, Athabascan, and Aleut—were permitted to carve ivory and each article must be certified. As a bonus, the proprietor, one more vivid Alaska character, introduced us to a handsome, month-old blue fox pup, called that because it is a color phase of the Arctic fox. He raises and trains one pup a year for breeding purposes.

Back on the road, we experienced a day so exquisite we felt we needed to photograph everything: mountains, rivers and each other. Every direction we looked another vista begged to be captured. Jim is very exacting about how and where people in his photos sit, stand or ride. Dave, reflecting on his ministerial past, muttered, "It's like being in a wedding. 'Stand here, do this, do that.'" We rode back and forth, too fast, too close to Jim, too far away, not cooperating. At last Jim got his photos. We took dozens of photos of each other with the dazzling scenery.

But how could we preserve a memory of the sound of rapids, the swish of willows in the wind, or the snap of branches as a moose wandered in the brush? How could we hold onto the smells of the woods, the subtle scent of fireweed, the brush of the breeze in our faces? My journal resurrected a memory: *The Tiekel River has many faces, rippling oxbows, white water rapids, braided sandbars, mountain currents.*

When we neared our Tiekel River destination, we heard the gently swirling sound of a trumpeter swan floating on a placid beaver pond. Beyond it hunkered an old beaver lodge, and farther on, a beaver dam demonstrated how nature's premier engineer calms a rushing mountain stream.

And then we came to the Tiekel River Lodge. The accommodations far surpassed our expectations. The four of us shared an oversized room with an equal number of beds, two to sleep in and two to spread our gear on. We had space enough for all the bikes, and an unpredictable shower. But it was *our* shower. Outside, a breeze dried our laundry as it hung from windows, doorknobs, ladders and barrel frames. It doesn't get much better than this for an overnight.

After facing the winds all the way from Glennallen, our Iowa City friends Steve and Sue Wolken arrived with an Alaska bicycling tour group. They and their companions stayed in luxury tents in the riverside campground—a lovely site but a long trek to the showers and restrooms. We moseyed down to the campground to see them and to talk with the tour owner to ask if he could assist Dave in repairing his broken seat bolt. He was distinctly ungracious in saying no.

Surprised but undaunted by the rebuff, we found lodge owner Mike, who jerry-rigged a radiator clamp to fix it. Ingenuity is in long supply among rural Alaska folks. During the radiator clamp surgery, we offered to pay Mike who first responded, "No!" He thought a bit and added, "Fifty cents for the radiator clamp." Paid!

That evening at a picnic table, the four of us feasted on steaming hot chili and gumbo in bread bowls, plus Dutch apple pie ala mode. Afterward, we strolled to the campground to see the tour group's amenities, complete with salmon and steaks for supper, coils to repel insects, screened tents to eat in, cushy pads to sleep on, and the rushing Tiekel River to lull them to sleep. But we felt happy doing our wilderness bliss ride our way.

🚲

Sweeping clouds backdropped our outdoor picnic breakfast of cereal, muffins and chewy pancakes. Awaiting us were mountains featuring long climbs to thirty-nine hundred feet, quixotic weather and fifty-six cycling miles to Valdez.

Before we left the Lodge, we bundled up in our wind jackets and tights and had rain pants handy. Throughout the day, we needed frequent stops to eat, drink, take off or put on another layer of clothing. Rain, wind, rain, wind. But the glory of biking in this landscape outweighed all the temporary discomforts of the elements.

Hungry from riding into the wind, we stopped at Worthington Glacier at lunchtime.

In the past century, the glacier has receded one thousand feet in length and an equal amount in depth, but nestled in the glacier, perfect picnic rocks awaited us. We created and ate our sandwiches there. Nearby, the biking group lounged in directors' chairs and polished off seafood linguini. We could not convince them to join us even when Jim tried to tempt them with the Matanuska radish-embellished tuna, jam, peanut butter and mustard sandwich he relished so much.

The Valdez Glacier area held the record for the heaviest snowfall in Alaska—over 974 inches fell in the winter of 1952-53 and once sixty-two inches of snow fell in a twenty-four hour period. To add to this, the ordinarily strong wind over the pass sometimes reached one hundred miles per hour. Before the discovery of Thompson Pass around 1900, many early explorers and miners came by steamboat to Valdez, then climbed the Valdez and Klutina Glaciers, continuing on to Copper Center. This resulted in many deaths and many more lost supplies in the Klutina River. Miners searched for gold as late in the season as they could, but before they were snowbound, tried to raft down the Copper River, often capsizing and drowning. Thompson Pass allowed them to bypass the glaciers and follow a trail through Keystone Canyon. I treasured the way historic and natural Alaska surrounded and surprised us each day.

Purple lupines and red fireweed blossomed on the highway's rocky shoulders to brighten our grey-sky day. According to my journal: *Going up Thompson Pass was a long but not grueling climb. A quick, steep downhill, one of the reasons we were glad to go north to south instead of the reverse. Mountains hid behind clouds and fog, more rain and chill. Still a long way into Valdez.*

This leg of the ride seemed especially long because we were wet and unable to see what we hoped to see, Keystone Canyon and mountains. We stopped several times to put on more clothes during this bitterly cold part of the day, especially before we whipped down into the flatland near Valdez. Cold seeped into every part of our bodies, our gloved fingers tingled. I had no more warm clothes to add.

We paused at an abandoned railroad tunnel and stood gape-mouthed at what people will battle over. A wooden sign explained:

This tunnel was hand-cut into the solid rock of Keystone Canyon and is all that is left of the railroad era when nine companies fought to take advantage of the short route from the coast to Copper Country. However, a feud interrupted progress. A gun battle was fought and the tunnel was never completed.

At last we rolled into Valdez and searched out our home for the night. The welcome from our hosts, Lynn and Jerry, made us quit shivering. Seeing our mud splattered condition, Lynn brought us a bucket of sudsy water and mentioned the detergent was Dawn which had been used to clean the seabirds after the Exxon Valdez oilspill. We scrubbed our rain suits, panniers, bikes, and Lynn washed and dried our laundry, a godsend. After we bathed, such bliss, we consumed warm-from-the-oven-apricot bread pudding topped with ice cream, and Jerry shared the M&M cookies he'd made. Warm welcome, indeed—an Arctic Shangri-La.

Their lovely home matched their grace and friendliness. I couldn't believe how immaculate it was, including the birch floors and flagstone Arctic entry. I put on a new pair of white cycling socks and wore them all over the house. When I took them off, they were still white! Lynn told us it is a custom in Alaska to remove your shoes when you enter someone's home, just like we knew was done in Hawaii and Japan. An idea worth emulating.

Sandy, Dave, Jim and I had promised to reward ourselves with an Alaskan salmon dinner when we got to Valdez, but none of us wanted to go out into the lousy weather. Instead, we asked our hosts if we could order pizza for them, us and their other guest. Lynn made a tossed salad while the rest of us talked pizza. Once again, Jim thought he was starving. Sandy and Dave worked overtime convincing him we didn't need two large and one medium pizzas. Consultation with Lynn and Jerry confirmed the pizzas would be Alaska-large.

When the pizzas arrived, we nearly choked. Alaska-large meant an eighteen-inch deep dish pizza. The seven of us ate and ate and still had enough for lunch on the ferry.

We spent an entertaining evening hearing more Alaska tales from our hosts. Her family had come during the Gold Rush of 1898 and her grandfather was a freighter who took miners' goods over the mountains via the glaciers. Jerry is a pilot and co-owns a plane. Lynn has taken flying lessons, has soloed but did not get her license. However, she said she would be able to land a plane in an emergency.

Jerry, a San Bernardino, California transplant, did not return there for many years after he came to Alaska. For thirty years he worked with the Department of Transportation. He had also been employed as a fisherman, which sounds like the one of the most trying jobs in the world because of wind, weather and the sea. He now does private snow removal in addition to their B&B. He chuckled while telling us during one blizzard, he had driven his front loader into a huge snowbank and, without realizing what was in it, lifted out a VW Beetle.

Jerry's barber had not quite finished his haircut when the Great Alaska Earthquake of 1964 struck. He bolted out of the chair and raced outside to see what he could do to help. Days later, he returned and asked the barber to finish the cut. One of the overwhelming tragedies of the earthquake was one hundred thirty-one people died, mostly because of tsunamis. A great slice of Valdez dropped off into Prince William Sound and everyone on the Port Valdez docks died. As a consequence, the entire town of Valdez was moved to another higher, safer location and remains an ice-free saltwater port.

🚲

Lynn and Jerry wished us well as we left their home the next day, leftover pizza and cookies in our panniers, to board the one hundred seventy passenger ferry and cross the Sound. We wheeled our bikes into the hold in preparation for our seven hour trip to Whittier. We had hoped for sunshine but grey water and grey clouds greeted us. A young local assured us that it was often this way near Valdez but the sky often turned blue and clear in other parts of Prince William Sound. As soon as the ferry passed by them, fishing boats immediately closed in behind and let out their nets. Later they would "purse up" the nets in order to capture the fish the ferry had attracted.

The allure of water, mountains, clouds and now cobalt sky spawned a lovely sail on the Sound. We had been told we would not come very near the Columbia Glacier so the passengers kept snapping photos, thinking that any moment the captain would divert the ferry. We came much closer than we had thought, although we could not hear the glacier calving as huge slabs slipped off the glacier into the ice-cluttered water.

The Columbia Glacier, the fourth largest tidewater glacier in Alaska, is open to the sea allowing icebergs to break off directly into the ocean. We saw only the lower ten to twelve miles of it with its two and a half mile wide face. Although the ice extended about sixteen hundred feet below the water, the height above measured only one hundred fifty to three hundred feet. At times, the glacier moved forward as much as sixteen feet a day but about half that much was the average.

Due to blue light not refracting the way other colors do, the surreal quality of the ice creates a startling crystalline turquoise. Dirty hunks of ice created quite a contrast to the aqua ice. Along the way, we had seen sea otters and sea lions in the Sound but we soon saw orcas, Inuit for killer whales, as they played and raced alongside the ferry. Snow-inlaid peaks reflecting in the Sound created more memorable sights.

Flanked by rocks streaming with waterfalls, a clamorous kittiwake colony filled the air with *kittee-wa-aake!* calls as we approached Whittier. In 1995, the town was connected to the outside world only by ferry and rail ferry, aboard the Alaska Railroad to Portage. Now a two point six mile rail tunnel has been converted to a one-lane combined highway-rail tunnel. Trains and cars take turns traveling through it.

We wheeled our bikes off the ferry, pushed them up the ramp into town. We wandered into a few stores, enjoyed our ice cream, gawked at the hundreds of boats and just took in the sights while waiting to board the train to Portage. When the time came, we loaded our bikes in the baggage car. Motorized vehicles, autos, buses, RVs, drove onto flatbed cars with their occupants in them, while we rode in the passenger cars. During the twelve mile ride, we crossed a marshy isthmus connecting the Kenai Peninsula to mainland Alaska, always accompanied by snowy mountains. We disembarked in Portage to bike the final fifteen miles to Girdwood, our night's destination. That totaled seven hours by ferry, twelve miles by rail, and fifteen miles by bicycle, arriving by late afternoon. Not our usual day.

As we wheeled toward Mount Alyeska, we looked up and glimpsed the red, orange and yellow wing of a paraglider floating above us in the cloud-punctuated sky—a lively welcome to Girdwood, a major resort and recreation area just an hour's drive from Anchorage. That translates into a day's bike ride. The great mountain overwhelmed the area with its grandeur.

It felt good to settle in for one more night on the road. Our Alaskana House host led us into his spacious home and down the stairs to a sizeable room. It took my breath away to see all the mounted creatures in every corner and on every ledge and level: mountain goat, bear, wolf, mountain lion, elk head. An eerie feeling enveloped me in the middle of the night when I got up to go to the bathroom and saw the reflection of light in their eyes.

🚲

An aura of excitement intermingled with an impulse to just keep going and not let our cycling end permeated our final day of riding from Girdwood to Anchorage. We lingered by the sea, searched for eagles, and savored the glory we'd experienced biking in Alaska. We laughed at a sign with silhouettes of a mama duck and two ducklings, warning us to be alert. The marshland bordering the highway produced just such denizens. Despite seeing an occasional car, a peaceful feeling stayed with us. All too soon a *Welcome to Anchorage* sign brought us back to reality. The streets broadened to four-lanes, traffic signals appeared on major corners, and we left rural Alaska behind, our thirtieth state and the only one we didn't bike totally across or around.

We retrieved our bike boxes from the Ramada Inn, spread our gear all over the concrete sidewalks in front, and began dismantling and packing our precious bicycles. I nearly always grieve the end of biking trips and this was no exception. The poignancy lasts until we launch into another phase of the trip or we begin planning another one. In this case, we would rent a car and spend the next week experiencing Denali National Park and visiting Dave's son in the Fairbanks area. It held a different kind of excitement until we returned to Anchorage, retrieved our bike boxes from the Ramada Inn again and caught the plane for the *outside*—Iowa City and home.

Memories? They abound. We cherish them and relish telling and retelling stories of people we met, places we went and experiences that wove themselves into the webs of our lives.

Here are two such Alaska stories:

🚲

ALASKA DREAMS—PART 1

Because we stayed mostly at B&Bs and rode bicycles on our Alaska trip, we had opportunities we don't always have to get to know some of the people who live in the land we are only traveling through. So it was with Lonny and Bart and their story.

Lonny grew up in Hudson, South Dakota so knew my birthplace, Akron, Iowa while Bart came from nearby Sioux Falls. They had moved to Alaska in 1986 after their youngest son graduated from high school. He stayed on in the Lower 48 to provide an income for the family. Three trips later, all the family's belongings were there and they settled into their new Alaska home, the Tazlina Lodge property. Their son rejoined the family in Alaska once Bart had a job. As a welder on the Trans-Alaska Pipeline, he traveled to Prudhoe Bay to The Slope* and worked until he had earned enough money to return and continue renovating their purchase.

Jim asked, "Had you been to Alaska prior to buying the lodge and moving there permanently?" Lonny said Bart had brought her there on a moose hunting trip in 1982. He and his hunting buddies had no success. Lonny, however, managed to bag one. With their car.

One of their daughters married a half-Inuit young man who is a hunter. At the fishing camp, he shot a bear described as "seven-foot square," a great hulking one. While we were at Tazlina, Lonny and Bart received word about a bear marauding the camp and eating all the stores including flour and muffin mixes. Camp neighbors expressed concern the bear would repeatedly return. Bart and Lonny didn't say it, but I had the feeling they would try to track it down and shoot it. Lonny told gruesome tales about bear attacks, one of which we would hear again from another B&B host down the road. It seems rural Alaska can be a very small town when it comes to the magic news grapevine.

The couple had gutted the lodge and worked on putting in new footings. She invited us to come see the interior. The original footings were five-pound coffee cans filled with concrete. The great 1964 earthquake had pushed them several feet out and the lodge walls rested on the ground, no matter which way the ground canted. The original bar had character: The lodge had been built with no concern for the sloping land. The bar and bases of the barstools had been cut to varying heights to accommodate this and to try to make the tops even with each other.

Progress was slow but apparent. The exterior logs had been totally stripped and painted and recently a green steel roof had been added. Bright blooms filled the window boxes and a new floor was being laid within the lodge, complete with plastic moisture barrier and foam insulation.

They hoped to have the lodge completed by January 1, 1996 to accommodate lodge-to-lodge dogsledders. Guests, particularly Northern Europeans eager to participate in Alaska's winter sports, would mush dogs with sleds about ninety miles and stay at lodges along the way. Lonny and Bart also expected to host a large contingent of Koreans and Japanese who already enjoyed Alaska in the summer.

Lonny contended the cabins were completed but the double bathhouse with a shower, sink, and toilet plus a bathtub with no water source, was usable only on one side. I couldn't imagine using it in the middle of winter.

I asked, "What about property insurance in the remote areas of Alaska?" Lonny responded there was no insurance because there were no local fire departments. We don't know if that is an accurate appraisal or not but that sobering thought recurred whenever we saw yet another burned out shell of a home or business. We had heard another version: Owners burned their homes and businesses because they couldn't make payments so wanted the insurance money.

In addition to welding, helping Lonny run the lodge and fish camp, Bart guided trips and flew his airplane for fun. The Tazlina Airport, just across the road from the Lodge, had the hilliest runway I've ever seen. Not only are many Alaskan runways hilly and bumpy, they are terrifyingly short. We watched pilots take off from and land at these rural airports and I could not fathom how they accomplished either. I believed Alaska's bush pilots were truly a breed apart, and virtually everyone we met was either a pilot or had parents or siblings who were.

Lonny and Bart owed no money to anyone. In their own way, they were far ahead of many in the world. They lived in a slightly dilapidated house that needed work. Lonny sighed as she looked at the flooring being put into the lodge, "There goes my new house." She added, "Living here is a hard life. Alaska is very unforgiving."

*THE SLOPE: Bart spoke of working on The Slope, the Alaska North Slope—the National Petroleum Reserve—the Prudhoe Bay Oil Field and the Arctic National Wildlife Refuge (ANWR.) The ANWR has been a subject of decades-long controversy between those who want to drill for oil within its boundaries and those who don't. Native populations, environmentalists and big oil interests continue on a collision course regarding this land, its wildlife and hydrocarbons. Mix that with money, politics and who to believe, the issue is only clear to those on a particular side of the conflict. What will become of this rich wild land and its denizens?

ALASKA DREAMS—PART 2 SUMMER, 2010

Sandy, Dave, Jim and I took a five-week driving trip from Iowa to Alaska and back. As we drove through Glennallen, we decided to see if Tazlina Lodge still existed because it was not listed in the *2010 Milepost*. We wondered if it had burned down, how it and the couple who owned it had fared since we bicycled in Alaska in 1995.

I can only describe our feelings as delighted when we saw the familiar but changed lodge still standing. The once dark brown log lodge with bright flowers gracing the window boxes had been stained grey. Faded plastic flowers stuck in the window boxes looked sad. The bright green metal roof remained the same. Different smaller cabins replaced some of the trees near the old bathhouse.

We alighted from the van to look around and take photos. Jim insisted the long cabin closest to the lodge was "ours" but it didn't resonate with me. Dave answered that question by opening the door and announcing, "This is the bathhouse." He added that it was now used for storage including 5-gallon buckets of unidentified stuff.

I walked behind the lodge looking for our cabin. Dave pointed to one that had been moved closer to the lodge he had just peeked in. "That's it." I opened the door and there it was, the canvas ceiling, two rooms, the far one being the step-down room, both rooms filled with cardboard boxes and luggage. I had just closed the door when we heard the motor of an Arctic Cat 4-wheeler that had experienced better days. A scruffy-appearing man dressed in grubby jeans, stained sweatshirt, and a faded grey baseball cap with an outline of Alaska initialed AK, drove it. He sported wild eyebrows, straggly hair and seven-day whiskers. The man's hands were knotted, arthritic, stained, with the middle finger and part of this right thumb missing. He fit an Alaska stereotype of a man who had lived a hard life. Neither friendly nor hostile, he greeted us, "What's going on here?"

"We stayed here the summer of 1995 and wanted to see if the lodge was still here."

He glanced up, gruff demeanor softening, "You did?" We recalled for him our bicycle trip and stay. When we reminded him of borrowing Old Blue for our excursion to Mendeltna Creek Lodge to eat supper, he grinned at the mention of the old Mercury Marquis. "It ran to two hundred eighty thousand miles. We drove about eighty thousand more miles after we bought it." The four of us knew where at least six of those miles came from. He continued by saying that Lodge down the hill opened sporadically. "When He's at home, the place is open. When He's on the Slope, She puts the Closed sign up, shuts the door and vamooses. Nobody knows where She goes."

A sudden memory made me ask, "Is your name Bart?"

"It is." He admitted work on their lodge hadn't made much progress since 1995. When we referred to the floor of the lodge being worked on, he shook his head slightly, "We probably haven't gotten much farther since then. We're getting old and you can't get anybody to do anything up here." He mentioned they had been building a house nearby, probably the one Lonny thought wouldn't be built because of redoing the lodge floor.

We plied our questions, "Do you still fly? Do you still have the fly-in fish camp? Do people still come for winter activities?'

Bart answered he still flies and occasionally has guests stay at the camp. Snowmobilers and cross-country skiers sometimes come. "It's really a lot of work to keep the lodge and cabins. We rent them out but there's no food. It's too much work for my wife to cook."

We recalled the big bear break-in at the camp. Bart replied, " Yeah, that bear broke some windows and they probably haven't all been fixed cuz if you fix 'em real well, they just come back and break 'em again." He said he had retired from working on the Slopes so spends more time in Tazlina now. His and Lonny's dreams of a thriving lodge and fish camp held no promise anymore. They still sold vehicles to help make ends meet. A couple of weeks earlier, Bart had sold an airplane. In turn, he bought one in Louisiana on E-Bay but didn't know how he was going to get it to Alaska. Dave facetiously suggested he drive his ATV there to pick it up. Bart didn't smile.

We took photos of Bart on his ATV, thanked him for visiting with us, and left with new memories and old ones rekindled. Tazlina had changed in some ways, as had Bart. They, well, Bart at least had grown older, more tired and more resigned to things staying about the same as they had been fifteen years ago. We imagined that Lonny had too. We drove down the three-mile hill to Mendeltna Creek Lodge to get something to drink. We felt more secure in the van than we had in Old Blue. A *Closed* sign filled a window. He must be on the Slope and She must have vamoosed again.

We drove back up the hill, honked and waved at Bart who chatted with the mailman. He smiled and waved back. We continued to ponder our visit to Tazlina Lodge and Bart. Dave opined, "I was curious about what we'd find. If we came back in another fifteen years, Bart would be older but everything else would pretty much be the same. I was surprised and pleased that he came to talk with us. But it was kinda sad to hear him when I asked when their lodge was closed and he said, 'Most of the time.'"

Sandy commented the new cabins were refreshing to see. They were an improvement over the old ones but still looked like they were just being used for storage. Jim echoed the feeling. "I'm sorry about the place. It has potential but it would need different owners and lots of money. The infrastructure is there. It needs cleaning up. I really wanted to see if the floor in the lodge was done."

I remembered Lonny's words from 1995, "Alaska is very unforgiving," and felt sorrow anew for Bart, Lonny and the other dreamers whose hopes and lives have been shattered by the harshness of life in Alaska.

A couple of evenings later in Skagway, as we ate supper we spoke with its former mayor and related our stories about Bart and our visit to Tazlina Lodge. Tom shook his head knowingly and smiled sadly, "Alaska dreams."

ALOHA EE KAUAI-1996

Riders: Jim/Jan. Distance: 216 miles

A late January snowstorm canceled our flight in Cedar Rapids but our travel agent daughter Tania booked us on a later one to Chicago. We barely made it, headed to Honolulu but missed our connection to Kauai. We overnighted in Oahu and grabbed an early morning plane to Lihue. Amazingly, our baggage including our bike boxes had caught up with us. We took a station wagon cab to our home base on the island, Kapa'a Sands, in the same complex as our friends, Betty and Dick Mitchell. The light airy feel of the condo, an expansive view of the ocean and being fifty feet from the surf and coral reef with its fish and sea turtles made us very happy.

Jim promptly assembled the bicycles and discovered a clip on my bike box had broken. The next morning, we took a brief ride to a nearby bike shop, succumbed to buying brilliantly colored Kauai biking shirts, yellow for Jim and fuchsia for me, and ordered a replacement clip. The shop proprietor's chit-chat delighted us. The temperatures on the island had been unseasonably cool recently, in the 60s. When he spoke to his sister that morning, she said her children refused to get out of bed to go to school because it was too cold. We chuckled and told him we had just left lots of snow and below zero temperatures.

We continued on and rode a ten-mile loop on back roads to Opaeka'a Falls and back to our condo. As we passed the closed but tidy appearing Cocoa Palms, we remembered what had once been a lively and gorgeous resort with a coconut grove planted by Kapule, the last queen of Kauai. On his R&R from Vietnam Jim and I had felt like royalty staying there, just as my grandparents had in 1966 when they celebrated their fiftieth anniversary. We saw the driveway still lined with majestic coconut palms, but gone were the tiki torches surrounding the ponds, and the rooms with enormous shell sinks. Hurricane Iniki's devastation had totally altered the resort's future.

Later that week, I phoned the resort's manager who said he hoped they would open in the spring of 1997. Unfortunately, the insurance company would only pay eight million dollars but the owners demanded the eighteen million dollar replacement cost. Stalemate and legal turmoil. Litigation continued for over a decade.

Because Dick and Betty had come to Kauai for many years, they had thoroughly scoped out beaches. Relaxing on nearly deserted Larson Beach, our picnic spot for the day, we watched waves and read. The beach looked smooth but rough coral sand irritated my tender feet. Memo to self: Stroll beach with sandals on.

⚲

The following day, I watched a cloudy Kauai sunrise from our lanai, contentedly contemplated the Pacific waves hoping to see migrating humpback whales. We just can't do that from our porch in Iowa City.

Also visible from Kapa'a was a mountain called Sleeping Giant. Legends abound of Menehune, industrious little people credited with marvelous construction of ancient stonework and often mischievous feats. The existence of the Sleeping Giant is attributed to them. The little people threw stones in an effort to waken him, only to leave him entombed forever in the rocks, or so the story goes. Jim and I strolled the beach to a little cove, then rode more miles trying to reach our goal of bicycling every paved road on the island. This time we headed into Lihue Town and its residential areas, which strangely enough, reminded us of similar spots we'd seen last year in Valdez, Alaska, simple homes and yards.

⚲

Another cool morning, we cycled again to nearby Opaeka'a Falls, stopping first at a heiau, one of many lava rock temples constructed of stones brought up by hand from the river below. Built by ancient Hawaiians, their worship focused on soothing the gods, invoking war, peace, health, good fishing and farming, or increasing the population. This particular place was considered the birthplace and homeland of Kauai's royalty or ali'i. A kahuna/priest conducted religious ceremonies whose rituals disappeared when the traditional Hawaiian religious system was largely abandoned after Kamehameha the Great died in 1819 and the 1820 arrival of Christian missionaries.

From the bluff we looked down on the Wailua River and out to the Pacific Ocean. We glimpsed kayakers on the river and an occasional excursion boat plying its way to the famed Fern Grotto, once off-limits to all but Hawaiian royalty. Obviously, that rule no longer applied since Jim and I had visited it in 1970.

That afternoon Dick, Betty, Jim and I drove north to the Princeville area to check out the roads Jim and I would bike on our around-the island trip. Kilauea Lighthouse, a favorite sight, illuminated the north shore of Kauai. An adjacent cliff provided nesting and rest sites for red-footed boobies and albatross.

Pounding surf and Ke'e Beach with its spectacular view of Na'Pali and the ethereal Bali Hai enthralled us. No doubt that view helped convince the producers of *South Pacific* to choose this location for filming the movie.

Back at the condo, we saw lots of windsurfers waiting for just the right wave. We settled in to watch them and their skills, or lack thereof—human beings challenging nature. We would do that soon.

⚬⚬

On February first, our goals included climbing an extraordinarily steep hill, seeing more of the interior of the island, going to the Arboretum and biking as close to the shield volcano Waialeale as we could on our road bikes. The name means rippling or overflowing water, appropriate for a summit reputed to be the wettest place on earth. I can't fathom anywhere that has averaged more than four hundred fifty inches, about thirty-seven feet, of precipitation annually since 1912. A record amount of nearly fifty-six feet fell in 1982, about five stories tall. All that on top of 5,208 foot Mount Waialeale. Where's the ark?

Near the entry to the Arboretum, the Wailua River crossed the road then quickly flowed down the mountain to the sea. We pedaled easily through the water and then spotted what I thought was a lovely downhill into it. That made Jim leery. "We'd have to bike back up!" I convinced him I wanted to do it anyway and set off by myself. He followed and neither of us had difficulty going up or down, the colorful native Hawaiian flora making any effort worthwhile. As we returned to Kapa'a Sands, irrigated orange groves provided a striking contrast to the deep red volcanic soil.

⚬⚬

A pleasantly cool morning greeted us as we took our snorkeling gear to nearby Lydgate Beach. A rocked wall protected us from the surf and made it better for my early brand of snorkeling. The water was cooler than I like it so it took me forever to edge my way in, but I loved the fish. Another goal included a trip to Kapaia Stitchery to buy fabric for a quilt for Baby Whozit, Mara and Doug's second baby, due in the spring. I had made Ryan, the soon-to-be-older brother's quilt from fabric chosen on the Big Island. Jim chose an aqua hippo and fish print for one side and stars for the other—another fun project.

Back at the condo, in preparation for our multi-day ride, we hauled our bike boxes to Betty and Dick's lanai and packed our snorkel gear in the trunk of their rental car. We'd check out of Kapa'a Sands the next morning.

⚬⚬

We began our ride around the perimeter of Kauai on February 3 by cycling to the north part of the island. Iowa's -30 degree temperatures reminded us of how happiness can be revved up by warmth.

183

Great scenic views in every direction and low mileage clamored for us to stop frequently to savor such moments.

We tucked into an early lunch of veggie, sesame seeds, sunflower hearts and anise pizza at a bakery/pizza shop. A Farmer's Market caught our attention so we strolled through it on our way to visit Kilauea's 1935 lava rock church. Built with stone provided by The Kilauea Sugar Company on land deeded to them, the earthy tones softened the appearance of the little church. Brilliant reds and blues of the Mother and Child and Good Shepherd stained-glass windows gave light and life to the simple wood and plaster sanctuary. Gravestones snugged up alongside the building dated to more than a century ago.

Back on our bicycles, we turned in a more westerly direction into the wind. That meant hard pedaling toward Ke'e Beach, the end of the road on this side of the island. We cycled parallel to the coast, turquoise water reflecting the sunshine and bringing smiles to our faces.

As we had when we drove this route earlier that week, we paused at the Hanalei River Valley overlook to admire the geometry of the patchwork taro fields. A bucolic view we had seen on postcards. Just beyond a hairpin curve, we spotted brown furry looking blobs. What were they? With the pali/seaside cliffs in the background, we knew we weren't in one of the Great Plains States. What to our wondering eyes should appear but bison! We found out as more and more bison meat was eaten in the Islands, taro had become scarcer, losing not only acreage but importance, specifically in making poi, a traditional dietary mainstay.

Our frequent hunger had to be assuaged so we ate at the Tahiti Nui Café in Hanalei. No poi or bison for us, we capped off our cream of chicken vegetable soup with apple pie for Jim and banana cream for me. Downtown, we happened on a funeral at a Latter Day Saints Church. We heard the blowing of the conch shell and witnessed a large funeral procession accompanied by men holding aloft tall ceremonial cylinders of red and gold feathers.

Every sea view begged to be photographed and the sound of the sea transfixed us. We even stopped at Lumahai Beach where Mitzi Gaynor "washed that man right out of my hair…" in *South Pacific*. Many ups and downs later, Ke'e Beach came into sight. We baptized our back tires just as we've done at the beginning of every RAGBRAI. Carrying or wheeling our bikes over the soft sand is difficult, so we settled for a bottle of ocean water poured on them. This beach is the farthest point one can travel on the north side of Kauai except on foot. From here an eleven mile hiking Kalalau Trail extends to Polihale/Barking Sands Beach which we will reach in a few days, the long way around the island on our bikes.

We retraced our route to Hanalei where we immersed ourselves in the ambience of the mission-ary era buildings: The white with green-trimmed Mission House, built in 1841 and the moss green Gothic church, the oldest church building in Kauai, built in 1912. My memory flipped back to the film of Michener's *Hawaii* where I had first seen these structures.

Smell of the sea and sound of the booming surf on Kauai's coast

By 4 o'clock, we had settled into our Hanalei Bay Resort room, ready for cleanup and laundry to dry in the breeze. HBR kitties lounged nearby, but always ready to pounce on any rodent foolish enough to come near. The one who curled up on our lanai, according to his collar, was identified as *HBR Trouble*. Views, both mauka/toward the mountains, and makai/toward the sea, made us sigh with contentment. Soon we ate in the Bali Hai Restaurant, mahimahi with papaya salsa and macadamia nut rice pilaf, a wonderful conclusion to our forty-nine mile day.

Our short twenty-seven mile return to Kapa'a meant we could stay in bed longer to watch the moon set. The Na'Pali Coast and vivid blue sky portended an A-one day, complete with poi pancakes for Jim and macadamia nut waffles for me. Small rocky waterfalls, bright orange bougainvillea arches, rows of monkey pod trees, as well as a massive overwrought concrete fountain of a clam shell with Neptune popping out the top, melded into our memories of this stunning resort.

I wanted to bike down to Anini Bay, a wildly spectacular spot on the coast. Jim didn't relish the idea of the sharp climb back to the main road, but he came anyway. I love the intensity and powerful sound of the surf filling our ears. What fun to re-ride yesterday's route from the opposite direction.

At a viewpoint overlooking Kapa'a, we spoke with a volunteer with the Fish and Wildlife Service. She enthusiastically explained the behavior of spinner dolphins and breaching whales which could be seen from there, saying breaching could be a part of a courtship ritual.

When we arrived at our overnight we got ready for the beach where Dick and Betty waited for us. Jim played in the swells as we watched sea turtles surfing and a man successfully catching fish using a simple noose. After pizza and brownies, sunburned Jim declared he needed rest. He added he would wear SPF 50 sunscreen from then on.

Wind. The instant we hit the highway, we knew we would face forty-five miles of wind. Light traffic helped but we had to cycle carefully to not be buffeted into vehicles. We continued our clockwise circuit of the island, first to the south and then the west. We forged on, biking excruciating hills with no reprieve. We even had to pedal going downhill, something I detest.

Surely gravity should help us swoop down. Some people claim such efforts are character-building. Frankly, I thought my character was sufficient, at least for that day. I felt so weary when we broke for early lunch I didn't care if I ate at all, practically a first. I tried to force myself but ended up packing the food in my panniers, and flung my drooping body back on my bike.

More hills. Then, at last, an exhilarating downhill—and ahead of us, the sparkling Pacific Ocean! Coffee fields flanked us and we could hear rushing water in the irrigation ditches. We stopped for another lunch where Jim ordered food and drink and I finished my sandwich from earlier.

Feeling restored, we set off to Waimea to see the sights, among them Russian Fort Elizabeth, named after Tsar Alexander's wife. In 1815 a Russian-American cargo vessel shipwrecked in Kauai en route to Sitka, Alaska where it was to pick up furs for trade. Kauai's King Kaaumkalauii confiscated the ship and cargo. After many convoluted machinations, Russians designed and built a fort, but were expelled from Hawaii instead of getting the promised one-half of Oahu. Eventually, this fort was used for other purposes including wars among the Hawaiians, as burial grounds, and saluting royal birthdays with its cannons. Little remains of it but the stories.

Also in Waimea we saw one of the many monuments to British explorer Captain James Cook who had arrived in Kauai in 1778 and became the first European to begin formal contact with the Islands. He named the chain The Sandwich Islands after his patron, the Earl of Sandwich. This statue, featuring a sextant and rolled map in his hands, is a duplicate of one we had seen in Whitby, England where, as a teenager, Cook had become fascinated with the sea and sailing. Jim and I had now seen monuments honoring him in England, New Zealand, Australia, Alaska, the Big Island of Hawaii and Kauai, all places Cook had been. This quote exemplifies his passion for exploration:

Ambition leads me not only farther than any other man has been before me, but as far as I think it possible for man to go.

As we mused about the intrepid Captain Cook, we shook our heads in wonder at how much he accomplished and how far he had traveled before being killed on the Big Island at age fifty-two. We were reminded of humorist Tom Lehrer's comment: *It's sobering to think that by the time Mozart was my age, he'd been dead two years."* We were well past fifty-two and still had miles to go that day as we pedaled on in our own discovery tour of Kauai.

We spotted a corn field followed by Chinese then Japanese cemeteries and, at last, our Coral by the Sea B&B. Our hosts Sharon and Fred showed us a comfortable studio apartment, our home for the next two nights. In our conversation, we learned their son Bryan needed math help so I promised to tutor him that evening before bedtime. In thanks, Fred gave me three fact-filled Hawaiian coloring books he had collaborated in writing.

We had arrived early so Jim and I decided to bike on toward Polihale Beach, not knowing if we could ride the whole way on our bikes. What a bumpy, pitted and pot holed road. We met a young Canadian couple riding mountain bikes and carrying backpacks as they came out of the sugar cane fields. They exclaimed over the beauty of the beach so we decided to try it, biking four and a half miles through the fields. A mile or so later Jim muttered, "Our road bikes aren't designed for this kind of rough road. Watch out." I tried to ignore his doom and gloom.

The people who had given us directions to the beach had warned us, "Remember to take a right at the monkey-pod tree." We followed that advice as well as the traffic signs on these cane roads, but Jim persevered with his litany of potential problems. Finally, when he had said, "Oh Honey, I don't know…" for about the fifteenth time, we came upon a sign for the campgrounds. Yes! We could do it! Was Captain Cook rubbing off on me?

Our bikes stalled in the sand so we pushed them up a gigantic fifty-foot tall, three hundred-foot deep sand dune. We were rewarded with a dazzling scene of Napali Coast to our right, nothing but beach to our left, and heart-pounding surf straight ahead. We had hoped to stay a while but we needed to pedal ten miles into the wind to return to our B&B. Sunset at 6:30 provided enough time to get water from the ocean to baptize our bikes' front wheels just as we'd done with our back ones at Ke'e Beach two days ago. The sand, as the name Barking Sands Beach implies, barked as we walked across it. Strange, having a beach talk to us.

Dragging our bicycles, we clambered back up and down the dune. Mounting them, we bumped along the road, remembered to turn left this time at the monkey pod tree, right at the stop sign, walked our bikes over the bridges and finally headed back to the terminus of Kaumaulii Highway and home. We felt so good! The headwinds had not affected us as much as we had feared and the miles went quickly.

We rubbed sand off our arms and legs as well as we could, scrubbed our hands and cycled downtown to a shopping center to eat. We chose Goodie Barn's excellent veggie burger. Jim heartily approved of Grandma Lucinska's potato salad. The finale, island favorite Lappert's famous and rich ice cream. Blue Bunny afficiando Jim said it tasted good but Blue Bunny was still better. We told Teddy, Goodie Barn's owner, that our meal would surely get us up to Koke'e Lodge and beyond the next day. Menehune Market provided more fixin's for that trip up Waimea Canyon. Then home to shower, do laundry and a well-deserved sleep. But only after Bryan and I shared our fun tutoring session.

🚲

CRANKING KAUAI'S CANYONS

My hands gripped the handlebars and tested the brakes. They both seemed to work, hands and brakes. I heard Jim encouraging me, "C'mon! Let's go!"

I gulped, "I'm scared. I don't think I can even make it across the road without falling." No matter that we stood at the edge of what Mark Twain called *The Grand Canyon of the Pacific*, I wasn't registering beauty right then. Trying to keep body and soul undamaged and together kept me occupied.

I checked the road for traffic and assessed the dizzying hill we needed to ride down. On our way from the lookout at the top of Waimea Canyon, we had turned into this pull-off, ostensibly to rest our hands from constant braking. Our hands felt strained, but I wanted to stop because I feared going too fast and totally losing control of my bicycle.

I knew I needed to start riding. But my invisible guardian angel screeched in my ear, "What are you? Crazy?" *No! Just terrified of smashing myself all over the roadway!*

Jim and I had begun the day with high hopes. We planned to make the long-anticipated forty-two mile ride up the less steep Koke'e Road to the famed Kalalu Valley Lookout, then dive down cascading Waimea Canyon Drive. In addition to food, we packed our rain gear, plus tights and long-sleeved shirts for warmth, but we didn't haul our panniers with us.

The road remained flat for about a mile and then it climbed up-up-up. We took our time on this demanding uphill, took a break whenever we needed to rest, sometimes only for a few seconds, embraced the scenery, snacked and kept hydrated. The higher we climbed, the more frequently we heard a mysterious laughing sound from a bird. Was that an editorial comment from the avian world? Jim called back, "That's rude! After all, we are moving!" Later we learned the bird must have been a reclusive denizen of the upland forest, the laughing thrush, one we heard but never saw.

A cloud cover kept us from really suffering from heat, but we poured perspiration. Despite no respite in ten miles of climbing, a few undulations broke the monotony of a straight uphill slog, much to our relief. Patches of thick fog popped up, disappeared and popped up again, raising concerns about safety. Whenever it cleared, we regained hope. At the point where Koke'e Road and

Waimea Canyon Drive converged, the increase in the number of vehicles surprised us. Finally, we realized that NASA as well as other sections of the Pacific Missile Range Facility had a presence there.

Generally courteous drivers prevailed but one incident unnerved us. During our early picnic lunch, Jim and I sat on a lava rock bridge set back from the road. We thought we would be safe there, but a Swiss woman driving a rental car came way too close for our comfort. At supper that evening, we spoke briefly with her and her daughter at The Goodie Bar Restaurant. The daughter and I recognized each other, even without the startled looks on our faces from the close call. The woman appeared oblivious to our earlier near-meeting.

After catching only a fleeting glimpse of Waimea Canyon, we reached Koke'e Lodge. Eagerly, we ordered the Lodge's famed chili, remembered from being here in 1970, and even more famous cornbread. True comfort food. In the small Koke'e Museum, home-video footage of the terrible destruction of Hurricane Iniki in September 1992 provided an absorbing and sobering exhibit. Four years after the storm, reminders of the hurricane, damaged, nearly destroyed homes and businesses, now lay all over the island.

We didn't linger because we wanted to experience the iconic Kalalau Valley Lookout. We got on our bikes to ride three enormously arduous miles. I again experienced how hard it was to get my feet back into my toeclips once I had stopped on those inclines. The view from the 4,120 feet above sea level Lookout to the Na Pali Cliffs—beyond spectacular. The sapphire to turquoise ocean, its edges trimmed in lacy froths, contrasted with the four-fifths of a mile deep valley of green, gold, russet, and sienna cliffs. Changing light mesmerized us.

We glided back to the Lodge and then sailed and climbed the road to the intersection of Canyon and Koke'e Roads. Jim wanted to return the way we had come. "It's so foggy we won't be able to see anything of the canyon anyway."

"I'd rather go the other way, down Waimea Canyon Road. Let's flag down the next driver to see about the weather conditions." We did and he said the fog cleared in two-to-three hundred feet. It did!

We'd seen signs admonishing drivers to *Descend in Low Gear*. Simple in a car, much more difficult on a bike. We hit the brakes again and again and again. I fought the urge to drag my feet to slow my descent to sea level. "I'm glad we biked up Kokee Road. I'm not sure we could have made it up the Canyon Road," Jim volunteered. Our hands ached from the effort required to apply the brakes sufficiently to stop. Periodically we had to in order to cool our wheel rims and prevent blowouts. Distant fog and intermittent sunlight subdued the views in the canyon. Scudding clouds entertained us by playing against the surface of green and red canyon walls.

Back at the pull-off I stood still, trying to convince myself to get on my bike and back on the route. I took a deep breath, hung on for dear life, prayed, *God, help me get into my toeclips*, and

189

headed perpendicularly across the road. I hoped to gain control before plunging into the tremendous downhill sweep. Jim and I plummeted down and surged up most of the hills the rest of the way into Waimea Town.

Relief filled us as we cycled the sea level surface back to our B&B village of Kekaha. Jim said, "Let's not get cleaned up right now. We won't want to leave once we are home. Let's just go eat." After a fresh fish and salad supper, we biked to the beach to watch the sunset.

Away from ferocious waves and rip tides, I waded in to relax my hot, weary feet. The sunset, gold-trimmed with gray clouds, mellowed us before we pedaled back to our B&B. We had sweet and happy dreams.

🚲

Early in the morning of our last day of biking, we heard rain. We hoped to relax and wait it out until the storm passed. We bade Sharon thank you and goodbye and left before 9 AM. The headwinds we had anticipated did not materialize but Mother Nature soaked us. We retraced some of our route to Lihue except for a long hill which we avoided. We stopped at Kaumakani to trudge down a sticky, red dirt road to the West Kauai Methodist Church. Our friends Norm and Cynthia Zimmerman had been Volunteers in Mission there a couple of years earlier, helping to repair it after Iniki's damage. The church looked great.

Getting the red clay off our bikes required a lot of scraping. Just as we finished, I had a flat. Then I broke the stem on an inner tube. The usually patient Jim began to get a bit frustrated, but, true to his role as my hero mechanic, he came through and soon we pedaled away—through more rain.

We decided to stop at one of Lappert's ice cream stores. You know, when in doubt, have ice cream. Somehow we had heard that a woman who worked there had come from Salina, Kansas where we once lived. Unfortunately, she had already left work that day but as we turned to leave, who should appear but Mr. Lappert himself. He looked older than the photos on the billboards portrayed him but we recognized him, a local celebrity. That brief encounter helped us get through the next truly grueling miles, especially those near the Lihue Airport.

At last, thrilled and relieved, we saw the Kapa'a Sands sign We had truly biked Kauai! For all the red dirt grunge we wore on ourselves and our bikes, we looked like we had rolled in it.

🚲

Two days were left of our vacation to do some of the things we hadn't had time to do, such as photograph the colorful plants around the condo complex. We spent our last sunset time at the Ancient Hawaiian Salt Pond reminding us that the art of making salt continued to be practiced even today.

We received an unsettling phone call from Mara who asked if I could come to Colorado soon after we arrived home. Her blood pressure was very high and her obstetrician wanted her to rest as much as possible—not an easy feat with a two plus year old. Tania arranged a flight for me to go two days after we arrived home. A UPS person came to take our bike boxes so we didn't have the emotional hassle of taking them with us. Sometimes the cost for transporting our bikes on the plane went up twenty-five dollars per bike from the time we had arrived. Thinking of our red dirt condition, we purchased red dirt shirts for our Boulder family. My red dirt socks and shoes came gratis.

Jim and I had a marvelous experience in Kauai, both fun and quiet time with Betty and Dick, and meeting our goals of biking throughout this wonder-filled island. Time came for us to go home and for me to continue to Colorado for Grandma duty.

A month later, our grateful family welcomed a healthy Cameron Charles, born sooner than hoped despite Mara's bedrest. During the time we waited, soon-to-be-big-brother Ryan and I made Cameron's quilt, played games, took hikes, cooked, baked, read books, sang songs and just enjoyed life together. During the seventy-one days I spent with our Colorado family, I learned that even though I could bike all over mountainous Kauai, an energetic and enthusiastic two-going-on-three year old and a newborn with reflux problems could wear me right down to the ground. I slept for a week when I returned to Iowa.

Once I recovered, Jim and I planned our next bicycle ride, this one down the superb coast of Oregon.

jb

WESTWARD, HO TO OREGON! 1996

Riders: Jennifer/Bernd, Jim/Jan. Distance: 444 miles.

Bicycling from Canada to Mexico had long been a dream of ours; we knew it would probably take us four separate trips to complete the 1850 miles. The 450 mile Oregon Coast Bicycle Route became our goal for the summer of 1996. We'd already ridden across Washington from the Oregon border to Canada with Tania in 1983. Two more vacations after that would complete the California portion of the Pacific Coast Route.

When Jennifer and Bernd learned of the plan, they immediately said, "We'd like to come too!"

"You would? That would be fantastic!" The four of us had a memorable ride in the Loire Valley in France three years earlier.

First, we figured out the complicated logistics: Jennifer and Bernd wanted to sightsee and hike in Northern California before biking. I would drive our van from Iowa City with our four bicycles to meet them in Smith River, California, where we'd also end the bike ride. They would leave their car there and the three of us would drive to Portland to get Jim who'd worked a few more days. Clatskanie, on the Oregon side of the Columbia River, was our next stop, where we'd deposit the van and begin cycling back to Smith River.

Once we'd biked eight days, we'd load the bikes on the top of their car and return to Clatskanie to retrieve our van. Jim and I would take the bikes home in the van and Jennifer and Bernd would have a few more days of vacation. In the middle of all this traveling back and forth across Oregon, we would be lucky enough to visit friends in Corvallis, as well as Becki Saltzman, Jennifer's college roommate, and family in Portland.

My part of the journey began early Tuesday, June 2, 1996. By 6 AM I was ready to leave, off to follow I-80 and the Oregon Trail. Jim, the number-lover, took a photo of the odometer which read 2662. He thought that was a good sign for the journey. The morning sun vied with little streams of fog in the valleys and ravines while I listened to, among other books, *Into the Wild* by Jon Krakauer and William Least Heat-Moon's *Blue Highways*. The latter wrote of his odyssey traveling America's blue highways, the two-lane roads marked in blue on old road maps. His experiences driving the Oregon Coast and up the Columbia River whetted my appetite even more for our venture. He said he was going miles and miles, staying on these country roads through the boonies (I thought of Ruble, the now rickety school, store and house near my growing up home,) the easy to miss spots on the roads. Sounded just like what we do on our biking trips.

I loved my drive to Oregon, despite driving a high-profile vehicle in the wind. I had plenty of time to listen to books and contemplate life and how we live it. When I arrived in Smith River Jennifer and Bernd were ready to roll. I unpacked the bike rack which Bernd put on their car and, in the process, strained his back. He tried to get comfortable in the van while Jennifer drove and I scrunched in the back with Jim's bike as my companion. We arrived in Corvallis to visit Nancy Ashby, Seattle days friend and the last member of the Ashby clan we visited during our rides, and her husband Milt Plocher. As we talked we meandered the town's tree-lined streets, past English house gardens on our way to *Nearly Normal's Gonzo Food*, home of terrific vegetarian food. We exchanged family and friend news and life tales, shared photos, and later toured their kitchen garden complete with blueberries, currants and cherries.

Early the next morning, Nancy's blueberry muffins nourished our bodies and souls. Jennifer, Bernd and I hustled to Portland's airport to pick Jim up and were back on the road by mid-morning.

We decided to motor down the Washington side of the Columbia River to Longview where Jim and I had begun our cross-Washington bicycle trip in 1983. As we drove across the Lewis and Clark Bridge we recognized all the negatives we didn't want to face on bikes: hair-raising, fast-moving traffic; steep approach, and unnervingly narrow, debris-filled shoulders. That changed our plan to begin our ride in Longview. We scouted another route, mentally calculating the length and grade of the hills.

We drove the van as close to the Columbia River as we could for a ritual dipping of the tires marking the connection of the Washington and Oregon biking routes. We discovered we couldn't ride or carry them far enough over rocks and rough areas so had our photos taken with the Lewis and Clark Bridge in the background. Jennifer, Jim and I wheeled our bikes to the highway to begin riding. Bernd drove back to our motel and then cycled to meet us.

About river valleys: in order to get out of a valley or gorge, going up is mandated. And up we went. Bernd's first hill measured three times as long contrasted with our first hill, a 7 percent grade, mile and a half long climb following the Lewis and Clark Trail and the Oregon Bicycle Route. On the way up, we paused at an overlook and suddenly saw Mount St. Helens with the Bridge in the foreground. As we pedaled away, we resisted repeatedly checking our rearview mirrors just to see the panorama. *Pay attention to the road, Jan!*

A mishap occurred when ecology and economy-minded Jennifer spotted a roll of still-wrapped paper towels along the road and stopped to rescue it. As she got back on her bike, her toe slipped and she toppled over. Scraped knee and leg bruises later, she gamely clambered back on her bike and continued on her way, muttering, "Biking is not my strong suit." Two long steep hills punctuated those thirteen miles of US Highway 30. Despite his painful back, Bernd cycled both ways and claimed he got double the fun and exercise.

We returned to our Clatskanie motel, and spent an inordinate amount of time sorting and repacking the panniers. After dinner and a quick market stop, we went to bed thinking about what we might have forgotten that we'd need on the ride. We'd leave the van at the motel.

🚲

Bernd discovered the panniers he'd borrowed wouldn't fit on his bike rack. So he used Jim's old yellow Kirtlands we'd brought along, just in case. Jennifer found the panniers she'd borrowed wouldn't work on her rack without hitting her heels with every pedal revolution. So she tried the ones Bernd had initially planned to use. Success. Repack. *My questions: Shouldn't road bike racks be universally compatible? Shouldn't we have figured out the pannier-rack situation before we left home? I feel like we'd already had a full day just getting on the road!*

Combed clouds against vivid blue skies, just right temperatures and shade going up the longest, steepest hill made an auspicious beginning. We paralleled the Oregon side of the Columbia River and enjoyed the views throughout the valley. The pungent smells of Washington's paper mills did not reach us but we could see the mills and surrounding area clearly. Rows and rows of quick-growing hybrid cottonwoods flourished in close proximity to them. A sign informed us these trees, planted in 1989 would be harvested in eight years.

As we bicycled toward Astoria, hues from crisp spring green to the deep evergreen of Douglas fir, hemlock, spruce and pine trees made me wish I was a watercolorist. Tree-rimmed flat farm fields bordered the ever-widening river. As we climbed higher, hill after gloriously foxglove-covered hill painted the roadsides. With my fuchsia shirt, mulberry panniers, and raspberry Borthwick bicycle, I nearly disappeared in the flowers.

A sign, *Summit Clatsop Crest Elevation 656*, amused us. To the eye it didn't seem like much but to the body it was a different tale: we climbed, descended and climbed again to gain that elevation.

Just as he did each day, whenever we stopped, Bernd whipped out a deck of cards. He was hooked on Hearts and needed to keep his competitive spirit intact. We happily complied and sat at a guardrail along the highway. The flat tops of our back-racks and panniers provided adequate space for making peanut butter sandwiches and slicing fruit but proved awkward for a game of Hearts.

Winds swept in from the Pacific Ocean into the mouth of the Columbia and down the gorge, so we were aware that headwinds from Clatskanie to Astoria would likely be as persistent as the hills. Still, we knew we'd made the right choice to design our route to approach Astoria from the east. Cyclists who dared to come from the north on the Pacific Coast Bike Way, face the daunting task of biking the four mile Astoria-Megler Bridge. Frightening tales riders tell about nearly being wind-tossed off the bridge convinced us to not even consider it. Pacific? That hardly describes this vast ocean and its effects.

By early afternoon we arrived in Astoria, the oldest American settlement west of the Rockies, at the mouth of the delta-less Columbia River. John Jacob Astor started a fur trading post there in 1811, the genesis of becoming America's first multi-millionaire. We took only a cursory look before we crossed the two-plus-miles long bridge to Warrenton, relieved the wind had not been as bad as we had feared. Accounts of coastal fog obliterating all but the approach to the bridge had unnerved us. Anyone using it would have to have faith this was actually a bridge to somewhere, as opposed to nowhere, and that the other end of it had not fallen into the bay.

Bernd and Jennifer welcomed to Oregon Coast Trail

We had no further perils to face that day, such as shifting sandbars, since we had arrived by bike. All we needed to do was reflect on our forty-two mile ride, buy some juicy Rainier cherries, idle in the sun and play more Hearts as we waited to check into the Shiloh Inn.

While Jim, Jennifer and I swam then mellowed out in the spa, Bernd soaked his tender back in the tub. Jim insisted that Jennifer or I go back to the room to see if Bernd was out yet. He said it again with more force. When neither of us made a move in that direction, he exclaimed, "I was only thinking…" Before he could get another word out, Jennifer and I burst out singing, *I'm only thinking of him, I'm only thinking of him…* from *Man of La Mancha.* We exploded with laughter and Jim spluttered. Jim checked. Bernd was out. We cleaned ourselves and our clothes and ate an excellent fish dinner at Shiloh's, except for meat-loving Jennifer, concluding a happy and satisfying first day of our Oregon Coast venture.

🚲

The thirty mile ride from Warrenton to Manzanita began with cloudy skies, cool temperatures and flat roads. Our first stop—Seaside's fantastic oceanside aquarium was a blast. As we stood outside, we heard a terrible racket. Immediately, the teacher in me wanted parents to quiet their kids so they wouldn't scare the seals. I laughed as I realized those "kids" were the stars of the show, the Harbor seals.

Two newborns lived in a tank with other seals, all clamoring to be fed. Poppy, with incredible breath control sounded like a chainsaw. A twelve year old raised her flipper as if she were raising her hand, demanding, "Me! Me! Feed me!" Splasher Pup soaked Jennifer and me as we tried to throw fish to the other seals, particularly to the infants. Pup looked a person straight in the eye and, if she wasn't fed precisely when she wanted, flipped her flipper and shot water right in the slacker's face! Another seal repeatedly flapped on her chest to attract attention. Once we had thrown all our fish to them, they totally ignored us. Our drenched and fishy-smelly selves amplified the ruckus with our laughter. The rest of the small but memorable aquarium consisted primarily of Oregon coastal species such as giant King Crab and a spectacular twenty-ray starfish.

The End of the Trail Statue of Meriwether Lewis, William Clark and their ever-loyal Newfoundland dog Seaman provided another of Seaside's unexpected highlights. The statue commemorates the end of their epic eighteen month, four thousand mile journey from St. Louis, Missouri to the Oregon Coast from May, 1804 to November, 1805.

Somehow Sacajawea received no mention there and she was the person who led Lewis and Clark through treacherous territory, translated for them, all the while caring for her infant son and demanding husband. When she learned the expedition had been given whale blubber by beach Indians, she insisted she had to go see "the big fish" since she had traveled so far. That wasn't all she deserved but at least she got to do that.

On our way to Manzanita, we met three brothers ranging in age from fifteen to twenty-two, from Pittsburgh, Pennsylvania where Jennifer and Bernd once lived. Two weeks earlier they had begun biking in Vancouver, British Columbia. They planned to meet their parents in San Diego in four weeks. We wondered if they would make it. To their credit, they were at a laundromat, always a good thing for bicyclists. Bernd and the eldest brother exchanged Pennsylvania mountain biking tales and trails.

As we cycled that day we mused that Cannon Beach probably got its name because of some cannon. Exactly. In the 1800s, one washed ashore from the ship *Shark* as it attempted to exit the Columbia River and caught on the shoals. Cannon Beach's iconic Haystack Rock, a two hundred thirty-five foot sea stack, a column of rock eroded by wind and water, is a seabird nesting refuge. This spectacular monolith enticed us to take many photos from sundry angles. We stared silently, mesmerized by the subtleties of the emerald to cobalt to gray waters. From a higher vantage point, shifting misty light enhanced the far-reaching beach, and cirrus clouds wisped high above. Puffins, cormorants, and gulls dotted the sky.

Naturally we stopped at Hug Beach to hug and walk along the pounding surf of this coastal wonderland. Stagecoaches once used the beach as a road to get around the promontory. They'd had to hug the cliff to avoid being swept out to sea, yet sometimes needed to drive in the surf. Good grief.

As cyclists know, climbing hills often has unheralded rewards—if the hills don't make you breathless, the vistas might. From our viewpoint at a cliff top near Manzanita, the seacoast funneled into the distance and frothy breakers resembled cotton candy strung along the shore.

Our motel in Manzanita was spotless, and the owner wanted to keep it that way, so he brought in old shower curtains for us to put our bicycles on. The three fish-lovers ordered barbecue salmon for our evening meal. Then, knowing we'd have time for a game of Hearts, Bernd pulled out the cards. We'd just begun playing when the waitress came over and abruptly said, "You can't do that. It's illegal in Oregon to play cards in a restaurant." We stopped, shrugged our shoulders, "At least we still have the salmon to look forward to." That is, until we saw it. We had no idea it would be a slab of salmon covered with plain old barbecue sauce.

⚲

Our sixty-four miles from Manzanita to Pacific City started with breakfast in a folksy café where regulars have their own coffee mugs lined up on shelves. We even had time enough for an illegal game of Hearts while we waited for our food.

Our route took us inland on quiet roads, away from Highway 101. We swapped traffic noise for several long lung-blaster hills, one taking nearly an hour to climb. We relished the tranquil scenes of

Holstein cattle grazing in woods-edged pastures, acres and acres of foxglove covered hillsides, and viney coastal highlands. Far below, breakers pounded the shoreline.

Once we rolled back onto Highway 101, we headed to the Tillamook Cheese Factory. During our self-guided tour of production areas, we ambled along elevated walkways and watched cheese being made and packaged. Best of all, we got to sample the smooth flavors of Tillamook cheese. What we purchased didn't last long.

Down the road, a passing pickup with two teenagers riding in the back swerved toward Bernd and me and yelled. We didn't feel too threatened. However, by the time they drove by Jim and Jennifer, they veered close to them and yelled, "Look out!" Jennifer memorized their Oregon license number plus a description of the vehicle and people which she wrote down and reported to the Sheriff's Department after we got to our motel. We don't know what, if anything, happened to them. We hope they were at least stopped and informed that bicyclists have legal rights to ride on most public roads and should not be harassed.

As we approached Pacific City, we encountered sand dunes encroaching on the highway. The fine blown sand made riding on the shoulder of the highway risky. The Inn at Pacific City, advertised that it catered to bicyclists. The owner made an excellent recommendation of where to eat. Bernd and I ordered sole almandine with mushrooms that literally melted in our mouths. After our arduous day and such a wonderful meal, we were all happy for sleep.

۶

By the next morning, Jennifer and Bernd had decided to advise the owner he needed to cater in a new mattress.

According to my journal, our July 3 fifty-six mile ride to Newport, was *another tough day—some beautiful off-US 101 routes.* Red clay, clear-cut slopes intermingled with glades which Jennifer described as "deep, dank, dark forest." The Sitka spruce, Douglas fir, Oregon grape, and vine maples entangled so thickly we could not see through them. Branches hanging within mere inches of our heads reminded me of the scary Winged Monkey Forest in the *Wizard of Oz.* But we escaped on our bicycles and cascaded to the main highway and the coastline.

Gazing ahead at a threatening sky, we dismounted as we approached the cape that Captain Cook had dubbed *Foulweather*, and grabbed our foul weather gear to fend off the rain, rising wind and dropping temperature. We had no doubt Captain Cook's first landfall on this coast had been in the midst of just such a bleak and blustery day in 1778. From our cliff top vantage point, we viewed what he could not, the ocean below roiling toward the bluffs, cutting into the mainland. Skinny headlands, houses precariously clinging to bluffs, all appeared as if any violent gale or drencher would wash them away. Yaquina Head Lighthouse stood proudly in the distance. Wind flapped at our Gore-tex jackets, chilling us as we swayed and braced ourselves against the gusts.

Because the next day was the Fourth of July, the traffic picked up tremendously by noon. Six miles from Lincoln City, it worsened, backed up by casino traffic. Most drivers drove considerately, we often went the same speed—slowly. One man at the wheel of a red pickup, Oregon vanity plate *PAPA*, repeatedly cut me off by drifting into the marked bicycle lane. I squelched the urge to rip his outside mirror off, turn it to him and explain, quietly and diplomatically of course, what the mirror was for. Perhaps PAPA needed a new license plate. MENACE came to mind.

It felt really good to arrive safely at the West Wind Motel, get off the bike, and relax in the spa. We chuckled at the motel's name. After all, we had just read the sign at Cape Foulweather: *P.S. Winds 100 MPH at this location are not unusual.* We believed the sign.

Happy Independence Day! That sentiment seemed appropriate for long distance riders. We exercised our independence that day by not relying on any vehicle except our bicycles, and the power came from our legs. What a great way to celebrate the Fourth of July.

Hallmarks of our ride from Newport to Florence, all fifty-one miles of it on US Highway 101, included tailwinds and hills. Traffic hassles disappeared and a smooth road surface soothed our bodies and spirits. Between Newport and Coos Bay, nearly one hundred miles away, incredible views awed us. In some places the mountains squeezed so close to the sea, the highway wound upward a thousand feet or more, crossing misty headlands. Seals, sea-lions and marvelous sea otters cluttered the air with their barks, evoking all sorts of sea dreams and memories in our heads.

In Seaside, Tillamook and all along the Oregon coast, we had been treated to pedaling across Conde McCullough's beautifully designed bridges. McCullough, head of Oregon's State Highway Department in the 1920s and '30s, creatively incorporated Art Deco and Gothic-inspired balustrades within the design of his bridges, his artistic and unique style delighted us. Many of his signature bridges, some up to fifty-four feet long, grace both blue and major highways. He also designed and built bridges for then newly-developing Pan-American Highway in Central and South America.

We four Iowans appreciated the fact that McCullough had been raised and educated in Iowa, and earned a degree in civil engineering from Iowa State College, now Iowa State University. We applauded his solutions to crossing bays, rivers and inlets, but our immediate concern was a solution to Bernd's tire problem. Ever since he'd had his first flat, we had searched for a new tire. At last, we found a real bike shop open for business in Waldport. We had checked in every town between Seaside and there, but all the shops listed in telephone directories and Bikecentennial information had closed. Unless you owned a mountain bike and could buy parts at Coast to Coast or Walmart, "Tant pis pour toi!" Too bad for you, as French teacher Jennifer would say.

We hit the jackpot with this owner and shop. He not only had the tire Bernd's bike required, he also provided valuable information regarding roads, tunnels, scenic viewpoints and traffic. He informed us, "Eleven thousand bicyclists stopped at my shop last year." Most of them, like our family, followed the Oregon Coast Bike Route or the Bikecentennial Route which vary slightly from each other.

Another biker at the store warned us about a biking panhandler Jeff who told a sad story of being robbed and now tried to connect with friends. His personable manner had convinced others to give him rather large sums of money. Our informant said we would recognize him by his long, dark hair. We welcomed the tip. It would be easy to be taken in by another cyclist if the story sounded plausible. We didn't see him that day.

I could hear the Waldport Bakery calling Bernd's and my names—we answered the call. The buttery pastries tasted terrific. We met friendly locals there, one of whom asked me if I could read a foreign language. I told him I couldn't but our daughter taught French and both she and her husband spoke and read German. He said someone had given him a package of instant rice and he could read neither German, French nor Italian. I sent him to the bike shop. With a smile, Bernd translated the simple directions for him.

A *Keep Our Parks Open* sign emblazoned on a bright yellow sheet attracted our attention. The sign referenced lost jobs, no open beaches, *tourism, businesses and children will suffer. YOU can help*. On the reverse side was a list of elected local, state and national officials to contact to ask that they *take action to make sure these Coastal Parks are not closed*. We don't know whether any of the parks closed in Oregon, although they did in California. The usually well-kept Oregon Coast Parks restroom facilities were among our favorite stopping spots.

Some state parks were in jeopardy because the cost of keeping them open, clean, and in good repair continued to rise. One idea put forth suggested keeping some parks open but with no parking (Right, a park with no parking) no rest rooms, and no picnic tables. In other words, no amenities. Those that would be kept full service would cater to RVs and their owners. It seemed inconvenience to day trippers could be easily overlooked. A few bicycle campers told us the campgrounds might be lovely in many ways, but tent areas were often near the RV dumping stations. Money talks, even in state parks. Those who have, have more and those who haven't, have even less.

We traveled on, spotted enticing tide pools and decided to stop for picnic and tide pool fun. The sea stars and sea urchins' vivid rosy colors made them easy to see. We didn't think they measured up to those at Point Lobos, California, our family's tide pool benchmark. But it was good to get off the bikes, stretch our legs and get close-up views of nature's miracles.

Back on the road, the wind picked up and buffeted us a bit although it mostly blew at our backs. The coastline's jagged rocks jutted out to sea and the road marched up and down providing postcard caliber views. Lighthouses perched on promontories and pounding surf added drama.

We arrived in Florence and to our dismay, discovered the motel washer didn't work. We did laundry the old-fashioned way, minus the washboard. Another treat is to dry our clothes complete-ly, in a dryer, without having to use a hair dryer. "A hair dryer?" queried Jennifer when we packed for the trip. "Why is Dad taking a hair dryer?" I explained it wasn't for hair but for drying the thick padding in biking shorts, or shoes, or at least warming them up before we put the damp ones on.

⚲

Breakfast at the Bridgewater Café in Old Town Florence became our first stop of the day. To no one's surprise, bridge architect extraordinaire Conde McCullough had designed the two-arched bridge the café overlooked. Four fat, clunky-looking pillars between the arches surprised us. I thought four other slender obelisks helped salvage the bridge's aesthetics.

Jennifer's hands still felt sore. A Coast-to-Coast Store in town sold what the bike shop owner had suggested using, black closed-foam pipe insulation. This solution cost only eighty-nine cents instead of the fifteen dollars needed to buy those especially designed for handlebars. Our favorite repair people did their job. Jennifer reported the soft, cushy handlebars made her hands feel better as we headed out into the clear, cold and, surprise, surprise, windy day.

The wind continued to clobber us throughout the day. Our goal, Charleston, was less than sixty miles away so we dawdled and even napped in a park in the middle of the day. Jennifer slept so soundly she said she began to dream. I propped my bicycle against a tree; it blew over, a portent of even more wind on the road. Lily ponds backdropped by the Oregon Dunes lured us to go farther into them for our picnic lunch, served with sand blown into our appropriately named sandwiches.

At North Bend, our route took us across a 5,305 foot long McCullough Bridge. This spectacular cantilevered bridge spanning Coos Bay could be scary anytime for bikers, but especially in the wind. Bernd had biked ahead of us and, because of his strength and biking skills, was able to keep up with traffic. Badly placed bridge signs informed us it was illegal for bicyclists to impede traffic. Readable only after we were on the bridge, the second sign said if we were using the sidewalk, we must walk our bikes. Had I been so foolish as to ride the bridge instead of walking it, I definitely would be frightened. With our heads down, it took fifteen minutes to struggle with a loaded bike to the other side of the bay fighting the powerful gusts. By the time we caught up to Bernd, he had eaten his ice cream cone and had time to relax.

As long as the wind remained at our backs in North Bend, biking went well. I found it impossible to keep the bike going straight after we turned west, and the crosswind walloped us. I finally dismounted and wobble-wheeled my bike the last few blocks until we headed south again. A few miles later, Bernd got another flat. Jennifer and I, both stellar mechanics, decided to let Bernd and Jim male bond over it. She and I just moseyed on down the road.

When the guys caught up, all four of us left Highway 101 to pursue a true-blue highway to Charleston, a pretty little fishing village turned tourist destination. Three of us oohed and aahed over Portside Restaurant's fresh seafood from the Pacific, *delivered daily by the finest local fishing fleet of Charleston Harbor*. Viewing the bay from our table enhanced the flavor.

The following clear, crisp Pacific coast morning, with Port Orford fifty-five miles away, we began riding the hills of Seven Devils Road. We assumed the seven devils alluded to the most precipitous, challenging ones, but we counted some lesser ones we deemed demons—and named them pride, sloth, greed, envy and such. Fortunately, the road carried little traffic so we thought we chose well. We noted disconcerting information, lots of logging and clear-cutting, as well as evidence of forest fires, with no attempt at reforestation.

Another windswept beach view emphasized our early morning—we thought we'd had wind. By late morning, we had *WIND*! Picnic time in the lee of some sea-grassed sand dunes— once again, we had sandwiches, emphasis on sand. The weather was too blustery to attempt to climb down a huge dune to the beach.

Later, we stopped to get Ben and Jerry's ice cream bars. When I looked at the nutritional information, I realized why I had never had one before and would never have one again. Unless I was riding my bicycle a long distance and there happened to be a roadside store that sold Ben and Jerry's ice cream and if we just happened to stop and I saw it, that is. Ambrosial!

We blew into Port Orford to our Home by the Sea B&B by mid-afternoon. Located on a small peninsula, it overlooked a quiet beach and bay. Our host Alan, a loquacious pleasant soul, took photos of us and made sure we could recognize the ubiquitous poison oak before he allowed us to shower and go out to explore the town.

Deciding where to eat can be an uncertain science, but we had no difficulty choosing where we wanted to go that evening, we just needed to read its moniker, *The Truculent Oyster and Peg Leg Saloon*. Alan approved our choice.

The more we learned about Port Orford, the fonder we became of it. While Astoria claimed the distinction of being the oldest American settlement west of the Mississippi, Port Orford boasted the title of earliest incorporated town on the Oregon Coast (1859) as well as the westernmost incorporated town in the contiguous United States. It developed into an art colony and was the only dry dock and best natural summer harbor between San Francisco and Puget Sound. Of importance to sailors, no dangerous sandbar crossings either.

After supper we strolled the beach and watched the offshore rocks, breeding sites for thousands of marine mammals and birds. Depending on the season, puffins, harbor seals, California grey whales in migration and more can be seen. Bernd's eyes lit up when he heard that windsurfing was excellent too, but we had no time for another of his favorite sports on this dedicated biking trip.

Back at the B&B, Jennifer and I accepted Alan's invitation to see the working port, home of one of the last wooden piers for commercial fishing on the west coast. As we walked under the pier, a seemingly vast forest of huge, barkless trees, I put my arms around one of the beams and could barely overlap my hands.

Well-informed Alan shared his ideas about a number of topics. Regarding fishing in the area, he theorized it was a dying way of life but people who fish were not yet willing to accept that. He thought they hoped the government or someone else "out there" would come to their rescue and pointed out a fishing boat owned by a father, son and daughter, the second and third generations who had never worked for anyone but the family operation. Alan showed us impressive piles of traps, nets, buoys to help us understand at least one aspect of the local economy. We stayed to talk with him until the stars came out.

I told Jim I would have liked to continue staying at the Home on the Sea to just read, relax, and enjoy the views. No chance of that. We had miles to pedal.

⚲

We awakened to a magnificent day with a panoramic view of the lovely bay. I went out to take photos of it and the pier in early morning light. For breakfast we ate waffles, organic strawberries (grapes for allergic Jennifer) and bananas, plus Alan's considerable conversation. According to Alan, another point of interest harkened back to World War II. The town was the only place in the continental United States where the Japanese torpedoed a ship. A Japanese man involved in the bombardment eventually returned to Port Orford several times, welcomed as a friend. Bombs had been dropped other places in Oregon and some previously unexploded ones killed a woman and children near Brookings, a town we'd pass through later in the day.

Alan snapped more pictures of us with the background of the bay and its rocks. They would become cherished photos.

Our last day of bicycling—sixty-six miles to the Oregon-California border plus thirteen more to Smith River and the car. The trip total, about 444 miles across this, Jim's and my thirty-first state.

A coastal mountain's name Humbug resulted from a hoaxer telling locals there were treasures to be found near it. Gullible folks hotfooted it to seek their fortunes, got lost, and spent lots of time climbing trees trying to find a geographic point of reference. At last, they spotted the mountain, searched for the treasure, gave up and dubbed it and their quest *Humbug*. They did manage to return to Port Orford. I'll bet they were plenty irritated at having been snookered.

Startlingly, instead of the prevailing northerlies, we had headwinds. As Bernd put it, "This is our longest, hilliest day and we're getting headwinds." Fortunately, it changed direction so we didn't have to face it all day, but still made the ride more taxing.

Nearby small coastal valleys protected from fierce winter sea winds have developed temperate zone rain forests. We found them curious, especially since we had lived near one such tiny pocket in Seattle. But here the Prehistoric Gardens tourist attraction had been created, populated by replicas of "lost world" creatures, such as dinosaurs. More than a bit kitschy but we enjoyed it, especially the vegetation. Huge tree ferns seemed right out of *Jurassic Park*.

Although models of the creatures did not attain the realism of those we see in exhibits now, these were started years ago and reflected the available information then. Seeing a dinosaur poking its head out through old giant evergreens amused us. One sign indicated Annual Rainfall in This Area: minimum rainfall in 1930 of just over four feet; maximum in 1953 of ten feet; average over six and a half feet with January being the wettest month. Another sign located the site of a moonshiner's hideout in the 1920s, well-concealed by the lush flora. Fun biking break for us.

Challenging uphills are one thing but tough downhills are quite another. As we zoomed down a long, steep curving grade, we veered toward the coast and emerged from the lee of a hill. A heavy-duty cross-current from the sea blasted us. I gasped with fear and pleaded, *Oh no! Keep the bike on the road!* I clutched the brakes and braced my body so my bike and I wouldn't be swept into the oncoming traffic or off the road. *Whew! Thank you, God!* My fright dissolved after I caught my breath and planted my feet safely on terra firma.

Portions of the roadway marked *Sunken Grade* had been repaired but remained sticky with tar or had collapsed, another concern. Alan had told us the natural settling of the earth along the Oregon coast required constant vigilance and repair by the Oregon Department of Transportation. We saw visual proof.

Part way up the next climb, Jennifer paused to pick up a moveable plastic GI Joe soldier figure dressed in camouflage. She glanced at his physique and, using her gruffest voice and sternest look, dubbed him *Manly Man* and tucked him into her back pocket. To our delight, when some bicyclists heading north stopped to chat, they saw him and said, "Oh you have Sergeant Slaughter." She growled, "Oh no! This is Manly Man." Eventually, our whole family knew him as Manly Man.* He continued to ride along, peering bravely of course, out of Jennifer's biking jersey the rest of the trip. From that time on, he traveled wherever Jennifer and Bernd did.

Way back at the bike shop in Waldport, we'd been warned about panhandler biker Jeff. At a scenic viewpoint in southern Oregon we came upon him as he spoke to a woman. He called out to me, "You've almost caught up with them! They just went by!" meaning Jennifer and Bernd. It took me a moment to realize who he was, using the ploy of acting as though he knew me. When I reached Jennifer and Bernd, they had also decided he was Jeff.

One reason we like riding some well-known bicycling routes is we see other long-distance cyclists, most very unlike freeloader Jeff. That last day of cycling, we talked to a young solo rider from Seattle, heading to visit his brother in San Francisco. He planned to take Amtrak back home. Then we spotted the couple from Anchorage whom we'd met after we left Clatskanie on day one.

A lone rider from Quebec occasionally appeared along the way. His dream since his teen-age years had been to ride to California and had hoped this would be the year. He said, "I plan to continue riding to Mexico but I'm getting tired. I might decide to stop sooner." He paused, thought a moment and added, "My wife and teenaged kids fully support me, but I don't know if I can go on. I really miss them." Knowing he had a sympathetic audience, he continued, "Unfortunately, there were a lot of things I didn't know when I started that have made the trip harder. I thought the panniers would keep my clothes dry. I didn't know I should put all my clothes and gear in plastic bags before putting them in my panniers. It took me three days to get everything dried out after the first rainy day." We invited him to ride with us the remainder of the day but he told us he needed to rest longer. We felt sad for him but left, and once again talked about how depressing it could be to ride alone so far and not be able to share the experience with someone else.

Many riders we met had not decided how they would return home but few wanted to ride north against the prevailing wind. An occasional cyclist did, but they rarely stopped to talk to us. They had our sympathy and we were grateful we'd ridden the other direction. Nearly all the bicyclists we met and talked to left indelible impressions on us. We believed we shared a kinship with them in our common goal of biking long distances in a sometimes harsh but spectacular land.

Later that morning, after crossing Gold Beach's impressive McCullough-designed bridge, we caught up with Bernd. He grinned and said, "You guys are getting a lot stronger." I wondered aloud how he knew. Jennifer explained, "At the beginning of the trip he was able to buy and eat his ice cream goodies before we caught up with him. Now, he can't get rid of the evidence, the wrappers, before we arrive." Oh, sly Bernd.

During our beyond breezy lunchtime, we tucked in behind a rock and seagrass to eat unsandy sandwiches we'd bought in Gold Beach. Then back to the task of hot weather hill-climbing.

At our afternoon rest stop, we lined our bikes up by the curb. Jennifer's bike blew over. I thought that was symbolic of the week. Among all the things Jennifer was, she was not an enthusiastic bicyclist. Early in the trip she told me, "I'm not riding because I love bicycling so much. I'm riding because I want to be with you and Dad." That brought tears to my eyes. The four of us being together had made the whole trip incredibly special.

Through hard work, we earned every vista of the Klamath Mountains and Pacific Ocean that day—stacked rocks poking their heads through the pounding surf, precipitous drop-offs to the sea, arches rising from the seabed. Everywhere we looked, we felt awed at the views that greeted us. How could there be so much beauty along this coastline? Sadly, we'd leave it the following day.

Finally we arrived at Brookings and Harbor, the last towns before reaching the California border. They are situated in a unique climate zone referred to as *Oregon's Banana Belt*. Mild to warm temperatures occur any month of the year due largely to its location on the Pacific Ocean at the foot of the Klamath Mountains. Winds compress and warm the air flowing onto the town, sort of like the Santa Ana winds of Southern California. This mild weather is also responsible for the ability to grow acres and acres of Easter lilies here as well as in Smith River, California. Ninety percent of the lilies sold at Easter are produced in these two areas resulting in each town disputing the other's claim of the title *World Capital of Easter Lilies*. We rode past those very lily fields, now just foliage because the blossoms were long gone, and into Smith River, the official end of our bicycling trip across impressive Oregon on its Pacific Coastal Road.

At our motel, we cleaned up and, in Jennifer and Bernd's car, drove to the nearby Jedediah Smith Redwood Park and Stout Grove area. Jennifer crowed, "WHEE!! Look at how easy these hills are!" We strolled through shimmering green, relishing not being on our bikes, living in the moment. Soon we would be thinking about our next adventure, but today we reflected on and rejoiced in the one we had just completed. It was good. Very, very good.

Dedicated to the ever-present memory of our greatly loved Jennifer and Bernd.
Born 4-20-1965 in Iowa City, Iowa and 4-20-1962 in Munich, Germany.
Died together 8-6-2001 in a white-water rafting tragedy on the
Arkansas River near Buena Vista, Colorado
We cherish them, who they were and all the beautiful memories they helped create
for so many people.

*Manly Man has continued to travel with members of our family, primarily Tania, all over the world.

ARKANSAS-1997

Riders: Betty, Sandy/Dave, Jim/Jan. Distance: 205 miles

Excitement and anxiety mixed as our biking crew planned our spring break ride across Arkansas. Several years had passed since Betty had been able to ride with us, ever since she had been diagnosed with aplastic anemia, a severe life-threatening blood disease which curtailed every aspect of her life. She had been very ill but after extensive treatment and many prayers, had been declared free of the disease. We all rejoiced at her recovery—our miracle friend would ride again.

Bikes hung on the van's bike rack as we headed off to the wilds of Texarkana, a town straddling the border of Texas and Arkansas. After off-loading the bikes, gear and their three female companions, Jim and Dave drove our van and a rented-in-Texarkana car to McGehee, a town near the Mississippi River, the endpoint of our bike ride. They returned in the rental and dropped it off. Already they had crossed Arkansas twice on this Palm Sunday.

While Jim and Dave did the car-van swap, Sandy, Betty and I didn't venture far into Texarkana, Texas but strolled the streets of its twin Texarkana, Arkansas. Pulitzer Prize-winning Ragtime composer/musician Scott Joplin had grown up here. A striking mural including a portrait of him with his hands on a piano keyboard, snatches of his music, covers of his most familiar songs, and a sash with *American Composer* emblazoned on it spanned a city block wall. Joplin's composition *The Entertainer*, made famous by the film *The Sting* immediately popped into my mind and stayed there the rest of the day.

On State Line Avenue, we circled the Confederate Memorial dedicated in 1918, which featured a soldier facing north above the statue of a Confederate mother. The inscription on the soldier's base reads: *To our loyal Confederates.* On the mother's base: *O Great Confederate Mothers, we would print your names on monuments, that men may read them as the years go by and tribute pay to you, who bore and nurtured sons and gave them solace on that darkest hour, when they came home with broken swords and guns.* (This statue, like many others, has become a point of controversy about whether it represents heritage or hate. Note the dedication date.)

🚲

Our usual first day photo had a slight twist: Downtown, again on State Line Avenue, Betty, Sandy and I stood with our bikes beneath a sign labeled Texarkana with an outline of Texas map on the reverse side. Dave stood under a similar map of Arkansas on the other. Just out of town, we received our official greeting on another sign: *Welcome to Arkansas, The Natural State, Home of President Bill Clinton.*

On this rolling hills day, we headed east on our bikes to Magnolia, crossing the wide Red River on country roads lined with pines, the state tree, as well as hickory, maple and oak trees. The pines are part of the great eastern pine forest which extend into the southern half of the state.

We began to spot what we would continue to see in great numbers, not migrating birds, although this area is part of the Great Mississippi River Flyway. Walmart, headquartered in Bentonville, Arkansas, had tentacles reaching everywhere in the US, Canada, Mexico, and even China at that time. We would not go a day without seeing the Walmart name, particularly on trucks.

Our day's destination was named for a staple in Southern gardens, the magnolia. We arrived too early in the season to see their glorious blooms lining the Courthouse square but instead delighted in the vivid yellow of daffodils. Magnolia had been the largest oil producing field in volume in the United States during World War II. A seven-part mural in the historic center of town depicts various aspects of work in the Magnolia Oil Fields in 1938. Originally though, the town had been founded as a cotton, farm produce and marketing town. Because we saw paper companies along the way, we knew lumbering was still prevalent.

🚲

The following day the weather turned chillier, overcast and with a touch of wind. We all worried about long hills and watched Betty for sign of fatigue. Shortly after lunch, through tears, she stopped and said, "I can't go on. You go on." Through our own tears, we discussed what we should do. We decided to rent a car to get Betty to our night's lodging.

Feeling overwhelmingly sad, we left her at a secure and warm restaurant and rode as fast as we could to our motel in El Dorado. Jim and Dave rented another car, rescued Betty, brought her to the motel, then drove back to McGehee to pick up our van. They returned to town with both vehicles thereby crossing Arkansas two more times, four times so far, and returned the rental car. El Dorado had been the heart of the 1920s oil bonanza in Southern Arkansas and became known as Arkansas' original boomtown, so Magnolia wasn't the only town affected by oil.

🚲

Betty volunteered to be the designated driver, an emotionally difficult position for anyone who really wanted to be bicycling. Despite this frustrating setback, she put on her sunny face and did what she had to do for the duration of this trip. The rest of us knew she would be determined to work hard so she could ride again in the future. We continued cycling while Betty found nooks and crannies, little specialty stores, museums and other interesting sights. And she read from the stash of books we'd stowed in the van.

Jim had booked us into what promised to be lovely Colvin B&B in Warren. The grey with white trim bungalow surrounded by a white picket fence certainly had curb appeal. A gorgeous dried flower wreath on the front door welcomed us. Betty, Jim and I were settling into our rooms when we heard a slight commotion and went out to find Sandy leaving the house, struggling to breathe. She is very allergic to dried eucalyptus, a major component not only in the front door wreath, but also in dried sconces hanging over their bed and near our door. We feared she wouldn't be able to stay in the house but she and Dave removed the sconces and opened the window to air out the room. She spent the night in the room but never felt comfortable.

Our Maundy Thursday ride took us from Warren to our McGehee B&B. The terrain flattened the closer we came to the Mississippi River, and we saw more and more of Arkansas' rice fields. Dave commented several times how surprised he was at their number and expanse. The state often leads the United States in production of rice. Rice producers there owe thanks to a Nebraskan who saw rice-growing potential in Arkansas after a hunting trip to Louisiana in the early 1900s, where he'd seen lots of rice growing.

We had concerns about the level of the Mississippi River even as we planned this trip. The longer it took us to ride to the river, the higher the water would be from melting snow and rains upriver. We had lots of daylight left so continued our ride from Warren all the way to the river, instead of stopping first in McGehee. We rode the last miles on a lonely two-track, rough-riding road on the levee.

The river had reached flood stage surrounding a little ranch-style house sitting on a newly formed island. In the distance, we saw a sizable tug pushing three barges down the river, we imagined to New Orleans. As we stood transfixed by the flow of water, we silently reflected on our quick 205 mile ride. It seemed we kind of heaved the sigh of, "Is it all over already?" then loaded the bikes on the van to return to McGehee.

Our accommodations at the Evans House B&B Inn, an English Tudor-style brick house, surrounded by brilliant fuchsia azaleas, included just one part of the B&B: the bedrooms, baths, kitchen and breakfast area. Being prohibited from going to the other section made sense since it accommodated a funeral home, a first for us. We found humor in our beds being normal beds, not leftover caskets, and most of us slept well. Unlike most other B&Bs, our hosts did not stay there so we prepared our own breakfast from supplies they left for us.

Good Friday we bundled ourselves back into the van to drive to Fairfield Bay, a popular retirement area in northern Arkansas where our good friends Petra and Dick Meraz lived and owned a gift store, The Apple Collection.

On our way, we crossed the now familiar bridge where Jim and Dave exclaimed in unison, "Eight!"

"Eight?"

"This is the eighth time we have crossed this bridge since we came to Arkansas last Saturday. Once on the way from Texarkana to McGehee and again on the way back. Once more when we took the second rental car to pick up the van and then on the way back. We biked across it yesterday then went over it twice while we hunted for someplace to eat. This time makes eight." That's a first in our bike trip statistics. Another first was Arkansas' place as state number thirty-two for Jim and me.

After a delightful visit with Petra and Dick, we headed north to Iowa City. We managed a stop at "Home of Throwed Rolls," Lambert's Café in Sikeston, Missouri where the servers throw rolls at/ to customers, so everyone needs to stay alert. The rolls tasted pretty good.

After a long day of driving, we arrived in Iowa City. We would spend Easter Sunday at home.

SOUTH DAKOTA-LAND OF GREAT SPACES-1997

Riders: Jim/Jan. Drop off: Betty. Distance: 454 miles

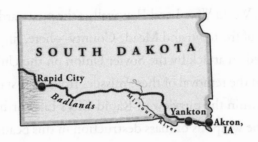

Logistics would be a problem for us no matter where Jim and I bicycled that autumn. We seriously contemplated bicycling across Nevada but decided not to when we couldn't figure out how to return to the van once we'd finished biking.

"How about South Dakota?" Jim queried. That had promise although how to do it would still need copious contemplation. After consulting with friend Betty, we came up with a solution using one van, one car and her help. Why the consultation with Betty? She would be caring for three of her grandchildren in Rapid City and would be able to drop us and our bikes off at the Wyoming border. The van would stay in Rapid City for its vacation.

It worked. We had a fun evening with Betty, David, Catie and Nick, and early the next morning the six of us headed for the Wyoming-South Dakota border. Betty had been one of our biking buddies for years making it hard to say goodbye and know that she would not be joining us—even for the first day.

She snapped our photos, then a brisk and lively westerly tailwind quickly swept Jim and me away. From the old road we traveled, the sound of I-90 was barely perceptible. A border of fall wildflowers with red Indian paintbrush and grass of gold to auburn to umber warmed the outlines of rugged rocks. A perfect start to another ride!

With apologies to unhatched chickens, "Don't count your miles before they're biked," became a dead-on adage for me that day. I foolishly calculated about how long it would take us to breeze to the corner where we would turn south into Rapid City. I figured we'd spend another leisurely evening with Betty and the children. "Ha!" countered Mother Nature. We'd gone only a few miles when pedaling started to get harder. Sure enough the wind switched and became a northerly sidewind. *Oh well, that won't be too bad since we'll be angling in a southeasterly direction soon anyway.* The farther we cycled the more it continued to change direction eventually coming out of the northeast then firmly blowing from the east, quartering into our faces. *Recalculate, Jan.*

We reached the town of Sturgis, home of the great motorcycle rally, which made a welcome food and rest stop for our windblown selves. Looming Bear Butte formed a dramatic backdrop for the town, as it had in the past for Fort Meade where soldiers trained for the Spanish-American War, the Pancho Villa Incursion, World Wars I and II as well as the westward expansion. Another historic drama had a role in the life of the town and Meade County—here, fifty ready-at-a-moment's-notice Minuteman missiles awaited an attack by the Soviet Union on the United States. In 1991 President George H. W. Bush ordered the removal of these missiles from alert status, profoundly affecting the economics of this region within the purview of Rapid City's Ellsworth Air Force Base. Who would have thought there would be weapons of mass destruction in this beautiful landscape? We could see the missile silos and were reminded that even small towns in seemingly out-of-the-way places can play remarkable roles in our nation's history.

Dusty and weary, Jim and I climbed the hills to where Betty, the children and a slobbery golden lab awaited our arrival. Warm welcome, hot showers and hearty lasagna made us content, for a while. After dinner Betty, with a look that made our hearts stop, said, "I have something to tell you. I had a phone call from Jennifer. Bernd has been in a serious bicycle accident. He's through surgery and is doing OK." We could barely breathe.

We immediately called Jennifer to get more information about Bernd's condition. She explained that they had gone bicycling with friends in the Sugar Bottom area north of Iowa City. Bernd and Steve decided to challenge the mountain bike trails while Jennifer and Laura contentedly rode at a more leisurely pace. Suddenly they heard Steve yell at them, "Bernd's wasted! I'm going for help! He's in the ravine!" In her shock at hearing the word *wasted*, Jennifer believed Bernd was dead and struggled to hold herself together to get to him.

She and Laura found Bernd alive but in horrific pain. While zipping down a steep incline, he had accelerated for the next climb and hit a wooden pallet bridge. His front tire slipped into a crack and he crashed, smashing his left femur. Once the ambulance arrived, it took forty-five minutes to get him on a back board and hoisted up by rope from the ravine to the ambulance and to the hospital.

Many pints of blood later, Bernd's life and leg had been saved by the gifted orthopedic surgeon, Dr. Charles Clark. When we told Jennifer we would come home right away, she emphatically responded, "No! Bernd would be so mad if you cut your bicycle trip short because of this. He's going to be all right and so am I. Besides, his parents are here."

Although our minds were whirling with doubt, we knew that when Jennifer used that voice, it would be best to heed her wishes. Bernd the adventurer would indeed be very upset if we abandoned this bicycle trip because of his accident. We spent a restless night tossed with prayers of gratitude. Bernd was alive and would be well again, albeit with a new titanium rod sustaining his femur.

🚲

The following morning, we hugged Betty, thanked her for all her help and friendship and rode into the sunrise. It took surprisingly little time to get out of Rapid City and its environs into the barren high plains of western South Dakota. Both Jim and I relish the harsh beauty of the plains and we filled the day with comments such as, "Look at that color—look at those grasses! They are glorious!" interspersed with, "I wonder how Bernd and Jennifer are doing." We had time aplenty that day to reflect on obstacles in life and how life can be totally transformed in a heartbeat. We knew Bernd would do everything he could to get back on his bicycle as soon as possible. And he would be back challenging gravity—how he loved what Jennifer described as "anything with adrenaline."

Winds. Ah, winds. As we bicycled through unforgiving landscapes, we contemplated what life must have been like for our pioneer ancestors. Sod houses, few trees, unpredictable water sources, and wind, always the wind. I remembered reading of pioneer women for whom the wind had become such an agony that they lost their minds. Bicycling in the wind was our choice. They had to live with it day in and day out.

Our goal that day—world-famous one-of-a-kind Wall Drug, home of ice cold water for weary travelers. It had also become the home for all kinds of *Made in China* souvenirs for weary parents to placate their pleading children. I recalled the first time my family had traveled there. In 1946 my parents, nine year old brother and I took a three week road trip to California following some of the routes that my then ten year old dad and his parents had traveled in 1925. When we got to Wall Drug, my mother, as always, made me brush my hair before I got out of the car so I would not look like what she called *The Wreck of the Hesperus,* a famous shipwreck. Keith and I had been told that we could choose one special souvenir on this trip. We spent lots of time pondering all the trinkets there. None of them enticed us, but we decided it would be fun to have our photos taken as we rode a mounted bucking horse.

All these years later, Jim and I approached Wall as memories filled my mind. A postal truck stopped and the mail man poked his head out the window, "Do you want a ride into town?"

"No thank you. It was thoughtful of you to stop but we're fine." Whenever we answer "We're fine!" as we ride our bicycles in some forsaken place, we know that to some people we must seem to be anything but fine.

We biked downtown to Wall Drug where we perused the merchandise, ate ice cream, and had our photos taken in front of the Wall Drug sign. The store's aura has been somewhat dimmed by time, increasing commercialism and by memories of a seven year old child who listened to her dad's Wall Drug stories from 1925. But the water was still cold, clear and refreshing.

Despite the nursery rhyme's promise of snow when the north wind blows, it blew briskly but no other sign of snow appeared as we headed south from Wall to the Badlands. Yet.

We were so excited to return to this national park, our first time since 1967 when we traversed the country with our three small daughters as we moved from Iowa City to a California army post. Only this time we'd be out in the elements, whatever they might be. Blue skies looked promising. We cheered at a wonderful surprise—the roads had been newly blacktopped! We just rocketed on that surface.

The Badlands' beauty, history, and geology fascinate visitors from all over the world. According to the Park Service information, …*the striking geologic deposits contain one of the world's greatest fossil beds*. Ancient mammals, saber-toothed cats, camels, three-toed horses and giant rhino-like creatures once roamed there. The park covers 244,000 acres and contains the largest protected mixed-grass prairie in the National Park system. Bison, pronghorn, whitetail and mule deer, coyotes, prairie dogs, turtles, snakes, raptors live here. Massive buttes, colorful spires and pinnacles with deep gorges reveal sedimentary layers of tan and gray sand and gravel, red and orange iron oxides, purple and yellow shale and white volcanic ash. Some of my favorite earth colors.

Captivated by the Badlands

Relishing the moment, we whooshed down into the bottom land, stopped to soak up the other-worldly feeling, and marveled at the monoliths encompassing us. We had never felt so much a part of the Badlands as we did at that moment, unencumbered by the steel cover of an auto. The smiles on our faces reflected our joy of the moment.

We saw few people or cars so it seemed as though we had this bad land to ourselves. As we drifted along the road, I fell behind Jim and noticed that a whole passel of dried Russian thistles had congregated on the road. I considered calling his attention to it by yelling a revised version of a recent movie, *The Russian thistles are coming! The Russian thistles are coming!* but decided not to. Surely he had seen how these tumble weeds shrouded the whole road.

Nyet. I should have remembered Jim's open-country penchant for playing games with his odometer, such as reaching 12345 or 12 miles per hour when we had bicycled 12 miles. The first tumbleweed swatted, startled and stunned him. How I wished I'd had a picture of him in the midst of this stampede of thistles.

The vistas from the overlooks reminded us that early ranchers intended to tame this wild land. Remnants of ranch houses and pockets of trees testified to the fortitude of those stalwart settlers, but also to nature having its way. As we had so many times before, we commented, "What a tough way to live!"

The 85 degree temperature made us thirsty and hungry. The Lodge's menu looked inviting so we cooled off there, enjoyed our lunch and reveled in a dessert that would become a favorite pleasure. Fruit of the Forest pie—raspberries, blueberries, strawberries—tasted as good as the name sounded.

Sated, we grabbed our bicycles and then realized we had an enormous hill to climb out of the basin. On full stomachs that could be a challenge—the blood wants to get on with digestion, and in climbing mode the leg muscles demand that blood supply. We went slowly, stopped at all the overlooks, walked short trails and enjoyed what pedal strokes and views offered us. Our bodies cooperated.

Too soon we left the stark spectacle of the Badlands to head to Kadoka for our overnight. We telephoned Jennifer who assured us, "Bernd is improving but he's in a lot of pain. You are doing the right thing so keep riding. Tell me about your trip because I want to tell him all the details." We did, although our hearts ached to be with them.

We had planned a relatively short day but exhilarating tailwinds blew us across the prairie faster than we had imagined. We stopped in Presho to cancel our motel reservation for the night and continued on to Kennebec. Even though the wind sped us along, I still found it tiring to be in that parching element.

The Budget Host in Kennebec lay next to a small, smoky, noisy café where we ate among the locals. There was no phone in our room so we asked if we could use the café phone. I stood in a storage closet straddling big containers of supplies to reach the telephone. When Jennifer answered, she wondered where we could be that there was so much noise. She gave more details about Bernd's condition and about the kinds of therapy he would undergo. She admitted she felt exhausted and that teaching her French classes at West High was tough when she really wanted to be with him. She didn't have any clear idea of when he would be discharged from the hospital but she had the house ready for him. She felt grateful his parents lived in Iowa City so they could assist in the transfer and in being with him at home. We wanted to be there but understood their decision. We slept more peacefully that night.

🚲

South Dakota allows cyclists to ride on the interstates when there are no other viable roads. So with some trepidation, especially on my part, onto I-90 we went. Although rumble-strips ribbed the shoulders, we still had enough space to ride comfortably. The traffic noise created the biggest handicap but the rest areas provided a big advantage. We stopped at one along the way to rest and snack. A young native American woman came over and asked, "What are you doing?" When we told her we were riding across South Dakota she looked at us incredulously, "You're doing what? Are you crazy?" We grinned at her and answered, "I guess maybe we are, just a bit." She shook her head in disbelief and walked off.

In addition to riding on the interstate, soon we'd get to cross the very broad Missouri River at Chamberlain, reminding me of the traditional folk song *Shenandoah, A-roll, a-rollaree, Across the wide Missouri...* a song thought to have originated with Canadian and American voyageurs or fur traders canoeing down this river. How exciting for us to contemplate what they and Lewis and Clark must have experienced when they first followed this great river.

We crossed the bridge and aimed for the highest vantage point overlooking it. The dramatic scene, enhanced by tall concrete tepee-like poles, tempted me to lie down in the center so I could look straight up at them piercing the cornflower blue sky. Humbling! We ate our lunch on the bluff, left the river vista and continued on to our overnight in Plankinton. There we would leave the interstate, head south toward Wagner and into another day of unknowns on the welcoming blue highways of South Dakota. We thought.

🚲

NEMESIS—A FORMIDABLE AND USUALLY VICTORIOUS RIVAL.

I tried to be stoic but I felt miserable. What had been an incredible bicycle ride across South Dakota had become a nightmare. When Jim and I turned south into my nemesis, the wind, our speed dropped to three point five miles per hour. When it gusted, we biked as slowly as two miles per hour—barely enough to stay upright. I tried to block the misery by singing in my head *They Call the Wind Mariah* but my choking sobs drowned out the music.

Two hours and seven miles later I alternately muttered or wailed, "This isn't fun anymore!" Jim sympathized but told me what I already knew: "Keep pedaling. We have to get to our motel in Wagner." There we'd find respite.

At the motel, without bothering to follow my usual routine of washing our sunglasses and cleaning and refilling the water bottles in preparation for the next day, I just collapsed on the bed. Eventually we both showered and mustered enough energy to eat supper at the nearby Pizza Ranch.

Early to bed to sleep soundly until 2 AM. Inspired by who knows what, I awakened, grabbed the telephone directory, went into the bathroom, turned on the light and combed the *Yellow Pages*. Rental cars, that's what I wanted. Just a simple Rent-a-Wreck would be sufficient, anything to get me off my bicycle and out of the wind. I searched and searched— no rental cars within seventy-five miles of Wagner.

The proverbial light bulb popped above my head with another idea: *Used Cars. We could buy a used car for one day, leave our bicycles as collateral, fetch our car from Akron, Iowa, come back and return the car to the dealer.* Wagner **did** have used car dealers. It made perfect sense to my wind-addled brain. Satisfied, I shut the telephone directory, turned off the light, happily shuffled back to bed and slept until six.

⚇

When Jim awoke, I eagerly informed him of my brainstorm, "I have an idea..." He did not seem as receptive as I had hoped but undeterred I continued, "It'd work and we'd get out of this wind!"

I knew his look very well—patient, fond, calm, and thoughtful. He cautioned, "Oh Honey, let's not make any rash decisions on empty stomachs." He knew after I've eaten breakfast, I'm much more likely to be rational—or perhaps just more malleable. He was right. I really didn't want to bail out of this trip. I would regret it if I did.

We returned to the Pizza Ranch, ate breakfast, and rode out to brave the South Dakota wind. But this seemed different than yesterday's headwind. This was a crosswind, a brutal crosswind that would...

But that's another story.

⚇

THIS ONE.

Autumn in South Dakota holds within it the possibility of nearly every kind of weather from blistering heat to snowfall, from drought to floods. As Jim and I bicycled the sixty-two miles from Wagner to Yankton, moderate temperatures and an overcast sky blessed us. Brewing crosswinds cursed us. By the end of the day, the winds weren't the only things that were cross.

That day proved that riding a bicycle in a steady crosswind can be vexing. We had to constantly battle the pressure of being either forced into the ditch on the right or propelled across the road to the left. Gusts exacerbated the situation. In the early mornings, our favorite time to ride, breezes are often mild and pleasant. As the earth warms, the velocity strengthens which can make cycling more taxing.

We weren't the only things responding to the airflow. Birds danced on the updrafts and, every mile or so, red-tailed hawks perched high in the trees. There they waited and watched for some unsuspecting creature to pop out of its burrow just in time to become a hawk snack. The sunflowered ditches crackled as the dried blossoms and leaves swayed in the zephyr and brome grass rippled bronze, buff and fawn. Birds, plants, and the smooth blacktop soothed our souls. True to form, the winds ratcheted up and by lunchtime the familiar dread encompassed us as we thought of the remaining miles to our overnight lodging.

In early afternoon our bucking, thrashing bikes, apparently brainwashed by the wind, seemed to have lives and wills of their own. I became a bicycle whisperer needing to tame my feral steed urging, "Come on, Borthwick, we can do this. We just gotta stick together." That fell on deaf ears.

Kerwham! I lost control of her as a gust grabbed and threw me across the road and nearly into the ditch. Fortunately, there were no oncoming cars. Gasping, I stopped, braced against my bike, "Jim, did you see that?" His worried expression said he had. Later he showed me a photo he had taken of me and Borthwick as we leaned into the wind. There was little time to ponder what might have happened to me other than scratches, bruises and irritated spirit had I been flung into the ditch.

A sky we midwesterners know and fear loomed ahead of us—deep, dark, whirling black, green and grey clouds, ominous tendrils snaking down. Distant lightning and thunder plied our senses. With the constant menace of the storm and the impending threat of an even greater one, what should we do? Our only choice—keep going.

Though our original plan had been to turn south earlier in the day, we had deliberately delayed turning into the storm. We were just four miles north of Yankton when Jim pointed to an upcoming intersection and hollered, "This is where we have to turn!" We did and hit a wall of wind that bested us.

We tried but couldn't even make one revolution of the pedals. Somehow we kept ourselves from falling over, dismounted, put our heads down and attempted to push our loaded bikes, a proverbial exercise in futility. We looked up and saw, not a knight in shining armor on a white horse, but a dirty old white pickup parked just yards from us. We knew that junk-filled Datsun could be our salvation. Buffeted and feeling battered, we waited until a man and little girl came out of the country café headed toward it. As we struggled toward the pickup, Jim shouted, "Could you give us a ride to our motel in Yankton? We can't ride our bikes in this wind."

With a friendly smile, the bearded man nodded, "Sure, just put your bikes in the back. It'll be crowded but you can get into the cab with us." With his help we hoisted our bikes into the pickup bed and climbed in. "We'll just stay back here and hang onto our bicycles to keep them from blowing away."

Four miles. Just four short, four long miles we couldn't ride. Four miles of our South Dakota route left unbicycled. We grimaced as we clung to our bikes and bounced into Yankton. By the time we arrived at the motel, unloaded the bikes, and thanked our Good Neighbor Sam who wouldn't take anything for his help, rain dumped on us. It looked like Noah's rain must have looked.

After a quick dash to the motel restaurant for supper, we returned to our room and turned on the television. The weather reports confirmed what we had experienced. The winds blew between fifty and sixty miles per hour with gusts over seventy-five. No wonder I nearly had an up close and personal encounter with a ditch. More sobering, however, a series of tornadoes south of Yankton damaged buildings, but fortunately with no loss of life.

For the moment, we hunkered in our own little motel room ark, out of the elements. Once again, we gave thanks for safety.

♺

The rain drizzled all night and showed no sign of letting up in the morning, our last day on the road. We briefly considered waiting to see if it would lessen but chose instead to don our rain gear and head down the road to Vermilion and on to our destination, Akron, Iowa.

The steady rain and light breeze made our experience a common-place rainy day on a bicycle. It was Sunday so when we reached Vermilion, the restaurants filled with post-church crowds. We had not dressed in our Sunday-go-to-meetin' clothes and some people looked askance at us as we walked in. Despite our efforts to shake most of the water off our bright yellow rain jackets and black pants, we still dripped. Our helmets protected our heads from injury but not from rain—we had wet hair, well-misted faces, blurry glasses and soggy shoes to boot. The hostess showed us to our booth where we attempted unsuccessfully to blend in. Except for the very pleasant server, our smiles were met with solemnity. Ah well, those poor folks didn't have a clue about what fun we'd been having the past few days.

Warm food and indoor plumbing do a great deal to hearten us savage bike riders. When the rain stopped, we were happy to be back on the road. Unfortunately, it began to rain again, I got a flat tire, and the mosquitoes viciously attacked the vulnerable tire changer and his helper. Fortunately, Jim fixed the tire as quickly as he could in between swats at the pests.

I love to stop at all the historic markers along our travel routes but Jim, not so much. When I pointed to the one titled *Giants in the Earth* he was emphatic with his, "No! Next time!" I knew O. E. Rolvaag had set his classic book in Spring Creek, Dakota Territory in this general area. But we chose to go on without stopping to learn more. Jim's reaction and swarms of circling mosquitoes made it easier to capitulate—the mosquitoes the deciding factor.

Crossing the Big Sioux River into Iowa was a cause for celebrating state number thirty-three. Akron, where we'd left our car with my stepsister Karen, lay eight miles away. We turned north onto Highway 12 and immediately, a car moving too fast and too close buzzed by us. We went from startled to angry to be so close to our ride's end and have to face another thoughtless driver.

When Karen came to the door, she was greeted by two of the wettest people she had ever seen. Her mouth dropped open, she stood speechless for a moment and then, always a photographer, said, "Let me get my camera!"

After wonderfully warming showers, we had a great hot supper and conversation with Karen, her husband Don, and her brother Stan. We couldn't stay the night but packed our bicycles and gear in our car and headed toward Rapid City. After our overnight in Kennebec, the same place we had stayed earlier in the week, we continued phase three of this trip, van retrieval. Several miles later, an unsettling sight awaited us. We glanced knowingly at each other and then chuckled. We'd had all kinds of weather on this trip but overnight, when the wind blew from the north, it had snowed. We sat safely, possibly smugly in our car, not on our bikes!

TEXAS THE LONE STAR STATE PART 2. CORPUS CHRISTI TO BRENHAM-1999

Riders: Jim/Jan. Distance: 221 miles

Logistically speaking, this was the most complex of our bicycle rides to date and the first foray with just the two of us. Jim and I had to get the van to the endpoint and us back to the starting point. We had mulled logistical questions for several days. "I've got it!" one of us would say. "We could start by…" The voice would taper off as a problem appeared with the idea that might have solved the *How do we do this* question. Eventually, we agreed on a plan and drove to south Texas.

The highlight of this Texas ride was another visit to our cousins in Kingsville, Jan and Mitch Nielsen, whom we had visited on the first leg of our Texas crossing. This time, instead of focusing on the vast King Ranch, they proudly introduced us to the emus Mitch and a partner had begun raising. These flightless six-feet tall, one-hundred fifty pound, three-toed birds need a fence to keep them in but with room to roam since they have a nine-foot stride and can run forty miles per hour. The claim is made that every part of the bird is usable from feathers to leather to cholesterol-free meat to fat which produces medicinal and health-building omega-3 oils. Their huge green eggs can be carved as art too. Mitch demonstrated his enthusiasm about the prospect of emu-farming for several years, at least until he broke his ankle while trying to catch one.

After we left the Nielsens, we headed to South Padre Island and the Port Aransas Bird Sanctuary. We have no idea how many species we saw during our brief visit, but throughout the year, almost five-hundred species of nearly eight-hundred species in North America come here. From whooping cranes to hummingbirds, birds have internal signals that guide them to this area. Thousands of hummers fly from nesting grounds both east and north before they fly over the Gulf of Mexico to their winter home in Mexico. Once they've gone, whooping cranes begin to arrive to overwinter here. We told ourselves we'd return some day when we could focus on birds instead of bikes.

Once we arrived in Corpus Christi, we checked into the motel where we would spend two nights, and left our bikes and gear. We walked a few blocks to rent a small car. Jim drove it and I drove the van which would be parked, with the hosts' consent, at the Brenham B&B. We had reservations there for Friday night after we completed segment two of the Texas ride. We returned to Corpus Christi, turned the rental car in and hoofed it back to the motel. After our overnight, we would begin our ride on our trusty bicycles.

🚲

We had allocated four to five days to bike the 221 miles. The first day a storm behind us blew us along much faster than we had anticipated, our route taking us along the Intracoastal Waterway paralleling the Gulf of Mexico. Once we left the Gulf, we turned north on Highway 71 at Palacios.

The countryside was enjoyable to ride through and the people we met showed their Texas conviviality. We missed seeing the plethora of bluebonnets we'd been treated to on Texas Trip 1. But tailwinds continued as we rode gently rolling Texas hills on our way through Halletsvillle and LaGrange on to Brenham, home of the famed Blue Bell Ice Cream.

First things first, we followed the adage *Life is uncertain. Eat dessert first.* We indulged our ice cream fantasies with Blue Bell Ice Cream. As usual, Jim felt compelled to compare his town's Blue Bunny Ice Cream with Brenham's Blue Bell. He admitted Blue Bell tasted good but, you guessed it, not as good as hard-to-beat Blue Bunny. What is it about the color blue and ice cream? Does it make for a totally different gastronomic experience? Or is it just eye-catching?

Always a good sign, our van had remained where we had left it at the B&B. Our gracious hostess gave us each a bottle of Spring Valley water which we had never tasted. I loved it and thought it had to be the best water I'd ever drunk. Jim and I had full run of the antiques and memorabilia-filled B&B so we sauntered from room to room looking at the furniture and accessories. Our hostess suggested we eat at a local French restaurant in a freshly restored Victorian storefront. It lived up to all she said—wonderfully prepared food with a much more up-scale ambiance than we had experienced earlier in our trip. Jim and I also looked better in our "civvies" than we had earlier in our biking clothes.

🚲

On our way back home, we traveled via our expected Texas Trip 3 route to Leesville, Louisiana. I jotted down the names of potential towns and motels where we might want to stay, and checked to see if there were places to eat along the way. Betty, Vicki, Tania, Darcy, Jim and I had stayed in a charming B&B in 1988 when we had cycled across Louisiana. Jim and I hoped it would still be in business so we could stay there again at the end of our final Texas trip. The house remained but the B&B had closed. Alas, we remember having such fun in the marvelous antique-filled house. We guessed we'd have to settle for a plain old motel.

We did a lot of sighing on the way back to Iowa City. It had been a very pleasant ride but a long way to drive for so few biking miles, but we already knew that was the way with spring break bike rides and trying to accomplish a goal.

THE GREAT IDAHO-MONTANA RIDE OF 1999

Riders: Sandy/Dave, Jim/Jan. Drop off, pick up: Norm/Cynthia Zimmerman. Distance: 530 miles

Once we began our quest to bicycle across the fifty states, we fine-tuned our wishes by inserting adventures we'd like to have along the way. Within seconds Jim added his long-time dream of biking The-Going-to-the-Sun Road in Glacier National Park.

Friends Cynthia and Norm Zimmerman had never been to Glacier so we recruited them to be the official van drivers. After overnighting at border town Newport, Washington, they took photos, waved goodbye and set off to wander through Yellowstone before meeting us in Glacier. Sandy, Dave, Jim and I would bike from the Washington border, across Idaho to Glacier where the Zimmermans would meet us.

We had just cycled past the Idaho border on Highway 2 when Jim started yelling and flailing, scaring us all. A bee had flown under his shirt and had stung him on the chest. He killed it, not with his shrieking but by slapping himself and the little beast. We put a chilled water bottle on the sting, the coldest thing we had until we got to a convenience store where we found ice. The wound swelled and stayed bright red for several days and the discomfort irritated Jim a lot. Not an auspicious way to begin an adventure. How is it that Webster defines adventure? *An undertaking of a hazardous nature.* Guess it was.

The trip across the Idaho only took a day and a half, but then Jim's Rules of Biking do not specify that border-to-opposite-border has to be the longest way across a state. So in Idaho, we biked the lovely panhandle, all forty-six miles as the crow flies, sixty-three the way we rode. Pine, spruce, hemlock, and aromatic cedars clotted the landscape of the northern rounded mountains.

Part of the state's topography is due to glacial action—ice sheets that extended south, retreated, then returned before retreating again when the ice melted.

We meandered along a small remnant of that warming, lapis-colored Lake Pend Oreille which in some places reaches a depth of over eleven-hundred feet, making it the fifth deepest freshwater lake in the country. Sandy and I especially liked that we were going through Sand Point, a town on the lake, home of Coldwater Creek Catalog Company at the time. I had seen their catalogs and had liked many of the items they carried. Jim and I found a small painting of a Rocky Mountain scene that we thought would be perfect for our Colorado condo. It was, as well as being flat and easy to carry in a pannier, definitely a plus for Jim. He's carried all kinds of things we've purchased on our biking trips: shirt and shorts and a Guatemalan vest in Wyoming; a Waterford crystal clock in Ireland; puffy biking shorts in Ohio; a purple woolen sweater on Prince Edward Island; a walrus tusk cribbage board in Alaska.

We left Highway 2 to follow a narrower road but still cruised along the lake toward Clark Fork Field Campus where we'd spend the night. When the turn-off sign for our cabin came into view, we all muttered, "Uh-oh." Its name? Mosquito Creek Road. Reality lived up to the name and we swatted the pests as we rode to Red Fir Cabin. Surprisingly, they didn't bother us as we ate supper at our picnic table. Maybe we had become less fragrant after we'd showered.

🚲

As we biked out, we traveled past a road leading to Ross Creek Cedar Grove. We didn't get to walk among the thousand-year old trees there, a price we sometimes pay by being on bikes and thinking that adding more miles to our day in the mountains might not be a wise choice. I felt dispirited at times when such decisions were made because I believed I was responsible since I rode so much more slowly than the others.

White blossoms fringed the peaceful route through scenic but ho-hum-named Cabinet Mountains. That setting helped compensate for missing the cedars. We turned back onto US Highway 2 once we crossed the wide Kootenai River, a major tributary of the Columbia River, until we reached Libby, downstream from the Libby Dam.

🚲

The Dam was constructed seventeen miles from town and formed Lake Koocanusa. All of us wondered about the name but decided since the lake extended into Canada, it made as much sense as the moniker Texarkana does. Later we learned that of the four Columbia River Treaty Dams, only Libby is in the USA while the other three are in Canada. Although it's more complex than that, the dams provide mutual benefits of sharing water between Canada and the USA, hence the *canusa* part of the name. The *Koo* part came about because the lake is formed from the Kootenai River. The look and sound of it resemble some of the indigenous names of the region.

Jan, Sandy and Dave pedaling along Lake Koocanusa

The four of us stopped to scrutinize the dam then continued to hug the shoreline up the west bank of the lake. This route reminded me of New York State's Finger Lakes, hills burgeoning with thick evergreen forests reflected in the water. Jim had chosen this part of the itinerary after reading an article in *Bicycling* magazine featuring this as one of the best rides in the country. Excellent and memorable choice. With all the forests, logging has been an economic source in the area for years.

Before we reached the northernmost stretch of the lake, we crossed it on the Koocanusa Bridge, the longest and highest bridge in Montana, standing two hundred seventy feet above the lake and measuring just over twenty-three hundred feet long. Some people think it really serves no purpose but surely the tiny local Amish community likes having access to nearby Eureka for supplies. For people like us who are not boaters or fishermen, but rather seeking out Montana's sights, it provided a wonderful window into the countryside.

Tucked in the woods, stood a simple pine wood store. We needed refreshment so stopped. Opening the door, we all felt a flash of, "We're in our home territory," because it reminded us of Stringtown, an Amish store near Iowa City. The staples even included one of our then-favorite snacks, salted dried peas. We love such surprises—both stores and snacks.

Our goal of the day, the lumber town of Eureka, sits on the banks of the Tobacco River. Naturally we wondered why its name since most tobacco growing we know of is in southern United

States. We learned early explorers ascertained the Indians there grew a native form of tobacco. Hurray for simplicity!

Biking upstream along the Tobacco River happened to be the only way we could get to Whitefish, our next destination. Highways rimmed with forests gave way to occasional pastureland and hayfields; aspen trees paraded their white bark splendor, edging out the evergreens; rushing water calmed to quiet, almost placid running streams; golden flower-filled meadows with boulders provided perfect places for picnics and relaxation. The river veered away and we began to parallel a railroad track the rest of the way to the town. Montana, blessed with a thousand lakes, certainly brought smiles to us lovers of water in a natural state.

As changing economies altered the lives of Whitefish's people, the town went from logging, farming and railroads in the first half of the twentieth century to its present focus on recreation and retirement. Skiing, golfing and fishing combined with the area's natural attractions have made Whitefish a different kind of center. We thought of it as one of the gateways to Glacier. The closer we came to the park, the more excited we became.

GOING TO THE SUN

Established in 1910, Montana's Glacier National Park became the United States' section of the Waterton-Glacier International Peace Park in 1932. Designated a World Heritage Site in 1995, it bridges the US and Canada as a symbol of their longtime friendship. Over two hundred crystal lakes dot its mountains but many glaciers have rapidly disappeared, a visually dramatic effect of global warming. Glacier's diverse terrain of windswept peaks, rolling grasslands, forested hillsides, and alpine tundra, plus ancient cedar forests, rugged snow-capped peaks and sapphire glacial lakes waited to beguile us. Nearly one thousand species of plants, as well as wildlife—marmots, moose, mountain lions, black bears, bald eagles, bighorn sheep, deer, mountain goats and grizzlies magnified this splendid place.

Long before any other people arrived and changed the landscape, Blackfeet, Salish and Kootenai Tribes had a close association with this area. One aspect of these indigenous cultures continues to be their humility and connection to the land: *Everything under the sky has a voice to speak with and knowledge to tell…humans are just one instrument in an ongoing orchestra of life.* Almost every aspect of tribal life has a spiritual ritual attached to it, from the way a tepee is set up to the way a hunter asks an animal's forgiveness before he kills it to feed his family. Gold diggers, buffalo hunters, oil seekers and coal miners all tried to make their fortunes in the mountains of what became Glacier and Waterton National Parks. Beyond the native people, the only ones who became successful were those who loved the area for its scenic beauty or its trade routes.

Saturday afternoon, Norm and Cynthia met us as we pulled into a parking lot at Sacred Dancing Lake, Lake MacDonald. We hadn't seen them since Monday so we had lots of tales to swap including one about mosquitoes on Lower Mosquito Road, a wonderful Amish Store and always the mountains and water. They enthused about Yellowstone's falls, geysers and wildlife. Happy to be together, we loaded our bikes onto the bike rack and checked into our log cabin accommodations to plan our next explorations.

🚲

Hikes along Glacier's many creeks and lakes filled the next morning: The Trail of Cedars, a boardwalk through the cool dark of towering old-growth cedar, hemlock and cottonwood; Avalanche Trail brought us to a spectacular same-named lake. Early explorers named it for the snow slides that tumbled and roared down the surrounding mountains in Glacier's long winters. I preferred hearing waterfalls instead of avalanches. A waterfall-rimmed cliff remains and Sperry Glacier still feeds the lake.

After lunch we decided we'd be better prepared to bike The Going-to-the-Sun Road after seeing the lay of the land up close, so we piled into the van for the preview. The theory sounded better than reality. To me, sitting up high in the van, the Going-To-See-The-Sun Road appeared more like "Falling-Over-The-Guardrail-Road" Our reconnaissance only served to spook me.

All the *What-ifs* of the upcoming adventure burbled up: *What if a car comes too close, where will I go? What if I hit a rough spot, will I topple over the wall and soar into the abyss? If that's the case, Lord,* I prayed, *take me home, take me home.* And the perennial What-if: *What if this is too tough for me and I need to bail out? What will I do? Norm and Cynthia will be long gone, off on their Montana junket.* So much for the comfort of knowing what lay ahead of us.

Norm chirruped, "You guys! It's scary enough just driving up the road. I'm sure glad Cynthia and I aren't riding our bikes." The rest of us whistled in the dark and voiced bicyclists' platitudes, "Oh, the hills always look steeper, the roads narrower and the drop-offs deeper when you are in a car rather than on a bike..." Yadda, yadda, yadda. Did we believe what we babbled? Yes, sort of...

Dinner that evening at Heaven's Peak Inn, a white tablecloth and cloth napkins affair, felt quite different from our usual sitting on the ground with our bikes, munching our tuna PBJ sandwiches. I welcomed the difference and the food too—fresh trout almandine for me. But even while we enjoyed this delectable meal, my mind kept flipping ahead to Tomorrow's Ride.

Back at our cabin, knowing that after early tomorrow morning we wouldn't see Norm and Cynthia again until we arrived in Havre, four days hence, we needed to repack our panniers. We collected cold weather gear for our early morning departure, filled water bottles, stowed everything we would not wear in zip-lock bags, hoped to get a good night's sleep while trying not to think about the morrow. Jim confided, "When I saw the terrain on our drive up Going-to-the-Sun, I asked myself, what are we doing?" Me too.

🚲

Monday: Up early, ate breakfast, dressed warmly including mittens and ear warmers, smiled for the camera, hopped in the van for a toasty ride to the northeast end of Lake McDonald where we'd stopped biking on Saturday. Off with the bicycles, on with the panniers, snugged sun-bright yellow pannier covers on them, the better to be seen. Checked the tires, the brakes. *Would we really need brakes going up this mountain? To keep ourselves from going backwards?* Turned flashing lights on, gloried in the pinking of dawn, smiled again for the cameras, hugged the Zimmermans, and pedaled off into that very sunrise. After all, we were riding The-Going-to-the-Sun Road.

What we'd now call research and development for this road required about fifteen years. Those doing it probably called it agony. The surveyors had to be roped together to traverse the rough mountainsides to get where they might be able to build a road. Road crews had to hike several miles and climb farther to go to work at their difficult and dangerous jobs.

In 1921, work began on this engineering marvel spanning fifty-two miles from West Glacier entrance, up to Logan Pass on the Continental Divide, to the east entrance at St. Mary. Inscribing the road from the natural masonry of Glacier Park's rocky cliffs had been dismissed by many experts as an impossible feat. The first designs had fifteen switchbacks at 8 percent grade, common in the Alps of Europe but way too many to please the supporters of what was then thought of as the Transmountain Highway. Redesign found a route which required one 180-degree switchback called The Loop. Once the design had been chosen, it took twelve more years of building until its dedication in 1933 as The Going-to-the-Sun-Road.

The construction of the road cost three lives, forty-two and a half million dollars, 490,000 pounds of explosives and presented a daunting task for equipment of the time. The men, armed only with hammers, shovels, hemp climbing ropes, *constructed scaffolding, scaled 100-foot ladders, and blasted through mountainsides at a rate of 100 feet per day* with dynamite and black powder. *(Pioneering the Road to the Sun, Flathead Beacon)* These workers began carving away the steep mountainsides to create a narrow dirt road. In addition to utilizing quarries, conservation-minded contractors saved rock removed during excavation which Russian stonemasons then used to build guard railings and huge stonework arches along the highway. Truly a classic mountain road, Going-to-the-Sun climbed 3300 vertical feet over the twelve miles, and twisted and turned through the landscape. It did not resemble a Zorro-like Z slash across the mountains.

Our challenges included being safe, enjoying every moment, taking photos, and following the rules of the road. One safety requirement for bicyclists coming from the west during summertime and enforced by the National Park Service, meant we had to be to the top of The Sun Road before 11 AM, an immutable deadline.

At first the four of us climbed gradually, then settled in for the twelve miles to the summit. When the road was designed during the 1920s, the recommended maximum grade for roads was 6 percent because at 7, cars had to shift down into second gear. I don't know about the others, but I shifted down and remained in my low gear the entire climb. My fears dissipating with every pedal stroke.

The surroundings transfixed all of us—an incredible narrow road winding among jagged mountains and cliffs, overlooks where we could see crystal clear glacial alpine lakes, sharp ridges, lodgepole pine and cedar-forested valleys, teeming flowering meadows and icy rushing streams. Every turn brought exquisite new vistas we could only try to absorb.

What I'd thought on Sunday were teensy rock guard walls, actually were seven miles of eighteen to twenty-four inch stonemasonry constructed of native rocks meant to keep us from tumbling over the edge. I would have designed them to be taller but, from the perspective of my bicycle saddle, I felt safe and secure.

Two tunnels, one on each side of Logan Pass, created novel echoing sensations for us as we biked through them. In the western tunnel, stalactites clung to the ceiling, and drilled grooves marked the spots where explosives had been placed to blast the road into existence. Two arches within it provided overlooks for travelers to see, among other sights, Heaven's Peak. A mile farther on, The Loop seemed to point toward Logan Pass, exactly where we were headed.

We relished the vast palette of green punctuated by red and yellow Indian paintbrush, glacier lilies, magenta fireweed; the crystal clarity of plunging waterfalls like Bird Woman Falls; The Weeping Wall where an exuberance of water seeped out splashing us and the road's asphalt; sedimentary stones of Garden Wall's rock face with bands of green, blue, orange and red countering the bright white quartzite veins. And always on sunshiny days, indigo mountain peaks collided with Big Sky blueness. Nature's extravagance.

Creation had already knocked our socks off when relics of the past, long black-fendered, red seventeen-passenger 1930s antique buses called jammers complete with roll-back canvas convertible tops, incongruously wended their way along this fabled road.

We kept going, going, going up. We felt the chill as we glided by a twelve-foot snowbank, remnant of last winter's road clearing. Mountain goats ignored us from their rocky domain as we reached Logan Pass. We made it before the 11 AM deadline, another Continental Divide crossing for us, elevation 6680 feet, backed by huge fields of snow. We marveled at all we had seen and wondered how long would it take us to assimilate this most amazing day, this day that wasn't over yet.

We wanted to stay at the Pass among the flowers and glory, to relish and rehash the ride up the mountain but knew many miles lay ahead of us. But the sky, snowfields, waterfalls, rocky precipices

Happiness is reaching the Going-to-the-Sun-Road summit! Jim, Jan, Dave, Sandy

held us there. We allowed ourselves photos and food, then began the long declines mixed with inclines to St. Mary. We repeatedly paused to try to capture the greatness and the nuances of this magical place. Views of Lake St. Mary stopped us mid-pedal stroke. We all wore our sky-blue Bike Montana shirts and discovered they morphed into the lake's Caribbean blue color.

The road emptied out at St. Mary, a small village on Blackfeet Indian Tribal land. We remembered the west side of Glacier's rain forest and contrasted it with the rain-shadowed east. Dry, windy, more austere, but oh, the beauty.

The excitement of the climb and descent diminished as we faced a long, slow ascent to the village of Kiowa. I began to struggle and wondered how I had made it up to Logan Pass that morning. Then, as I was thinking drab thoughts and nit-picking at my capabilities, I made a discovery, one I could have lived forever without knowing. A fly began to buzz around my head. I swatted it away. Well, what I thought was away, but eager as it was, it returned and continued its course around me. I slapped at it again, totally ineffectually. The fly settled in, apparently content to fly near my right ear, its irritating sound reminding me of how I hated flies. I glanced up to see Dave, Jim and Sandy pulling away from me and my new companion. Drat! I decided I would stop to see if I could distract the little pest and then zoom away from it. Well, as zoomy as I could get, under the circumstances my little ploy worked—for a few seconds. Before I got to my top climbing speed, it buzzed up and seemed to perch in the air again by my right ear. Defeated, I thought *Whatever lesson can I learn right now from this irritating situation?* My Aha! moment was not momentous but did soothe me ever so minimally. I glanced down at my odometer and determined this: The top speed of this particular fly, and maybe even others, was seven miles per hour. So we kept company for the next few climbing miles until it couldn't keep up when I spotted a sign of the Promised Land—Kiowa Motel.

◪

We pedaled away from Glacier Park and Kiowa and faced the early morning sun. Before us lay the vista of Great Plains wheat fields. Behind us the mountains. Out of habit and nearly in unison, we checked our rear view mirrors and slammed on our brakes. "Look at that!" Still straddling our bikes, we spun our bodies around and gasped at the grandeur and majesty of the Northern Rockies. Our tear-filled eyes embraced the Montana landscape—brilliant azure sky, wind-rippled golden wheat fields, glowing mauve mountains. Jim murmured, *O Beautiful, for spacious skies, for amber waves of grain, For purple mountain majesty above the fruited plain...*

In that moment we experienced *America the Beautiful,* a moment which would remain with us the rest of our lives. We tell the story to all who will listen. Each time my skin tingles.

Leaving mountains by car, bicycle, plane or train, has always been hard for me. I never want to go. I want to stay enveloped in them. Even though I may be leaving dramatic beauty for another kind, I mentally cling to the mountains. For a while.

We shook ourselves free of reverie and headed into the high golden plains of Big Sky country. I rolled a Clint Eastwood title around in my brain—*High Plains Drifter.* That's what we were doing now, drifting across Montana on US Highway 2, willing big and little adventures to cross our paths.

Forty-seven miles from Kiowa to Cut Bank meant we had plenty of time to flow with the spirit of that day. What better place to benefit from it than immersing ourselves in Browning's irresistible Museum of the Plains Indians? Who can imagine dyeing porcupine quills to ornament deerskin clothing? Or fashioning eagle feathers into incredible headdresses? Who can dream of the exquisite love that created cradleboards? The four of us absorbed all we could, then lost in our own thoughts, continued pedal-drifting to the next prairie towns.

Abandoned grain elevators, lone, forsaken farmhouses miles from anywhere inspired us to reminisce about Midwest farms going bankrupt, then being deserted. And everywhere we looked, chamois-colored wheat fields. We pondered in silence, our hearts and minds grasping at how to express the awe and poignancy of what we had seen and felt that morning.

After such an emotional high, the day became miles and miles of miles and miles, cut by railroad tracks and ranch roads leading into the distance. Ahead more plains, behind fading rugged snow-capped Rockies. A sign woke us from our reveries: *Cut Bank's Newest Motel Glacier Gateway*

Inn East End Next to 27' Penguin. Penguin? Then we saw it. There stood a red-capped, big-footed, blue-eyed cartoon penguin on a rock labeled *Welcome to Cut Bank, MT. Coldest Spot in the Nation.* Often reported that way, even though quixotic chinook wind can change the temperature by one hundred degrees within twenty-four hours. The penguin statue and a high railroad trestle spanning the cut bank for which the town was named, comprised its highlights.

Traveling east the following day, the stark attraction of the plains continued to overwhelm the horizons. We pedaled on. Our goal, Chester, a small town planted in the rolling hills of central Montana.

We had just checked into our motel when we heard the news of the deaths of John Kennedy, Jr., his wife and her sister in a plane crash. Plane crashes always elicit a visceral reaction in me. My thirty-three-year old brother Keith died in 1971 in a mid-air collision over the mountains northeast of Los Angeles. What tragic loss of life in both accidents. Such sorrow for them, their families, our family. I prayed silent prayers.

The smoky bar atmosphere of the café adjacent to the motel didn't appeal to us so we searched the *Yellow Pages* and the streets for a restaurant. We found The Red Rose, a supper club advertised as open to the public, even wanderers like us. Riding seventy miles had made us hungry. We appeared to be the first and perhaps the last patrons of the night.

The proprietor greeted, seated, and handed us menus. We relaxed and reflected on the day's events until Mr. Supper Club came to take our order. We ordered our entrees and inadvertently hit a touchy-button by asking to have our salad dressings served on the side. Mr. Club erupted in a tirade: "I know how to dress a salad! This is my job—it's my life! I don't need anybody telling me how to do it!"

Sufficiently cowed, we said nothing until he had returned to the kitchen. We knew Chester did not have a glut of eating places so we opted to stay, grin and bear it. The food tasted all right, not outstanding but it was sustenance. We wondered if Mr. Club's outburst represented his anxiety at having few patrons, if he might lose his business.

Half-way through the meal, the electricity went off and left us poking around our food. But even in dusky, summer sunset light we could see—the dressings had been served on the side.

Our last day of bicycling brought us past thousands of acres of wheat fields. A little burg along the way, Rudyard, advertised by announcing its population at one time consisted of *596 Nice People-1 Old Sore Head! RIP SNORTING & RARING for BUSINESS.* The now diminished town still names a Sore Head for special events. A little farther down the road, Kremlin distinguishes itself from the Russian city by adding USA STYLE, in case someone wondered.

Soon we came upon our B&B just outside Havre. There was no missing it with multiple *West Prairie Inn* signs as well as an old grain wagon in a field, a super-size tepee in the yard, outbuildings labeled *Antiques* and an early-1920s motorcar, small American flags waving from the front fenders, parked next to a wooden sidewalk leading to the house. The owners' love of the outdoors, particularly fly fishing was reflected in the décor of the bedrooms, a woven creel, canoe paddle, Gone Fishin' sign dangled from the old oak wall phone. As we spoke with them, we learned that our hostess taught a women-only fly fishing course, a first for us.

Once Cynthia and Norm arrived with the van, we headed into town for supper and a tour of just-opened *Havre Beneath the Streets*. In 1904 a fire destroyed most of the town. Both residents and businesses decided to move into their basements while the town was rebuilt. Although meant as temporary shelter, it became more permanent than expected. A series of tunnels connected the businesses including an underground bank, funeral parlor, and even a drugstore with a soda fountain. A saloon, meat market, an opium den as well as a bordello have become part of the tour. Once Havre had been rebuilt, Chinese railroad workers continued living in the underground spaces owned by the railroad. Rampant racism made it safer there than other places in town. So went our unexpected Havre history lesson.

Once again a bike trip ended and we needed to pack up and hop back in the van for the long drive home. We wondered how long it would be before we could return to complete our Montana ride and continue across North Dakota. We could hardly wait.

MEANDERING MISSOURI'S KATY TRAIL-1999

Riders: Sandy/Dave, Betty, Barb Goff, Jim/Jan. Distance: 319 miles

The idea of cycling Missouri's Katy Trail, the longest Rail-to-Trail in the country, in autumn became an invitation we couldn't refuse. We answered with a resounding "Yes!" even though we knew the trail was not completed.

The Katy runs two hundred forty miles along the route of the former Missouri-Kansas-Texas (MKT) Railroad, following over one hundred miles of Lewis and Clark's route up the Missouri River. Our group traveled in the opposite direction of the great explorers. Crushed limestone made a hard, flat surface with negligible elevation change. Mostly, I liked that feature but, imagine, sometimes I yearned for a hill. The trail had opened in the east from St. Charles to Sedalia in 1996 and the remainder, from Sedalia to Clinton in 1999, just after we completed our ride. The Great Flood of 1993 had damaged about seventy-five miles of the original one hundred twenty-six miles of the trail, so considerable restoration had to take place.

After an Iowa football game, we trundled off to Missouri, left our van at our motel end-point in St. Charles and drove experienced rider Barb's van to Harrisonville in western Missouri. From there we cycled fourteen miles on State Highway 2 to touch the Kansas border then returned, making possible our border-to-opposite-border ride.

🚲

The following morning we rode to the Katy Trail itself. Rolling hills, mostly gentle, covered with autumn tinged trees, rusty red metal roofed barns and Amish buggies along the roadways painted picturesque rural scenes reminding me of Pennsylvania hills.

When we connected with the flat trail's newly opened portion at Sedalia Trailhead, we found it soft and difficult to ride on. The firmer older sections were easier but presented another hazard—prickly vines growing across the packed rock and soil surface. Their stickers punctured and caused nine flat tires, mere prelude to a later trip across Arizona-New Mexico's record of fourteen. Avoiding all of them—impossible—since some trees nearly met over the trail and copious fallen leaves covered many of the ubiquitous tormenters. Fortunately, no poison ivy, snakes or weather hazards bothered us.

Sedalia, home of a memorable 1895 Victorian depot and museum provided an excellent spot for us to launch onto the completed portion of the Katy Trail. The community also hosts the annual Scott Joplin Ragtime Festival, a second spot we have cycled through where Joplin had made his indelible mark. Naturally, many of the towns on the Katy had their genesis when the railroad reached there. Businesses that popped up often included general and drug stores, hotels, harness and saddle shops, barbershops, blacksmiths, wagon shops, and shoemakers. An exception was Boonville, where the trail joins the Missouri River. One of the state's oldest surviving towns, it is also where the first battle west of the Mississippi River took place during the Civil War. After we passed its Mission style depot we crossed the river to reconnect with the trail. We remained on the north side of the river from that point on.

Historically, we had arrived in the central Missouri area known as Boonslick Country, called that after Daniel Boone's two sons made salt from a nearby salt springs, Boone's Lick, in the early 1800s. We hit the village of New Franklin at noontime which, in this town, meant head to the Silver Liners Senior Center to join the locals for lunch. Betty had discovered this gem in her trip preparation, so it was a no-brainer to eat taco salad and enjoy local conversation and color for a two-dollar donation.

White blocky church towers marked nearby towns while both wooden and iron framework bridges spanned the Missouri as well as local creeks. French names such as Rocheport caught our eyes in Boone County, compliments of the early French voyageurs, trappers and missionaries. We enjoyed marvelous views of the river as we passed towering limestone and sandstone bluffs carved by the elements and the river, and pedaled through a dark and only true tunnel of the trail, a 243-foot long one cut for trains into solid rock in the 1890s.

Pumpkins! Pumpkins piled everywhere in Hartsville: Brightly colored pumpkins, enormous, just huge, regular to tiny, awaited their annual October Pumpkin Fest. The sandy soil here provided a perfect growing environment for these autumn gems. A flying witch, arms and legs straight from the impact, splattered around an electrical pole. Straw-filled dummies of an old couple in a buckboard attached to a corn-husk horse in its traces amused us too.

We had reservations in town at the century-old Globe Hotel. Recently renovated after the devastating floods of 1993, its old tin-roofed bay window, grey with white trim porch, white roses and gold fall flowers suited this lovely Victorian hotel in the charming village. This area became a garden spot of the county because of the fertility of rich river bottom—soil, fruits, vegetables, grasses and grains thrive here.

☙

Hermann, named Missouri's most beautiful town, would be our next overnight. Vineyards and wineries provide the most important economic power in the area. The town, much like our Iowa neighbors the Amanas, was founded by a society with nearly utopian goals where it could continue traditional German culture based on farming, industry and commerce.

In 1843, Eduard Muehl and his brother-in-law began publishing the first newspaper in Hermann, the *Hermanner Wochenblatt*, the Hermann Weekly. Muehl, known as a fiery radical freethinker, early and outspoken critic of slavery, was a proponent of cultivation of grapes with the purpose of quality wine production. Expressing his views, particularly regarding slavery, required courage since many in his community were slaveholders. He supported teaching German in the schools to help preserve Hermann's identity as a community of German immigrants. He died in 1854 from cholera, the newspaper was sold and renamed *Hermanner Volksblatt*. His life and work interested me because his great-grandson, Sig Muehl married Lois Muehl, a woman I and many other Iowa City area writers consider to be our mentor and light.

We had to cross the Missouri River to get to town. A local pickup driver, another Good Neighbor Sam, noticed us riding from the Katy and, knowing how narrow and treacherous the bridge could be, blocked traffic for us by driving behind us.

This pretty town featured lots of brick buildings and gardens. We stayed in an old home with a pottery studio and had it to ourselves. Friends of Sandy and Dave's, Doug and Ellie Norris, joined us for supper at a local restaurant, an uproarious meal with stories told, perhaps exaggerated, by those two quiet and sedate (?) Methodist pastors. I knew my mother would not have approved of such boisterous behavior, especially in a public place. Tsk, tsk.

☙

Our final day of cycling brought us to St. Charles where we would end our trip. We reminisced about the things we liked best about our Katy Trail ride: The gigantic limestone escarpments lining the trail on one side with the river on the other; open stretches with harvested croplands; Riverview Traders Camping Store; Herb's, where we sat on a great porch and relaxed with our treats; arched stone viaducts; barges and tugboats hauling gravel on the wide Missouri; autumn colors of green to tan to muted rust to deep crimson. I loved the neat little pull-off places with benches tucked under riverside trees inviting us to sit and ponder the river; eagles soaring overhead, swirling currents and eddies creating designs on the water. From our Oregon trip we recognized the iconic brown Lewis and Clark Trail sign with of one of them pointing, maybe at the future. We would see it again on later treks.

All of us were eager to complete the ride and enjoy the accomplishment. At the end of this final day, however, Betty tipped over just feet from where the trip was to end. She had Addison's Disease so her body did not produce enough adrenaline. In her handlebar bag, she always carried a kit which contained an injection to overcome any bad reaction if she needed it. She told us she did not need it right then, but we still worried about her. We gathered her and her bicycle up and walked them to the van where she waited until the rest of us completed the last bit of our route in St. Charles, the oldest city on the Mississippi River.

Celebrating the crossing of another state, Jim and my thirty-fifth, we packed our bikes on our van and headed west to retrieve Barb's. On our way home, as always, plans for our next ride were the main topic of conversation. Come springtime, we'd be back on the open road, ready for new vistas.

THE TENNESSEE BICYCLE WALTZ IN MY OLD KENTUCKY HOME–2000

Riders: Sandy/Dave, Jim/Jan. Distance: 337 miles

Living in Iowa City has many advantages, among them the opportunities to hear and see people who have made impacts on our world. For example, the experience of hearing Bishop Desmond Tutu speak generated a series of events that expanded well beyond his words.

The date, Monday, February 8, 1999; the venue, the University of Iowa's Carver-Hawkeye Arena. Jim and I arrived early in expectation of a large crowd. We seated ourselves and immediately overheard some people talking about one of our favorite topics: bicycling.

We looked around and recognized Chuck Offenburger, *The Des Moines Register's* Iowa Boy columnist, and his wife, Carla. As part of his job and his love of bicycling, Chuck takes part in RAGBRAI each year. We introduced ourselves to them and to a local couple they were speaking with, Retha and Ray Haas.

Chuck went into spasms of delight when Jim mentioned we planned to bicycle across Tennessee and Kentucky. He had graduated from Vanderbilt University in Nashville, and his good college friend, Doug Bates, lived sixty miles away in Centerville, Tennessee. He enthusiastically spoke about his recent ride in Tennessee and Kentucky and offered to send us some of his route maps. Yes!

As the six of us discussed bicycle trips, we realized Ray and Retha were avid cyclists too. Later on, through riding bikes together and working in our local Habitat for Humanity, they have become two of our best friends. We feel grateful to Bishop Tutu for not only speaking eloquently on

Human Rights and the Truth and Reconciliation Process but also bringing us together with people who have become special in our lives.

Just over one year later, in April 2000, Sandy, Dave, Jim and I drove to Florence, Alabama where we would begin our Tennessee-Kentucky cross-states ride. Dave and Jim did the van/rental car shuffle between Florence and Henderson, Kentucky while Sandy and I spent a relaxing day, meandering through town until their return.

One of Florence's two lakes was created by the damming of the Tennessee River by the Tennessee Valley Authority, part of President Franklin Roosevelt's New Deal Plans. Wilson Dam, begun in 1918, integrated both ancient Roman and Greek architecture into its structure, and was acquired by the TVA in 1933.

The town celebrates native son, Father of the Blues W. C. Handy by the preservation of the log cabin in which he was born, and an annual ten-day long W. C. Handy Music Festival. We couldn't stick around long enough for the pickin' and playin' at the summer festival three months hence.

The first of several days of rain plagued us as we headed our bikes north toward Waynesboro, Tennessee, nearly fifty miles away. Although it is a few miles off the famed Natchez Trace Parkway, this county seat town of twenty-two hundred often serves as an overnight stop for cyclists riding the Trace. Happily for us, the rain enhanced the lime green leaves popping out on the trees lining the quiet highway. Often when it is raining we have to remind ourselves that hydration includes inside the body. We had plenty of it outside.

🚲

Ineffectually, we hoped for better weather the second day. Not only did it rain buckets, but Dave kept breaking spokes on his wheels. He desperately wished for a bicycle shop. We hadn't seen one on the route and thought perhaps Centerville, our next overnight might have one. No such luck. Why do spokes break? Some people say because of impact. Others swear that uneven spoke tension leads to one breaking. If one breaks and tension is not tightened on all of them, more spokes will break. What I do know is it leads to irritation if it happens more than once.

But back to our situation in Tennessee. We had chosen to stay in Centerville precisely because of information from Chuck Offenburger. He had written us about his friend, "Doug loves to have Iowans drop in, especially on bikes." We called the number we had for Douglas T. Bates III and told him of our connection to the Offenburgers and of Dave's plight.

He gamely responded, "Go on over to our house. My wife is leaving to take our daughter back to college in Nashville, but you can have one of our cars to go to a bike shop there." What? He didn't know us and he was willing to loan us his car? When asked about trusting us, he responded, "You're Iowans. You're on bicycles. You're friends of Chuck's." Not only that, they didn't have a rack for Dave's bike so they unloaded their station wagon of college gear and gave that to Jim and Dave to drive to the bike shop.

Astonished and grateful, once again we had solid proof of so many incredibly generous people out there who trust others whether they know them or not. As we thought about it, Jim and I recalled stopping a group of six young touring cyclists on the road near our home and inviting them to stay overnight. They had responded with surprise and skepticism but had decided to stay, cook their own supper and do laundry while Jim and I continued with our original plans to go out with friends. The following day, Sandy, Dave, Jim and I biked to West Branch with them.

After we settled into our motel rooms, Sandy and I spent a now sunny afternoon wandering the streets getting acquainted with another unfamiliar town, Centerville. Jim and Dave drove about sixty miles to the closest bike shop on the edge of Nashville to get the new spokes for Dave's wheel. Does this seem like a bike trip pattern—Jim and Dave driving somewhere and Sandy and I exploring towns?

Among other things, Sandy and I learned that Grand Ole Opry's Minnie Pearl, the funny lady with the $1.98 price tag hanging from her straw hat, had been born in Centerville. But in her comedy act, she always said she was from Grinder's Switch. Although that sounds like a made-up name, it isn't. It also isn't a town, it's a place near an old depot behind the nearby county fairgrounds. At one time there was a main railroad with a spur called Grinder's Switch coming off it. Sarah Ophelia Colley (Minnie Pearl's given name) would watch her well-to-do lumberman father and his workers load lumber from his sawmill onto train cars there. This positive experience, among others of her childhood, influenced her to end her 1980 *Minnie Pearl: An Autobiography* in this way: "I wish for all of you a Grinder's Switch."

Sandy and I finished our town tour and returned to our rooms to again wait for Jim and Dave's return, this time at our own Grinder's Switch Motel where Doug would pick us up for a tour of his beloved home town.

The next morning, we joined Doug and his wife Molly downtown at a breakfast gathering spot, Breece's Café. He introduced us to people there as friends of a friend from Iowa who were spending their vacation biking through Tennessee and Kentucky. He saw their faces and added, "Really." What a treat to spend a bit of time with him, his wife wasn't able to stay, before he headed off to his law office on the square. The Bates family has had members practicing law in Tennessee since 1871, with the exception of five years during the 1920s and during World War II. He was the sixth in four generations. Quite a legacy, sounding wonderfully southern.

With that happy interlude in our memories, we again headed north toward Kentucky. Unfortunately, the skies did not reflect Doug's sunny disposition. It rained and then rained some more.

241

Rolling hills of Kentucky

Creeks rose and overflowed in the spring green. Rivers had begun to top their banks, including Duck River just outside Centerville. We carefully eyed the ditches, streams and rivers and kept our yellow rain gear on much longer than we had hoped to.

When the rain paused, we stopped for snacks along weed-pocked rocks near the rising waters. Despite the rain and maybe due to the cool temperatures, most trees had not leafed out. But the redbuds claimed the day! Their lively fuchsia blooms against green pastures enticed us to whip out our cameras to freeze the moment. Then our eyes caught the bold pink of what we learned were star-shaped butterfly pentas. What luck! More smiles from us celebrating gently rolling landscape and warmer temperatures—and blossoms.

The relaxed pace of this forty mile day of biking ended with a night in Waverly, a quiet county seat in Humphreys County. The quietness of the area undoubtedly enticed Jesse James to settle near here with his wife in the 1870s. Reportedly, they lived as normal a life as they would ever know for a couple of years before returning to Nashville where his brother Frank lived. An Iowa connection: during the Civil War this town was established as a Federal US Civil War fort where the 8th Iowa Cavalry had been assigned.

🚲

On another short-mileage day of forty-five miles, we biked to Dover, a gateway to the famous Land Between the Lakes. Horse farms graced the land along the highways, and occasional blacktop roads flanked with blossoming trees made us wonder what lay at the end of them. Maybe more ponds, streams, small lakes and forests like we'd been seeing, or perhaps another horse farm.

🚲

We left Dover on The Trace, not the Natchez Trace but the Woodlands Trace National Scenic Byway, and cycled past Fort Donelson National Battlefield. This Trace was a 45 mile paved roadway, the main north-south route through the Land Between the Lakes. The Land Between the Lakes National Recreation Area refers to the 170,000 acre peninsula between Kentucky Lake formed by the Tennessee River and Lake Barkley with the Cumberland River running through it.

This area encompasses a restored native habitat for bison, fallow deer, elk, eagles and other wildlife. Some, like the bison and elk, were indigenous (Really!) and had lived there as late as the 1800s, when overhunting and habitat degradation eliminated them.

As we neared the Kentucky border, we saw a massive, stone walled, pyramid-shaped construction with a pit in the middle, standing alongside The Trace. This Great Western Furnace was a reminder of the heyday of one of the few industrial areas in the south. Impressed with the good condition of its limestone block walls, we were surprised to learn it had only produced for one year, starting in 1852. However, it had produced over thirteen hundred tons of iron within thirty-four weeks.

A stiff breeze made us alert and eager to get to our overnight destination of Grand Rivers where The Trace ended. I enjoy these names that evoke the grandeur of the natural beauty of the area and say geographically where they are located.

🚲

After our night there, we crossed the Cumberland River on our way to Princeton. None of us had known until we arrived there that the tragic removal of Cherokee Indians, among others, from their homelands in Tennessee, Alabama, North Carolina and Georgia to Oklahoma Territory on The Trail of Tears in 1838-39, came as far north as this part of southern Kentucky. A tavern built in 1797, turned into art gallery, is the only original building still standing on what is now the Trail of Tears National Historic Trail.

The following two days of bicycling on scenic highways, past trails, lakes, grasslands and forests, had a wonderful calming rhythm to them. We didn't have to hurry because we biked less than fifty miles per day. We hadn't biked so few daily miles since we had cycled in the Netherlands. However, this landscape rolled and did not resemble the Dutch countryside.

Our accommodations in Henderson, on the Ohio River, delighted us. The two-story, red brick Victorian L & N Bed and Breakfast is part of the historic Main Street. Its back door opens to a view of the railroad tracks which still carries over fifty trains a day alongside the inn. We heard them during the night but weren't disturbed, rather lulled by the rumbling sounds. The B&B had been meticulously renovated and maintained by very gracious hosts, Norris and Mary Elizabeth Priest. Sparkling stained glass windows and a gorgeous carved and curved oak staircase added to the charm.

Henderson had been founded and mapped with the help of Daniel Boone in 1797, but even more fascinating to us was the impact that the naturalist, John James Audubon, had on the city. He once owned a gristmill on the Ohio River and spent years studying and painting the bird life in wooded acres nearby. Because Henderson lies on a migratory bird flyway, it must have been a perfect place for him to live and work. Our visit enhanced our appreciation of the bird sanctuary and memorial dedicated to Audubon as well as the extensive collection of original Audubon art and memorabilia in the museum.

The day we left Henderson truly must have been a slow news day. I was interviewed by a TV reporter and photographed riding my bike. At breakfast, a live radio broadcast featured Jim as he explained our goal of bicycling across all fifty states, mentioning that states number thirty-six and thirty-seven had been claimed by Tennessee and Kentucky.

Content and dry in our van, the over four hundred mile trip home seemed laid-back. Unfortunately, rain continued to pound Tennessee. Our hearts went out to the affected people when we saw newscasts and videos of the floods—we knew we could have been cycling in the midst of it all.

CHICO HOT SPRINGS, MONTANA THROUGH WYOMING TO BOULDER, COLORADO-2000

Riders: Sandy/Dave, Jim/Jan. Distance: 405 miles

July of 2000 brought the Down Home Family Reunion to Chico Hot Springs, Montana, where cousins Suzee and Steve Branch hosted a marvelous gathering with many of our far-flung family. Long-time friends Sandy and Dave Schuldt joined us as honorary Down Family members. After the reunion they, Jim and I rode our bicycles to Boulder, Colorado.

CHICO HOT SPRINGS TO MAMMOTH HOT SPRINGS (DO I DETECT A VOLCANIC PATTERN?)

After Jim's Saturday panic of realizing he had forgotten to pack his biking shoes, a trip to Livingston with Dave to find a bike shop, buying a pair that didn't really fit, our wonderful sons-in-law Doug and Bernd swept into action. Bernd presented his biking shoes to Jim who declared they were too big. Doug rallied and offered his shoe inserts which made Bernd's shoes fit just fine.

Sunday our family arose early to finish packing, get baggage into our van, and hope we had everything we needed in our panniers. Logistics determined that part of our Boulder family would haul our panniers in their vehicle to our overnight in Yellowstone and Doug would drive our van to Boulder. Tania took the all-important photos, we four riders said our goodbyes and set out to conquer Wyoming.

Highway 89, a lovely route with great shoulders, paralleled the Yellowstone River which flowed north to the Missouri River. The road gradually climbed to 6259 feet from Chico Hot Springs' mile-high and Emigrant's even lower altitude. Near-desert vegetation, sere grasses gradually gave way to scrubby bushes and sparsely wooded hills. We faced heat—up to 98 degrees plus headwinds—creating a challenge even going downhill when we could only get up to nine mph. Mara, Tania, Ryan and Cameron caught up and checked on us mid-morning on their way to drop our panniers off, see some museums and continue on home to Boulder. I envied them their AC.

Of geographical interest, we paused on the forty-fifth parallel of latitude—halfway between Equator and North Pole. Of human interest, as we pedaled along a couple in a red pickup truck took our photos. We fully expected them to reappear to try to sell us the prints but they didn't. Maybe they just thought we were crazy people doing what we were doing in the heat. We might have agreed with them on that.

A short time later we approached a rest stop and saw our nephew and niece Steve and Marie at the side of the road videotaping and photographing us. We had been looking for them but hadn't seen them pass us. Marie will always remember Yellowstone National Park, not only for its amazing geysers and other wonders, but because of an incident there on the way to the reunion. She, Mom Down and I had been standing in a restroom line when we heard a shrill complaining voice, "I can't see anything here at Yellowstone. There are too many trees." Before soft-spoken Marie could even think about it, she heard herself say, "Then you should have gone to Disneyland!" She looked startled at her own comment but Mom and I loved her zing.

Steve and Marie left and we crossed the highway to the exotically named Cinnabar Store, a welcome oasis on this desert-temp day. We walked in, I spotted a gorgeous fuchsia, black and azure Guatemalan woven vest, tried it on and bought it. I loved it then, love it still. While there, we decided to have our first lunch, delicious wild rice and black bean soup. Adding cool drinks, we had a very refreshing respite. Then back on our bikes to head to Gardiner where we would eat pie.

We could hardly believe the views enveloping us—high western valleys flanked by stunning mountain ranges, wildly rugged peaks, big horn sheep gazing at us from their rocky crags. What an opportunity for a calendar photographer, and for us who were not!

Rustic letters engraved on the Roosevelt Arch at Gardiner welcomed us: *For the Benefit and Enjoyment of the People.* Constructed by the US Army stationed at Fort Yellowstone, an active fort from 1886-1918 and the future site of Mammoth Hot Springs, President Theodore Roosevelt had laid the cornerstone in 1903.

Next came the serious business of climbing nearly five miles of 6 to 7 percent grade in suffocating heat. We took frequent breaks and drank quarts of water. When we knew we would make it, we relaxed at the bottom of the last climb and talked with a local. He described the temperatures as like Las Vegas, creating extreme fire danger in this hottest summer people remembered in northwest Wyoming.

Elk, as opposed to The Elks as in the Fraternal Order of, soundlessly greeted us at the hotel and kept on grazing. Meager cross-ventilation made our cabin a bit less than miserable. After we ate mouthwatering trout or salmon with pasta dinners, Sandy and I climbed a short path up to the Mammoth Hot Spring Terraces, chalky white travertine testaments to hot springs cascading over limestone formations, ever changing, ever growing.

Jim, the weary but with happy feet thanks to the cobbled together shoe fitting, went to bed while the rest of us elected to hear a presentation on *Music and Yellowstone*. The musician-speaker enriched his colorful tale by telling of his attack by and narrow escape from a mama bear protecting her cubs from his encroachment—a close encounter of the ursine kind.

We went to bed with windows and drapes flung wide open to let the slight breeze in. Before morning, the air became cool and comfortable and so did we.

⚲

MAMMOTH HOT SPRINGS TO OLD FAITHFUL, 57 MILES, 95 DEGREES

We stood outside the hotel and gazed at our surroundings. Yellowstone, home of ten thousand thermal features, three hundred of them geysers. Unparalleled in all the world, this array of geothermal phenomena took our breath away—and I'm not referring to the sulphur smell that permeates the air. Mud pots, steam vents/fumeroles, hot springs, geysers, all evidence of its volcanic past and present active earth. This history echoes huge eruptions two million years ago, one point three million years ago and sixty-four thousand years ago. At one point the major volcano collapsed and formed a thirty by forty mile caldera. Today we would cycle along one ridge of the caldera as we rode from Norris to Madison. Imagine that.

We biked off to face more inclines but Sandy and I couldn't resist a mile and a half loop to admire the hot springs formations of orange, gold, red, cream—colors of dawn and sunset.

Impressive pine forest scenery marked some of the day. However, in 1988 a wildland fire swept through one-third of the National Park. Now vast hillsides of tree skeletons, ashy grey earth with slashes of white, acres and acres of blowdown looking like a wild game of giant pick-up sticks, stretched along the mountains and valleys. But hope appeared in the struggling baby pine trees, popping up from the ash after the fireweed, one of the first plants to appear after forest fires. Once trees grow again and block the sunlight, the fireweed dies, leaving its seeds to await another fire and after that, sunlight to sprout again.

At our picnic spot at Norris, we had a surprise visitor, a scrawny looking coyote who circled us, hoping for a handout. He didn't get one. We continued on planning to see the marvelous scenery along the Gibbon River to Madison Junction we'd heard about. Unfortunately, heavy traffic consumed our energy and made it impossible to appreciate our surroundings—we couldn't even savor the fact we traced the edge of the caldera. The 14 mile trip from Norris became even more difficult because of the chopped up road surface. Most drivers treated us well but some rude ones stood out.

Jan and the wildfire remains

No shoulder existed except at turn-offs so as cyclists, we had no place to ride except on the road. An RV driver pulled up behind Sandy and blared over his loudspeaker, "Get inside the white line!" Startled, she had no place to go to get away from this seemingly dangerous and frightening man.

Fortunately, the road from Madison to Old Faithful had a shoulder. As we climbed one hill, we spotted three people who stood beside their car waiting for us, cousin Dick Joslin, his sister and her husband. During the reunion, they had been based in a campground north of Chico Hot Springs but now toured Yellowstone—a delightful surprise for us. We stopped to chat, then moved on and hoped to see them again.

Visions of Yellowstone: thermal springs, hot pots plopping bubbles, paint pots, gold to green treacle trickling from volcanic waters to swift-moving streams, placid lily pad ponds, a pelican drifting on a lake or in the sky, a bleak post-apocalyptic landscape of the eight hundred thousand acres of fire-destroyed forest. But, along with vast but intermittent signs of the Fire of 1988, lovely broad vistas of flowering meadows and geysers bordered the road the rest of the way to Old Faithful.

Once we arrived at the hotel to check into our cabin, Dick and company intercepted and informed us that Old Faithful would erupt in twenty minutes. In all his over seventy years this was

Dick's first opportunity to see this wonder—he had never been to Yellowstone before. The dramatic eruption captivated him and we enjoyed it even more seeing his reactions.

We said our goodbyes and rolled our bicycles to our cozy cabins. The only challenge came when we had to carry our loaded bikes up five steps to our room. We sat down, cooled off on the steps and chatted with our neighbors, a couple from California, who complimented us about our bicycling efforts. All along this trip, people have been saying how they admired what we are doing, honking and yelling drivers excluded. They sometimes subtly asked our ages. Dick had even gone so far as to say it was thrilling to see us riding by in our matching sky blue Montana jerseys. Wow! We were thrilling!

Before we ate supper at the Old Faithful Inn, we rambled about this rustic architectural gem with huge beams supported by Y-shaped logs. I remember being impressed by it when my family visited it in the '40s. The food at the sweltering restaurant ranged from very good to just all right. Another surprise awaited us as we looked around the room and saw someone we knew who wasn't a family member. Jim and I approached and greeted him, "Hi, Steve."

He glanced up, "I remember you! You were on the Inside Passage cruise a couple of years ago. You're the bicyclists."

Obviously, Steve Hurt, our excellent tour guide when we took our mothers to Alaska in 1998, possessed a terrific memory. We asked what he was doing now. "I'm leading bus tours for old people, not active people like you. Mostly I take them to national parks." We chatted a bit more, thanked him again for the way he'd made the Alaska trip so memorable for our mothers and us, and bid him farewell. This unexpected encounter with Steve reminded us how fortunate we have been to meet such cordial and interesting people as we rambled about the seemingly smaller and smaller world.

On our way back to our still overheated cabin, we stopped at Hamilton General Store for our food supplies for the next day. Part of the extra heat had to do with our routine of doing our laundry when we shower. We then hang the clothes up in the breezier places, like windows, which cuts off that very breeze from us. We didn't know what critters might come around the cabin during the night to try on our colorful biking jerseys so didn't want to dry anything outside. I decided to read until I got sleepy, page two to be exact, when my book fell down and my eyes closed for the night.

🚲

OLD FAITHFUL TO JACKSON LAKE LODGE, 67 MILES, 88 DEGREES

On a brisk, pretty morning we packed up and headed to breakfast at the striking new Snow Lodge, constructed with lots of beams and branches to resemble a forest canopy.

Our ride to West Thumb, then two miles farther to Grant Village was far more pleasant than I'd thought it might be. I had seen the route from a car last Friday and things looked different from a bicycle seat, in this case, better. We crossed the Continental Divide three times today, the first two at altitudes of 8,262 and 8,391 feet before we arrived in West Thumb. That helped us earn our lunches, but none of the climbs managed to get to the lung-burner stage I had anticipated. The third crossing, south of Grant Village, lay within the Yellowstone Caldera as the first two had.

We stopped at Grant Village in hopes of seeing Nancy Procter, our guide from Jim's and my last February's snowshoeing and cross-country skiing Yellowstone Institute Winter Course. She had been a valuable guide with many resources including a deep appreciation of two favorite environmental writers of ours, both born in Iowa—Aldo Leopold, who wrote *A Sand County Almanac*, and Wallace Stegner, *Angle of Repose*. She was away leading a three day trip so we just left a note.

While we roamed the visitors' center, we met a man from a remote village in northern Manitoba where he teaches computer science. He had cycled from there and planned to continue to Glacier, Banff and home. He really traveled light. His rank odor proved it. His Spartan equipment included two small front panniers, a handlebar bag, no rear panniers but a sturdy plastic, bear-resistant barrel on his rear rack, along with his sleeping bag, tent and quantities of water. In contrast, our bikes looked severely overloaded. My journal notes *Me-thinks he has only one change of clothing and a bit of warm and rain gear. We have lots of comforts including snacks, changes of clothing, including clothing for dinner and bedtime.*

We traversed the last up-the-hill-over-the-Divide in the park while reveling in the bucolic setting of sharply rising mountains and evergreen trees. Our next picnic spot at the beginning of Lewis Lake permitted more relaxing time to watch a white pelican dive for its lunch. We just dived into our panniers for ours.

Road construction confronted us, with crews laying chip seal, definitely an improvement in road quality despite my generally negative reaction to chip seal. Most of the drivers, however, were inconsiderate and sped past us, throwing up gravel, rocks and chips plus a lot of dust. Yuck!

We were relieved to make it safely to Jackson Lake Lodge. Only one room was available for us, fortunately, a large one so we and our bicycles had enough space. Hanging laundry was a bit tricky so Jim pulled a "Manitoba Man" and didn't do his that night. Luckily, he did not emit an unpleasant stench.

Behind the lodge, a local moose waded in a pond, appropriately dubbed Moose Willows. A large enthusiastic crowd gathered to see what he would do. He did exactly what moose do and eventually wandered out of the pond into the willows. Now you see him. Now you don't. An excellent young pianist entertained us by playing everything from pop, ragtime to classical during dinner. Our attentions were divided between music and moose as we munched our Haagen-Dazs almond fudge bars. Dee-licious!

For years in my family farm home, a trio of sepia photos of the Grand Tetons hung. I loved them so hoped to see that scene again in real life. Sadly, in addition to their massive destruction, Idaho's forest fires created a haze over them, dimming the view of these otherwise spectacular mountains.

JACKSON LAKE LODGE TO DUBOIS 62 MILES WITH RAIN ON THE PASS, EVENTUALLY 95 DEGREES

Trying to evade tooth-rattling potholes on the five miles from the Lodge to Moran Junction quickly woke us up after a light breakfast failed to. From there we had a fun tailwind push to the Hatchet Ranch and Motel where we devoured breakfast number two. We admired the fact that the Hatchet Ranch people, in conjunction with a National Trust group, purchased and set aside land for wildlife preservation. We need more civic-minded people and groups like them.

Cycling up Togwotee Pass at 9,658 feet seemed intimidating, especially after we had just eaten—we really needed blood to flow to our legs but a lot of it went to our stomachs. It began to rain, not hard, just enough for us to put our yellow front pannier covers on. The gentle cooling rain refreshed our bodies and spirits.

Despite the beauty of the ride, we hated to leave the dramatic Tetons behind. The valleys that opened up as we rode made us realize again how dazzlingly stunning and truly grand our country is. We kept turning around or checking our rearview mirrors to see the Tetons fade until we could see them no more.

Within a few miles we ate lunch and danced around trying to avoid mosquitoes and eat our sandwiches at the same time. Dave had blood running down his leg from one bite and the rest of us developed itchy welts to commemorate the event.

At the Tie Hackers Memorial, a bas-relief limestone monument overlooking the Wind River, we learned about these skilled and hard-working men and their importance to the development of thousands of miles of railroad in the west. A multitude of Irish and Scandinavians became tie hackers chopping down trees and slicing the timber into eight and a half foot ties. These vital ties would be skidded/dragged down the mountain by mules or horses and floated downriver. We hadn't been working as hard as the tie-hackers had but nevertheless felt a kinship as we rode into Dubois, overheated and weary in miserably sweltering weather.

Bordering the town to the south, lakes and glaciers carved the towering granite peaks delineating the Continental Divide along the Wind River Range's one hundred mile crest. To the north of DuBois, Yellowstone's volcanic activity had formed the Absaroka Range. The Whiskey Mountains, named for the reputed whiskey stills found there during Prohibition, also jut up where the largest wintering herd of big horn sheep in the area feed. Mountains everywhere!

Main street, called Ramshorn, lined with attractively restored brick buildings from the late 1800s and early 1900s, impressed us. There was a lot of money in Dubois although much of it came from elsewhere. An incredible number of new, often huge homes were being constructed in the area, many owned by Hollywood actors. Hunting, snowmobiling, fishing and other outdoor pursuits help Dubois thrive. The old western culture was being lost but the town and local people will survive. No doubt the townspeople ask themselves which is the greater loss.

🚲

DUBOIS TO LANDER 83 LONG MILES, 98 DEGREES 5,367 FEET, FORT WASHAKIE 5,570 FEET

After breakfast at the Cowboy Café, we left Dubois on a glorious downhill into the Valley of the Wind River. Gorgeous hues ranging from beige to red to purple windswept rocks created a vivid contrast to the green foliage that grew along the swiftly flowing Wind River. What an exquisite ride, just flowing and dipping like the river itself. My heart sang the whole way.

We stopped in Crowheart, 6,078 feet, for juice and a bit of rest. A little general store with a bit of everything became a convenience store/hardware store with hunting and fishing supplies. The proprietor Kathy busied herself with unloading new inventory of products from dog food to athletic drinks. In the distance, dramatic Crowheart Butte dominated the area but a marker focused on highly regarded Shoshone Chief Washakie. He was not only a fierce warrior, but a skilled diplomat and leader as well. He was so admired, the people of Wyoming chose him to represent them with a statue in the Capitol Building in Washington, D.C.. His greatest sorrow was the government of the United States did not keep their treaties with the Shoshone. He was buried with full military honors.

We rode with ups, downs and blazing hot temperatures and a slowly flattening tire, Dave's. He pumped it up a couple of times and made it to town where he and Jim discovered a tiny sliver of metal, probably from steel-belted radial tires. Itsy-bitsy menaces.

I rode around town trying to get information about Chief Washakie and Sacajawea's burial sites. We found his at the edge of town but hers was a couple of miles farther out in a cemetery—a very poignant and moving sight. Flowers, mostly plastic which would last in the heat, abounded. Lovely carved headstones or simple rocks painted white had basic life information written on them. The monuments to Sacajawea and her two sons inspired us to contemplate her extraordinary contribution to the Lewis and Clark Expedition. Her efforts had been absolutely crucial to the eventual expansion of our country. I thought deeply about the sacrifices she had made and the risks she had taken. I again felt sorrow that so many women in all times of history have not been recognized for what they have done. I'm so glad we stopped there to honor her.

Sixteen more 98 degree miles and we would be in Lander, known as the City of Bronze because of all its statuary. When we arrived, my mileage read over eighty miles. I logged more than the others because I had biked around Fort Washakie. What a relief to be in Lander and have a chance to cool off and clean up. It took so long to get to our motel on the east side of town, I began to wonder if we would ever get there. I am not a stalwart pioneer. I like AC.

Sandy and Dave had inherited plumbing problems. Dave had been ready to shower, grabbed the water control handle, turned it and water squirted straight out of the faucet while he still had the handle in his hand. Eventually they moved to a new room where the plumbing held no surprises.

Soon our water pipes began roaring every five minutes. The plumber said they'd probably stop after all the guests finished showering. Wrong. We had to leave the faucet running more than a trickle and I had to hop up several times to adjust the flow to get rid of the noise. We told the manager what we had done and left to eat at Amaretti's. Italian music played and wonderfully relaxing, subdued atmosphere plus terrific food made the evening very special. I had salmon over spinach on whipped sweet potatoes with a sweet potato vinaigrette. When I went to the restroom, Italian language tapes played for our educational enjoyment. What contrasts we had been treated to that day.

High Plains drifters

LAYOVER DAY IN LANDER, 95 DEGREES

My journal entry begins: *Wonderful, wonderful layover day.* I love them. Most of us do, especially when blistering conditions exist outdoors and we can have an indoor retreat if we want.

Our large motel room had an entire wall of windows overlooking the Popo Agie (popo-shia) River. A riverside campground and its occupants provided us, especially Jim, with endless entertainment. We watched dogs wandering, people putting up tents, tents collapsing, tents being blown into the air, Scouts arriving. After breakfast and laundry, we walked downtown. I hoped to find a new pair of shorts. I did and found a shirt too. Jim bought a butterfly tote bag for his mom, a butterfly enthusiast. We bought groceries at Mr. D's and commented on seeing a truck marked Harker's Meats, headquartered in Jim's hometown in northwest Iowa, in the middle of Wyoming cattle country. Bowls of soup for lunch at Mom's Malts followed by napping, writing, reading and watching the nearby campground activities made a great low-key afternoon.

Before supper, Jim and I strolled down to Gabel Street, a dead-end, two-block street. Why? Gabel is my maiden name and we rarely see anything with that name, unlike my married name Down which is announced on old elevators, *Going down,* or written on newer elevator buttons, tagged on warm winter merchandise, conjoined with arrows telling people where to go. You get the idea. We took a Jan and a Gabel Street sign photo to go with the ones we'd taken of the marvelous western-themed sculptures in parks and on the streets. We were really impressed with Lander.

After our delicious Thai dinner we thought we'd head to bed but Jim noticed my bike had a flat tire. Another wire poke. I was just getting ready to shower when he asked my help so I did—in my altogether. Then I decided to lubricate my bike chain. At least I didn't get any of my clothes greasy. I showered, went to bed. Too frequent blasting noise from the water pipes serenaded us all night long.

🚲

LANDER TO SWEETWATER JUNCTION 6800 FEET; JEFFREY CITY 6357 FEET, 59.26 MILES, 85 DEGREES NICE TEMPERATURE ALL DAY

At breakfast we met an impressive Mormon Handcart re-enactor group. They planned to walk on the Oregon Mormon Trail to go to South Pass, the only natural route through the Rocky Mountains to the West Coast. They would pull the same kinds of handcarts as their ancestors had on their way to Salt Lake. This fascinated us as an aspect of history, but additionally, we live in a community, Iowa City, where handcarts were crafted for the long trek west in the 1800s, as exemplified by our Mormon Handcart Park and Mormon Trek Boulevard.

The winds treated us to changes all day long, coming from every direction but nevertheless cooling us. Likewise, in every direction we enjoyed incredible vistas, remote roads leading to who knows where, flocks of sheep, one led by a llama, herd of wild horses, some of the thousands of antelope living between Lander and Jeffrey City, and always, the brown, beige, rose, grey tough grasses flowing in the breeze.

Except for Dave running over a dead skunk, the whole atmosphere created an altogether satisfying day. Still we felt glad to get to Jeffrey City, whose population shrunk to one-hundred after its heyday as a uranium mining boom town. We looked forward to arriving here after we had heard fellow-cyclist Mary Palmberg tell about staying here when she bicycled cross-country with a Women Tours group. She had described it to a T, including the condition and position of the lone telephone booth, wavering in the wind in the motel parking lot, and a once classy neon top hat sign supposedly designed to appeal to travelers in this barren country. Why wasn't it a Stetson?

JC Motel had its problems—no working AC, cross-ventilation or hot or even tepid water. Sandy and Dave's TV didn't work and when he reported it, the creaky-appearing manager unplugged his own TV loaded it on a hay wagon, climbed on his red Massey-Ferguson tractor, hauled to their room and lugged it in. A bit snowy reception but…

We ate at the only café in town, the Split Rock Café whose owner was preparing for a wedding reception dance that night so was very busy. We liked the food very much—I had Indian bread taco, and a big dish of ice cream which cost seventy-five cents. An Adventure Cycling group stayed at the motel too and one member gave us information regarding going through Sinclair, Wyoming.

We voiced our hope the wedding dance crowd would be at least semi-quiet when they came back to the motel. We went outside and were awestruck by the handsome young men we saw, totally spiffed up in their white shirts, black string ties, black jackets, black jeans and black stetsons. As we hoped, eventually the wedding guests became quiet and we rested well.

jj

JEFFREY CITY TO RAWLINS 70.49 MILES, 87 DEGREES, WESTERLY WINDS 14-29 MPH, PLUS SOME HEADWINDS; TWO CONTINENTAL DIVIDE CROSSINGS AS THEY FORM THE GREAT DIVIDE BASIN

After our good night's sleep, things started going downhill. (Why downhill is a generally negative expression, I don't know, especially on a bicycle trip when it should be a positive.) The one and only restaurant's sign said *Open at 7 AM*. By 7:20 no one had come to open it and we needed to get on the road before the heat of the day hit us. We went next door to the convenience store and bought rock-hard, tasteless Danishes, some juice and yogurt, as did quite a few of the Adventure Cycling cyclists. (Sixteen bicyclists stayed at the motel last night.) We returned to the motel to eat and finally left for Rawlins.

We headed toward Split Rock, from whence the café got its name, a landmark once used by trappers, emigrants and others, including Pony Express riders. Extraordinary granite mountains flanked us and we mused, "No wonder the rock hunter from New Jersey we'd met yesterday had been so taken with them."

A tremendous number of motorcyclists passed us, many of whom were headed to the huge rally in Sturgis, South Dakota. At Muddy Gap, Dave and I whooped with joy when we found *Twin Bings,* a candy we knew as kids as *Cherry Bings.* They were still manufactured in Sioux City, Iowa, where Jim and Dave once lived. We each bought one and it felt like a trip back to our childhoods. Dave and I still liked the sweet cherry flavor.

The highway became very busy but we rode the wide and not overly bumpy shoulder. The up-hills along this stretch had double lines so we felt pretty safe. After a demanding slope, we coasted into Rawlins where trees broke up the bleakness of the last miles. We ate lots of veggies for supper, bought fresh fruit for the next two days, topped off the evening with phone conversations with several family members which soothed us before we slept.

⚶

RAWLINS TO RIVERSIDE 60.97 MILES, 84 DEGREES, MOSTLY WESTERLY WINDS 15-30 MPH WITH HIGHER GUSTS.

Getting out of Rawlins created no problems because we took a road parallel to I-80, unlike the Adventure Cyclists who had been routed onto a construction zone on the interstate. We had to ride its wide shoulder for nearly twelve miles, noisy but otherwise pleasant. Jim, the inveterate counter, reported that 232 vehicles passed us including eleven motorcycles.

Shortly after we turned south toward Saratoga, Jim noticed Dave's rear wheel shimmied—another broken spoke. They trued the wheel as well as they could and we all tried to think of ways to get the wheel fixed before we rode Trail Ridge Road on Thursday. Tricky winds made riding very difficult as well. The sun played hopscotch with the clouds and we really reveled in the cooler temperatures when it slipped under the clouds.

Some cyclists going the opposite direction said they were on the *Tour of the Peaks*. Jim queried them about a mechanic and one of the riders told us to look for the Ryder truck. When we saw it, Dave stopped and the driver told him where to find the mechanic in the town of Riverside. What a relief to think this wheel shimmy problem could be so easily fixed. That's not always true with on-the-road situations.

We continued cycling through the lovely green North Platte River Valley. Astonishing to us, some of the homes bordered on English country manor size. As we approached the Riverside/Encampment area, we noticed a forest fire about five miles southeast. Caused by lightning, it had started August 2 but the day we arrived the firefighters had been released to go home. We saw a truckload of them plus more in individual cars. All the people standing along the street cheered and clapped as they passed by. We joined them, the least we could do to thank them for serving such dangerous duty.

We arrived in Riverside and found the cycling group. Their trip, a total of over six hundred miles in seven days. The ride plan for that day included 124 miles, a lot of it against the wind. One mechanic couldn't help Dave but when another one rode in, he was able to pull the freewheel and fix the wheel for him. Despite Dave's offer, he would take no remuneration. That increased our already favorable impression of the riders of the Tour. They offered us fruit and drink and complimented us about bicycling with panniers. One went so far as to say he wished he could be doing what we were.

A sixty-nine year old man with *Tour of the Peaks* told us he was totally out of his league with the other riders. He mentioned he had ridden from his home in Denver to his high school fiftieth reunion in Akron, Ohio, unlike many of his classmates who were barely mobile. Jim and I both thought he looked familiar and recognized his story. During the night, I remembered that Mara had sent us a clipping from *The Denver Post* about him and his ride to Ohio. We also met a rider who in 1999 had set a RAAM (Ride Across America) record of just over five days. We were incredulous. RAAM begins in Oceanside, California and ends in Annapolis, Maryland, climbs 175,000 feet and traverses three major mountain ranges. The competitors ride as long and as fast as they can, stopping briefly to eat, nap and do other things necessary for life, but all of it quickly. I can't imagine riding all night with only short breaks, let alone day after day. No wonder the Denver man felt outclassed.

Later on, when I thanked the mechanic, he was very modest and as I left I said, "God bless you." On many levels, we felt blessed by this group.

The Bear Trap Cabins had an indoor bathroom which we shared among the four of us, and a sink/stove/refrigerator combination. Everything seemed clean but the cabin had very poor cross-ventilation. We discovered outdoors was 20 degrees cooler but an open door invited mosquitoes in. The adjoining Bar and Grill served good food.

After supper we walked to a well-kept park nearby, then to the convenience store for juice. While we stood there, two enterprising teenage boys approached and asked, "Can we clean your windshields?" We told them we had none and had only our bikes. As quick as a flash one responded, "Can we clean your reflectors?"

🚲

RIVERSIDE, WY TO WALDEN, CO 50.43 MILES, WHAT WE CALLED LONG HILL PASS 8200 FEET, WALDEN 8099 FEET, 89 DEGREES, TOP SPEED 39.1 MPH

Our room finally cooled off during the night and became downright blanket weather by 4 AM. Fortunately, the AC that squeaked and squawked all evening shut off once it cooled. What an exquisite day to bicycle with prevailing pleasant temperatures. We thought the morning's ride had to be one of the prettiest we've ever taken—the North Platte River Valley with mountains all around and wheat fields spread before us.

We met a lone cyclist on the road and stopped to speak with him. Personable Colby Prevos from Washington, D.C., distinctive because of the huge real antlers attached to his helmet, had just returned from his Ivory Coast Peace Corps stint. He had cycled from D.C., spent two and a half weeks in Estes Park where he rode Trail Ridge Road several times just for fun and then proceeded with his cross-country trip. While talking with him, we learned he knew Heidi, a young woman who had worked with Dave as a peer minister at Iowa City's Wesley House. The more miles we rode, the smaller the world became.

For miles and miles today, we bicycled along vast Big Creek Ranch in Wyoming which seemed to meld into State Line Ranch in Colorado. I use the term meld because both ranches used the same brand and had the same white buildings with red roofs. We could not imagine how many acres were owned by this individual/group/conglomerate.

Due to the lack of any other shade at lunchtime, we huddled in the shadow of the iconic brown board with white print *Welcome to Colorful Colorado* signs. That meant we had just crossed state number thirty-eight. We rode in the sun, heat and wind that afternoon. Arriving at our overnight town of Walden, our celebration consisted of a trip to the soda fountain—root beer float, chocolate soda, chocolate shake and chocolate malt—just like the good old days.

Sometimes the condition of our motels was so awful, not clean, comfortable or cozy, it forced us to find other less reprehensible ones, like here in Walden. Sandy's comment? "We seem to be going from dump to dump to dump." The second motel had new fixtures in the bathroom plus hot water. Were we coming up in the world?

For our evening's entertainment, Sandy and I took a walk in a cemetery across from our motel. We paid special attention to the sayings and special carvings on them; many had mountain scenes, most appropriate since they were a dominant part of the culture and environment.

Since we last stayed in Walden in 1989 on our first cross-Colorado ride, much had been done to update and beautify the town, including installing street signs with moose symbols. Walden claims the title of *Moose Viewing Capitol of Colorado.* Jim said more than moose exist among the denizens of the area. He came face-to-face with a badger as it ran across the road, into the ditch, then back up to the road where it hissed at him.

🚲

WALDEN TO GRANBY 64.7 MILES, 41-89 DEGREES, WILLOW CREEK PASS 9683 FEET, GRANBY 8367 FEET

The owner of our breakfast place, the Coffee Cup Café, intrigued us with stories, then whipped out her autograph book with Mary Palmberg and her tour group's names. She also had a map of the world with pins for locations and autographs of all her foreign visitors. A fun way to start the day since a few miles later, Dave broke another spoke. Hence, another truing session. His wheel didn't wobble quite so much but he rode carefully the rest of the day. I stopped to write a message and put it in a rancher's mailbox to tell him/her that one of the cattle appeared to have an injured leg. It hobbled to the pond but looked dreadfully in pain. The farm girl emerges.

Other delights of the day—seeing the green trees of the mountains and smelling the pine tree fragrance, followed by climbing five miles up Willow Creek Pass and swooping down the other side like birds. Jim and Dave spied a moose among the willows but Sandy and I sped by without a clue to what we missed. Dave one-upped us in the animal count by spotting a marmot.

We took a short stop at Windy Gap Refuge Lake just before pedaling into Granby. Shakes and floats at Mrs. Z's enticed us before Dave located a bike shop. Closed! We only had seven more miles to go to our B&B but those miles provided some difficult moments. Winds switched over and over and the heat felt miserable. Finally, with help from the wind, we sailed the last bit to our lodging. Dave contacted the bike shop in Grand Lake but their mechanic wouldn't be in until 9 AM the next day, too late for us. So Jim and Dave had more truing to do, this time on a deck overlooking lovely Lake Granby and the western slopes of the Rocky Mountains. Jim announced "His wheel will be okay unless he hits another hole."

After we showered, we took *Big Brown,* our hosts' old van into Grand Lake to eat. Usually the restaurant was open but not that night so the van conveyed us to the Terrace Inn, offering considerably higher class food than we've been eating—trout, salmon, Caribbean chicken, wild rice. That and peach yogurt filled up all the hungry corners.

⚙

NORTH OF GRANBY TO ESTES PARK VIA TRAIL RIDGE ROAD 40-82 DEGREES, GRANBY 8367 FEET, ENTRANCE TO ROCKY MOUNTAIN NATIONAL PARK 8709 FEET, HIGHEST POINT 12,183 FEET, TO ESTES PARK 7522 FEET. WINDS FROM ALL AROUND.

We repacked our panniers so Lisa, Sandy's daughter, could pick them up from the B&B and take them so we didn't have to carry them over Trail Ridge Road. We planned to just take foul weather gear, food, juice, water and sunscreen. Because we had miles to cover before noon, we planned a 6 AM start, just before sunrise. Thunderstorm danger rises in the afternoon in the mountains and we didn't want to get caught in one.

HEROES AND GOATS

Grand Lake, Colorado to Estes Park seemed like a big hunk of real estate to bicycle in one day, especially since our route would reach 12,183 feet in altitude. But riding All-American Trail Ridge Road topped one of Jim's life goals. He, Sandy, Dave and I awakened that August day with eagerness and trepidation.

After a stand-up breakfast of muesli, blueberries, bananas and juice in our motel room, we opened the door to see the rosy glow of sunrise pinking the lake and backlighting the silhouetted sailboats. *My Lord! What a morning!* Immediately early morning wildlife appeared—a moose and her baby foraged in the willows, a fox scurried across the road as a V of geese soared overhead. A kamikaze chipmunk scampered between our bikes, a herd of female elk grazed with their calves.

Jim had difficulty with one cleat and discovered a screw had nearly fallen out. He fixed it and we resumed our ride. We all felt excited and perhaps a bit awed by what we had planned for the day. Sandy and I discussed it and we both felt capable of the climb over Trail Ridge Road. However, we knew the vagaries of weather could impede us with wind, rain, heat, or lightning, whatever nature might throw at us. The ranger at the entrance raved about our endeavor which encouraged us too.

Our slow uphill through montane valleys passed the wonderfully named Never Summer Ranch, pine smell permeating our senses. Rustles in the willows revealed another mama and baby moose. Just before Lisa arrived, an iconic Hartford Insurance logo bull elk hulked on the side of the road. Contrasting his astonishing size with a mere bicycle and not knowing the protocol for bike riders passing a regal wapiti, we proceeded with caution, took his photo and hustled on.

Sandy and Dave had carefully driven, measured and scouted this route for rest areas, hairpin curves, passes, potential food and facility stops. Without my panniers, I did not stay in my "granniest" of granny gears all the time! Yay! When the terrain steepened significantly we began to feel the effects of diminished oxygen. Reactions of people in vehicles passing us sharpened our oxygen-deprived state when they shouted, "Way to go!" with thumbs up, honking and whooping and even clapping. Without their encouragement would we have found the extra oxygen we needed to reach such heights?

Grateful for the shade of trees that helped cool us as we climbed, we stopped frequently for water and snacks, making sure we stayed hydrated. Spectacular scenes in the valley of the Colorado helped spur us on.

Milner Pass, our eighth crossing of the Continental Divide on this trip, lay at 10,759 feet, but the highest point on the road measured 12,183 feet. Once my brain had more oxygen, I remembered the Continental Divide designation dealt with where the water flowed, to the Pacific or to the Mississippi River even if it was not the highest spot on the road.

Once we left the pass, a really frightening sight concerned us, an older driver of a Cadillac who seemed to have no sense of responsibility and who must have thought he owned the road. He truly was a menace after he nearly caused three accidents with bicycles and cars within five minutes.

As we pulled into the Alpine Visitor Center parking lot, people stopped, clapped, cheered and greeted us like celebrities, some saying, "You are tough! I'm really proud of you!" We often hear, "You are crazy!" and we expected some who saw us riding in thought that too. One gentleman approached us and stammered, "Well, you...well, you aren't eighteen anymore either!" We said three of us were in our sixties and the fourth was pushing it. He shook his head and grinned.

A woman in a wheelchair approached me and asked about the fires in Montana since we all wore our Cycle Montana shirts. She congratulated us for what we were doing and mentioned my age. I told her, I'd be sixty-one the following day. She replied, "I'm sixty-eight but I used to be active." I told her, "Our bodies often change what we can do but you have spirit." This poignant moment reminded me once again of how vulnerable we can be and how fortunate the four of us have been with good health and strength.

We relished the views and attention, chatted with onlookers and ate our purchased lunch. Mine tasted awful. Getting out of the parking lot managed to be trickier than we had imagined. Jim went out first, then a car cut off Dave who caught his tire in a drain and tipped over, knocking his handlebars and seat askew. Unhurt, he straightened everything and proceeded on. We completed our climb to the tundra and highest point on Trail Ridge. We met Lisa again at Rock Cut where we thanked her profusely for making the climb so much easier and Sandy told her she could go on home.

We glanced at the western sky. How quickly it had become a menacing black, promising one of the summer afternoon storms that frequently races through these mountains. At this altitude, there would be lightning, so we needed to move fast to get down the mountain to shelter. As we descended, we became cognizant of the dangerous drop-off on the right side of the road. A moment of carelessness would have caused quite a tumble to the glacier-fed moraine lakes far below.

Moments later we noted not only the changing weather. We had been the happy recipients of support and cheers, but at warp speed they switched to heckles and jeers. We became scapregoats. No longer in danger of falling off the mountain, we had to contend with having no shoulder, a solid wall of rock on the right, and nowhere to go except down the mountain road. Many drivers did not understand that and yelled at us. "Get off the road you idiots!" was the kindest of the abrasive to downright nasty comments made about our inconveniencing them by riding too slowly on what they thought were *their* roads. They readily shared their views with us but we had no time to reciprocate with the "You can thank bicyclists and the League of American Wheelmen for taking the forefront in getting roads paved…" lecture. How fine the line between hero and goat!

With roiling sky, distant thunder and impatient motorists spurring us on, we pedaled past evocatively named Lava Cliffs, Iceberg Pass, Forest Canyon, Rainbow Curve, and Beaver Ponds.

We prayed for safety, not just from the impending storm. I exhaled a huge "Whew!" as we turned left at Deer Ridge Junction and swooshed into the Big Thompson River Valley leaving most of the cars and their all too verbal passengers. Behind us lay tumult and ahead, refuge in Estes Park. After a brief but necessary stop at the Fall River Visitor Center, we raced into town to our reward at The Malt Shoppe.

Treats in hand, we relaxed on benches outside the shop and celebrated our safe journey. We overheard a blonde woman exclaiming to someone, "Did you get caught in the hail up on Trail Ridge Road? What a terrible storm! We're so glad to be out of it." We four eavesdroppers nodded in agreement. I thought, *We're glad to be out of it, too. We preferred our ice in ice cream.* None of us bothered to ask her if she had seen four crazy people on bicycles up there for fear of what she might say.

We meandered the bike path that rounds the lake and cut off to our motel—a very cheering sight. As we cleaned up, Jim repeated over and over, "We biked Trail Ridge Road. We biked Trail Ridge Road." He added that the whole day went much faster than he wanted it to, after all, this day had been on his Bucket List. As for me, I had decided that in addition to never bicycling across

Wyoming again, I didn't need to bike Trail Ridge Road again either, but I was oh so glad I had done it once.

By the time we were ready for dinner with Dick and Betty Mitchell, four of us were yawning. This had been a VERY BIG DAY. But first we got to tell our tales to our friends. Before going to bed, Jim and I repacked all our gear to take only what we needed the following day in our panniers so Sandy and Dave could take the rest back to Iowa City. The conundrum was, I couldn't remember what I'd packed for Chico and the Family Reunion that still might be clean and in Boulder. Right then I determined that, given the opportunity, I could get used to just packing in a garbage bag!

Our hot, hot room didn't cool off until midnight. When I opened the door and just stood there, Jim wondered what I was doing. I just needed cool mountain air.

MY 61ST BIRTHDAY, ESTES PARK 7522 FEET TO BOULDER 5239 FEET, 40 MILES, COOL TO NEARLY 90 DEGREES IN BOULDER, MILD ESE WINDS

We joined Sandy and Dave before 6 AM for a celebratory birthday breakfast at the Egg and I. They gave me a delightful Kokopelli bicycle magnet. Jim and I returned to the bike path with our lightened gear and continued around Estes Lake. The stunning views of the Rockies in our rearview mirrors demanded we stop. Yesterday we had been up there—biking over them! We stopped three women walkers to ask how to get onto Highway 36. In the ensuing conversation, they learned it was my birthday and where we had been biking. Their enthusiasm and good wishes included, "You are such inspirations!" and sent us off feeling even better.

I reflected on people's responses to our venture, from "What are you? Crazy?" to "I admire you but I can't imagine doing that," to "You inspire me." I'm not including the invectives of those who want us off the road completely and are very willing to drive us there. I guess we have reached the age, state of gray-hairedness, plus lines in our faces, to think some people could take heart and consider that older people can do physically demanding activities, even if they seem a bit foolhardy.

A four-mile climb followed by a fifteen mile descent into the town of Lyons required little braking to maintain a reasonable speed. Traffic increased as we approached the town but it didn't detract from the ride. We stopped for pecan waffles at Andrea's German Restaurant and called Mara to let her know we were about twenty miles away and would be at their house by noon, barring mechanical problems, headwinds or other glitches.

The pleasant ups and downs from Lyons to Boulder meant we could pedal slowly enough to appreciate our surroundings including the amazing growth in Boulder County. We arrived in the city and soon connected to the bike trail that led us to Mara and Doug's neighborhood. We arrived shortly before noon when Mara, Ryan and Cameron returned from the barn where she stabled her horse Michael. Time for more family fun. What a super ending to a memory-filled adventure.

⚲

NEBRASKA-COAL CAR COUNTING COUNTRY-2001

Riders: Sandy/Dave, Jim/Jan. Drop-off, pick up: Cousin Dick. Distance: 495 miles

We four Iowa Citians followed our noses to the kitchen where Dick was preparing his famous pancakes. He knew how to feed bicyclists! Not only that but we would all leave his home in Omaha and share a first for him—his first opportunity to travel to western Nebraska. The beautiful day was made even better by seeing the countryside, especially the green rolling Sandhills, through Dick's eyes.

We drove to Chimney Rock forty-two years after Jim and I had seen it on our honeymoon, and noticed the pinnacle had eroded over the years. Our repeated comment, "How welcome the sight of the rock must have been to pioneers traveling through or settling in the area." Thousands of them had carved their names in the soft surface of the then three-hundred foot landmark.

After checking into our Scottsbluff motel, the bikers changed clothes to begin our ride to the Nebraska-Wyoming border. The terrain and wind at our backs made an easy ride through Holly Sugar Beet country. Dick picked us up at the state line in time for supper where we discussed how the town was a major railroad center and how the railroad would be a big part of the landscape for us during the first half of our biking route. We retreated to our rooms to repack our gear, some to send with the van and the rest to go into our panniers. Dick was incredulous at all the last details of preparation. Most important, the following day the ride would begin in earnest.

The late May dawn brought us clear blue skies and 30-degree temperatures. Sandy, Dave, Jim and I got up early, had our motel breakfast with Dick and cycled on our way before 8 AM. Dick returned home to Omaha with our van after doing his family duty of helping us with transportation. He planned to pick us up at the Iowa border at the end of our ride.

The cool, crisp day and azure skies continued. At least to begin with. From State Highway 2 which strikes out through the famed Sandhills, we could see all the way back to Scottsbluff and to reddish-gold rock formations, especially iconic Chimney Rock.

This first full day of cycling in Nebraska entailed some longer climbs than we had expected. As we turned north toward Alliance. BANG! Direct wind in our faces. We struggled the three miles to Angora, collapsed and decided to eat lunch using the food we carry with us—PBJ sandwiches with added tuna for more protein, bananas, apples, carrots, Sandy's old-fashioned cowboy cookies and fruit juice. No time to relax, we hopped on our bikes again.

Suddenly the sting of sleet pelted our faces. We'd seen the irrigation spray sweeping across the highway from over one hundred feet away and, at first I thought it was water until I realized it was ice, creating its own bit of misery. Bicycling was not a happy pursuit that day.

The wind did not mellow after lunch. Jim saved me by letting me draft him part of the time. I couldn't always keep up so that meant facing headwinds without protection. The entire afternoon challenged us, particularly the last dozen of the fifty-two miles. We stopped frequently to fuel up, and put gloves and ear warmers on. Sandy suffers from the cold so she put on virtually every warm thing she had brought along. So did I, as the temperature dropped from sixty to thirty degrees.

At last we saw the Alliance water tower but knew it was still several miles away. We pedaled and pedaled but it seemed we would never get there. We finally turned our backs to the wind and zipped to our Holiday Inn Express—sweet relief. The helpful and personable motel staff held the doors open for us to bring our bikes in and then brought us hot water for hot chocolate. Sweet delight.

Jim and I took turns standing in the steaming shower trying to warm up. We did our laundry and went next door to Arby's to have pasta. We had no energy to walk very far in the cold. After we returned to the motel I called my mother and glanced at my bike. It had a flat tire. Jim changed it, repaired the tube and was prepared to relax when he looked down. "Blarst!" Another flat tire. After the unwelcome reprise, he needed to shower again.

The Weather Channel advised us of frost warnings for the next morning with possible snow, northwest winds (that's OK) and highs of mid-30 to mid-50 temperatures. No question about it, we'd layer our shirts and pants and pull on our warmest gloves.

🚲

True to the forecast, on Monday May 21, we encountered northwest winds and chilly temperatures. We bundled up, bought some fruit after breakfast and hit the road before 8. At times, favorable tail-or-quarter-winds helped us sail. At others we still worked hard to earn our lunches and to warm up. However, when the wind gusted to thirty-nine miles per hour, working hard didn't help much.

We frequently laugh at people's perceptions of various states, especially when they comment, "Iowa is so flat." They need to bike the Loess Hills which parallel the Big Sioux and Missouri rivers on the west and the Iowa River Valley slopes as well as bluffs along the Mississippi. Nebraska is another much maligned state regarding topography. Many folks have only seen the state along Interstate 80 and the Platte River. Our biking route did not take us near either. We bicycled in the Sandhills.

Mixed prairie grass stabilized the sand dunes in Nebraska's National Natural Landmark Sandhills which cover an area of about twenty thousand square miles, about one-fourth of the state. Some dunes are over three hundred feet tall. Most of the land has never been broken by a plow for crop production so the Sandhills have been designated an ecoregion, an intact natural habitat.

That doesn't mean that farmers didn't try to grow crops, some did in the late 1800s. By the twentieth century, part of the land produced crops due to the development of center pivot irrigation. That's the kind that creates the huge circles of green we see when flying over the Great Plains. Mostly though, ranchers discovered the grassland provided well for beef cattle. They work to keep the dunes stable with grass so the land does not revert to the desert of long ago. Their half million cattle need places to graze. More cattle but fewer people as the human population declines and younger people move into the cities. Hence the many shrinking towns we saw.

An aspect of the Sandhills that absolutely thrilled us? Water, yes, water in this semi-arid region. The immense (about the size of Lake Huron) but shrinking Ogallala Aquifer lies beneath the Sandhills. Thousands of pothole lakes, wetlands, and some larger shallow sandy-bottomed lakes grace the landscape. As part of the great central flyway, waterbirds, especially Sandhill cranes, ducks and geese, use the lakes as resting places in their migrations. Some, such as the ones we saw in May, stick around for longer periods of time. Our springtime view: gorgeous rolling grass-covered dunes and lots of birds. A feast for our eyes.

We passed through several little villages such as Bingham, with a whopping population of twenty, a one-room schoolhouse, post office and Missouri Synod Lutheran Church. We pulled in where its steps made a perfect place to eat lunch. Same good fare as yesterday.

About ten miles later we came to the largest of the small towns we encountered that day, Ashby, with a sign enticing us with "Best Beef in Ashby." Ashby had about two hundred people and a post office. For all we knew the crowded café, the only one we saw, might have had the only beef in town. For this second lunch of the day, two of us had veggie soup, the other two had chili, the beef in the chili undoubtedly the best in Ashby. Our waitress, all dressed up in her Sunday-go-to-meeting clothes, told us, "I'm going to a wedding." She wanted all the patrons to hurry up and eat so she could be on her way. She handed the checks to us before we'd finished eating and didn't ask if we wanted dessert. No banter today.

Nine miles later we arrived in the county seat Hyannis. Sandy had me in her viewfinder in front of our Hyannis Hotel lodging when we heard someone call from across the street. "Were you biking south of Alliance yesterday? I saw some people on bikes working very hard."

"That was us."

"My name is Shepherd. I'm a retired rancher so now I live in the house across the street." He indicated an attractive sand-colored stucco house. "I ran my ranch south of town. Eighteen thousand acres." When we commented on the size he explained it was the smallest of the extra-large ranches. Sandy and I compared our family farms. Her dad farmed eight hundred, a lot from my perspective since my dad had a half section, three hundred twenty acres. When we recovered from our eighteen thousand acre shock, we asked him farming and ranching questions including, "Is is true there is a Nebraska law that stipulates only Nebraskans can buy ranches or farms?"

"No. But if foreigners want to buy land, there are restrictions." He did not enumerate them but added he greatly opposed too much trade with other parts of the world if US farmers and ranchers were adversely affected. When we mentioned all the sugar beets and pinto beans we've been seeing, he told us sugar beets grew well in the Nebraska Panhandle, especially now with good irrigation systems. Low humidity and aridity in the western part of the state created a perfect climate for beans so Nebraska has become first in the nation for dry beans production.

Mr. Shepherd skipped from agriculture to history. He informed us his wife was the grand daughter of the first sheriff in the area, Bud Moran. Sandy and I remembered reading about this colorful character. According to history, this region had become a favorite hiding place for fugitives from the law. The governor realized the outlaws ruled the territory so appointed R. M. Bud Moran as sheriff in 1886. Mr. Moran accepted. After posting a warning to cattle rustlers, he broke up the gangs and captured the Cherokee Kid, among other dangerous characters.

We hated to stop this fascinating and farming/ranching/history conversation but thanked Mr. Shepherd and told him goodbye. Jim and Dave had finished checking in to the hotel and we needed to get cleaned up. The guys had carried the bikes up the steep back stairs and locked them together at the end of the skinny hallway.

After showering, we went shopping and sightseeing. The Flower Shop sign said *Closed* because of a funeral. The grocery store across the way had postcards and better yet, stocked my favorite brand Henry Reinhardt Original Recipe Root Beer from a brewery dating back to 1856. We strolled about town and contemplated climbing Main Street's very steep hill to see a windmill, but chose instead to visit the courthouse museum. Its eclectic collections ranged from a vast display of salt and pepper shakers, a history of the town doctor, to photos of early day Hyannis.

We hiked to the edge of town to the cemetery overlooking Hyannis and the subdued colors of the Sandhills. Locating the oldest graves and recognizing several of the local names we had seen at the museum highlighted our walk.

Sandy took special note of the name Thurmond and related that her dad always came from Illinois to Hyannis to buy cattle from a man named Thurmond. My dad came from northwest Iowa to buy his in Valentine, a town on the northernmost edge of the Sandhills.

With a tiring day behind us and the air growing chill, we hurried back to the hotel for dinner. We remembered some of the day's subtle highlights: blowing sand; the astonishing number of bee-hives; the lone swan (they mate for life so we wondered what had happened to her/his mate;) fifteen miles of wonderfully smooth road; courteous truck and car drivers; a box turtle crawling across the road. Great day, great memories.

🚲

MAY 22-HYANNIS TO THEDFORD, GRANDMA ADAMS BORN 105 YEARS AGO

A rancher approached us at breakfast and asked, "Have you been riding horses?" Before we could respond he added, "Have they been getting enough oats?" We laughed and told him we were feeding them as well as we could. He chuckled at his witticism, turned and strode away.

As we left Hyannis, the bank time and temperature sign indicated 7:48 and 45 degrees. Speaking of vital statistics for a cyclist, a twenty-three miles per hour wind caught and blew us down the road while the sun tantalized us by playing peek-a-boo. Waterfowl, primarily ducks of all sorts, floated on umpteen pothole lakes dappling the often barren landscape, a terrain that soon morphed into rolling green hills. The sand-adapted grasses, bluestem, switchgrass and grama, created a palette of beige, ecru, brown, russet to emerald tickled with burgundy. An artist's and bicyclist's dream.

We rolled through the day, reveling in the landscape, colors, tailwind and appreciating time amid nature to ponder our experiences. When people ask about being bored while riding, my answer is "Never!" There is always something to see, hear, smell, contemplate, often little things we might miss while zooming by in a car. Sometimes I felt weary when riding but that was due to lack of energy not lack of ways to savor my immediate world.

Sandhills and windmills seem to go hand in hand. Unsurprisingly, we came upon many windmills among the pottery, bronzes, paintings, sculptures and photographs at the Thedford Art Gallery. What a delight to discover such an exhibit in a town of 170 people, and what a treat to have traveled by bicycle and been rewarded so richly.

Among other things, our next stop, the Rodeway Inn, had washers and dryers which meant really clean clothes we didn't have to hand-scrub. At dinner the four of us discussed the most memorable moments of the day in addition to Sandhills scenery. Competitive spirits Jim and Dave talked about the game they developed—CCCC—otherwise known as Coal Car Counting Competition. The whistle and sounds of trains punctuated our long periods of time spent in the saddle, and nearly all of them hauled coal from Wyoming to coal-powered utility plants in the Midwest. Inveterate train car counter Jim, quickly recruited Dave to fall into that same pattern. After seeing a train pass, one of them would loudly announce 116. The other countered with, "Don't you know how to count? There were 109."

And so it went throughout the day. Many days we saw more trains than cars and trucks. Sandy and I laughed, shook our heads and commented on the maturity level of our beloved husbands and their little/big boy competitiveness. Jim also kept track of the trains we saw that day: The first three consisted of oil tankers, then coal and another coal. Then he decided to keep track of the number of cars: 118, 170, 149, 160+, the next one slipped behind a hill, 115… At that time, more than 140 trains a day sped through this central part of the state making it America's busiest train corridor.

⚲

"THEY'RE SO POOR…" MAY 23 THEDFORD TO BROKEN BOW

Breakfast at the motel was marginal at best. A dried out sweet roll and a miniscule glass of juice didn't prepare us for the exertions of the day. Despite that disappointing start, we received the gift of a prairie-wind-filled day, thirty mile per hour breezes with gusts to forty-one.

Absolutely crystalline blue skies backdropped the Nebraska National Forest, originally hand-planted but now germinating in nature's way. Even though I knew ponderosa pines grew in abundance in northwest Nebraska, I had never thought of the state as having a national forest, especially the center of the state. The Forest had originally been founded with the hope of providing timber for cutting. It never reached that magnitude but the Nursery supplies up to 4.5 million high quality bareroot conifer and hardwood seedlings per year. It also serves as the seed bank for the Rocky Mountain region. Who would have thought that amid the prairie grass there would be the largest hand-planted forest in the United States?

Hoping to augment our skimpy breakfast, we cycled into Halsey but wondered if we'd find any food there. We relaxed too soon thinking a sign for a grocery store meant an operating business. No. As we pedaled slowly down the street/highway, I glimpsed a neon sign down a side street, possibly Main Street, indicating an eating place. Eagerly we hopped off our bikes and went inside. We asked a woman whom we supposed to be the owner, "Could we have some breakfast?"

She hemmed and hawed but eventually said, "Well, I guess so." Perplexed by her attitude since we appeared to be her only customers, I thought maybe she didn't usually serve breakfast this late in the morning. Once we sat down and asked her questions about the town and her café, our hostess Evelyn's more affable nature appeared. Along with oatmeal, toast and scrambled eggs, she dispensed insights into the area. She and her husband bought the restaurant thirty years ago and raised their eight children in Halsey although seven of them lived elsewhere "…because there's nothing for them here." Their youngest son, twenty-one years old, lived at home but she didn't offer what his job was. I thought, *What a constrained life they live. They can't travel often because they can't leave the business. They only managed to see their architect son in Phoenix two years after he'd built a new home.*

Evelyn said that Halsey had shrunk to fifty people, mostly elderly, and businesses closed. "We might have to start stocking bread, juice and the like." As we prepared to leave, she expressed concern about our safety telling us to be careful, especially of the trucks. Jim had his hand on the door when she stopped us. She proudly showed us a laminated article from the *Omaha World-Herald* praising their restaurant, *The Double TT*, the food and the ambiance. To me her pride symbolized the heart of a tiny rural town. Although the glory days of their eatery might be over, she and her husband helped fill a great need in the community—a place of sustenance, not just for food but for the spirit.

As we left, we complimented her on the friendliness of Nebraskans. She responded, "They're so poor, they don't have anything better to do than talk to people." We biked on and mulled over our conversation with her and the plight of small towns.

At a gas station north of the next town Dunning, we discovered a treasure: a wall of shelves filled with Sand Hills Pottery. Without hesitation, Jim chose a deep aqua mug with Sandhills etched on it. Norm Van Diest, the owner, asked if we'd like to see more pottery. We said yes and he called his wife to let her know we were coming. A quick ride later, we were up to our elbows in Marlene Van Diest's pottery shop. We learned she had just returned from Jim's and my old stomping ground of Northwest Iowa. She had visited her sister in LeMars, Jim's hometown; cousins in Merrill, my family farm's address and Akron, my birthplace. Jim chose another mug, I found a small covered casserole and Sandy and Dave bought a bowl all of which Marlene packed and mailed to our homes. Fun stop for small world connections and for pottery.

About fifteen miles farther, in Custer County but still on Highway 2, a lovely vision of a church tower appeared on the horizon. We knew the Cathedral of the Sandhills in Anselmo would be a perfect spot for lunch. Sitting on its front steps to eat continued a recurrent theme of a long line of churches at whose entrance we have shared bountiful, and not so bountiful repasts. Church steps always seem to be welcoming strangers to eat there or enter. Better yet, this church welcomed us with unlocked doors beneath a tower that reminded me of the now obscured Gothic tower at the University of Iowa Hospital in our town, Iowa City.

I caught my breath as I walked into the peaceful sanctuary of St. Anselm Catholic Church. Pale aqua carpet outlined with mauve matched the ceiling and arched ribs; dusty rose wainscot set off the gold framed Stations of the Cross; stained glass windows with slightly pointed Gothic-Revival arches lit the room; an elegantly simple altarpiece trimmed with a Gothic carving focused my eyes. I wanted to stay there and just be.

Anselmo sits on the border of the Sandhills to the north and west and cattle country, corn and alfalfa croplands to the east and south. Too soon, the road called and we left our time of respite, and blew on toward Broken Bow. Then Jim had a brainstorm.

WIND RIDER

Jim is a very competitive man, with himself, with others and sometimes with nature. So it was in Nebraska, slightly more than thirteen miles west of Broken Bow. We had a brisk tailwind with temperatures cool enough to make us don our wind jackets.

Tailwinds can be godsends to weary bicyclists, boosting them out of the doldrums, spurring them up challenging hills, or just giving them a break from arduous cycling. On the other hand, tailwinds can make them feel warmer, a pleasant thing when the weather is nippy but quite another on a hot, humid day. When we send our friends off on their bicycles, many of us still call out a line from an old Irish blessing: "May the wind be at your backs!" This wind was. Jim Down is a great ponderer of tailwind power.

The countryside featured cloned rolling hills plus steeper down-and-uphills. The Great Ponderer declared: "I'm gonna see how far I can go without pedaling!" He shoved off, settling into what he hoped would be the most advantageous body position for riding the wind. Sandy, Dave and I intermittently rode the wind but pedaled when our meager momentum threatened to topple us. Jim went on, his legs locked in place over the pedals.

Sometimes he'd sail, other times he wobbled, wavered and realigned his body to propel himself forward. But he didn't pedal. His speed fell to just over two miles per hour, barely enough to remain upright. A break in the road, a shift in body position, or a little draft moved him onward. Still he didn't pedal. At times we were certain he didn't have enough oomph to get up a hill, but he lurched and bobbed on. The rest of us pedaled.

He unzipped his jacket, it poofed up and, as the maize Michelin man, he zigzagged on, prisoner of his competitive spirit and the westerly zephyr. His jacket was now a sail. He did not pedal.

His smile was broad as he announced how many miles he had been blowing: Three miles, four miles, five. I was impressed. Six miles, seven. Ah, this downhill will get him over the next roller but beyond that was a steeper hill. He couldn't possibly make that. And yet he did. He pogoed his bicycle, urging it onward, pleading, "Come on, Klein!" The bike and the wind did his bidding.

We took heart when we saw the *Broken Bow 6 miles* sign. Jim easily clicked off the rolling eighth, ninth, and tenth miles. He waggled his shoulders, "I'm getting stiff riding in the same position. I can't move."

We cheered him on, "You can do it."

Eleven. We could see Broken Bow's water tower clearly now. We were relieved that it wasn't like the plains of Kansas where we had to bike fifteen miles from the place we spotted the grain elevators until we finally reached them.

Twelve miles. Not much farther; he's going to make it.

The long last gentle slope into town assured him of victory. Thirteen. We passed the water tower and he rolled on. "What if I can't unclip my cleats? I'm frozen!" he wailed. We pictured a tumble of Jim and bicycle but were unwilling to let him ricochet off us to stop him. The only advice we could think of was, "Head for the grass! You can fall on it instead of on us!" He was incredulous. He had expected sacrifice from his wife and friends.

There would be no broken bones as we arrived in Broken Bow. Jim turned his bike at the Court House, headed up a slight incline into the wind, slowed, managed to extract his feet from the cleats, dropped his bike and hobbled away exulting, "Thirteen point thirty-eight miles!"

The adversary had been conquered. Jim owned a new personal best Riding the Wind record, thanks to the wind, gravity, a billowing jacket, and the staunch support of his riding companions. His time: one hour twenty-eight minutes. That's important to a Wind Rider.

MAY 24 BROKEN BOW TO ORD, MARA AND DOUG'S 9TH ANNIVERSARY

Morning greeted us with chilly northwest winds of twenty to thirty miles per hour and sprinkles off and on. We could see our breath when we departed Broken Bow and plunged into the green rolling hills that reminded us so much of Northwest Iowa. We discovered we would travel on an initial fourteen mile detour for Highway 2 driven by lots of discourteous drivers, in direct contrast to drivers we had previously encountered. It seemed this crop thought bicyclists didn't belong on the highway so cut us off, drove too close to us, and generally made us uncomfortable and a little nervous.

What a pleasure to get back on Highway 2 to reach Arcadia and read a century historical marker which stated *Arcadians are simply and contentedly anticipating tomorrow.* Reading on, we learned they had endured locusts, tornadoes, blizzards and droughts in their past. They seemed to think as survivors they could outlast even more catastrophes. Simple but good food made a happy lunch at Two Sisters. Not a penny had been spent on decor—we hoped they spent it on food. Before we went in, a windshield replacer from Kearney told us of his fascination with our trip and our gear. He hesitantly asked, "Are you all over 60?" He continued, " I want my wife to bicycle with me but she's not interested at all. I can hardly wait to tell her about you." We hoped she'd at least listen to him.

While we ate, rain came down hard but from then on just off and on. Mud splattered us, but that's not unusual. Six miles east of Arcadia, a couple of long uphills and headwinds made pedaling more strenuous but not as difficult as Sunday's ride from Scottsbluff. None of it approached our South Dakota experience. Jim gave me respite by breaking the wind some of the time.

When we arrived at Ord after 2, we decided to go to McD's close to our motel. We each enjoyed an ice cream dish of some sort but especially liked warming up and relaxing. We asked other patrons where to go for a good meal. Despite being a county seat and having a population of over two thousand, Ord has McD's, a Veteran's Club, a Pizza Hut way out of town and a restaurant where "our source" said the owner smokes and cooks at the same time. We appreciated the tip.

The guys went to check in and Sandy and I stayed and chatted with a variety of locals. When Jim and Dave first left several of the people didn't realize Sandy and I remained. They chirped away, "Look at them! Why are they dressed that way? Weren't there four of them?"

We filled them in on the details. One man offered, "Don't go to any of the cafés in town but there is a good one in North Loup (about twelve miles away) and one at a sale barn in Ericsson."

He forgot we were on bicycles. He followed that with a good bit of his life story, complete with surgery and cardiac rehab details. Amused, Sandy commented, "He's the Neal Sherrick of Ord." Her dad, Neal, a gregarious and outgoing farmer was apt to stretch a point or two to make a good story better.

We walked all over downtown then back to McD's for supper and the Pump and Pantry for Blue Bunny ice cream treats.

🚲

MAY 25 ORD TO ALBION 66.77 MILES, 34 DEGREES TO LOW 70s. NW WIND 18-25 MPH, WIND CHILL 24 DEGREES IN AM

I don't care to ever repeat the lousy breakfast I ate. Fortunately the pretty landscape and blue sky appealed to us. We asked each other, "How many shades of green do we have names for? Emerald, sage, pea, jade, pine, kelly, olive, grass, lime, avocado, chartreuse. We thought we saw all of them that day.

Another thing we saw that day as well as other days—Zimmatics. Irrigation systems are big business in Nebraska and other Great Plains States so we saw lots of them including Zimmatic, which is manufactured locally, as well as Taylor and Valley. To this day, we comment on irrigation systems and recall this Nebraska bike trip.

Once we turned east, riding became easier although we sometimes felt blown about. We ate at the Ranch Café at the sale barn. No auctions now in the off-season but we appreciated the second breakfast. Our waitress/cook/owner told us that half of her new house was still in O'Neill and the other half had been delayed elsewhere on the truck delivering it. She stated, "I'm really excited about getting it together."

The hilly terrain became much drier, with cactus and yucca becoming the primary vegetation. Spalding's Antlers Bar and Café was our lunch spot. We met a woman there whose sister lives in Odebolt, the Down Family hometown. The still hilly nineteen miles to Albion gave us the heeby-jeebies. West of Broken Bow virtually every driver had been careful and courteous. East of there a lot of people seemed to have lost their sense of safety or courtesy. At least we didn't have horrific truck traffic.

For the people who insist that Nebraska is flat, we invite them to drive or better yet bike the hills after hills after hills on this route. That pattern would continue the following two days as well. The weather became warm enough for us to get down to our shorts and shirts, a pleasant reprieve from jackets and tights. Our low-key evening in Albion included a visit to check out old buildings in this county seat downtown and eating at Junction 14 and 91 Café.

🚲

MAY 26 JENNIFER AND BERND'S 10TH ANNIVERSARY, ALBION TO CLARKSON 50 MILES, 70 DEGREES, NW TO N WINDS—EASY GOING SOMETIMES AND VERY DIFFICULT OTHERWISE

After our big bowls of oatmeal at the Dew Drop Inn we commenced our ride. The scenery looked like the hills Jim and I grew up with. We hit a very rough twelve miles of striated road surface. We committed to riding it then wondered if we had made the right decision. Nearing the end, Dave took a vote on whether to turn back and find another way. Sandy and I voted to go ahead and told Dave if he wanted to go back and come another way, we'd meet him in Clarkson. He continued on. After four miles we stopped in Lindsay to go to The Watering Hole. Jim and Sandy had what they thought to be scrumptious cinnamon rolls. I had a root beer float so our bill, including a bottle of grapefruit juice totaled $2.60—way too cheap. I told that to the proprietor and she said she tells locals they think nothing of paying big bucks in Omaha but don't want prices to increase at home. She added, "And we probably work harder than they do in Omaha too! I make all the cinnamon rolls every day." We agreed with her.

An older lady told us she used to have a ten-speed bike when they first came here. She went on, "This woman is the best cook in the world and you should come back for lunch. Those cheapskate executives from other towns come and eat and never leave a tip. They act like they're too good to live here!" She told us Zimmatic irrigation systems were designed and built in Lindsay and once employed 500 people.

Another gem, an older man, showed interest in our ride so asked lots of questions and told us stories: A man always called his wife affectionate names after sixty-five years of marriage but when someone mentioned it to him, he responded sheepishly, "I forgot her name about ten years ago." The other tale concerned a man who drank too much and said, "I have to drive home because I'm too drunk to walk." All in all, Lindsay provided an entertaining and educational interlude.

We continued cycling the DOT-created striated road. Finally we got to the Humphrey turnoff and decided to go into town. A pretty town, made so by people who showed a lot of pride. Our first stop had to be the stunning St. Francis of Assisi Roman Catholic Church. For miles we saw the steeple rise above the prairie and hills, so had no trouble finding it. Father Getsell greeted us and happily showed us its special features—dramatic lighting that sets off the nooks and crannies, beautiful wall and ceiling murals, an outstanding rose St. Francis window placed in 1980. Adjoining the church a former Franciscan monastery now lies empty of monks who left a few years earlier. A convent also closed, the last nuns leaving about three months before we visited. Humphrey has a population of 700, many of them young families, but the church claims 1400 members and 300 students in its kindergarten through twelfth grade school.

The gazebo in City Park lies in the middle of a pond. We had a windblown lunch in one of the picnic shelters but chose not to go for a swim in the pool. I made a startling discovery in the public women's restroom. When I walked into the darkened building, the lights flipped on. *Motion sensor lights.* I jumped when a male voice began speaking. I stopped and then realized a radio had begun to play, again automatically. So did the toilets, the water and hand dryer. I wondered how the town financed all this technology, far beyond what most small towns could afford. It must have been as prosperous as it appeared. What a refreshing stop.

Back on the road we discovered the wind had changed and had grown stronger. So we had more work to do! We pedaled down the streets at Clarkson about 2:30 and searched for Annie's B&B, home of Anne Cerv, her husband Adam and their daughters Madison and Cully. Anne, an art teacher, had cleverly decorated the house. Jim's and my room took the persona of the fisherman's room, complete with rods, reels, creels, fishing flies and an evergreen tree at the end of the bed.

We walked around town after our lemonade and date bread snack on the upstairs porch of this 1890 home. A bride and groom would also stay at the B&B that night. We saw them and heard the entourage going up and down the street on a hay rack while horns honked and blared. The group had been in the Brass Rail Restaurant for a while but had left before we ate there.

While we relaxed on the porch enjoying the evening, we pondered the question of how will it work when seven of us share the bathroom tonight? Sandy, remembering an old Midwest tradition, suggested we short-sheet the bridal couple's bed. We didn't. We also decided not to shivaree them either, another old Midwest tradition of serenading the newlyweds by banging on pots and pans while circling the house.

🚲

MAY 27 GRANDSON RYAN'S 8TH BIRTHDAY, CLARKSON TO IOWA BORDER 63 MILES

At breakfast Jim announced another of his major accomplishments yesterday: At one point his odometer read 12345.67!

We pedaled out after B&B photos and enjoyed the experience of practically no wind with mild enough temperatures for us to strip down to shirts and shorts within a few miles. Because we were intent on getting to the ice cream store in Blair to meet Dick by 2 PM, we didn't cycle around the towns on the route. We did functional things like eat, drink and use the bathrooms.

The farmland looked beautiful with many farmers out working the fields. We noticed a definite increase in the use of terraces along with grassed waterways. My dad would have had a fit about some of the conservation practices farther west where lots of straight up and down the hills instead of contour planting seemed to be the practice.

Jim called Dick from Nickerson where we resumed long and steady hills of nearly a mile, or slightly less. By this time the heavy traffic had eased so we felt more comfortable. Even strong-legged Dave admitted he hoped every steep hill would be the last. He said he spent a lot of time distracting himself from thinking it by focusing on what he might treat himself to at the ice cream store. Smart bicyclist.

The last downhill allowed us to whiz into Blair, a town with tidy streets and renovated store-fronts. Dick awaited us at the Goodrich (est. 1932) Ice Cream Store. Jim had told him last week that we wouldn't be there before 2 PM. We arrived at 1:57 —pretty good timing. We celebrated with ice cream, a black raspberry sundae for Jim and an orange Casanova, fancy name for an orange milkshake for me. Feeling refreshed, we felt ready for our few miles to Nebraska's eastern border, the Missouri River.

Dick met us there and took the welcome to Iowa photos as we celebrated completing state number thirty-five. After we returned to Dick's house, Sandy and Dave left for Iowa City. Jim and I said our goodbyes to Dick with, "We'll see you in two weeks at Erika's wedding," another family affair. We continued on to Lincoln to our motel, called grandson Ryan to wish him a Happy Birthday. When I asked him how it felt to be eight, he responded, "Not any different than six or seven." I sang the Happy Birthday song and Jim quacked it. Ryan quickly added, "Hi Grampa Duck." We told him we'd see him the next day and would join him for his putt-putt golf party too.

Family fun in Colorado capped off this across Nebraska ride. This time, we did stay on Interstate 80. Amazing how quickly the miles sped by and how flat the land. But in the distance, we saw the edges of the scenic Sandhills.

THE FINAL EASTERN TREK-BY THREE TREKS AND A KLEIN* NEW HAMPSHIRE & MAINE-2001

Riders: Sandy/Dave, Jim/Jan. Distance: 345 miles

Sandy, Dave and Jim had already had a stellar bicycling year, cycling around the Big Island of Hawaii while I nursed a badly broken wrist. In the late spring, I had joined the other three in our trek across Nebraska. Now we were on the cusp of another adventure, riding across New Hampshire and Maine. Stops to visit Jane and Bill, Sandy's sister and brother-in-law in Michigan with a lovely drive along the northern coast of Lake Ontario into Quebec punctuated our trip. A highlight came in Kingston, Ontario on July 1, Canada Day, where the town celebrated the occasion with a visit from the Tall Ships. We visited an Anglican Cathedral where a male choir sang *The Sailors' Hymn*. I always choke up hearing it.

Sandy, spotter extraordinaire of bakeries, pointed to a tiny one just across from the cathedral. We floated right into the store on the most heavenly aroma of freshly baked bread and goodies of all kinds. Cinnamon roll experts Sandy and Dave succumbed to what they claimed (again) was one of the best cinnamon rolls ever.

We passed through Montreal, and after sixty miles of Vermont's rural landscape, arrived in New Hampshire. We drove along the Connecticut River to our destination Lancaster, in plenty of time to unload bikes and van and be ready to go out. Betty Oglesby's friends, Peg and Bill Fischang, had invited us to dinner. We met this gracious pair and appreciated the tour of their new specially constructed timber beam home. They answered every question they could about the house, its design,

276

why they retired in New Hampshire, their past lives plus a host of questions about beekeeping, Bill's hobby. He had spent his career as an entomologist at Purdue University. Peg told of her enthusiasm for yoga. We enjoyed their company enormously and Sandy and I looked forward to spending the next day with them while Jim and Dave did the routine van/rental car shuffle.

*Sandy, Jim and I rode our Trek bicycles while Dave rode his Klein.

欯

Our transportation authorities, Jim and Dave, began their early morning travels and Sandy and I decided to bike to Mount Orne Bridge, the long covered bridge over the Connecticut River near Luneberg. We biked downstream trying to find Luneberg but obviously didn't go far enough and never did. We crossed the river, rode up the Vermont side, recrossed it near Lancaster, then bought a few groceries for our ride and tidied up before Peg and Bill picked us up.

Our lunch at Mount Washington Hotel would wait while we explored the area. Overlooks and historical markers helped us become thoroughly entranced by the Presidential Range. We climbed the stone Weeks Fire Tower for awe-inspiring 360 degree views. The town of Jefferson claimed fame with homes remaining from the Grand Hotel period, some used as summer and others permanent abodes. We edged Martin's Pond where Bill had taught Betty to kayak, then relished the excellent meal at Mount Washington Hotel and admired the spectacular grounds.

The final treat on our agenda was a visit to Garland Mill, the oldest (1856) continuously operating water-powered lumber mill in the United States, where Peg and Bill had the lumber for their home milled. It was a stark contrast to the last mill we had seen on our West Virginia journey. We were invited to see the inner workings of both places, one depicting the past and Sam and Jack Sanders' computer-operated mill charging into the future. What a sight. Peg and Bill dropped us off at our motel and we secured a promise from them to visit us in Iowa City. Friends of special friends become our friends.

After combing downtown and the attractive UC Congregational and United Methodist Churches, Sandy and I went to see the beautifully paneled jury room of the Old Court House. We continued to a small covered bridge built in 1852 spanning the Israel River.

New Hampshire's landscape began to change about a century ago, from open fields and small farms to the second most forested state, percentage wise in the country, after Maine. The Great North Woods consists of twenty-six million acres of land in Quebec, New York, Vermont, New Hampshire and Maine, and Lancaster is considered to be the gateway to New Hampshire's region of these woods.

Jim and Dave returned from their duty at 9:15 PM. Fifteen minutes later, we were in bed.

欯

LANCASTER, NEW HAMPSHIRE TO BETHEL, MAINE 55.5 MILES

The four of us left our motel and ate an unremarkable breakfast downtown. The Vermont-New Hampshire border beckoned so we biked there to officially begin our ride.

New England's covered bridges are so beautiful and the one in Lancaster, the 1911 wooden Howe truss bridge, a true gem, is recognized on the National Register of Historic Places. Two-hundred sixty-six feet long, it replaced the first bridge constructed here in 1860-1870s which existed as a toll bridge until 1908 when a log jam destroyed it. In 1969 a highway salt truck dropped through the deck but landed on the ice below. After a twelve-week renovation a rededication took place, the bridge reopened, a perfect photo op for us.

I saw a young man driving by and asked him if the street we were on led to North Road and then on to Highway 2. He said it did. Five minutes later, he returned to make sure that was really what we wanted, not North Highway 3. How thoughtful of him. After he left I wondered if he was also concerned that North Road was awfully hilly for bicyclists of our tender ages. Nevertheless, we always appreciate the kindness of those we meet along the way.

Indeed, the North Road was replete with lots of ups and downs but had a great surface. Unfortunately, I had the first day jitters. First I thought my front wheel was out of true. I checked and it was fine. Then I thought my panniers were unbalanced. They were, so we fixed that by moving some gear from one side to the other. Then I thought the repair person at the bike shop had not properly adjusted my headset last week. Upon checking, it appeared to be straight. Then I thought my brakes were rubbing—not an auspicious beginning. I was also a bit concerned because I had just begun a new medication. I had been diagnosed with high blood pressure three days before we left home, and I really didn't know how the medication would affect me. Except for the panniers, everything else was just me, struggling.

Fortunately, beautiful tree-filled hills and valleys everywhere enthralled us. We hated to exchange the pastoral qualities of North Road for Highway 2, but were obliged to, at least until we reached Gorham.

The number of hikers in the parking lots just off the Appalachian Trail surprised us. Whenever I heard about hiking the Appalachian Trail, I thought of Bill Bryson's book *A Walk in the Woods: Rediscovering America on the Appalachian Trail.* One of the reasons he decided to challenge the Trail was, as he said so vividly, It would get him fit "after years of waddle-some sloth." Not being particularly concerned about waddle-some sloth, our love of cycling, adventure, discovering more of our country, and fitness embraced some reasons for our quest.

We crossed into Maine, nicknamed The Pine Tree State denoted on the state flag featuring a single pine in the center. Even after decades of logging and development, 90 percent of Maine is still forested, so some people call its forests the heart of Maine.

Easy riding in the woods

Jim caught sight of a rural bike/hike/mountain gear store. It was like a magnet we were unable to resist. We really didn't need anything but we all love such stores. We checked out water bottles, road bikes, mountain bikes, backpacks.

"Need anything for the bike trip?"

"No."

"Not even new biking gloves?"

"No. Are there any biking tights that have ankle zippers?"

"I don't see any, just ones with elastic at the ankles."

"Look at these shirts. They are great—love the material. I like the vents in back."

"Remember anything you buy, you have to carry the rest of the trip."

"Yeah, I know."

The only thing we got was advice from the owner about optimal biking roads heading toward Gorham. "Three and a half miles out of Gorham, there is another North Road. You'll love it."

Gorham, with its campus of the University of Southern Maine, has become a bedroom community of Portland. However since 1764, industries included agriculture, water power for manufacturing textiles, clothing, and carpets. Lumber products—barrels, chairs, wagons, sleighs and boxes, paper pulp mills, granite and marble works added to the economy. With the construction of a nearby dam, many mills flooded. Times and the economy can change.

The bike/hike store owner was right on. This North Road was an absolute joy with an excellent surface and hills mostly gentle dips and ups with a few short, steep huffer-puffers thrown in. Tunnels of green and occasional birch groves backed by magnificent pines took our breath away. We pondered the age of the huge pines since their trunks were too large for me to get my arms around to hug.

Basically, we followed the Androscoggin River all the way to Bethel. It dropped one thousand feet from headwaters to the sea, about eight feet per mile, which makes this large volume, swift-flowing river an excellent power source. Lucky for us, the roads alongside also provide excellent downhills for cyclists. Unfortunately, due to textile mills, paper-making factories and other industries on its banks, pollution has taken its toll, reportedly so bad one fourteen-mile stretch requires oxygen bubblers to prevent fish from suffocating. Somehow brook, rainbow, and brown trout as well as landlocked salmon and small mouth bass have managed to survive. Farming is the principal occupation in the area, on land originally cleared by Native Americans. It's supposed to be prime moose-watching territory too but we didn't see any.

In Bethel, Jim and Dave wanted to show Sandy and me the gorgeous homes turned Bed and Breakfasts—dozens of them—which they had seen as they shuttled our van to Maine before the ride. Our inn for the night had been purchased by our hosts several years ago and their renovations and restorations looked good to us. So did their beds. Before we parted for the evening, the four of us contemplated the question, "What will you remember most about today?" Nothing about industries or food, just one first and last answer, "One really long steep hill."

🚲

BETHEL TO FARMINGTON 53.85 MILES

Independence Day arrived and we set out on a route a ranger had recommended. Although crushed rock sometimes forms a difficult surface, this mostly hard-packed rock road wending through outstanding scenery seemed perfect to us. It also edged the Androscoggin River, known as Andy Valley to the locals, which had more traffic and more taxing short and quick hills. But oh, the joy of the views! We hated to end the peace of a back road at East Peru/Mexico. We hurried to Rumford—Sandy had told us she wanted to be part of the Fourth of July parade there. After all, we had flags on our bikes. She added she would also be happy just to have a fried dough boy. We made it and she had her treat and we saw the parade.

We decided we were quite international on this trip having already been in Canada near Paris, London, Moscow, near Berlin (pronounced BER lin in New Hampshire.) And now Peru and Mexico. Somewhere along the way we saw a sign that read *Thanks for coming Ayuh!* Yes, truly cosmopolitan. Except in jest, we did not adopt the Maine *Ayuh,* meaning agreement.

Puzzle of the day: Was Jim's odometer reading of 1776 on this Fourth of July serendipitous or an auspicious sign from the universe?

🚲

FARMINGTON TO BINGHAM 44.15 MILES

After bulking up with cinnamon rolls and Maine blueberry pancakes which reminded us of the picture book *Blueberries for Sal,* we headed out of our overnight town, not on Highway 2, to grapple with the hills. We continued to take backroads affording pastoral scenes and lots of time to listen to birds. Jim and I heard a meadowlark song and decided it had to be an Eastern meadowlark, or as Jim put it, a meadowlark with a Down East accent. A problem with backroads —the generally awful surface. Frost heaves had really created a bumpy mess. Long downhills teased us but fear of getting a wheel caught in one of the cracks made us brake more than we wanted to. One of the pluses—lack of traffic. A snowmobile path following a railroad track tempted us with its nice terrain to cycle but deep sand instead of crushed rock covered the track. We all knew sand would not be a good choice for us.

A few sprinkles cooled us off, then more sprinkles. Just when Jim decided to put a cover on his handlebar bag, rain dumped. Some thunder accompanied the rain but we didn't see any lightning. We'd had enough pyrotechnics the previous night while we tried to sleep.

🚲

BINGHAM TO MILO 52.69 MILES

Hills. Hills. More hills including one three and-a-half miler at 10 percent grade. Dave called that day "the hardest day I've ridden in two years, including Going-to-the-Sun Highway and Trail Ridge Road." We decided since not every one of us could bike it all, this trip could be called *Bike New Hampshire and Bike-Hike Maine.* At points the road surface became so uneven and treacherous, I had a hard time even looking at the scenery because I had to keep my eyes glued to the road. At least this route followed the rocky Piscataquis River—wonderful rolling Native American name. Although our Gifford's ice cream didn't have one, it had a descriptive, hard to resist flavor—Maine Black Bear, blackberries dipped in chocolate. Yum.

Once again we saw lots of moose tracks but no moose today, except for the cute little moose Santa figure I bought. Would we ever see a live moose in Maine's moose country?

At Abbott's Village we came upon a relief map which gave us an overview of the terrain we'd bicycled. We were amazed. We'd ridden some downhills that could have been fun but broken road surfaces made us slow down until the brakes became hot. Dave let 'er rip so went forty-three plus miles per hour, Jim over forty, Sandy and I attained thirty-eight, fast enough considering those conditions. We biked on wide-shoulders the last pleasant miles to Milo.

Our B&B hosts Frieda and Everett Cook showed us our loft room over his furniture-making shop. My journal said, *If we don't clobber ourselves on the ends of the beds, etc. we'll probably be OK.* That meant every time we had to leave to go to the bathroom.

Of the nineteen people who came for dinner, thirteen belonged to one family, the Currans, including ten brothers and sisters. All had been educated beyond high school, mostly as teachers and nurses. Our host Frieda, the youngest of eighteen children, said she and Everett had lived in Alaska then moved to Milo, and had started this B&B seven years ago when the Curran family wanted to have a reunion. Our dinner menu included pork loin roast, mashed potatoes, cooked carrots, broccoli casserole, tossed salad, rolls, applesauce, strawberry shortcake and "bust your girdle." Ingredients for the latter dessert consisted of a lethal combination of Oreo cookies, peanut butter cups, and hot fudge sauce with a whipped topping.

After dinner we strolled downtown and happened onto another bit of Americana—a Kiwanis auction. We caught the action of one woman waving at a friend and then fearing she had bought a Moosehead mirror. She breathed a sigh of relief when someone else bid higher. We thought a lot of junk, spelled with *k* not *que,* was up for bids.

Our loft beds felt fine but the trips up and down the steep stairs were a bit of a nightmare for our nocturnal visits, but we didn't have to navigate our way through table saws or wood piles. Frieda let us use her washer and dryer so that helped make up for the location of the bathroom and the chilly night there. Frieda and Everett do all the B&B work themselves—a lot of very hard work.

🚲

MILO TO MILLINOCKET 42.5 MILES

Our French toast breakfast gave us plenty of fuel for a much less extreme terrain, wonderful temperature, light winds, mostly gentle ups and downs with a few stiffer hills, and fewer buckled and rough roads. Good fortune.

Many moose tracks and wallows enticed us to play with the moose name even though once again we didn't see any moose. Moseying for Moose. Mooning for Moose. Moving for Moose. Where's da Moose. When I'm calling Moo-oo-oo-oo-oo-oo-oose. We wondered where all the moose and deer were since they reportedly exist in greater numbers now than one hundred years ago. Despite not seeing moose, we spotted Mount Katahdin, the endpoint of the Appalachian Trail. What a magnificent goal for through-hikers.

⚲

MILLINOCKET TO SHERMAN MILLS 35 MILES

Today featured cool to comfortably warm temperatures with mostly friendly ups and downs, gentle breezes, pleasant vistas, and quiet rivers that occasionally tumulted over natural rock dams. Always we looked for moose. We sang for moose, we mooed for moose. All the places they ordinarily frequent, especially at dawn or dusk, such as willow stands—empty. We meandered all day since this was a short-mileage day.

As we went up a small rise, we looked up and, at last, saw a mama moose and her baby exiting the woods onto a gravel side road. We stopped, transfixed as the mama glanced at us (do moose with their limited eyesight ever glance at anything?) then whirled around and headed back into the woods. The baby, not yet educated in fear, gazed at us a few moments longer, realized that her/his mama was no longer alongside, turned and followed. A magical moment for us. She, so huge and dark brown, and the baby so small and cinnamon colored, were exactly what we had hoped for. Not enough time to take a photo but sufficient to totally impress us. This sighting, a fox scampering in front of Dave early today and the red-cockaded woodpecker we saw fly across the road to a tree, fulfilled our desire to see wildlife. And we had been serenaded all day by a chorus of birds in the forest.

This seemingly tractless Maine North Woods meant we observed lots of logging, a paper recycling facility and, next to it another Great Northern paper plant. A friend had told us International Paper owns about half (reportedly two million acres) of the North Woods of Maine which created lots of questions about conservation and logging practices. Many farms have been labeled "tree farms" with one sign further explaining the trees were grown for International Paper.

We read that most of Maine's woods have been harvested two or three times, now mechanically cut and replanted. It is obvious that paper and lumber companies drive the economic engines of this area. They develop the roads used by the public, including outdoors people such as campers, hunters, canoeists, fishermen and mountain bikers.

On a totally different note, we picnicked at the Stacyville Pentecostal Church—not on the front step as we usually do for there were none, but on the front ramp. The outhouse in back seemed to be built for very tall people because even the extra step didn't quite make it easily accessible for all of us. The plastic toilet ring was a welcome accommodation so we didn't worry about splinters, and mosquitoes did not attack as ferociously as those in the woods, all privy virtues we really appreciated.

⚲

SHERMAN MILLS TO HOULTON THEN SWEET WATER INN 60 MILES

Our last bicycling day began with overcast skies, forecast of a 60 percent chance of rain, and humidity that would do justice to a rain forest. The day's theme, a gauntlet of hills, miles and miles and miles of them, so challenging that Dave said he checked his tires while riding to see if he had a flat. He didn't. None of us had a flat that week and only a few sprinkles of rain.

Highlights of the day for Sandy included all the potato fields and logging trucks. Flowers and homes caught my attention but I especially noted many differences in income levels. Many people picked strawberries while many others sat watching the roads, lots of them young people. I wondered about the unemployment numbers.

We rode to the border of Maine and Canada but could not cross it. All traffic had to go to I-95. We couldn't envision what direction or road we would have taken if we had intended to continue riding into New Brunswick. But Jim and I had successfully survived the crossing of states number forty and forty-one. We had thirteen more miles to go to our B&B, the well-named Sweetwater Inn, had just that—excellent sweet water.

Our hosts, Rue and Phil Geishecker, both musicians, prepared a terrific salmon dinner with snow peas, freshly picked greens, potatoes and strawberry cheesecake. Phil played jazz guitar during dinner and Rue entertained us with a medley of American songs on her violin afterward. Appropriately, their Maine coon cats were musically named Dolce and Presto, and their cuddly, attention-seeking dog was Banjo. What a lovely woodsy home, excellent conversationalists, fascinating people with eclectic backgrounds. Thanks to Jim for finding these warm and accommodating people with a B&B to match.

Whenever I reminisce about the New Hampshire-Maine ride, I get wistful and misty-eyed. As Sandy described it, *Shortly after this ride, we lost our innocence.* We had blithely biked along totally unaware what the next months would bring. I had long poignant phone conversations with our daughter Jennifer. I reflected on her seeming loneliness but thought it was because Bernd was working in Houston during the weeks we were gone from Iowa City. We knew they had had another in-vitro attempt at achieving a pregnancy, which ultimately would not be successful. We didn't suspect what Jennifer in her heart of hearts knew—soon she and Bernd would die together. We came to understand this later when we pieced things together—things she'd said, a poem she had written, what she'd done such as pay off their mortgage and write a will. When she handed her will to Jim she said, "Now I can die." Jennifer was known for her quirky sense of humor so we thought she was being facetious. Because my mother was sitting nearby, we didn't say anything more than, "Oh, Jennifer!" Jim glanced at the will and saw she had named him executor.

"You don't want me as your executor. You want someone your age like your sisters."

"No Dad, I want you."

She had written a poem with the little magnetized poetry words that were the rage then, her words those Emily Dickinson had often used. We found it on their refrigerator and now keep it on ours:

This Simple Tomb Is For Ourselves;
Dew Covered Bone Lain Blank
And Night Counted Our Tender Names
Twice.

On August 6, 2001 Jennifer and Bernd died in a white-water rafting tragedy on the
Arkansas River near Buena Vista, Colorado. Five weeks later 9-11 occurred.
And early the following month, Sandy was diagnosed with breast cancer. Our Innocence
was indeed over.

TEXAS THE LONE STAR STATE PART 3. BRENHAM, TX TO LEESVILLE, LA-2003

Riders: Betty, Barb, Mary Palmberg, new friends from Women Tours, Jim/Jan. Distance: 275 miles

When Jim and I learned our former neighbor Mary Palmberg planned to join a Women Tours bike ride across the United States from California to Florida, we asked her about the route. Amazingly, it would be in the area of east Texas we had envisioned riding during spring break, exactly when she'd be there.

Navasota became the meeting point for the four Iowa Citians and the Tour. But first we had to get our van to Leesburg, Louisiana. We drove our van to Brenham where Texas Part 2 had ended. Using Enterprise, we did the familiar rental car-van switcheroo taking us to Leesville and back again. We arrived in time to check out Brenham's Victorian buildings and again savor some of the town's fabled Blue Bell ice cream.

♾

JIM AND THE TEXAS BLUEBONNET BIKERS

Eagerly we began Jim's and my last phase of our three-part journey across Texas, and Betty and Barb's first by pedaling twenty-six miles to Navasota. Bluebonnets and Indian paintbrush embroidering the roadside meadows further lightened our hearts. We rode across the Brazos River, sometimes used to delineate between East and West Texas, then arrived at Washington-on-the-Brazos Historical Park. The scene of the signing of the Texas Declaration of Independence and the drafting of the Constitution of the new Republic of Texas in 1836, it celebrates its role as the "Birthplace of Texas."

286

Miniature ponies raised by the Sisters of the Poor St. Clare Monastery made us smile and, of course we couldn't resist petting them. We also celebrated because the highway now had a paved shoulder.

That evening we connected with Mary and her "touring family" at their motel for a meet, greet and eat—good food at a gas station café. We loved hearing the stories of their cycling journey along the southern tier of the country. Among other experiences, due to terrain and weather, they had encountered some harrowing circumstances in eastern California, especially heat which made it difficult to remain hydrated.

The next day we rode to our overnight in Cleveland while they biked to Coldspring. (We stayed in a different town since WomenTours had rented all the motel rooms in one!) Our 50 mile proximity to Houston surprised me because East Texas Piney Woods in Sam Houston National Forest felt like a remote area.

We pedaled a couple of hours to join Mary and the others. According to an East Texas Forest Trail brochure, a pass-through town Kountze, called *The Big Light in the Big Thicket,* considers itself the "gateway to the vast impenetrable woods that were once hideouts for smugglers, outlaws and service-dodging Texans." (Think Civil War.) Swamp, desert, barrens and piney woods intersect there. The Big Thicket, at one time, possessed nearly every kind of hardwood and pine native to this part of Texas. Once over-logged, now it exists as a protected national preserve. The fascinating history and ecology of the area surprised us, much different from the drier, hotter Texas we had experienced on our earlier bike trips.

At lunchtime, the Iowa City group picnicked at a house construction site after Mary asked permission from the woman who lived there. The owner even brought out some chairs for us to use as tables. True to being the traveling foodies that cyclists are, we also stopped for an afternoon snack of cherry cobbler, although Mary heartily recommended an okra/tomato/ onion concoction.

We continued cycling through fragrant piney woods past Lumberton and on to Silsbee, both originally logging camps and sawmills, now bustling towns. Like other rides, some logging trucks carried logs that looked precariously fastened, nerve-wracking for bicyclists and motorists too.

In addition to welcoming us to ride with them, Tour members and staff, from their mobile kitchen, fed us a scrumptious supper of spaghetti with a choice of veggie marinara or pesto sauce, plus green salad, fruit, cookies and cake, then an equally delicious and filling breakfast in the morning. What an array of food! The four of us concurred we could have gotten used to those meals and service. Jim enjoyed being the only man among these awesome women. Mary had posted descriptions to go with photos of their adventures and personnel every day since they left San Diego, so we felt connected to and admired them. What a commitment to cycle all the way to St. Augustine, Florida and what a gift for us to have had a taste of their ride. I'm not just talking food here.

🚲

After breakfast, we bid Mary and our new friends safe travels, the traditional *Wind at your backs* blessing, then pedaled into the morning sun, still wishing we could join in riding the rest of the way to St. Augustine. We continued to Kirbyville, named for John Henry Kirby, known as *Prince of the Pines,* since his company produced more Southern Pine lumber than any other in the world. Lumber ruled.

To shorten the final day of biking, we altered our route to Bleakwood and rode blue highways, quieter, less-trafficked byways. We commented how appropriate the town's name must have seemed for anyone who felt grim at being surrounded by seemingly unending forests.

Shortly after, we reached the Sabine River where thousands of acres of bottomland had never been cleared.

Our last miles to Leesville, Louisiana led us over that river which forms part of the border between Texas and Louisiana. Reaching this line meant Jim and I had crossed forty-two states and we had cycled a continuous route across Texas, Louisiana, Mississippi, Alabama and into Florida. We cheered each other on, "Only eight more to go!"

Part of the call of the road involves learning more of the history and geography of the places we visit. In history, this river delineated part of the Spanish-American, then the Mexican-American and lastly, the Texan-American international boundaries. We continued on Highway 8 paralleling Nolan's Trace to Leesville. Its mustang smuggler namesake, Philip Nolan, moved horses from Spanish Texas to Natchez, Mississippi and New Orleans. He came to an untimely end near the Brazos River where Spanish troops captured him. Fortunately, we escaped his fate and rolled safely into Leesville.

🚲

We traveled home to snowy Iowa with happy memories of bicycling with old and new friends and through immense, green Texas forests.

🚲

288

MO-NO-KOTA RIDE-MONTANA-NORTH DAKOTA-2003

Riders: Betty, Sandy/Dave, Jim/Jan. SAG drivers: Betty, Sandy, Dave. Distance: 602 miles

How exciting for us to return to the middle of Montana where we had finished our Idaho-Montana biking adventure four years ago. This time, Sandy, Dave and Betty would alternately bike and drive our van, while Jim and I made sure we rode every single mile, border-to-opposite-border per the Dictum, AKA Rule of Rides.

Our route, made simple by continuing on US Highway 2, started with Havre as the launch site. Dave, Jim and I, wearing our sky blue Bike Montana shirts, pedaled off leaving Betty and Sandy to drive the van. We chuckled at the brown and white Havre sign:

Cowpunchers, miners, and soldiers are tolerably virile persons as a rule. When they went to town in the frontier days seeking surcease from vocational cares and solace in the cup that cheers, it was just as well for the urbanites to either brace themselves or take to cover. The citizens of any town willing and able to be host city for a combination of the above diamonds in the rough had to be quick on the draw and used to inhaling powder smoke.

Unexpectedly, a pale pink stuccoed adobe church of American Southwest architecture and topped by two simple crosses, appeared. Who would have expected such a structure standing starkly against the lapis Big Sky of the Great Plains? Alongside the church lay a cemetery, tough soil studded with scattered tufts of hardy prairie grass and white wooden crosses. Poignant mementos of the dead—flowers, flags, helmets, mugs—decorated the rock and wood-limned gravesites.

The broad-shouldered road ran straight through the flat to rolling landscape creating a seemingly endless pathway, a perfect backdrop for stellar photos of our cycling team. Roadside signs kept us apprised of earlier Montana history, especially of outlaws. One described rustlers as *hombres prone to disregard the customary respect accorded other people's brands.* Another extolled buffalo as meaning life to both Plains and Mountain Indians. Pemmican, dried and pulverized buffalo meat, kept indefinitely, and reportedly had food value of one pound worth ten pounds of fresh meat. Tanned skin and rawhide were used for robes, tepees, shields, stretchers, travois, canoes, and bedding, while bones and horns became utensils and tools. Our education by signs continued: *The buffalo played a prominent part in many of their religious rites and jealousy of hereditary hunting ground brought on most of the inter-tribal wars.*

🚲

Along the way, a serendipitous occurrence gave us new depth of understanding of long-distance cycling. A flash of crimson wrapped around a hunched figure by the road caught our attention. Closer, we could see a bicycle propped nearby. A slender shivering man hunkered there with his lightweight rain jacket pulled as far as possible over his knees. He looked cold and miserable.

We stopped and inquired, "Are you OK? Do you need help?" When he answered, "I'm just resting…and my bike has some mechanical issues," we huddled around him to shelter him from the wind. After we introduced ourselves, Chris Burton explained he was from Britain, had retired from the police force, lived part time in Spain, and was solo biking across the North American continent, planning to end his journey in Cape Breton, Canada. "My wife isn't very happy about this dream of mine. She doesn't like the idea, thinks it costs too much money, and is constantly worried about me and my safety."

When we asked about his bike, he said the gears weren't working well, his wheel seemed out of true, his rear fender rubbed. "I didn't get a new bike for the trip because of the expense. I didn't want to spend extra money on clothes either but now I think I'm not well-prepared for this changeable climate." From the paucity of warm stuff among his gear, we had to agree. Jim and Dave, both capable bike trouble-shooters, offered their help in doing a short-term fix so Chris could get back on the road. He accepted, so they tweaked this and that (that's bike talk for I don't know what they did). We invited him to not only ride but also stay in motels with us for as long as he wanted to. Gratefulness swept across his face. Our new friend joined us.

We cycled together, took lots of photos with Chris, and then ate our lunch at a moss-spackled picnic table, sheltered from the wind between two metal buildings. Out of his panniers, Dave pulled a Quaker Oats container filled with Sandy's specialty Cowboy Cookies. Chris was duly impressed. He hadn't had any "homemade biscuits" since he'd left England, and had never had the Cowboy variety.

On the roadside, a rose granite monument honored the men and women of the proud As-siniboine and Sioux Tribes of Fort Peck Reservation who have served in the military. Noted was the *"extremely high ratio of military participants in time of adversity. From the time of the historical frontier wars to the Vietnam Era, these men and women have defended and died for their homeland during peacetime and war. These monuments are a humble and perpetual symbol of appreciation to those ancestral and modern-day warriors and service people who alongside their non-Indian comrades unselfishly gave their life* (sic) *defending the preservation of freedom."* Who would not be moved by that tribute?

Another sign indicated we were approaching Wolf Point, a town on the Reservation, population of 2600, home of the oldest rodeo in the state. Once there, we took a walk in the downtown and then sauntered back to our bikes. Joe, a local Native American stopped us and began to ask questions, the usual ones we are asked on bike trips. What are you doing? Where are you going? How long is it going to take you? Chris's accent and answers obviously intrigued him, especially when Joe found out he had been a police officer in London. He asked Chris what years and upon hearing the answer added, "I was there with the Marines during some of that time."

He questioned Chris, "Do you remember the 1968 Grosvenor Square demonstrations against the Vietnam War?" Chris did. Joe responded, "I was there as a guard at the US Embassy on the Square." In disbelief, Chris told him, "I was on the roof of the MacDonald House, right on the Square too." The rest of us stood with our mouths agape at this fortuitous meeting. Imagine these diverse men, a Plains Indian from a reservation in Montana who had been a US Marine happening on a former firearms officer born and bred in London, sharing stories of the same tumultuous event and place. Our chance and memorable meeting with Joe and hearing his story, reinforced the words on the monument outside Wolf Point. We hated to leave him, but had to get to our overnight motel. Sandy, Dave, Jim and I had been moved by Chris and Joe, their meeting and the bonding that occurred among all of us. We only wish Betty could have been with us but she was driving the van.

A nearby bike shop provided Chris with equipment including a rear-view mirror, one of many potentially lifesaving safety items. Dave and Chris worked on the bike, trued the wheels so they didn't wobble, and adjusted the brakes. The bike would not be perfect but at least they improved safety and comfort.

🚲

The following day, we parted ways with Chris and rode at our own pace through eastern Montana, paralleling the Missouri River, although our route had fewer twists, turns, bends and curves. In Culbertson we saw Chris again, savored a quick reunion and wished him Godspeed for the last time. He had connected with two other cyclists and planned to ride Highway 2 halfway into North Dakota with them, whereas we would turn south at Williston in the west of the state. Our group talked about him and what he had added to our bicycling memories. What a wonder to be with someone for such a short period of time who truly impressed us with a slice of his life. We hoped he would remember to write us. He did. He safely returned to England, built a house in Alicante, Spain, and moved there with his wife.

In the Culbertson area, cattle industry in the 1880s included settlers raising horses for the US Cavalry's posts in North Dakota and Montana. The semi-arid climate of the area and the 1909

291

homestead laws allowed three hundred twenty acres instead of the former one hundred sixty and in turn, impelled dryland farming—not using irrigation and planting drought-resistant crops.

A gold, green and black welcome sign highlighting Theodore Roosevelt stood at the Montana-North Dakota border. A national park celebrated him in the state too. Another guide-post featured the iconic silhouette of Lewis and Clark, Lewis pointing the way for the same-named Trail. A CanAm Highway label showcased a bright red maple leaf and a blue star. I had forgotten how close we were to Canada but Jim and I did remember we had just crossed our forty-third state.

Sandy, Jan and Betty cycling a North Dakota Highway

I had also forgotten how music can sometimes help make a ride simpler—or not. We had each brought some of our favorite CDs to listen to as we passed the van-riding miles en route to Havre. Betty provided the rage musical of the moment, *Mamma Mia*. The title song became one of my earworms, fun for a while and then not so much. As we cycled the spectacular and round-rocky hills outlining the Missouri River valley, I remembered that. I kept hearing the quick and bouncy title song by ABBA but I was neither, not bouncy and definitely not quick as I muscled my way up the inclines and dipped down again and again. The rhythm beating in my brain had no resemblance to the stuttering pulse of my pedaling. The views, including bison calves and adults, made up for my erratic cadence but the song stuck in my head.

Flatland Fort Union fascinated us with its reconstructed walls, Indian trade house, and stone bastions. The archaeological discoveries and artifacts housed here clarified its life as a fur trading post beginning in 1828. The Assiniboine and six other Plains Indian tribes came here to barter buffalo robes and smaller animal pelts for such things as blankets, guns, beads, and cloth.

Our layover in Williston's El Rancho Motor Hotel brought another chance pleasure. While we checked in, another couple pedaled in, heavily laden with what looked like fully packed German brand Ortlieb panniers. Naturally, we gravitated to each other and decided to meet for supper to share stories. The man was seventy-five and the woman fifty-seven. He told us of his dream of cycling around the world. She explained to Sandy, Betty and me: "I'm not on this trip because I love bicycling so much. I'm here because I love my husband." She added, "He makes sure we only bike about fifty miles a day and then we stay at motels. He wants me to be happy too." They had been on the road for eighteen months, including a long stay in Turkey where she had been ill and hospitalized. Recovery time meant a month's delay in their journey. The Turkish people had welcomed and cared for them beyond their imaginations. They continued their journey through Asia and on to North America, but we thought he could have gone on and on. What an inspiration! We traveled vicariously with them via his blog once we were home, and dreamed of possibilities.

A favorite overnight? Rural Midstate B&B conjured a stereotypic North Dakota ranch. Our host, Grace Faul, served a delicious dinner and breakfast. She explained she and her husband are particularly busy in the fall when hunters from all over the Upper Midwest take advantage of the pheasants in their vast wheatfields. Another dinner guest joined us and while discussing the snowbird phenomenon, she remarked, "My husband and I go south for winter too."

We queried her further, "Where do you go?"

"Lincoln." We Iowans stifled our laughter. Lincoln was west to us but to those living in North Dakota, we supposed going south, even to Lincoln, made sense. Well, sort of.

Originally, we had hoped we would end this junket at the same border spot we had begun our Minnesota ride so long ago. Alas, we didn't have the time to cycle that far south (even though it wasn't Lincoln) but settled on getting to the state line, the end of our forty-fourth state.

As I reflected on the two phases of our Washington State to Minnesota tour, I focused on the Great Plains. Beyond wheat, to me its greatest commodity might be the openness and immensity of the sky. It created a sense of endlessness with no confining borders—a place to really breathe. We had.

In memory of our dearly loved Betty Oglesby.
We miss her friendship, cheery smile, giving heart and strong faith.
December 19, 1933-August 22, 2013

CALIFORNIA, HERE WE COME!!-2003

Riders: Sandy/Dave, Jim/Jan. Drop off: Michelle Pick up: Tim Schuldt, Dave's nephew. Distance: 236 miles

In our eagerness to complete our goal of bicycling across all the states, we delayed another dream, that of cycling down the California coast. That would wait. Now we followed the old song, "California, here we come..."

Cousins Charles and Kerstin Wolle hosted us for dinner the night before our ride, this one from their hometown Genoa, Nevada, elevation 4806 feet, to San Francisco Bay, California, elevation sea level or thereabouts. Kerstin, a superlative cook, prepared an excellent lasagna that suited what was coming our way, a long distance tour across state number forty-five.

An early September morning departure meant wearing warm clothes which we hoped we could shed as we pedaled to 8573 foot Carson Pass. We followed Foothills Road up Emigrant Trail onto a highway briefly paralleling the old Pony Express Route. The slight then steadily increasing incline took us past vast stands of pine and palisade-like rocks with vertical striated faces. Jackets and tights came off. Slightly worn and ramshackle but picturesque cabins laid claim to small parcels of pastureland. Going up we experienced the meaning of the eight miles of 8 percent grade curving road. For me, I focused on breathing, *In through your nose...out through your mouth...Again... Again,* set small goals of *Count your pedal strokes until you get to the next curve...and the next...* adding *You can do this* for encouragement. Mostly that worked.

A blessedly flat open meadow, dappled with yellow flowers and watered by a meandering stream was marked with boulders. I gave sighs of relief for a few brief downhills and gave another kind of sigh when up-up-up steepened the grade to 10 percent.

Carson Pass had been named for the western frontier's skilled trailblazing guide and hunter Kit Carson. According to the sign in 1843 *Carson led the first crossing of the Great Salt Desert, a route later adopted by the Pony Express. The following year he made a daring winter passing through the Sierra Nevada…Carson Pass became one of the most popular crossings along the Emigrant Trail.* What a trek that must have been. It seemed hard enough on a bike riding paved roads. And it wasn't winter.

At the Pass, we looked way down on lapis-colored Red Lake. "How can Red Lake be blue?" Sandy asked. We didn't know but was it was bluer than the sky and reflecting the surrounding mountains and trees. As we continued, I squinted at the road ahead and gulped. More grey granite blocks with hearty pines poking through. But suddenly relief came from a downhill into Kirkwood where we'd spend the night.

♾

We eagerly greeted the morning knowing more 7 percent grade uphills and downhills faced us. I wondered what color Silver Lake would be—but suspected it had more to do with mining than with color. After another unrelenting climb, we looked back at the now cobalt lake.

A sobering sign pointed to evocatively named Tragedy Spring Road where three names carved on a tree referred to members of the Mormon Battalion who had been killed near the spring. Not far away lay the Maiden's Grave marked with a stone erected by guests at Kirkwood for a young woman from Iowa. The historical marker inscribed: *Broken dreams and hope, carried 2000 miles through scorching deserts and over lofty mountains. At last…the sight of the promise land (sic). Those of you who visit this grave carry a torch of love and hope (which this young girl lost,) and pass it on, to generations unborn. Rechall Melton was laid to rest here, on a cold and frosty morning, Oct. 4, 1850. Bless (sic) are the pure of heart for they shall see God.* The details on these signs compelled us to ponder the pioneers' plight as they traversed the Sierras on this rugged Emigrant Trail.

As we dropped in altitude, aspen mixed in with pines and gentle rolls replaced precipitous inclines. Twisty turns, tight corners, and no shoulders described our beautiful back-to-nature route to Placerville. We could simply reach out and touch trees along this narrow road as we zigzagged along the contours of the mountains. I noticed my hands had become sore from braking so much and I occasionally pedaled, not because I needed the power, but I needed to keep my legs loose. Approaching more inhabited territory, open fields interspersed with horse farms and vineyards.

Michelle awaited us in Placerville where we ate lunch with her. Our early arrival made it possible for the guys to drive her car to Charles and Kerstin's home to retrieve the van. After they returned, she drove back to her home in Sacramento. That evening Doug and Ellie Norris who then lived in California, joined us again for a celebratory dinner. They were becoming quite the bike trip groupies and we all loved being with them. Being fellow-seminarians had certainly bonded Dave and Doug.

🚲

Folsom became a special memory because of an unusual coincidence. As we pedaled past the Folsom Prison, we learned that Johnny Cash had died that day. His performance of the *Folsom Prison Blues* had been one of my brother's favorite Johnny Cash songs and there we were, cycling by it. I never think of one without thinking of the other.

The flat American Trail through Sacramento was fun to ride most of the time. A causeway over the Sacramento River, fields and marshlands created three miles of intense noise and vibration from the highway. Less frenetic portions of highways lay along fields of grain, hay and rice. The sometimes paved, sometimes dirt or gravel bike route on a frontage road paralleled it. We didn't linger in either Sacramento or on the quiet stretches of the bike trail since our overnight was in Davis, home of the University of California-Davis. The feel of the town reminded us of our town, home of The University of Iowa.

🚲

Our route continued through the Sacramento Valley, the northern part of California's Central Valley. A Jim expression, "We need to hustle…" came to mind as we steadily cycled to reach the ferry terminal on San Pablo Bay, the northernmost part of San Francisco Bay. It was to be a family affair. Our nieces Kevin Marie and Renee were to meet us there as would Dave's nephew Tim, keeper of the van.

Tim arrived and Dave regaled him with biking tales. We waited for our nieces but they didn't come. We called their home number but no one answered. We were really disappointed because we hadn't seen them in a long time. Eventually, we gave up and decided we had to leave.*

Our biking had ended at the terminal but the fun had not. Jim had been making noises about cycling across Nevada and Utah sometime soon. He especially wanted to ride Highway 50, the Loneliest Highway in the USA across Nevada. Once again another opportunity awaited us after this ride ended. We drove the highway and located places to stay, nature call spots, sights to further explore, while Sandy took notes. In two years, we would thank her profusely for the information, wisdom and wit.

🚲

*Once we arrived home, we received the message that Kevin had been stung by a bee; an allergic reaction had necessitated a trip to the emergency room. Our disappointment was replaced with great relief that she was OK now.

🚲

BIG ISLAND HOLOHOLO: RAMBLE AROUND FOR PLEASURE-2004

Riders: Jim/Jan. Distance: 237 miles

When we stepped off the plane, I breathed in the soft Hawaiian air. I'm always excited when we arrive, but this time had another layer of meaning. I was going to bicycle around the Big Island, a feat Jim had accomplished three years earlier with Sandy and Dave. I hadn't ridden with them because my broken wrist, suffered in an ice skating mishap, had not yet healed. When my internist informed me my bone density was that of a decades younger person, I wailed, "Oh no! That means I'm just a klutz."

This time it would just be the two of us. I have never quite figured out Jim's motive for planning this trip as he did but he had decided we would circumnavigate the island in four days instead of the five they had used. The distance was not great and we would go counterclockwise to reap the benefit of the prevailing winds, but terrain and quixotic winds can create formidable challenges.

We grabbed our gear from the luggage carousel and caught a van cab to our hotel. An added benefit—the hotel would store our bike boxes without charge until we returned. We arrived in our room early enough in the day to assemble our bicycles, pack our panniers, prepare our other gear for storage, have supper and still get to bed at a good time.

The Big Island has the most diverse climates of the Hawaiian chain, ranging from lush tropical near Hilo on the wet windward side, to subarctic on the two most prominent mountains, Mauna Loa and Mauna Kea. The fact that lava has increased the size of the island by 550 acres since 1983, lends credence to it being geologically the youngest of the present islands.

The following morning, Jim and I began our journey at just above sea level. Within a quarter of a mile, we climbed our first hill, it felt like a mountain, on Kamehameha III Road. I puffed and wheezed, onward and upward to connect with Hamalaloa, the Highway Belt Road which rings the island. It continued rising but not as steeply. On each previous trip to the Big Island we had driven these now familiar roads, but things looked different from a bicycle seat than from a car window, and felt much more intimate and every rise took extra effort.

In too many spots, this essentially shoulderless highway can be harrowing. We rode carefully and checked our mirrors frequently to keep track of vehicles approaching from the rear. We had no close calls. Brisk ups and downs prodded us to remember the volcanic origins of Hawaii. Although wooded areas exist, including macadamia nut orchards along the way, we saw where lava flows had inundated the land in recent years as well as long ago. In late March 1868 tremors and earthquakes rattled the Ka'u District land for five days. On the sixth day, violent quakes shook the earth and fiery hell broke through. Lava rivers surged down hills, devouring everything in their paths, villages, people, livestock. In moments a tsunami swept away whatever had been left near the shore. The triple punch of earthquake, lava and tsunami altered Ka'u's topography forever. Cinder cones toppled and landslides completed the devastation. Now gray-green patches of valiant hardy grasses and trees poke their heads through the lava. The land heals itself, slowly and inexorably.

Scenic turnouts allowed us refreshing views of the Pacific Ocean. Squinting into the expanse of ever changing salt waters, our indelibly imprinted fourth-grade geography lessons reminded us that only islands existed between us and far away Asia.

Whether on a bike or in a car, a favorite stop on this route always beckoned to us. This permanent roadside stand sold macadamia nuts, oranges, nectarines, pineapple, coffee and other island treats. A family, originally from Uganda, has owned and operated the business for decades. This shady oasis offered another respite from the road—sky chairs, hanging canvas sling chairs offering a perfect way to unwind, swing lazily and relish juice-filled fruit. Leaving that relaxation, a problem. But Jim and the road called, mostly Jim.

Our first day's goal meant reaching our B&B near South Point, Ka Lae, the southernmost spot in the United States. We were tempted to turn down the buckling chip-seal road that led there, past wind generators and on to dramatic lava ledges to watch the confluence of ocean currents. We consoled ourselves with the promise we would explore it the following week with our family.

We spied a small country store in Kahuku and went in to buy food for the night's supper. Amid DVDs, toys, plastic snorkel sets, candy, soda and chips, we found what we hoped would be passable chicken/veggie and rice microwave dinners. Purchases made, we strapped the boxes on our rear bike racks and pedaled on.

We found our rural B&B just off the highway. We explained to our host that we needed to heat our supper and also would leave well before he served breakfast to other guests. He showed us the microwave and assured us he would prepare an early sack breakfast for us. We mentioned we had stayed in Naalehu town at Becky's B&B three years earlier. He remembered the shocking news that two years afterward, the husband killed his wife.

Later, in checking the *Hawaii Tribune-Herald* archives, a different story was reported. A horrible event had occurred but the father had killed his eight-year old daughter in retaliation against his estranged wife. What a heart wrenching tragedy.

🚲

Unnecessarily, we set our alarm. Nature's own, a Hawaiian rooster, crowed his wake-up call well before five. Just after daybreak, we gulped down our sack breakfast and pedaled away, happy for the safety of daylight.

One of my favorite sections of Big Island coastline overlooks roiling Hanu'apo Bay. We stopped high on a bluff and gazed down to the rocky crags below, some outlined by sandy beaches and pounded by surf. What we'd passed resembled the gently sloping emerald meadows of the tip of southwest Ireland's Dingle Peninsula, green dropping sharply over a pali/ cliff to white tipped waves. Ahead, a damaged wooden jetty clung to a rocky spit of land poking its head into the sea. In the distant low-lying coastal plain, trees ringed placid salt ponds.

Jan biking a favorite coastline overlooking Hanu`apo Bay

We sighed as we pulled ourselves out of our reveries. We hated to leave this idyllic scene but the joyful rush of a fantastic downhill swoop parallel to the bay obliterated that regret. Even though we knew our reality would change, too soon we fell into the throes of a steady forty mile uphill climb to the eponymous Village of Volcano. The town perches on the edge of Kilauea Caldera, traditional home of Pele, goddess of fire and volcanoes.

One of the casualties of cutting our trip to a four-day ride—the opportunity to stop to enjoy at length some of the character of the route, such as Kilauea's petroglyphs. Again, I semi-successfully comforted myself with the knowledge we soon would see them with our family.

Jim seemed to pedal more easily while I slogged up the hill, but my mind did little happy dances every 500 feet of altitude gain, as we passed signs saying, 1,000, 1,500, 2,000 feet. I was grateful no rain fell during the entire climb as it had for Jim and Dave in 2001. However, at 3,000-feet, mist dampened us and we needed to grab our rain jackets.

I had not trained vigorously enough for a February bike trip, so stopped frequently to eat, drink and stretch. Nearly five hours later we reached the 4026 foot elevation at the top. We ate lunch and roamed the Visitors' Center before it dawned on us we had twenty-five more miles to go to our B&B in Hilo. No need to panic because getting to town was mostly downhill. We hadn't counted on two hiccups.

All at once biting rain hammered us, stung our faces and nearly blinded us. I don't see well without my glasses but they streamed with icy water so I tried riding without them. Not a good idea so I quickly put them back on. I tugged my hood forward and my helmet brim down but not so much I couldn't see the white lines on the road. We hoped our flashing lights alerted motorists to drive cautiously. We just kept on keeping on.

Wide shoulders kept us off the highway proper as we determinedly progressed toward Hilo. Just when we thought the sky looked brighter physically and psychologically, Jim's front tire went flat. Rain still fell, though not as hard, but it's difficult to remove the front panniers and change a tire in wet conditions. He did the work while I played my role of sous mechanic, handing him tools and wrapping up the wretched tube.

Because our Dolphin Bay B&B included a kitchen, we made a lightning fast stop at a grocery store to get food we could quickly prepare for supper. We had cycled across much of Hilo and twilight had fallen by the time we squished up to the door. Soon wet clothes draped our apartment, but truly dripping stuff went in the shower after we did. Hot supper soothed our bodies and souls.

Seventy miles of changing altitudes and scenery, from oceanscapes to lava fields and down to sea level tropical Hilo. Quite enough delights and frights for one day. Sleep came soon.

🚲

Most of the roads leading to Waimea from Hilo featured wide shoulders. Serpentine valleys spilling their water out into the sea commanded where and how the roads lay, creating surprising scenes and a challenging ride. We passed the spot where a tsunami had devastated a village and swept an entire school with its children out to sea in the 1940s. What a painful reality for people on the island.

We spotted snow-capped Mauna Kea, glimpsed the glimmer of the observatory atop it and reminisced about our evenings spent star-and-planet-gazing just below it. The altitude, clarity of the air, lack of dust and light pollution is said to make the summit one of the best locations in the world for such an endeavor, some say the very best. Our experiences there had been thrilling.

At a time-worn general store, Jim and I enjoyed some nut-covered chocolate Maxxum ice cream bars. We began a conversation with two other cyclists, a woman and a man who did most of the talking. He told us that once they decided to bike around the island, he went to Walmart to buy his wife the cheapest bike he could find, a very heavy steel-framed one. He already had his biking equipment—need I mention it was of a much better quality and lighter weight? He didn't want to spend the money for a bicycle helmet for her either so found an old motorcycle helmet which looked like it weighed ten pounds. Jim and I were aghast. The woman sat there silently listening. He also didn't want to spend money on any kind of a pannier or saddlebag for her clothes so purchased a huge wire basket to hang on her handlebar. He acted very proud of what he had done, while the two of us wondered how his wife could stand him or the circumstances. She mustered a weak smile as we told them goodbye and wished them safe travels. As we discussed the incident later, we concurred that he probably treated her this way all the time. What a jerk! We felt angry at him and so sorry for her.

At Hanaloa, we eagerly left the new road and turned onto the Old Highway, a road we had happened upon years before when we circled the island in a rental car. Coming from the northeast, the narrow winding road was mostly uphill. Jim and I relished the rural feel of this byway, occasional clusters of houses, tunnel of trees nearly enclosing us, intriguing caves in the roadside bluffs. Nearly zero traffic blessed us until we popped out on the newer highway at the edge of Waimea. We had forgotten what a long ride it was from that edge to the Town center. We were ready for the day's ride to be over.

⚲

WAIMEA WINDS

Jim, Sandy and Dave had raved about the downhill ride from Waimea to the coastal road where the cycling leg of the Iron Man Classic takes place. "You'll feel just like you are soaring! You'll love it and the tailwind is terrific." I had hoped to ride and enjoy the thrill of that hill— someday. That day had come.

Jim and I awakened in our Waimea motel in eager anticipation of this day. We had it all planned out. We'd sail down the eight-mile hill to the coast and finish the day by enjoying the last forty miles to Keauhou Kona where we'd spend the next two weeks. Jim wouldn't bike the whole way but would stop at the airport to rent a van since he'd already circumnavigated the island in 2001. We'd say goodbye at the airport entrance and I'd ride solo the rest of the way.

Best laid plans…The instant we stepped outside the motel room, the wind whipped at us. *Oh no. This doesn't look good.* My heart sank. The prevailing wind which we expected to be at our backs had turned into a quartering wind at our right, from the northwest. That would be the worst. We could be blown into traffic if we weren't careful .

After breakfast we loaded the gear on our bikes and, with trepidation, plunged into early morning traffic in this northern Hawaii ranching community. Immediately, the wind blasted us. We had to slam on our brakes to maintain some control, then concentrate and make judicious use of them. Passing vehicles offered little protection from the gusts. After a mile in town, we hit the open highway, right in line of the gale's full force. Occasionally, hillocks momentarily shielded us, but we could only travel thirty to forty yards before we had to stop to put a foot down, both for safety and for release of tension, not the most efficient way to ride. Coast, light brake, coast, stop. Pull over to regain balance, coast, light brake, coast, full brake, stop. Over and over and over.

Fear of being pushed into oncoming traffic and cars and trucks passing us kept us in a state of chronic preparedness. Our wind-wearied bodies, aching, braking hands (or was it *Achy-braky Hearts?*) and battered psyches cheated us out of the promised great ride, assured by those who have no control over the weather. Not only did we face winds, we had to focus totally on the road, and couldn't appreciate the beauty of this part of the island. Because we'd been there before, we knew we biked through spectacular stretches of cattle-studded emerald meadows, rolling hills fringed with evergreens and grey-green ironwood trees. We could only do what we had been doing.

I'd anticipated exhilaration, not adrenaline-pumping blasts necessary to keep ourselves safe. I felt like we were in an Iron Man event and the wind was winning. When we turned left onto Queen Kaahumanu Highway paralleling the west coast, gratefulness filled me at being spared to ride more miles that day and we hoped, others.

Still forty-seven miles left to reach our condo. The rest of the ride played out much as I'd imagined, except for an unplanned stop at a fire station along the route with a plea to use their restroom. The fireman hesitated but eventually led me to the most blindingly clean necessary room I've ever seen.

We picnicked in the shade of plantings at the gate to Waikoloa, one of the ritziest golf resorts in Hawaii. No one bothered us as we sat on the curb and ate our simple sandwiches, chips and carrots lunch. Jim and I kissed each other goodbye at the airport where he biked to the car rental then drove to meet me at the condo.

Alone, I pedaled the last fifteen miles through the old industrial district of North Kona, on the main streets of Kailua-Kona, and south along the rocky beaches of the western shoreline. It was comforting to spot the Kailua Pier, Hulihee Palace which had been the summer home of Hawaiian royalty, and the oldest church on the island, Mokuaikaua Church. I zipped by the farmer's market, the tiny chapel of Saints Peter and Paul, and lastly, our favorite Kahaluu snorkeling beach.

I had reached one-fourth of a mile of our home-for-two-weeks when Jim passed me in the rental van. Drat! I had hoped to beat him in my own little Iron Woman race.

BUT WHAT ABOUT THE VAN?

I had long dreamed of bicycling in the American Southwest in the spring. I wanted to experience the blooming desert from a snail's pace instead of zooming by in a car, looking at blurry plants and wishing for a desert plant guide with equally blurry photos so I could identify them. If only we could solve a major logistical problem. What? Logistics again?

We asked each other, "Where are our kids when we need them?" For many years of our bicycling mania, our daughters, their friends and children of our cycling buddies had managed to help us do The Transportation Thing. They'd drop us off at the beginning of the ride route, go to the beach, a scenic area or a nearby city to play while the oldsters huffed and puffed across a state. At week's end the offspring would come to retrieve us and we'd head for home. Now they were all grown up and making their ways in the world. But we'd really like them to be teenagers again at least for this California to Texas bike trip.

"Who else could we ask? Who is retired?" We framed the question more appealingly. "Who would like to spend part of April delighting in the beauty of the Southwest desert in bloom?" That is, after they'd sent us on our way and before they gathered us up at the finish.

"What about cousin Linda? She lives in Tucson and if we got there on a Friday, she could go with us to the California border then drive the van back to Tucson and be ready to teach on Monday," Jim suggested.

"That's an idea although it would take her entire weekend. But how would we get the van to the Texas border from her house?" Another dilemma. "Who else do we know in Arizona?" Our high school classmate Bob Whelan and his wife Judy! "But they're in Lake Havasu City and that would involve them driving the van and a car across two states. That's too much to ask. Who else?"

Sandy offered, "Doug and Ellie Norris live in Mesa part of the time. They loved being part of the bike rides in Missouri and California. Maybe they could do it for us." Sandy and Dave checked with them about joining the cadre of people who'd helped us in our quest to bicycle across all the states. Doug was excited about the prospect, Ellie had other obligations.

Part 1: Pick Doug up and drive to Lake Havasu City to see Bob, the new mayor of the town, and Judy. It'd be fun to get a river tour from hizzoner. After that visit, Doug would take us the remaining way to the California-Arizona border, drop us off and return to Mesa with our van.

These are some of the things I love about bike trips. We get to see old friends and new places. But we still had to get the van from Mesa to the New Mexico-Texas state line.

Once again, Sandy to the rescue—her sister and brother-in-law. "Jane and Bill are always asking what they can do to help with the bike rides. Maybe they'd come to Arizona. And they've never really traveled in New Mexico."

Plan: Jane and Bill Nash fly to Phoenix, retrieve the van from Doug and Ellie, sightsee, meet rest of us at Texas border; bundle bikes, gear and selves, drive to Colorado. Jane and Bill fly to Michigan, Sandy and Dave drive home, Jim and I visit family in Boulder. Fait accompli!

Relieved, we smiled at our good fortune and set about Part 2—getting our bodies in as good shape as our plans. April would be here soon.

CRUISING THE CACTI (ROADRUNNER ROULETTE) ARIZONA-NEW MEXICO 2004

Riders: Sandy/Dave, Jim/Jan. Drop off: Doug Norris. Pick up: Jane/Bill Nash. Distance: 874 miles

Spring in the desert! What a treat! After layovers in Boulder and Fort Collins, the four of us drove our van to Mesa. Doug, bike trip groupie extraordinaire, became our drop-off hero.

Our next stop was to visit friends Bob and Judy in Lake Havasu City who led us on a tour of the town where Bob had been mayor. Judy's family had owned a boat business which she and Bob took over so, we enjoyed a ride on the Colorado River to see London Bridge which the city had purchased from Britain. Obviously, someone had offered to sell it, Lake Havasu City had taken the bait and purchased it—an extra spark of excitement for tourists. Too soon we had to leave to get to our overnight at Ehrenberg, Arizona on the California border.

The first joy of the day after Doug left with the van? We crossed the Colorado River from California into Arizona. The second was getting to bike, totally unfettered, on a ten-mile section of Interstate 10 closed to other traffic. What freedom to use both lanes to ride around hairpin curves and plunging downhills. Exiting to Quartzsite we continued our upward climb to Hope. In the scrubby wasteland outside of town, a possibly prophetic sign stopped us: *You're now beyond Hope.* That could be.

After abundant winter rainfalls, the desert produced a passel of flowers and shrubs. Spiky red-bloomed ocatilla, white prickly poppy, yellow turpentine bushes, fuchsia locoweed, yucca and on and on. We whipped out our cameras to try to capture the density of beauty in this otherwise parched land. Our motel in Salome, advertised as *Where she danced,* topped our landscape wonders with a towering—at least six times my height—seven-armed saguaro.

Jan is beyond Hope

Mountains ranging to over 5600 feet surrounded us as we climbed to Wickenburg and made us work. So did the first of repeated flat tires on the trip. Recovery came quickly and we continued to town for dinner with Dave and Sandy's daughter-in-law Natalie's parents.

We barreled down the mountain from Wickenburg and into the suburbs feeling increasingly confident. The traffic didn't look too bad, and we thought finding the bicycle trail would be the only challenge of the day. Our route through the northwestern part of the metropolitan area had pockets of convenience stores, tire repair shops, schools, automobile dealers, plus large tracts of walled homes, and spring was in the air.

Stomach-clutching traffic in cities makes me apprehensive about biking there, but Phoenix promised to be different. The bike maps showed what should be an uncrowded, safe and smooth surfaced route paralleling a canal. Forty miles through the city should be a unique experience. Our map showed a four-lane street crossing over the Arizona Canal with the bike trail angling east down from the bridge. "Oh no! We missed it! Come back!" came the shout.

We stopped to strategize how to get across the now swiftly moving traffic to access the trail. Jim and Dave wanted to wait for a break and sprint to safety on the other side. Sandy and I spotted traffic signals and a crosswalk farther on and opted for that more cautious approach. I remained close behind her as we hopped on our bikes. Just then Jim hollered, "Now!" Sandy slammed on her brakes so she could follow Jim, and mid-pedal, I had to make a quick dismount. Well, that was what flashed through my head.

This was Sandy's first long-distance ride since she had been treated for breast cancer with surgery, radiation and chemotherapy two years earlier. There was no way I would jeopardize her trip by running into her. My feet were already clipped into the pedals and I couldn't get them out fast enough.

Fortunately	Unfortunately
I tipped over instead of hitting Sandy and her bike.	The stone wall next to me didn't break my fall.
I flipped over the wall rather gracefully, if I may say so.	I landed on the rocks two feet below.
They were rounded river rocks.	I landed upside down.
My panniers broke my fall.	My feet remained clipped into the pedals.
My companions were able to free me from my pedal prison.	My handlebars entangled in the grate.
They didn't take photos before they released me.	I felt bruised and shaken.
Jim and Dave eventually extracted my bike.	We still had fifteen miles to go to our motel.
Neither my bike nor I had any broken parts.	I felt a bit creaky.
We arrived safely.	I had no "hurry" left in me.

Fortunately, a hot shower helped heal my physical and psychic wounds, and that night we ate pizza at Organ Stop Pizza with Doug and Ellie. The atmosphere, food, company and Mighty Wurlitzer Organ music filled us with new energy. Tomorrow was a day for play and sight-seeing.

As we celebrated our layover day, Jim, cousin Linda from Tucson, and I enjoyed strolling and admiring the delightful statuary Mesa has assembled on their downtown street corners. We loved being with her. That evening we drove our van to the Barleens Arizona Opry in Apache Junction. Roast beef, mashed potatoes and all the trimmings dinner plus a wonderful musical event performed by several generations of the Barleen Family delighted us. Sandy's older daughter Lisa had married Bob Barleen whose grandfather originated this business many years ago. We loved hearing the verbal patter of the performers as well as their musical virtuosity. Attesting to musical genius, one member who plays as many as thirty-two different instruments has a vocal range of five octaves. No ordinary musicians, these.

⚙

A new day and back on the road, Sandy, Dave, Jim and I pedaled on Highway 60 through the Superstition Mountains, labeled *Extreme Grade* on our map. Our biggest challenge lay ahead —the twelve hundred foot long Queen Creek Tunnel. Not only did we continue climbing the 6 percent grade in the dimly lit tunnel, the clamor of traffic made my ears ring. Thrilled to have survived the passage, I still felt the clanging in my head in open air. While I tried to regain my equilibrium by hanging over my handlebars at the side of the road, Sandy and Dave giggled at me and Jim took my photo. Hmph! At least twelve miles of winding 6 percent mostly downhill came soon after that. Sounds good but it was difficult to see the rocky palisades and other scenery while trying to control speed, focus on safety and not careen over a cliff.

Our day's seventy-five miles ended in Globe, one of the many towns founded because of the discovery of silver and copper. In this case, once the copper mining operations closed, the old mine workings served as water supply for the area. *Would it be safe to drink?* The town features a number of buildings listed on the National Historic Register and its history as a true frontier town included stagecoach robberies, lynchings, murders and a number of outlaws. The Clanton Brothers came there after the gunfight at the OK Corral in Tombstone. After our overnight stay, we quietly bicycled through it, no gunfight, no outlaws. We did drink the water.

⚙

Our next miles took us past the Pyramid Mountains to Lordsburg, New Mexico. The topography, desert plants and climate did not change appreciably as we crossed into the new state. The greatest change would come the following day, Easter Sunday.

⚙

A PIECE OF CAKE
In arid regions of the world surface winds pick up silt and sand and suspend them in the air to form dust storms. Up to this point, our experience had been limited to spotting cyclonic dust devils at a safe distance. Our first direct encounter with a dust storm came as we stood in our Lordsburg motel room, drop-jawed at not being able to see the restaurant across the parking lot.

We had transitioned to the harsh Sonoran Desert country of southwest New Mexico and had seen *Caution: Dust Storm* and *Zero Visibility Possible* signs all along this stretch. Reflecting on the day, a coiled snake hissing at each of us had been our only incident. I was happy to be off the bike because of a bad cold. The following day we'd celebrate Easter by riding sixty miles east to Deming.

The weather channel forecast strong easterly winds Sunday as well as strong westerly winds Monday. For two of us, there was only one intelligent thing to do: simply take an early layover day Sunday, then blow into Deming on Monday. Two impediments to this decision—our spouses adamantly opposed the idea. They would not deviate from our planned itinerary. We would bicycle tomorrow. Dave shrugged off our arguments with a smug, "A piece of cake." Inwardly, I gagged. *I detest that phrase! Why tempt fate?*

Sandy and I faced the choice between the smart one to remain here in our Lordsburg motel for an extra day or to stay the course and go on with our favorite bicycle mechanics. To use an old western expression, too weak and lily-livered to stand up to them, we opted to forge on.

🚲

Easter Sunday morning. East wind. Bold brazen cold east wind. Still, high spirits prevailed when we took the balloons Sandy had brought to breakfast to share with and thank the wait staff. After all, they had to work that day.

Gear loaded on our bicycles, layers of clothing to protect us from the shivery wind, we headed to Interstate 10. As in other remote areas of the United States, in this lightly populated corner of New Mexico bicyclists could legally ride the interstate since there were few viable roads to choose from. We had just entered the on-ramp when the full impact of what we were attempting hit us. I could barely pedal into the ferocious wind. Jim came to my rescue and yelled, "Tuck in behind me." More protected there, at least I could manage to make the same progress he did. Under my breath I muttered, *Why are we doing this? This is so stupid. We shouldn't have started out today. Hubris.*

We rode on the shoulder of the interstate whenever we could but potentially tire flattening debris made conditions dangerous to stay there. Fortunately, the passing traffic—everything did pass us—seemed generally mindful and moved to the inside lane, so being sucked into their drafts didn't seem likely.

Not one thing improved throughout the morning, we agonized every inch of the way. The nineteen miles to the only stopover of the day took us over three hours. Buffeted by wind. Buffeted by cars. Buffeted by semis. Dirt blew in our faces. We grimly greeted each mile marker with gritted and gritty teeth.

Rain, hail, sleet, snow bombarded us. At last in the distance we saw the oasis where we could escape the relentless thirty to forty mile per hour headwind. A graveled parking lot puddling with icy water welcomed us. Shuddering "Brrrrr!" we locked up our bikes. At least one of us prayed some foolish soul would steal at least one of them so we couldn't ride any farther, and staggered into the tourist haven. Any other time we might have said, "What a tourist trap!" But the warm windless store had indoor restrooms, beverages, and amazing to us, Blue Bunny ice cream bars. They had limited appeal that day.

Minutes later other travelers burst into the store and reported a horrific accident a few miles back. A car had rear-ended a semi during a dust storm's parallel to a whiteout. Fatalities had occurred and we realized we could have been in the midst of the tragedy. We somberly thought of and prayed for those poor people.

We wandered aimlessly around the aisles, fingered souvenir key chains, Indian blankets, carved horses, ojo de Dios, post cards, but not the potted cactus, and contemplated our next move. We needed to ride over forty miles to get to Deming, with no services along the way. April's limited daylight hours made us ask, "Can we meet the challenge? Should we even try?"

We finally agreed to return to Lordsburg. We believed we would be blown all the way back by the ill-tempered east wind and, considering the wind's velocity, within a reasonable length of time. Jim called the Lordsburg motel to see if they had a vacancy. They said we could have the same rooms. He contacted the motel in Deming to ask if we could cancel our rooms for that night and make reservations for the next. No problem there either. We breathed sighs of relief, reveled in the last bit of warmth and headed out to the road.

Sandy and I pedaled up the interstate ramp ahead of Jim and Dave and groaned when we realized while we were thawing out, the wind had switched and had become a cruel north cross-wind. Woefully, we cranked on. We had no cell phones so after a couple of miles when we didn't see the guys behind us, we doubled back to check if there had been trouble. They had just finished repairing Jim's tire, flat number seven for the four of us on this trip. We had bicycled thousands of miles together and had never had so many flats! Our dearly beloveds seemed astonished we had returned to see what had befallen them. It seemed perfectly reasonable to Sandy and me.

The elements did not improve. The sky roiled with ominous clouds. Another storm moved in, with wind, sleet and falling temperatures, ten degrees in the last hour. Pelted, hammered, and lambasted not only from the skies but from vehicles zooming by, we looked like dirty sleet-sodden bundles of no-longer-waterproof Gore-Tex.

After a few miles I shouted, "I'm stopping!" dropped my bike on the interstate shoulder and plunged into the ditch seeking refuge. The others followed. We couldn't scrunch into the much-too-small culverts, but cowered there, each in our own culvert trying to get out of the wind —after first checking for snakes, scorpions and other critters. But what self-respecting creatures would be out of their holes or dens in this weather? Bicyclists, that's who.

We hunkered down for nearly thirty minutes until the major part of the front had passed. We gingerly stood up, stretched our stiff bodies and scrabbled out of the ditch. The wind continued its about-face until it came from the west and the sleet morphed to rain. We plugged away in drizzly headwinds for a long time. A very long time. The amount of time to return to Lordsburg? The same as we had taken to ride from there. Untiringly the weather taunted us, and at the last just as we approached town, with sunshine.

Eventually we warmed up; eventually our clothes dried; eventually we forgave ourselves. We did not forget the choices we had made that begot this tale. But please do not use the phrase *A piece of cake* within my hearing. I know what that cake tastes like. I have no desire to bite into it again.

As far as recriminations go, I was too tired to make even a mediocre attempt at *Sandy and I told you so,* and I didn't trust myself to not go too far in what I said. So I did the next best things—I showered, ate supper and went to bed. However, years later when I disagreed with Jim and Dave about potential biking decisions, I confess to making not-so veiled references to certain dimwitted decisions in the past.

⚲

Monday a blue sky, moderate temperatures and westerly winds prevailed. Sandy and I could barely smile at our husbands for our exhausting experiences the previous day. Easter Sunday. Resurrection. I suppose we felt a bit resurrected, albeit a day late.

As Sandy and I had said yesterday before our fateful ride, if we took our layover day on Sunday and waited until Monday, we would have sailed the sixty miles to Deming, pedaling, yes, but not struggling and miserable. No dust storms, no rattlesnakes, no harsh anything bothered us that beautiful day. We celebrated our arrival in Deming with a phone call and visit to Mr. Winter, a then sparky eighty-one-year old father of Sherry Rohrig, once a fellow teacher of mine at Lemme School. When he asked about our trip so far, I gave him a few more details than he probably wanted. His cogent response, "Well, if it was all easy, you wouldn't appreciate it." Right Mr. Winter, a perspective I sorely needed.

This town offered something else I needed—a walking tour. I didn't go on an official tour of historic Deming, but used a guide book I'd picked up. I wandered down evocatively named Silver and Pine Streets to enjoy the late 1800s and early 1900s buildings: art deco Luna Mimbres Museum, named after an ancient native group; Greek-columned Custom House; classic brick Baker Hotel; wood over adobe with stepped parapets Old Star Barber Shop. On and on, the downtown commercial buildings are part of the historic zone, some on the State Historic Registry and National Registry of Historic Places. It was a restorative walk.

⚲

Pedaling east sixty-five miles to Las Cruces, meaning crossroads, a sense of weariness hit us, particularly when flat tires did too. Checking the map, we realized we were less than fifty miles north of El Paso, Texas. Did we want to change our route and hit the border there? No, we had friends to visit in Alamogordo and so much more to see in parts of New Mexico we'd never traveled before.

Flat tire repaired, we chugged along, at least I did, into this attractive city, the second largest in the state. This city was to have been our layover day, except for the Easter wind, rain, sleet and snow snafu. So we made do with a cursory glimpse of the southwestern architecture and read about the joys of retiring here, as recommended by various money magazines. The only place we retired that day was to our beds, hoping to be refreshed enough for our next day's excursion.

Our day's ride took us another sixty-five miles northeast to Alamogordo with the White Sands Missile Range within view. As we pedaled on, we became more and more aware of the presence of the military as well as our nation's space program, including the Missile Range. This enormous complex is the largest military base in the United States, about thirty-two hundred square miles. Military weapons and equipment are tested there and have been since WWII. NASA used it as a landing site during the Space Shuttle operations as well as missile, flight and satellite tests before launch.

From the highway, we could see the bright white gypsum dunes of White Sands National Monument shining in the sun. An hour's drive north of there is ground zero where the first atomic bomb Trinity was detonated, beginning the Atomic Age. This Tularosa Basin landscape has been used and abused for so many reasons, not all of them military. It has been used for film-making, car racing, hunting range, parties, sand skiing, mining the dunes, picnicking, and an annual "Play Day."

We had a great time with friends Tom and Priscilla Mitchell at dinner that evening. Years earlier, Tom, originally from Iowa City and son of good friends, had been assigned to Holloman Air Force Base where he met and married Priscilla. Our excellent Chinese dinner satisfied our appetite for food but our fondness for laughter was sated by Tom who entertained us all.

At breakfast, Sandy told us she would not be able to continue riding. The cumulative effects of wind, tough terrain, and lack of a true layover day had been debilitating for her. She called sightseeing Jane and Bill who came to pick her up. Sandy joined them for a couple of days then planned to bike with us when she felt more rested. It felt awful to go without her but we all knew riding while exhausted is not good for bodies, spirits or safety. So Dave, Jim and I sadly pedaled north without her to Carrizozo, fifty-seven miles away. Flanking us on the east and uplifting our spirits were the snow-capped Sacramento Mountains.

While we cycled in the Tularosa Basin, we saw pistachio orchards, a relatively new crop here in New Mexico. In the southwest part of the state, we had noticed that chili peppers were popular crops in addition to the more usual hay and sorghum. We had time while riding to mull over what dishes we'd like these products in.

Eighty miles to Vaughn with a slight altitude gain to 5978 feet kept us occupied most of the day, our last day accompanied by mountains. I would miss them when they were gone, but for the time being, their presence and the occasional topping of snow made us feel better.

As the day warmed, we made use of shade for travelers provided by a length of corrugated steel fastened to two poles nearly perpendicular to the ground. Two additional poles angled with larger sheets of steel attached. Simple but effective in our otherwise shadeless environment. The burned brown of drought grass provided forage for a herd of antelope, but I thought they would also have liked the shade of the shelter.

Fort Sumner had its beginnings when the West was being settled by whites, although the region was already the homeland of Native Americans. Known historically as the terminus of *The Long Walk* for a beleaguered group of Apaches, this four hundred mile eighteen day walk, as with forced movements of other native groups, had a high death toll. Insufficient food, water, and care of pregnant women and sick people, as well as cruelty made survival difficult. For those who managed to live, a few years later the US government allowed them to return to their homeland. *How many times in history must people deprive others, whom they conceive of as inferior, of their homes, security and freedom?*

Good news too! The three sightseers joined us in Fort Sumner, Sandy planned to bike the rest of the way to the Texas border. Jane and Bill would take our rear panniers with them in the van, lightening our loads. We kept our front low-riders to carry jackets, sunscreen and food, whatever we might need during the day.

We welcomed the flat terrain and wide highway shoulder to Clovis, our last town in New Mexico. The first time I'd heard the name was when I learned of the archaeologists' discovery of the Clovis point, a finely honed spear head made by early indigenous people. Although the landscape seemed very brown and dry to us, irrigation in this High Plains region has made cattle ranching and farming corn, sorghum, potatoes and other crops possible. But it was still early spring.

Texico lay about ten miles away just on the border with Farwell as its Texas counterpart. We laughed when we saw the mileage sign which told us we were thirty miles from Muleshoe, Texas. There has to be a story behind that name. We pedaled into the Texas border town where Jane and Bill waited with cameras ready. We'd just added two more states, numbers forty-seven and forty-eight, to our list of, "Been there! Done that!"

This adventure required an addendum to tell more of the tale. Here is one, a letter addressed to Dave.

Open letter to a cycling companion:

DESERT MOON

What happens when you have made some minor mistakes about preparation for a long-distance bicycle ride? For instance, you bought a beautiful new multi-hued Klein mountain bike before heading for a spring desert jaunt across Southwestern United States. You replaced the really knobby tires with less knobby ones for a smoother ride on highways. Remaining true to your success with your road bike, you pumped up the tires as you would have, for sufficient traction and with the opportunity for greater speed. You knew the downside would be a harsher ride, but you had new cushy-bottom biking shorts, and besides, you really like speed.

About a hundred miles after leaving the California border with us, your wife and friends, you began to feel hotspots on your derriere. That's like blisters you know will follow hot-spots on your feet. Big sigh.

You had been prescient enough to bring along bicyclists' favorite Bag Balm which should take care of your now fully-realized saddle sores. For any farmer or farm kid, it is well-known that Bag Balm contains lanolin, often used on cows' udders to soothe chapped and dry skin. The FDA initially approved it for use on animals but not for humans, but that didn't mean it wouldn't be utilized by two-legged creatures seeking relief.

Something you didn't know though was Bag Balm had been used by Allied troops in World War II to protect their weapons from rust. Well, you didn't suffer from rustiness but did like the mild analgesic on your nether regions.

One application of balm per day proved insufficient so periodically you announced, "See you later!" The rest of us took the hint and kept riding while you treated your wounds. We often stopped on rural bridges, propped our bikes on the metal railings, stretched, snacked, occasionally addressed the calls of nature, then rode on, a perfect opportunity for you to continue your ministrations.

Your routine always included conscientiously checking for traffic. Generally, none existed, this being the Mojave Desert wilderness. You faced away from the highway, dropped your drawers and began applying the pacifying balm. Once, to your chagrin, you heard an engine, glanced up and saw a tour bus racing by. The driver grinned widely as he laid on the horn and his passengers waved wildly. Sheepishly, you finished daubing the salve, pulled up your shorts and caught up with us to relate your adventure. You provided a welcome break, laughter and memorable tale for your fellow cyclists, but no doubt for the bus driver and tourists too.

Your owies slowly healed, but the constant pressure of perching on a narrow bicycle saddle hurt your pride as well as making the ride painful. You stood up whenever you could to relieve the misery—not an easy feat riding that way for hours.

A few days later, we parked alongside another bridge for our morning snack. We knew the drill so took off when you retrieved your Bag Balm from your pannier. Again you squinted in both directions of our route. No traffic. Good, you thought, no humiliating but amusing reprise of your previous exposure. You decided to face the highway so you could see what might sneak up on you. You needed to focus on your job. Even your diminished hearing picked up the clamor. You rechecked the road and whirled around as a train roared behind you. The engineer hit the whistle and waved. Caught again.

We, your compassionate biking companions, teased you mercilessly about your "need to moon." None of your defensive tactics quieted us. We decided your experiences of desert mooning deserved to be memorialized in poetry, not an ode or an elegy but at least a limerick. Here are three modest examples:

There once was a man named Dave
Who used Bag Balm in order to save
His poor derriere
But to be more than fair
He preferred a whistle and wave.

There once was a cyclist named Dave
Who started to rant and to rave
He had saddle sores
On his delicate pores
Modesty he could no longer save.

There once was a cyclist named Dave
Whose condition was very grave
Just where he sot
Saddle sores he begot
He mooned folks, that black-hearted knave.

MIDDLE OF NOWHERE-THE LONELIEST ROAD IN AMERICA NEVADA-UTAH 2005

Riders: Retha/Ray Haas, Dave, cousin Kerstin Wolle, Jim/Jan. SAG: Cousin Charles Wolle.
Distance Nevada: 415 miles. Distance Utah: 487 miles. Total distance: 902 miles

When Sandy, Dave, Jim and I completed our east to west crossing of California in 2003, we immediately began to discuss where to bike next. Jim had an idea. "How about Highway 50 across Nevada? Then go on through Utah too. That'd be great." Pause. "And we could scout the route on our way home now."

We did just that. Sandy took meticulous notes that indicated VIPs—Very Important Places. For example: *Day 2, mile 3.0—Photo-op at Down's Lane; mile 4.0—last potty stop for a long time; mile 37.5—Abandoned white car. Day 3, mile 5.2—Three trees on right-potty stop. Day 4 —Big, big, steep, steep hill leaving Austin (2.6 miles). Day 5—No services-83 miles. Day 6—Ely lots of services!! Red Apple Family Restaurant (don't order a scone, French toast not great, oatmeal sets world record for large size).*

But of all the places we saw that day, Middlegate Station made the greatest impression on all of us. We didn't require Sandy's notes to remember it well. There in the middle of Nevada's nowhere stood a complex of low-slung, weathered wooden buildings. Prominent among them, next to the motel rooms, sat a small one with a half-moon incised on the door. What did that portend?

Sandy's comments on details of interest and usefulness to us as long-distance bike riders, helped us formulate our plans two years hence when the Middle of Nowhere ride would come to pass. During that planning, we learned The Loneliest Road in America was in the middle of something else, the area in Nevada called the Pony Express Territory. Things began to shape up to be a history lesson too.

Finding an efficient way to get our van from Genoa in the west of Nevada to Fruita, Colorado where we would complete our crossing of the fifty United States was the next task. Jim had enlisted his cousin Charles to be the SAG driver and his wife Kerstin to cycle with us. Perfect! Charles, a federal judge who now lives in Nevada but has an office in Des Moines, wrote the extended Down Family a letter which included this information:

I sit in my Des Moines US Courthouse office thinking some of you may think our 2005 plans are of some interest. Attached is Jim and Jan Down's amazing schedule to complete their bicycling across all 50 states. To test the difficulty, Kerstin and I will join their cross-Nevada pedaling…I drive their van while J & J, Kerstin and several friends bicycle east to the towns/motels listed—distances in miles/day of 74, 47, 62, 68, 73, 64 and 89. Oh yes, also across 6-8 mountain passes and valleys. A true trek.

He goes on to explain the complex picking up and leaving of cars, vans, and airplanes back to Iowa for another cousin's memorial service. Some of these original plans were altered several times before it all worked. Jim, in an earlier missive had added, "All of this is subject to change." Indeed. Charles responded:

Amazing planning! Timing is OK with Kerstin and me. Another possibility: Each day Charles drives ahead to next stop, parks vehicle, and rides back to join the pack, then rides to car with pack. At Delta, Utah, Kerstin and I figure a way to fly home to Reno.

Or not. Keep us posted!

The groundwork had been laid, tweaks followed, but eventually, a couple of weeks before the ride began, we had a basic plan we hoped to follow. Not everything went as we had hoped, but a necessary attribute of long-distance cyclists is flexibility.

🚲

TO MIDDLEGATE AND ON…MAY, 2005

Jim and I awaited Sandy and Dave's arrival in Boulder, Colorado where we visited our family. Sandy would join her daughter Lisa, son-in-law Bob, and grandson Logan in Loveland. It seemed strange and sadder still that Sandy could no longer bicycle long distances with us because of health issues. We had bicycled thousands of miles together over the years, sharing adventures, misadventures, memories, laughter and thoughts. That she would not be with us on this trip made me sorrowful.

Driving west, the interstate miles flipped by quickly. Once Dave, Jim and I arrived in Fruita, our eventual endpoint in a couple of weeks, we traveled along what we hoped would be our biking route in eastern Utah, an old highway just off I-70. A few stretches would be okay but most of it consisted of crushed rock, pitted surface—very hard on the body even riding in the van. We decided we would not bike it. Time would tell.

By the time we arrived in Delta, Utah Retha and Ray had been cycling around and had thoroughly explored the town. Dave would have plenty of time to do that when Jim and I were in Iowa for cousin Mary's memorial.

🚲

We left Retha and Ray's van at the motel in Delta for their return trip to Iowa. Then the five of us traveled in our van to Genoa, Nevada where Charles and Kerstin live. We had fun appraising what we would traverse the following days. Sandy's voluminous notes regarding this part of the route continued to provide valuable and humorous information. She had indicated mileage and steepness of the route and seeing some of it made us gulp a bit. Well, at least I did, but I don't know if Ray ever does when facing a challenge. I just hoped we would all be strong enough by the time we reached those hills to have few problems.

We arrived in Genoa early enough for us to drive up nearby Carson Pass. All of us had biked it within the past two years as we had ridden into California. It had been a tough climb and looked totally different now with lots of snow and the lake still frozen. What we had done earlier impressed us now. The wind whipped at us when we got out of the van so when Retha posed for a photo, she shivered and looked as though she was hanging onto the rocky ledge overlooking the lake.

We checked into our motel room and proceeded past flooded fields to Charles and Kerstin's home. Kerstin had prepared a flavorful lasagna and salad served with energizing lingonberry juice.

We took the bikes off/out of the van to put them into the Wolles' garage to get an efficient start the next day, then returned to the motel. Jim and Dave checked out two places for breakfast —a too-smoky casino and Jimmy G's next door.

🚲

GENOA TO FALLON 74.4 MILES BY BICYCLE

Up early for breakfast. Jim decided to break with tradition and not order oatmeal and dry whole wheat toast, instead ordering multigrain-buckwheat pancakes. Dave feigned being aghast at the change in Jim's diet, and laughingly told the waitress to put dry oatmeal on the top of Jim's pancakes. She did.

Off to Charles and Kerstin's and the beginning leg of our bicycle ride across Nevada. As planned, Kerstin bicycled with us and Charles captained the van as SAG driver. The air felt chill but we warmed up quickly and soon took off our tights and long sleeved jerseys. Snow-capped mountains created a perfect backdrop for us, and western meadowlarks sang.

The ride to Carson City went as planned and we skirted the main part of the city. We relaxed more once we left it behind. With blue sky and a breeze at our backs, we fairly sailed all day long, sometimes averaging over sixteen miles per hour. Great fun, especially for a first day!

As we entered Fallon, we could not resist the call of the giant root beer mug sign at Bob's Root Beer Drive-In, a quintessential root beer stand. The matchless thirst quencher became our reward for a good day biking. After a wait for our four rooms to be ready, we finally cleaned up and walked to the Churchill County Museum.

Road signs near town had touted the museum as *The Best Little Museum on The Loneliest Road in America*. It showcased the lives of Native Americans who inhabited the area many years ago. My favorite exhibit demonstrated how to make houses and boats out of tule reeds— lots of practice and patience. Another showed the hardships settlers and emigrants endured as they crossed the most treacherous part of the trail west, dubbed the 40-Mile Desert.

We also popped across the Lincoln Highway to the Overland Hotel and Saloon. We had read and believed the article that touted it as a must-see for visitors to Fallon. The quirky collection of whatever hung from the ceiling of the bar brought laughs and the antiques brought oohs and aahs. Quirky? Among the chaps, fish, moose and deer mounts hung a bedpan, an ox yoke and a car door. Amid the beer bottles on display were three boxes containing the ashes of three deceased customers. So the story goes, they had no family and had spent a lot of time in the saloon. It seemed only fitting…

Fallon traced its roots back to the California Gold Rush and western migration. At the turn of the twentieth century, the nearby Newlands Project became the first land reclamation project in the United States. It diverted water from the Truckee and Carson Rivers, reclaimed the land from the desert, and transformed the 40-Mile Desert into productive farms and ranches.

After an Italian dinner, we bought fruit and bread for the following day's lunch, while Ray purchased a rearview mirror and extra tire tube for Kerstin's bicycle. Although she is a strong rider, she'd never been on a long-distance bicycle ride before and needed such vital safety equipment.

⏚

FALLON TO MIDDLEGATE STATION 64.4 MILES

Middlegate Station Day! During breakfast Jim, Dave and I recalled our scouting trip in 2003. Here we were doing the real thing, but sadly without Sandy. Slight breeze at our backs, we continued to bike through the green Lahontan Valley, an agricultural oasis, where we saw the results of the reclamation project we had learned about at the museum.

Sandy's notes indicated a four mile uphill to Sand Springs Pass, followed ten miles later by an over three mile uphill to Drumm Summit. Among landmarks she had listed an abandoned white car. We saw it.

Just east of Fallon we came upon a land-locked US Naval Air Station. Over the years, it had been upgraded to full Naval Air Station to prepare crews for jet operations and became one of the premier training bases in the country. Periodically throughout the day, we looked up to see planes overhead, we assumed from NAS Fallon, the headquarters of Top Gun, the elite Navy Fighter Weapons School. Tom Cruise did not seem to be in residence.

Shades of caramel to fawn to sepia tinged the monochromatic landscape. Names and signs attested to that color scheme: Salt Wells, Sand Mountain, Carson Sink Stations, Soda Lake, Sand Dike. The names sounded remote, isolated, dry, lonely. To us, they also spell the harsh unrelenting beauty of salt flats, sand and rocks.

Once upon a time, this region lay beneath an immense inland sea, Lake Lahontan. It had covered Grimes Point Archaeological Area and receded by the time human population moved into the region. It contained an assemblage of over 150 basalt boulders covered with ancient Native American petroglyphs, etched into the rock sometime between 5000 BCE and 1500 CE. Many archaeologists think they were part of ritual practices by tribal shamans to ensure successful hunting, since the site is on the seasonal routes of migrating animals. The designs include circular and wavy lines, zig-zags, stripes, dots, asterisks, snakes, horned toads, goats and human figures. My mind conjured up seeing ancient people creating petroglyphs, but zoomed back to the present as a jet swept through the sky. *What were the stories behind these petroglyphs?*

We think we know the story behind another piece of art created along the roadway. Someone, perhaps besotted with bikes, chose dark brown round stones to create the outline of a bicycle. Not quite a petroglyph, but still a welcoming message, especially to us cyclists.

A few miles beyond Salt Wells, the Loneliest Telephone Booth in America caught our attention, a six hundred foot tall sand dune looming behind it. The locals got a lot of mileage out of the phrase *the Loneliest...* After our photo-op phone calls, we read the signage about Sand Mountain. *The giant dune was created by wind-carried sand from the beaches of a prehistoric inland sea that once covered much of Nevada.* That would be Lake Lahontan which had extended over 8500 square miles from the Great Basin in the east, and west to the Sacramento River. Its legacy includes mountain ranges, caves and terraces carved by waves, including the ripples we saw in the hills surrounding us as we biked through this vast scene. The Northern Paiutes call this landmark Kwazi, the name of the snake they believe inhabits the dune, its backbone forming the crest of the mountain. The mountain changes shape every day as the winds deposit new sand, resculpting the old form. Unfortunately, lots of four-wheeled ATVs roar up and down it, adding their own reshaping.

Over the years Sand Mountain had become a landmark for Native Americans, prospectors and pioneers, as well as for Pony Express riders. Adjacent to the huge dune, the ruins of the original Sand Springs Pony Express Station alerted us to the fact that much of Highway 50 in Nevada parallels the old route. This rapid (ten days to California) mail service, used from April, 1860 to October, 1861, started in St. Joseph, Missouri and culminated 1900 miles later in Sacramento. The stations had been built about ten miles apart, the distance a horse could gallop without becoming too tired. Posters advertising for potential riders said: *Wanted: Young, skinny, wiry fellows not over eighteen. Must be expert riders, willing to risk death daily. Orphans preferred. Pay $25 per week.*

We cyclists on our fancy 27 gear bicycles reflected on the differences and similarities between the brave Pony Express riders and us. We were not young, skinny, wiry or orphaned and definitely over 18. Although we don't change our steeds every ten miles, we often go five miles at our top gallop. We rely on our endurance and ability just like the early missive senders relied on those young men charged with carrying precious letters. The contrasts made us feel a tiny bit of kinship with those stalwart young men.

Overcoming Drumm Summit and passing Fairview Peak Earthquake Fault Road signaled that we were very close to the long-awaited Middlegate Station. Favorable tailwinds propelled us there early in the afternoon.

A bit of history: The Gold Rush meant more traffic along this overland route, so in 1859 it was established and named by James Simpson. He called the cuts in the mountains, gates, hence, West Gate, Middle Gate and East Gate. Middlegate became an Overland Stage Station for freight and stagecoaches crossing the country. In 1860 the Pony Express began using it as a home station to provide room and board for the riders.

When the Gold Rush ended, Middlegate lost its role and was no longer used. In the 1940s a Bureau of Land Management auction sold it, the new owner Ida Ferguson began its restoration. The Lincoln Highway provided vital business but the highway had been rerouted in the early 1960s and her bar and café suffered. Ida sold Middlegate and retired. It was sold and resold, still having no phones or electricity. But it did have the aforementioned one-holer. In 1984 the Stevenson family purchased the property and resumed restoration, bit by bit, work that continues.

Two signs welcomed us. A round one said:

Old Middlegate Station

Gas, Food, Ice

Historic Middlegate Station

A rectangular one read:

Welcome to Middlegate

In the Middle of Nowhere

Elevation 4,600 feet

Population 17 ~~18~~

The number 18 had been crossed off.

Because we had arrived earlier than expected, we caucused to determine if we would ride farther or stop then. We decided to shorten the next day's ride to Austin by continuing to bike thirteen more miles to Cold Springs, home of the Cold Springs Pony Express Station and the same named

Telegraph Station. That they are juxtaposed to each other is ironic. The telegraph is the very thing that made the Pony Express obsolete.

A mile and a half down the road, Ray heard something and said, "I don't like that sound." It was the group's first and last flat of the entire trip. He wheeled his bike into a roadside parking area for repair. We pulled in behind him and found ourselves under the famed Old Shoe Tree, festooned with shoes of all sizes and types. Sneakers, hiking boots, oxfords, sandals, baby shoes, wing-tips, strappy high heels all hung from the seventy foot cottonwood's substantial branches. This American folk icon, constantly in the making, fascinated us. We speculated about its possible genesis and what possessed people to continue to toss shoes into its silver-green leafed branches. We discovered several variations on a theme comprise the tree's creation myth. Here is one:

In the early 1990s, a young couple married in Colorado and subsequently traveled toward California. As sometimes happens, they began to argue and the husband pulled over to the side of the road under this big cottonwood tree. He left his wife there, apparently hoping her anger would subside while he cooled off with a beer at Middlegate Station. After drinking his beer, he returned to the tree and his wife. Small wonder, she was still furious. He grabbed a pair of her shoes, threw them into the tree and returned to the bar in another attempt of calm down. This time when he returned to his wife, they came to a truce. He tried to retrieve her shoes but did not succeed. They left them there, supposedly forever hanging from a limb. Other wayfarers saw the dangling shoes and, inspired by them, tossed their own shoes into the branches. Some reported it took them more than one or two heaves to get them to stay on the tree.

Many of the shoes appeared to be in wearable condition, maybe tossed on a whim. None of us contributed our biking shoes. A pink plastic flamingo added a splash of color. Someone created and nailed a sock-shaped plaque to the tree:

The largest Shoe Tree in the world…
My friend as you're driving by
Would you leave a pair of shoes
For now you have aplenty
So what have you to lose.
Someday someone may come walking
Bare feet so bruised and sore
To him, I'll find a pair of shoes—

Charles summed it up, "Perhaps we will never know the *sole* reason for the Old Shoe Tree." Ray quickly changed his flat and we forged on to Cold Springs. I noticed riding had become more difficult but thought we might be tiring, considering the time of day. Wrong. We had been slowly climbing, something that only became apparent to me when we returned to Middlegate in the van with Charles. How deceptive our perceptions can be.

A herd of wild mustangs grazing near the highway evoked an aura of the Old West. Mustangs and burros are part of 38,000 equines allowed to roam freely on rural lands in ten western states. Supposedly, they have a very long life span due to their insusceptibility to disease and lack of predators. According to the Bureau of Land Management, their numbers can double every four years, so a vigorous adoption program is in place. But those are just facts and figures. We were spellbound by the wild character and beauty of these horses.

We relaxed at Cold Springs, Retha and I slowly swinging on the porch swing and sipping our thirst quenchers. When we felt sufficiently rested, we read the historic markers. The Rock Creek/ Cold Springs Station highway historic marker relates this information:

The Pony Express Cold Springs Station (fresh horse, blacksmith services, and wagon repair facilities… available here) was constructed in 1860… transcontinental line was completed between Sacramento and Omaha in 1861 and abandoned in August, 1869. The coming of the transcontinental railroad and its parallel telegraph line…spelled the demise of both the telegraph line and the stage route here.

On our return to Middlegate Station, we rode in the van with our bikes in or on it. Once we'd arrived, we continued relaxing on our front porch overlooking a rickety buckboard and rusted hull of a wheel-less 1930s motorcar. Charles delighted us with a performance of his original limericks. I cannot, for the life of me, remember any of them.

We became beneficiaries of whatever restorations had been made. Our accommodations were many things, but clean and comfortable they were not. Dave tried to get the swamp cooler going in his room but it wouldn't cooperate. He kneeled down to look into it, turned it back on and was lambasted by a huge cloud of dust before it hit the opposite wall of his room. He burst out of the door, dirty-faced, roaring and coughing. He pacified himself by saying, "Well, it'll cool off soon so I won't need it."

After showering, we moved on to the only watering hole for the hoi polloi, the dimly lit but not gloomy café/bar of Old Middlegate Station. The flutter of thousands of dollars of paper money nailed to the ceiling caught our eyes. Not Monopoly money but genuine US currency, plus some foreign bills, most discolored by greasy residue from burgers and fries.

Curiosities and tokens from the area's past covered every wall, shelf and window sill. Old West guns, knives, hats, chewing tobacco tins, wagon wheels, soda bottles, old-timey gadgets, Pony Express memorabilia, wanted posters and badges. It conjured up a carnival of once bright, but now dull remnants of history. Military patrons' bright squadron and unit patches contrasted with the clutter of vintage knickknacks.

Russ and Freeda Stevenson, owners of the café, gave free coffee and soda to the troops, and encouraged them to write messages with their unit designations on the currency stapled to the ceiling. Boisterous members of the military, welcomed by equally hearty staff, flocked in for the trademark burgers and fries.

Bar patrons, local or otherwise, sat quietly or noisily, but the site of the most action was the Henhouse Grill with its tin rooster doodads. The quick, efficient cook, an expert in the burgeoning burger field, kept things moving. (I might have said she beefed up the bailiwick for bingeing burger biters, but thought better of it.)

The menu touted *The Best Burgers in the West*. Plain burgers, priced at $4.50, included 1/3 pound of ground beef, toasted bun, lettuce, tomato, pickles, sweet red onion and chips. The Middlegate Monster Burger, a full pound of ground beef on toasted sourdough mini-loaf with all the trimmings, cost $9.95. Despite having grown up on a cattle and hog raising farm, I chose the savory chicken fajitas.

Visits to restrooms in cafés often add glimpses into the culture and history of a locale. This one, wallpapered with quips, western wisdom, vintage newspapers, rusty keys and horseshoes, did not disappoint. The Old Middlegate Station Bar definitely lived up to the distinctive decor of small-town Nevada saloons, the Sagebrush Saloons. They also kept their own unique hours and advertised, *We open when we open and we close when we close.*

After supper, we strolled beyond the motel area toward the sunset on a preserved remnant of the old Lincoln Highway, once a 3,143 mile highway bisecting the lower forty-eight states from New York to San Francisco. We contentedly watched the sky change colors and stars pop out. Because this is Nevada and desert country with considerable military presence, our conversations turned to UFOs and time-worn comments about such an area: "I think they hide aliens out in that part of the desert." There are signs everywhere that say, *Watch for low-flying aircraft.*

Charles, with his propensity to browse and buy at flea markets, invited us to mill around the one in front of our rooms. He had kept the vendors happy with his purchases earlier in the day. They included a large, shocking-pink plastic horseshoe, a small soft pillow, and a navy blue sweatshirt with the sleeves and neck cut off. At the end of the trip, he presented this bounty to us. The pink horseshoe worked perfectly to prop open our cooler to dry once it had been emptied. As for the other things…

⚲

GRANDMA ADAMS BORN 109 YEARS AGO. MIDDLEGATE TO AUSTIN 62 MILES

The temperature cooled during the night so we welcomed the warmth of the morning sun. Charles amused us, his rapt audience, at breakfast. He is alone in the van most of the day, at least when he is not at flea markets or chatting up locals. I think he stores up his comments until we are all together.

While we waited for our food at the café, a young sailor came in. We recognized him from photos we had seen the previous night near our table. One showed a unit of sailors and the other a lone sailor, white cap forward on his forehead and an American flag slightly behind him. We spoke to him and he said he had come last night and was so happy to be home!

After our hearty breakfasts of oatmeal or eggs and toast, Kerstin, with her wonderful Swedish accent, pleaded with Charles, "Sveethaht, please do not buy anything more at the flea markets." He did not seem to heed her plea.

Because we had already ridden to Cold Springs the day before, we piled into the van to return there to begin our day's ride. That is an advantage of having a SAG van with us. We can ride more or fewer miles than anticipated but still stay in the motel rooms we have already reserved.

We passed The Old Shoe Tree and smiled at the playfulness of it. Never in our wildest imaginations would we have believed that five years later, in early January, 2011 vandals cut it down, destroying this whimsical and charming landmark. Charles asked this poignant question when he told us of its demise, "Why would anyone cut down the Shoe Tree we so admired?" According to the *Reno Gazette-Journal*, that is the question many people asked. And a Facebook page appeared, titled *Middlegate Shoe Tree—Rest in Peace*. Freeda Stevenson, an owner of Old Middlegate Station, planned a memorial on the site for mid-February.

As we biked toward Austin, great weather accompanied us. I felt strong as we climbed the summits of New Pass and Mount Airy—a wonderful feeling. Seeing the other mountains from Mt. Airy made us think we had returned to spectacular Alaska. Biking the hill into Austin heated us up and but gave us plenty of time to read the signs and billboards advertising Austin's Historical Museum, the Loneliest Road, as well as Pony Express Territory. A bronze plaque featuring a map of the route from St. Joseph to Sacramento offered this information:

The Pony Express Trail passed four miles north of Austin through...Park and Dry Creek Station. 1960-1961 National Pony Express Centennial Association Dwight D. Eisenhower—Chairman

In 1919 Dwight Eisenhower participated in a harrowing cross-country Army caravan on the Lincoln Highway. We wondered if that helped convince him of the need for an interstate system of highways which he signed into law in 1956 during his presidency.

Our muster headed out to see the town. Silver had been discovered here in 1862 so the town grew up around the silver and gold mines which produced about $50 million dollars. The National Historic Register listed several buildings, one of which was St. Augustine Roman Catholic Church. In the nineteenth century a priest had been so dynamic that many, many people attended services. Being an enterprising man, he decided to charge one dollar per person to attend mass. That didn't go over very well.

When evening fell, we photographed the three steeples that created a stunning skyline against the moonlit sky, then rushed to our Lincoln Motel once the mosquitoes came out to enjoy us as their evening snacks.

🚲

AUSTIN TO EUREKA 71 MILES

Ever since we had driven the route in September, 2003 I had been dreading the steep and long mile climb out of Austin. Polishing off my breakfast at the International Hotel, I mentally tried to prepare myself. As we wended our way up the 7484 foot mountain pass, I felt as though we were climbing into that beautiful sunrise sky, and discovered it had not been as difficult as I had imagined but I was thankful Charles had the extra weight of our panniers in the van. Right after Austin Summit came Bob Scotts Summit at 7195-feet and several miles farther, Hickson Pass topped out at 6594 feet. Glorious downhills—long, flowing ones—delighted us. I reached 38.1 miles per hour which somehow registered as 252.7 miles per hour on my odometer/speedometer!

Once we had left the summits behind, we hit the memorable Bean Flats section. Ray led a fast pace line across the thirty miles of the flats, rejuvenating and exciting us, which particularly helped Kerstin and me. Later on, when the going got tough again, Kerstin asked, "Ray, can we do that parade thing again?" We all laughed in appreciation of that apt description, one we fondly recall whenever we are in other rough riding spots. Fortunately, snow-capped peaks, the trilling melody of the meadowlarks and blue skies blessed us as they had so many times during this trip, lending serenity to our lives.

We ended our biking day with an uphill into *Friendliest and Loneliest* Eureka at 6481 feet, located in a draw in the Diamond Mountains. Population, six hundred. The Nevada Centennial Marker on the edge of town recorded this:

In 1864 Eureka developed the first important lead-silver deposits in the nation and during the furious boom of the 80s had 16 smelters, over 100 saloons, a population of 10,000 and a railroad…Production began to fall off in 1883 and by 1891 the smelters closed, their sites marked by the huge slag piles at both ends of Main Street.

After we did our usual chores, we strolled the downtown. We all loved this town which, obviously, the residents do as well. Their pride showed through the beautifully renovated buildings, among them, the Opera House. Live performances occur every year, one of which, a Celtic cowboy singer, was to perform the following Friday. The interior of the opera house features old-style paintings on its stage curtain—what a treat to be able to see it. The venue can be rented for one hundred dollars for twenty-four hours, and has a full kitchen so weddings and receptions can be held there.

The Eureka County Courthouse had been dismantled brick by brick, a new foundation poured, then reassembled. Originally, it had been built on a spring, not particularly good planning. The rich, dark wooden wainscoting and trim was designed in the Eastlake style prevalent in the late 1880s. Pressed tin ceilings added to the beauty of the Italianate building. The Sentinel Museum, behind the courthouse, housed the newspaper's original press room with all of the printing presses starting from the same period. The rest of the museum portrayed mining and other local life, particularly focusing on the boomtown which resulted from lead and silver strikes two decades earlier.

This cultural sweep through town stirred up our appetites. We chose to eat at the Eureka Café, home of Chinese and American food. As Sandy, Dave, Jim and I had in 2003, we all ordered Chinese—fresh and filling food. The Hong Kong born proprietor grew up in Canton, China, seemed to know all the locals, and appeared happy to chat about them, the town and our trip.

⚲

MARA AND DOUG'S 13TH ANNIVERSARY. EUREKA TO ELY 73 MILES

We began the day with a before-sunrise breakfast. This would be a long day as well as Kerstin's last bicycling day, and included three summits and one pass. It could prove to be challenging, though some of the last miles were supposed to be downhill. As with all days, it was a pleasure to see Charles and the van along the way. That has simplified our food and water carrying. Kerstin says she will not be eating any Clif Bars for a while since that has been what she has eaten along the road.

Snowcapped mountains backdropped our day but Pinto Summit began our nearly five mile climb to Pancake Summit. Then we relished the not quite as long downhill swoosh. After biking past irrigated fields on one side and sagebrush on the other, we started our over eight mile uphill to Little Antelope Summit. I noted in my journal *Some of these uphills are 8 percenters and that is steep. The downhills are long and eat up the miles.* That included a seven-miler off Little Antelope. Three short miles later we started the fourteen mile climb to 7,588 foot Robinson Pass. Days like this were either feast or famine but definitely reality for us.

By the time we arrived in Ely, six of us felt hot and tired. For some reason, Charles seemed unfazed by the day's rigors. Kerstin called her friend who would fly her and her bike home. For her first small plane ride, she discovered she'd have to be at Ely's airport by 4:30. She cleaned up and gathered her few belongings while the guys took her bike apart to fit in the airplane seats. We all wished her a good flight home and told her how happy her joining us made us feel.

When Charles returned from the airport, we went to supper at The Jailhouse. True to its name, many booths were behind bars, perfect for Judge Charles Wolle. Having him as our SAG wagon driver was an experience like no other. We've had different SAGs over the years, mainly our kids and friends who usually dropped us off and picked us up. But Charles headed a class of his own. He drove every mile of our Nevada route, often lagging behind us, then spurting ahead. He climbed hills, hunted rocks, picked up litter and chatted with anyone he had come upon as he went from place to place. He'd suddenly appear on the crest of a mountain, van unseen, and surprise us with his presence. He stopped to join us for snacks and lunch. He regaled us with tales of his flea market conquests. He delighted us with his jokes, original limericks, trivia questions, poetry he had written, comments about law cases, and philosophical discourses from Kierkegaard to Mormonism. Then he would disappear only to unexpectedly pop up again.

⚲

ELY TO NEVADA-UTAH BORDER 64 MILES.

Cool, crisp air greeted us and we remarked how gorgeous the scenery was and what a pleasant surprise to have the verdant valley open up after so many passes. Snowcapped mountains looked ever so much like the Tetons in the film *Shane.* One patch of snow surprised us—as if it might be a comment on what we were doing, the snow formed a perfect question mark.

After a long chilly descent, we stopped at Major's Place to warm up. This Basque-owned bar and restaurant, American flag flying high, was open and we took full advantage of it. Best of all at least to me, was a fenced-in carrocampo, better known as a shepherd's or sheep wagon, complete with a Basque flag. Once these enclosed wagons dotted the countryside in the West, wherever sheep were grazed, and often the shepherds were Basque. I was so excited by the wagon because it reminded me of my family's trip through Wyoming in 1946 when we went way into the Little Big Horn Mountains to try to find Dad's gold miner cousin Wes. Periodically, we had seen the shepherds' wagons and, even at seven years old, it made me think about the hardships and solitude the shepherds endured. I'd never been this close to one. However, I think none of them had a sign similar to this one: *Basque Hotel and Condo.* The bar manager told us the owner of the bar stays in the wagon when he's had too much to drink and doesn't want to drive home to Elko.

Four riders and the SAG wagon

Before we left this crossing, we looked across the valley to the Snake Mountain Range in the east. Aware of how deceiving distances can be in open country, we asked each other how far we thought the distance might be. The guesses ranged from four to twelve miles. None of us looked at Sandy's notes for the correct nineteen mile answer. The eight mile downhill at 8 percent grade proved to be very cold but better than uphill. Then we turned into the wind for another eleven miles—time for one of Kerstin's parades before heading up the next steep pass. My legs complained of the abuse. So did my mind.

We made it but I nearly didn't. Sometimes when we are riding, especially at a distance from the others, time becomes a precious opportunity to meditate, contemplate and remember. In a melancholy state, I became despairing at our loss of Jennifer and Bernd who died four years earlier. I wasn't paying attention to what I needed to—the road and traffic. I remember my head was down as I struggled up yet another steep hill, engaged only with their memory and my grief. Suddenly Dave's voice broke through my reverie, "Jan!" I looked up and saw a semi barreling straight at me while it passed another vehicle. I jerked my bike off the road onto the shoulder where I stood gasping. Dave pulled over, "I thought you saw it! When I realized you hadn't, I yelled."

Shaking from fright, I thanked him profusely and explained, "I was in another world and wasn't paying attention." I thanked him over and over for saving my life. He stayed until he knew I'd be okay then pedaled off. I've never forgotten that what he did made the rest of my life possible. I am obliged to use it to do what I can to honor that gift.

We arrived in Border, Nevada cheered and took our end-of-state photos and celebrated crossing state number forty-nine. Once we'd cleaned up we hopped into the van to drive to Wheeler Park, part of the Great Basin National Park established in 1986. At the top, we admired sublime views of the valley floor of the Great Basin. No foray into this area would be complete without stopping to give homage to one of the oldest and largest groves of the incredibly long-lived Bristlecone Pines. These trees, gnarled and shorter than I had imagined, are the earth's oldest living plants with life-spans that can exceed four thousand years. What a bonus to our already laden with joys bicycle trip.

Dinner at the Border Inn, this one highlighted by intense conversation by Jim, Ray and Charles with Dave primarily as a rapt observer. Retha and I sat at the table, as we had every night of the trip, stunned at their ability to maneuver nearly every topic we had been discussing into a sports report, complete with statistics. Among these four, they can quote them (or at least lead us to believe they know what they are talking about) particularly about baseball, football, basketball, tennis and golf. After all, Charles and Jim had been discussing and arguing sports since Jim was six years old and Charles nine. We heard about RBIs from the 1946 World Series when the St. Louis Cardinals beat the Boston Red Sox. Yardage from the 1953 Rose Bowl. Assists of Hawkeyes' BJ Armstrong. Merits of Bjorn Borg versus Roger Federer.

Each male had a favorite baseball team: Ray-Philadelphia Phillies; Jim-Boston Red Sox; Charles-Cincinnati Reds; Dave-Chicago Cubs. They spoke of the idols of the past, Ted Williams for Jim, fellow Iowan Bob Feller for Dave, Ray's was Hank Aaron. Sometimes Dave joined in the banter but preferred to listen and smile at the repartee. Could you hear Retha and my eyes roll?

🚲

JENNIFER AND BERND'S WEDDING 14 YEARS AGO. NEVADA BORDER TO DELTA, UTAH 91 MILES

Because of our motel's location in relation to the café, we awoke at 6:30 AM Mountain Daylight Time and ate breakfast at 6:00 AM Pacific Daylight Time, It was a late start for us. We looked ahead to eighty-three miles with no services, portending a spun-out, hard day. Thankfully, Charles was still our SAG driver.

Something to look forward to?

We climbed two passes followed by pleasant lengthy downhills and a fickle wind that blew at us from all directions, no matter what direction we turned. This became a day with parts we just slogged through with other parts we felt awe at the stark beauty. No snow showed on the mountains for a while until we saw the Wasatch Range near Delta, Utah.

Once again, Ray was a hero to me. He is truly the strongest biker I've ever ridden with and he headed a paceline that kept our average speed at thirteen point four miles per hour over ninety-one miles of riding. He doggedly stayed in front of us for much of that sometimes tedious sagebrush-infested stretch, keeping our pace steady and positive. Retha, Jim and Dave spelled Ray in that leadership by cycling to the front and pulling us along too. Then Ray could relax and ready himself for the next time at the fore. I would have been very hard-pressed to have made it to ten miles per hour without them. Sagebrush and more sagebrush marked the last miles into Delta.

About Ray. Throughout the Nevada ride, Ray made it possible for me to ride with more ease than I would have been able to manage otherwise. He often rode behind or beside me, talking about the vistas, other cycling experiences, interesting things he'd seen or done. He asked questions which I answered when I could breathe well enough to. He made me think, laugh and enjoy the journey even more than I already did. When I struggle on my own, I tend to get a bit gloomy and focus on just getting through this patch. Then I miss seeing the beauty of the wilderness and nature that surrounds me. I thank him for being there.

We arrived just before 5 PM, cleaned up and returned to the same restaurant we'd eaten at the previous week. The server recognized us and seemed pleased and cheerful. Retha and I did the laundry while Ray cleaned their van and Jim answered questions from a reporter for our local *Iowa City Press-Citizen*. Then I answered some, followed by Dave. She wanted us to email her a photo which our daughter, Tania, found on her laptop and emailed her. Once again, Tania to the rescue.

Whenever I think of Delta, I remember what a pivotal point it became in this ride: where Ray and Retha's van had been left, where at least one of us stayed five nights and the rest of us two or three. But another thing that always comes back to me was the Delta area's role during World War II. It had been selected to be the location of the Topaz Internment/Concentration Camp for people of Japanese descent. A commemorative sign in Delta read:

Sixteen miles west at Abraham is the location of a bleak desert concentration camp, one of ten in Western America. In all, 110,000 persons of Japanese ancestry were interned against their will during World War II. They were victims of wartime hysteria, social animosity, and economic opportunism... kept behind barbed wire fence and guarded by armed sentries for no justifiable reason. The internees, two-thirds of whom were American citizens, and the majority of whom were women and children, not only endured the bitter physical discomforts of the desert, but sustained a shocking affront to their sense of justice and human dignity. May this grim episode of basic American principles gone astray remind us to work for understanding and goodwill and justice in an enlightened America today.

The former residents of Topaz remember with grateful appreciation the friendliness and understanding with which the people of Delta received us during the period of our trial and despair.

How sobering to know what was done in the name of patriotism. And I wonder if we have changed—have we allowed our basic American principles to go astray again or are we working for understanding, good will and justice? Have we become more enlightened?

Still in Delta: Repacking panniers for the three of us continuing the bicycle ride. "Whaddaya takin' along? I don't want to carry stuff that I won't need. I'd rather send it in the van."

"I dunno for sure. There's stuff I didn't wear while we were biking across Nevada that I'll probably leave. I don't imagine we'll need it in Utah either. I'll be able to layer enough to keep warm."

"Are you taking your rain pants?"

"You know me. I never take them unless I absolutely have to. I've already stashed them in the van. I'll just take my tights like I always do. They're warm enough and they dry off fast after they get wet."

"Well, if Jan Down's not taking rain pants, I won't either. I hope I won't need 'em."

So it was settled. Jim, Dave and I would pack our extra gear, including rain pants, in the van that Ray would be dropping off at our endpoint, Fruita, Colorado. Retha would drive their van there, pick Ray up and they'd head home to Iowa City.

GRANDSON RYAN'S 12TH BIRTHDAY. WE SCATTER TO THE WINDS.

Our mattress felt so comfortable, it was hard to get up! We called Ryan from the restaurant and the six of us sang *Happy Birthday* to him. Jim got a rental car for those of us flying to Iowa. Everyone except Dave who stayed in Delta, readied themselves to leave. Retha was teary-eyed and we all felt sad as they left. We'd had such a marvelous time together. Bike trips are like that. We spend long intense hours with each other for days, this time for seven. We face the joys and vicissitudes of biking, we eat, laugh, sight-see, discuss everything from poetry to religion to baseball to roadkill, and we do all of it together. Then *Boom!* It's cold turkey. The trip ends and we go our separate ways and might not see each other for weeks.

Soon the remaining three of us, Jim, Dave and I would continue east from Delta and meander along to Capitol Reef National Park. Then we'd head north to Green River, cross the Colorado border and finish in Fruita, the end of Jim's and my rides across all fifty of the United States.

But first, Charles, Jim and I had to catch flights from Salt Lake City to Denver to Omaha, to go to Iowa for the memorial service of a dear young cousin, Mary Down Parker who had recently died of breast cancer. Dave stayed in Delta to await our return. Tania met us at our motel in Omaha where she and I stayed up to talk. Jim went to sleep.

MEMORIAL WEEKEND OMAHA-ODEBOLT, IOWA-OMAHA-SALT LAKE CITY-DELTA

What a gorgeous drive with Tania from Omaha to Odebolt, the older Down Family's home. Although Jim and I had grown up in Iowa, we traveled through towns we'd heard of but had never visited—Woodbine and Dow City among them. We arrived at the Odebolt Cemetery just in time for the committal of Mary's ashes. The cemetery looked beautiful with all the American flags flying, flowers gracing graves, bright blue sky and brisk, crisp wind.

We were so glad we had been able to come. Family and friends spoke eloquently of Mary, with many tears and much laughter for this wonderful person. After the heartfelt and poignant memorial service and lunch shared with family and friends, Jim and I returned to Delta and Charles went to his office in Des Moines.

We reflected with Dave about the weekend, then noticed he had a surprise for us. He meticulously cleaned our bikes and everything sparkled, ready for the rest of the ride.

DELTA TO SALINA 73 MILES

A good night's sleep on a wonderful bed made me just want to snuggle in for a few more hours, but we had seventy-three miles to pedal before we could sleep again. Jim hurried to return the rental car and rode my bike, which he had put in the trunk, back to the motel. What a sight—a long-legged man on my scrunchy-for-him bike. His panniers refused to slide back on his bike and, unfortunately, Sandy wasn't with us to use all her favorite made-up words for such recalcitrance. Eventually, we rode off for our last meal at the Ranch Motel and said goodbye to our now favorite server, Maran.

My journal says: *Cloudy skies and slight breezes accompanied us on our long but not very steep climbs. Surprisingly, my knees hurt, a rare occurrence for me. We won no speed records—the weight of our panniers slowed us down after we hadn't had to carry them last week, thanks to Sag Driver, Charles. A brief stint on the interstate was OK but an otherwise nice downhill had so much litter on it.*

The rest of the day consisted of gradual climbs and more good downhills, without the projected rain. I really felt tired when we arrived at our pleasant motel. Delicious Italian food helped resurrect me so I could stay awake at least until eight o'clock. I called my mother who read part of our local newspaper's article about Jim, me and bicycling. The writer had misunderstood some things but that is not unusual for a telephone interview.

At our motel, a curious eighty plus year old appearing man asked how we chose our routes and how many miles we rode each day. We told him what we have told many people before: We try to choose scenic but safe low-traffic routes. We prefer riding no more than seventy miles a day but sometimes because of no towns or facilities, we ride farther than that.

MEMORIAL DAY SALINA TO BICKNELL 63.48 MILES

The following morning, as I stood outside the motel with my bike, the same gentleman approached me. We exchanged greetings. He hemmed and hawed a bit before he asked, "How far are you going today?" I told him it would be about sixty-three miles. Then came the question he really wanted to ask. "How old are you?"

His flat "Oh" when I said sixty-five registered disappointment. He walked away. Amused, I wondered a bit about his response until I realized I had been out in the sun for days. My face probably looked rather weather-beaten, wrinkled and old so he undoubtedly hoped I'd make a better story for him to tell. Maybe I should have said I was seventy-five or eighty. Alas, he'd have to make that part up. By this time, Jim and Dave had paid the motel bill and off we went into more dramatic desert country.

HOT CHOCOLATE, PICKLE PIE AND OTHER JOYS

Turning south onto Highway 24, we could feel gusts of wind and see a furious-looking storm cloud framing the snow-capped mountains. To the west, we saw more darkening clouds and a rainbow. The rainbow meant hope but these clouds meant only one thing. We were in for some very foul weather, and no shelter, no culverts, no buildings, no respite appeared. The three of us conferred by shouting at each other through the wind and agreed the most prudent thing to do was bike as fast as we could in hopes of getting to the next town, Sigurd, before the storm hammered us.

Soon we could see the outlines of the town against the pulsing ebony sky. We spied a county park sign *Shelter.* Wind-driven rain pelted us as we hustled off our bikes. Standing in the lee of a

Dave and Jan heading into the storm

building, we saw a substantial-looking picnic pavilion a few yards away. We grabbed our bikes and scrambled to get under the roof, then realized the rain blew at such an angle we would get soaked anyway. A free-standing fireplace offered some relief from the wind as we hunkered down to get out of some of the splattering rain. Then I heard the first but definitely not the last of the complaints.

"I'm cold! Why didn't I bring my rain pants? It's your fault, Jan. You told us not to bring them. I'm freezing."

"I didn't tell you not to bring them. I just told you I wasn't bringing mine. Move in closer."

"That's not helping. I'm getting wet."

"Be glad you put your tights on."

"But they're not enough. I need my rain pants." Moan and whinge. Moan and whinge.

"Yes, it's miserable but we'll survive. The rain'll be over soon." Soon didn't come for another thirty minutes and who knows how many belly-aches.

Eventually the rain ceased as rain always does. We cranked our stiff bodies up, stretched, and rolled our bikes out of the pavilion. Now we could ride into Sigurd and find a nice warm dry café that served hot chocolate. A powerful tenet of my belief system is *Hot chocolate will soothe a lot of miseries.*

And it did. The only thing it didn't fix was the misery of listening to two formerly adult males grumble about how cold they'd been and how they wouldn't listen to the lone female in the group anymore. There could be only one thing I could think of to alleviate the situation: "Another cup of hot chocolate please, light on the whipped cream, heavy on the sprinkles." Pause. "And could I please have a cinnamon roll too?"

🚲

After the warming hot chocolate and gooey cinnamon roll, we felt ready to roll too. Jim, Dave and I knew the uphill out of town looked long, at least twenty-three miles but not too steep. In my journal, I described it: *The terrain was up-up-up, cottonwood trees for a while and then scrub pine and sage.* As we climbed, the clouds evaporated into the mountain-desert sky. The air felt crisp but we generated our own heat as we pedaled, so took off our rain gear and tights. Later the jackets went on again due to downhills and wind. Jim and Dave, stronger, faster climbers than I am, rode ahead and I took my usual back of the pack position. Another plus—polite traffic.

We spent the rest of the morning climbing, dipping, climbing, dipping. At one point, we looked down on an impressive green view of Grass Valley. Its place in Utah history involved a massacre, followed later by Brigham Young's representatives and Native Americans sealing a peace accord with a handshake. Unlike so many others in US history, the accord lasted.

As we often do, we ate our picnic of sandwiches, cookies and lots of juice and water, this time overlooking Koosharem Reservoir at an altitude just over 7,000 feet. To arrive at the 8,406 foot summit, we biked two two-mile long stretches of slow and steady 8 percent grade. For me, very slow and sometimes wobbly climbing.

Our altitude chart showed a precipitous downhill soon. I get butterflies in anticipation of really steep hills, either up or down. This one definitely made me swallow hard with its brutal straight decline, far beyond a simple swoosh down a hill. The wind hit squarely at our backs. I watched Dave fly down and sighed my relief when I saw no sloping curves to accelerate our speeds. He checked his odometer. He topped out at forty-nine point six miles per hour.

Breathless with fear of falling and being maimed the rest of my life, I managed to remain upright at forty-five point two miles per hour. Afraid of braking and sliding or braking too hard and blowing a tire, I just let 'er rip. I prayed *God, please take care of us and keep us safe even though we aren't doing a very good job of it ourselves.* I couldn't wait until we had our feet safely on terra firma and I could breathe again.

Jim came after me and went forty-three point three but would have gone faster had treacherous crosswinds not convinced him to slow down. We gained enough momentum to sail partway up the next hill but steepness made it impossible to coast to the top. That brought me back to slow slogging. My heart beat fast not from fright but from exertion. We stopped to relax a bit at the top.

We arrived at Bicknell and our motel shortly after 3:30, an hour and a half sooner than we had expected. We ate supper at the motel restaurant, one of two in the town, then strolled over to nearby Sun Glow Café to check when they'd open in the morning. That's when we discovered their unusual homemade pies. First we read the framed news articles posted on the wall, then decided who would order which pie. Jim picked pickle pie, I chose pinto bean and Dave ordered buttermilk. The pickle pie tasted similar to mincemeat with finely chopped sweet pickles in a clove-flavored base. My pinto bean, the one we thought tasted best, had flavors of a less sweet pecan pie. Our least favored buttermilk pie seemed to lack a truly describable taste, maybe a bit lemony. We have told the pickle pie café story over and over and would recommend traveling through Bicknell in order to eat desserts with a surprising twist.

⬧

BICKNELL TO HANKSVILLE, 58.45 MILES

What a beautiful, brisk morning—perfect for all our uphills and downhills! We decided this would be our dawdling day so we spent time taking lots of photos and didn't try to set any land speed records. Once again, the song of the meadowlarks went with us. They have truly sung us across Nevada and Utah—how exhilarating to hear them.

Capitol Reef National Park appeared burnished in the early morning oblique light. Thousands of photos waited to be taken in each aspect of the light. Unfortunately, we couldn't dawdle that much. Once we entered the park, we loved the 8 percent downhill to the Visitors' Center. There we met a young Chinese woman now living in Chicago, who traveled with her mother from Tienjin.

She was thrilled to hear that a friend of ours had been born there and that Jim and I had been there on our first visit to China. Jim added he had been to China four times and I, three. Another delightful moment with people we just happened to meet.

How can I describe Capitol Reef? Grand, stunning, colorful—no adjective ever quite manages to capture its rich but often stark beauty. According to Park information, a remarkable geological phenomenon makes Capitol Reef what it is, a waterpocket fold:

...a long (100 miles) wrinkle in the earth's surface, the defining geologic feature of this majestic national park...creates a dramatic landscape...in the heart of rock country.

Erosion and exposure created water pockets which eroded the plateau to form cliffs, domes, canyons, arches, natural bridges and monoliths. Seeing all of this magnificence overwhelmed us as we cycled through the park. So the story goes, one of the massive, stunning white Navajo sandstone formations reminded settlers of the United States Capitol—hence the name, Capitol Reef. As we struggled to get our minds wrapped around this astonishing park, I felt like a kid looking at clouds and seeing whales, turtles, and other critters. Everywhere the rocks looked like something else to me, pipe organs, pyramids, chimneys, temples, spires. No wonder the Mormon Temple in Salt Lake City looks like it does, with natural beauty as its model. Sandstone dominates the landscape with layer after layer of varying depths, textures and colors from red to yellow to white, while shale brings blue-gray to the palette. Pinons, junipers and cottonwoods contribute their own shades of green.

Leaving Capitol Reef

Adding to the amazing landscape, in the 1800s Mormon settlers founded the small town of Fruita, this one in Utah not Colorado, and in the process planted fruit trees. The orchards, all within the park, expanded and eventually numbered over twenty-five hundred cherry, apple, pear, mulberry, peach and apricot trees. We repeatedly crossed the Fremont River that morning, and near the Visitors' Center and orchards, trees on its banks looked lush and a breeze cooled us.

Once we left the park, signs of devastation to fragile life forms on the hills became apparent. Four-wheelers have become Big Business in this area but with a great cost to the land. Otherwise, farming along with tourism comprise the primary spurs to local economy.

We stopped for refreshments at Luna Mesa Oasis, a restaurant-motel-campground-horse rides -four-wheeler center. The owner and her daughter told us about the county. It appears she does everything that needs to be done to keep the area going.

On our very pleasant ride into Hanksville, we went from 7200 to 430 feet in elevation—quite a change from yesterday's climbing. Another 8 percent downhill before Luna Mesa made it even more fun.

🚲

HANKSVILLE TO GREEN RIVER 59 MILES

We lucked out with another fresh, blue-sky morning with excellent road surface and wide shoulders. Yay! The route consisted of ups and downs but nothing too steep going up, and one really good forty-four point eight miles per hour downhill. I had imagined the scenery might be sagebrush but we saw superb vistas of red sandstone castles and cathedrals. Magnifique!

The only sour note of the day. Gnats! Zillions of them attacked us whenever we stopped or even biked slower than ten miles per hour. Well, now we know the top speed of gnats. And we did what we could—pedaled a lot, stopped briefly to get food out of the panniers, and went on, snacking as we rode. When the breeze picked up, it kept some of the gnats away but the pesky pests did what they do best—annoy and try to bite. We decided not to eat lunch on the road so kept going in hopes of having lunch in Green River. It worked.

A ten mile stretch of riding on I-70 was mostly flat, then a short, steep uphill and down into town. We ate lunch at Arby's then went to the John Wesley Powell Museum right on the Green River, a couple of doors down from the Comfort Inn where we'd stay. We watched an eighty-minute film of Powell's 1869 expedition down the Green and Colorado Rivers. We thought the film had been well done and enjoyed it, but you know what happens when bicyclists sit in comfy chairs in a dark room with soothing music and voices. We each took little catnaps. The museum too was informative and made us realize again that adventurous people often do amazing-to-sometimes-crazy things.

We were about to leave the museum when we heard a roll of thunder, not distant, but close by. We pedaled toward the motel but mistakenly took a quick turn into the Holiday Inn Express next door but made it to our motel safely. Before we left for supper, a tremendous clap of thunder and crack of a lightning bolt startled us. After we ate our meal and enjoyed our river view, we returned to the museum to buy two iconic Native American story-teller figurines for our grandsons, Ryan and Cameron.

The following day would be our last day!

⚏

GREEN RIVER, UTAH TO FRUITA, COLORADO 92.59 MILES

Dark clouds blotted the sky, making us apprehensive about the morning weather. We had biked on I-70, but still and all, it was the interstate.

As we bike, Jim always, and I mean always, keeps a lookout for coins along the road.

A long time ago, he got the idea that finding a coin on a bike trip made it what he called "a real trip." I have no idea how that concept stuck in his brain. (An aside: As we cycled with Jennifer and Bernd in the Loire Valley in France, we came to the last day and Jim had not yet found a coin. He began fretting about it so Jennifer, surreptitiously she thought, biked ahead and salted the road with some well-spaced French coins. Jim spotted them and immediately accused us, "You put them there so finding them doesn't make a real trip!" We had tried. He was too clever to fall for it.) Back to Utah as we bicycled on I-70, Jim found more than a dollar in change along the highway. He was ecstatic! A real trip!

We eventually chose to take the Old Highway for eleven miles. That meant a very rough surface but no traffic, and to me, a wonderful remote feeling. We couldn't even hear the interstate traffic! We stopped at Thompson's Spring, the only services the entire day. A whole bevy of people descended on the convenience store at one time. The proprietor told us that eighteen yearling bears, orphaned in Utah and raised in Idaho, waited in a trailer out front. We went out to see what we could see and learned that later today, they would be released at two or three locations nearer the Colorado border. A local newspaper reporter from *The Emery County Progress* was with the entourage. She interviewed us, took our photo, and later sent us the article she had written.

When we returned to the interstate, the wind beat us in the faces for the next fifty miles. About five miles west of the Utah-Colorado border, we returned to the potholed Old Highway to cycle through the countryside. A totally battered and pock-marked white obelisk marked the border—it looked like someone had taken potshots at it. We took the requisite "We did it!" border photos, but Jim and I felt both overwhelmed and underwhelmed. We had reached our goal of biking border-to-opposite-border across all fifty states, but that reality had not yet sunk in.

The old road improved, we turned and the thirty to forty mile per hour wind caught and pushed us into Fruita. A package of chocolate and a congratulations card from friends Nellie and Harry Weber awaited us at our motel. Sweet in many ways. Extra-creative Lisa Barleen surprised us with gorgeous t-shirts commemorating this occasion. Jim's and my white ones featured a stylized bicycle and rider written in pastel rainbow colors. The lilac printed words surrounding the bicycle read *We did 50 border to border on two wheels!* A colorful map of the United States covered the back. What a thoughtful memento of our journey and the people who supported us the whole way.

We roared with laughter when we saw Dave's blue shirt printed with these words: *I Survived the Ups and Downs.* The double meaning was not missed!

We called our families and friends, including our biking buddies Retha, Ray, and Betty to announce, "Done!" They cheered with us.

The following day, we would travel in our van back to Boulder and, eventually home. Our twenty-six year mission had been completed. Or had it?

Jim and Jan: Mission accomplished. Fifty states crossed. Now what?

FROM THE END TO THE BEGINNING: TYING THE BOW RIDE ACROSS COLORADO-2006

Riders: Retha/Ray, Dave, Brett Rojec, Jim/Jan. Van exchanges:
Retha, Ray, Dave, Jim. Distance: 533 miles.

"How about a west to east ride across Colorado this summer?" we asked three of the Nevada-Utah riders. The question hung in the air approximately three seconds before unanimous "Yes!" responses came. To make it even more official, Jim and I knew we had to tie the bow. To us that meant connecting the end of our last ride across the fifty states, Nevada and Utah, to our first ride after RAGBRAI, in Kansas. We weren't ready for the dream to be finished and needed another long-distance ride—we created *From the End to the Beginning—Tying the Bow Ride Across Colorado.*

A few months later, we rendezvoused at our condo in Keystone, Colorado, transferred gear to our van and headed to Fruita, the endpoint of our Fifty State Conquest. Dave would join us for the whole ride and Retha and Ray for the first half.

FRUITA TO PARACHUTE 60 MILES

Five of the happiest bicyclists you've ever seen flashed their smiles at a volunteer photographer before we left the motel. After cycling through Fruita's industrial area, we continued on past rich red rocky buttes, dry sand-colored western flatlands contrasting with green irrigated hayfields and fruit orchards.

A mouth-watering sign beckoned to us: *PALISADES PEACHES!* As we turned into the flag-adorned roadside stand, a woman met us holding out rosy ripe peaches. Juice squirted and rolled down our chins and no other sound could be heard from us except for murmurs of delight. Bushel baskets of ripened peaches stood on flatbed trailers just waiting for someone to buy them or, in our case, photograph their beauty. We each purchased enough to hold us until we got to other roadside stands we hoped to find along the way. A short walk into the orchard, a chuckle at the misshapen peaches labeled *Misfits* who sported drawn-on eyes, brows and smiles, and we left this little bit of fruit-filled paradise.

Climbing gradually most of the way from Fruita, paralleling I-70 or the Colorado River, we hoped we could eventually relax and let a downhill do its work. Finally, just before Parachute, our overnight destination, we reached the summit and glided into town.

PARACHUTE TO GLENWOOD SPRINGS 43 MILES

Near the town of Rifle, the sandstone and shale Roan Cliffs tower three thousand feet over the highway. We learned that wherever these cliffs are, oil and natural gas interests want access. That means a struggle of benefits versus harm to ecology of the area will continue for years. At that moment, however, we were only aware of their grandeur and the great rock we found to eat our picnic lunch on and repair another flat tire.

Because we cycled only forty-three miles going to Glenwood Springs, we had time to explore this town located in the narrow valley. The Roaring Fork and Colorado Rivers converge here where extensive hot springs and other geothermal features exist. We took a tram up to an adventure/amusement park where Ray rode the speedy Alpine Coaster, kind of a roller coaster— with his hand ever ready on the brake lever. At thirteen hundred feet above the town and river, we were treated to a bird's-eye view of the valley, the surrounding red mountains as well as the serpentine course of the clay-toned rivers.

🚲

GLENWOOD SPRINGS TO AVON 55 MILES

We left town by riding up the Glenwood Canyon Bike Path, close to or tucked under the interstate, often dropping under a ledge just feet from the flow of the Colorado River. I-70 streams sinuously through the canyon, with other deciduous trees instead of cottonwoods as partners. Looking up at the bright rusty-red walls, black pinnacles and cliffs crowned with evergreens, I felt very small. Knowing we could spend neither the time nor the energy to hike to a favorite spot, Hanging Lake, we dallied at a trailside lake with its evocative reflections of the surrounding rock formations.

Dotsero sits on the Eagle River at the base of Colorado's most recent active volcano which erupted about four thousand years ago. There we found our way, traveling beside rough grass and tree-covered hillsides intermixed with sand-to-red-rock-colored terraces and pinnacles all the way to Avon.

As we cycled to the center of town, our eyes were immediately captured by a magnificent sight—a larger than life bronze sculpture of four wild horses, eyes ablaze, galloping hoofs, manes flying, muscled bodies in the air—*The Spirit of Wild Things*. We hustled off our bikes to pose for photos with it for our own rendering of that magnetic spirit.

⚲

AVON TO KEYSTONE 51 MILES

Biking from Avon's altitude of 7431 feet to 10,666 feet at Vail Pass, we had our work cut out for us. But first, needing calories, we pedaled eight miles to Vail, past red rock shale with both scrubby shrubs and evergreens, to check for more food.

Then it was time for the Vail Pass challenge which included an exceedingly sharp turn on a killer section. If you miss a gear change, it is unforgiving and continuing to pedal can be impossible. Strong rider Dave did and had to walk a short distance out of it which really upset him. He didn't know it, but he sometimes became the canary in the coal mine for me. If he had trouble, I knew difficulty lay ahead. I tried to do what he hadn't, such as shift well before hitting the tough spot. The route weaved into mountains and valleys then back to the stream, all the while indulging in occasional leg-burning angles. We survived the pass and breathed deep sighs of relief when we summited it. Hurray for us!

We celebrated with Ray by sharing his energy-restoring half-gallon of milk, photos of us with the lake, fuchsia fireweed, and lined up along a wall at the top. We felt ready to take the downhill plunge to the bottom of Vail Pass on the other side. Because I know the path to Copper from other rides, I felt happy to be getting a free downhill ride. Then, just before entering Copper, I looked at my bike rack and knew my yellow raincoat had disappeared. I remembered I had it at the top so needed to return—another long climb back up the mountain we had just sailed down. Compassionate Ray volunteered to go with me so back we went. A worker had just picked the jacket up and was about to put it in a storage unit when we arrived. We intercepted her and thanked her for its recovery. Then down the hill from the Pass again. *This was really getting to be a very long day and we still had lots of miles to go before we were in Keystone.*

Ray and I caught up with the others and headed into Frisco where we ate at The Butterhorn, a favorite spot for lunch in Summit County. About twelve miles later, the others rode while I slogged into The Pines at Keystone where our condo is. Photos and a bountiful dinner with Connie and John Carlson memorialized this day. How good it felt to sleep in our own bed at our condo.

⚲

Retha and Ray wanted to bike Hoosier Pass before they had to return to Iowa, Dave and Jim drove to Fruita to rescue our van and get some more peaches. I had fun with Connie on our low-key day, and also did laundry. The pass-climbers reached their goal and returned to Keystone. Tomorrow, they'd drive Dave's and their vans to Tribune, Kansas where they'd leave one van for the remaining three of us when we finished tying the bow across Colorado.

KEYSTONE TO FAIRPLAY 36 MILES

A tights and wind-jacket morning greeted Dave, Jim and me as we headed out from Keystone to Frisco then Breckenridge to begin the climb to 11,542 foot Hoosier Pass. A long, steady but pleasant enough slope led us to grueling parts of the pass. One incline triggered a memory of Retha exclaiming, "Holy crap!" as she cycled that section of the route. I agreed with her designation for this steep, totally unforgiving, leg-burning double hairpin curve that crawled on before us. Or was it that I crawled along trying to best it? No matter the answer to that question, to us it will be forever known as Holy Crap Hill.

Once we topped Hoosier Pass, the land opened up to reveal what is known as South Park, a huge wide-open bowl of gorgeous rangeland, surrounded by mountains in Park County. Ranches and small towns provided the population. Old hotels, a café or two, an occasional library and convenience/grocery stores, stipple the Main Streets. Small to diminutive structures, repeatedly repaired but often slumping, form much of the housing stock in the tiniest of towns.

The United States' highest incorporated municipality at 10,578 feet, Alma provided a quick stop after our descent on the south side from Hoosier Pass. Its history centers on silver, lead and zinc mining plus entertainment for the miners, since a nearby town didn't allow gambling and saloons. The area mines once produced over a million dollars each year but when the ore petered out and smallpox hit, the town was nearly decimated.

Another eight miles and Fairplay came into view. I'd never heard of it until 1980 when a friend cycling part of the cross-country Bikecentennial route said she would be riding from there through Kansas. The town, founded like many of the towns in Park County, came into being during the Pikes Peak Gold Rush. We stayed there that night so we had plenty of time to explore South Park City Museum, an open air representation of the county's mining camps-cum-boomtowns from the 1860s until the turn of the century.

One of my favorite exhibits was the Father Dyer Chapel, a former hotel relocated and reassembled log by log by itinerant Reverend John Dyer and another pastor, to become a Methodist Church. Its six small wooden pews and embroidered wall hanging *Cheerful Givers* and painted Psalm 121, *I will lift up mine eyes unto the hills from whence cometh my help…* added to the humble atmosphere. The array of dozens of structures—drug store, feed store and stable, school, Leather/Morgue/Coffin Maker shop—plus a shoot-out on the dusty streets culminating in a shotgun wedding, added drama to this town. Dioramas of mines gave us a close-up view of conditions endured by the miners.

As part of a special street event, Jim and Dave looked jaunty in their biking tights and jerseys, forgoing their usual helmets, one wearing a black ten-gallon Stetson and the other a sombrero. The transformation was nearly complete when they stood next to buckskin and chestnut horses instead of their usual steel Klein and Trek biking steeds, no lariats attached.

FAIRPLAY TO CANON CITY 77 MILES

The countryside seemed to flow as we glided through Park County—graceful rolling to flat land surrounded by mountain ranges named Mosquito, Park, Tarryall, Buffalo Peaks, and Thirty-nine Mile Volcanic Field. Dubbed South Park by settlers, we called it peaceful and just plain pretty. Hay, cattle and horses stoked the economy, and oxbows in the streams watered the crops.

A special family friend, intrepid thirteen year old Brett Rojec, joined us for the rest of the day. His earlier cycling experience included biking a challenging week long ride of Colorado's mountains and passes, and Juvenile Diabetes fund-raising ride and later, RAGBRAI with his mom, Patti. He, Tania, Patti, and his younger siblings, Stewart and Molly, met us at an overlook about twenty miles west of Canon City where they had been picnicking. He, Dave, Jim and I waved goodbye to the others and hit the pavement again. A delightful cycling companion, Brett rode eagerly and very competently with us. Later, Dave commented on how mature he was in his interactions with adults. Brett now recalls his introduction to Jim's famed tuna, peanut butter and jelly sandwiches and pronounced them delicious.

Soon we arrived in Canon City where the cheering squad waited for us at a playground. After a chat and rundown of this afternoon's events on the road, they returned to Denver with Brett. It had been a delightful interlude for us.

CANON CITY TO FOWLER 74 MILES

We left Canon City's high desert land to continue our slow decline to the High Plains of Eastern Colorado. Mountains still fringed us as we moved east, but after passing through Pueblo, they soon disappeared into our rear view mirrors and our memories.

FOWLER TO EADS 80 MILES

We awoke to fog, possibly compliments of the Arkansas River, which made grazing horses resemble ethereal beings. It lifted shortly after we latched onto Highway 96, where we continued following the TransAmerica Bicycling Trail extending from Yorktown, Virginia to Astoria, Oregon. How refreshing to discover this section, The Prairie Horizons Trail, which passes through the High Plains of Colorado and was adopted by three counties in Colorado. They had come together to work on planning and signage on this one hundred plus miles of trail corridor extending into Kansas.

The colorful blue to sunset-colored trail signs indicating bike as well as biker comfort information made life better. One such sign directed us to what became our most memorable potty-break. (See "Woods, Porta-potties and Other Joys.")

EADS TO TRIBUNE, KANSAS 58 MILES

The home stretch, well at least the last miles of riding to our goal of Tribune, Kansas. Excitement about finishing this part of our trip nearly overwhelmed me. We would truly be tying the bow on our bike rides, pedaling from the end of the fiftieth state, Utah, to the beginning of the first state that wasn't Iowa. There was a feeling of accomplishment that I hadn't felt after we reached the Utah-Colorado border last year. I thought I was almost content. For years my own philosophy included being wary of contentment. I rather thought being content meant not wanting more challenges, accepting the status quo and thinking there were few surprises that were worth pursuing. I wanted to keep moving, keep the challenges coming and pushing some but not all boundaries.

Then something came over me and I knew I had one more goal to accomplish that day—my own version of a victory lap.

BICYCLING BLUES

"So the last will be first and the first will be last." Matthew 20:16*

I had never been so discouraged about long distance bicycle touring. Not even when Jim and I faced the unrelenting South Dakota winds and I wanted to trade my bicycle for a car. That wind was of nature. Wind and whimsies of nature change.

My problem: I just couldn't keep up with my riding partners Jim, Sandy and Dave no matter how much effort I put into it. We'd start riding at the same time and in moments, I would be hundreds of yards behind them. I didn't expect them to slow their own natural tempo to stay with me. It's difficult and tedious to bicycle long distances at someone else's pace, either slower or faster. Sandy often rode with me but I knew it was at a cost to her.

Part of my problem was pride. But being humbled day after day can be bitter medicine. The three of them would stop to wait for me but by the time I caught up with them, they'd be ready to head off and I was ready to take a break. Resting too long made muscles cool off and stiffen up. Not resting enough, I became grumpy and disillusioned. And when Jim told me to go ahead, they'd catch up with me, the statement rankled—I often hadn't had the break I needed.

Within that disillusionment lurked some self-pity. Intellectually I knew they were being patient but I still felt rebuffed. Grimly, I kept going, internally muttering but not telling my companions what I was experiencing. I knew I wouldn't quit but I couldn't figure out what I needed to do differently except bike faster. Therein lay the core of the problem.

Once our trips were over, we felt joy with our accomplishments, thrilled at all we had seen, and my misery at being slower than the others faded. Within hours, we'd begin planning another bicycle adventure and I'd be excited about long-distance bicycling all over again.

🚲

My internist suggested I begin indoor cycling/spinning classes. The first time I went to the gym, I had no idea what to expect. The cycles were sturdy, stable and easy to pedal when there was little pressure applied to the freewheel. The more pressure applied, the harder one had to pedal. The first time my instructor, now a dear friend, told us to stand and pedal I was certain I would pitch over the handlebars. I continued to sit and pedal and felt irritated at my temerity at not even trying to stand.

By the second session, I had convinced myself that I wouldn't and couldn't tip the cycle over, fall off, nor launch over the handlebars. What a wonderfully freeing revelation. From that point on, I loved my spinning classes. The combination of lifting weights and spinning made me stronger.

348

Consistently pushing myself for one hour made me realize I could forge longer and harder and still have energy to expend at the end of class. A welcome side effect—my blood pressure dropped and I could stop taking medicine for it.

I would never be the fastest wheel on the road but I was faster and more powerful than I'd ever been. My riding partners complimented me on my improvement. That had two effects. One, I was happy about it and two, I experienced pressure to continue performing at that level. That combination of emotions kept me on edge.

Fast forward to our Tribute Ride in 2006, the one from Utah to Kansas that tied the bow on our fifty-state crossings. We had crossed Colorado from north to south in 1989, finished our final state, Utah, in 2005 and later crossed Colorado, this time from west to east to Kansas, thereby tying the bow. We ended the journey in Tribune, Kansas, a few miles beyond the exact spot where we had begun our cross-state rides in 1980.

On a sunny blue-sky day on the high plains of eastern Colorado, Dave, Jim and I rode the final stretch to the border. About eight miles from Kansas we stopped briefly for a nature break. A few minutes later I started out twenty-five yards before Jim and a bit more from Dave. Without even contemplating it, I was suddenly seized with an idea: I would not allow them to pass or even catch up with me. Jim saw me leave and later said he thought we'd ride the last miles together. *Ha! I said to myself. I'll make sure he can't catch me.* I could see Dave in my rearview mirror and was determined he would not get near me either.

They tried to overtake me but realized every time they threatened to come closer, I'd pedal faster. Both were aware of my motivation, after all, we'd ridden thousands and thousands of miles together. For once, I wanted to be first, first across a border, first to welcome them to Kansas, first to stop and wait for them, even if only for a few seconds.

As Jim and Dave crossed the border, they laughed, "What got into you?" and "Wow! Where did that come from?"

"I wanted to be first."

Years have passed since that heady moment—those years and many experiences including my body not cooperating as it once did. I may never again be first in that same way, but that is all right with me. I've had my moment. I only needed to do it once.

Once is enough.

⚲

* *Yes, I took liberties with my interpretation of the scripture; my apologies to gospel writer Matthew.*

COASTING CALIFORNIA'S COAST PART 1-2008

Riders: Retha/Ray, Dave, Jim/Jan. Drop off, pick up: Sandy.
Distance: 476 plus wandering miles in the Redwoods

In the intervening years since crossing Colorado, Dave, Sandy, Ray, Retha, Jim and I talked about another long-distance bike trip. All of us had bicycled across California, but a ride down the Pacific Coast Highway still called out names. Jim confessed, "I'm addicted! I'm not ready to stop riding long distances. I know Jan and I have completed our goal of riding across all the states but we still want to ride the California coast. She and I have ridden across Washington and Oregon, add California and we'll have bicycled all the way from Canada to Mexico. The coast route will be spectacular! It'd be fun! Let's do it!"

Excitement reigned in early April 2008 after we completed our bicycle trip plans. Part 1 of the two-part adventure would begin at Oregon's border and follow the California coast to Half-Moon Bay. Part 2, a later trip, would take us to the Mexican border. Sadly, Sandy was unable to ride with us.

Inauspiciously, Dave, Jim and I began our van trek from Iowa City, facing rain, sleet and big fluffy snowflakes. The Haases would fly to Reno where we'd pick them up. We visited our family in cold, windy Boulder, Jim attended his Board meeting in Keystone, Dave enjoyed time with his sister and soon we continued west on I-70 to Reno. Retha and Ray arrived, the doorknob to our motel room fell off and we couldn't get in, but we still managed to leave for Sacramento the following day to pick up Sandy. She'd been staying with her daughter Michelle, son-in-law Will and active toddler grandson Griffin. We proceeded to Smith River, California where five of us would commence riding.

Long striking mountain crossings made us remember how brave, and possibly foolhardy our forebears had been as they made their way west. A friend noted, "Of course there is nothing foolhardy about riding bikes down steep, treacherous roadways with cars traveling over fifty miles per hour." Point well taken. On the coast we spent the evening readying bikes, adjusting panniers, and repacking all our gear. From our rooms we could hear the thundering waves but couldn't see the ocean. Jim and I had fond memories of staying in this same motel with Jennifer and Bernd when we four had cycled the Oregon coast.

🚲

SMITH RIVER TO ORICK 57.5 MILES

After breakfast and photos, Sandy drove back to Sacramento to resume Mimi duty with Griffin. She so loves to bicycle but her health doesn't allow long distance touring anymore. We hugged her in a teary goodbye.

The chilly, overcast morning made us appreciate even more the beauty of Easter lilies grown in Smith River, a fraction of the 90 percent this area brings to the US markets. I heard Psst… psst… psst…Lucky Jim got to fix my thorn-punched tire which had interrupted our six miles of riding through bucolic farmland.

A great second breakfast at the Apple Peddler motivated us. Then *The Hill*, a challenging three and a half mile, 6-7 percent grade made my first outdoor bicycling day of the year miserable. I felt old and used up. Everyone else waited for me as I crept up at four miles per hour. My body and brain clenched at the thought of climbing a second big hill that day, supposedly a worse one. Nothing like psyching myself out.

We ate our picnic lunch at a blackish sand beach under cloud-spattered blue skies. As we rode, we heard crashing breakers and saw captivating views back to Crescent City—exactly as we had imagined riding along the coast would be. And we caught our first glimpses of redwoods.

Sweet relief! We arrived at our goal, Orick, without hitting another monster hill. An eccentric eighty-two year old woman operated the Palm Motel and Café there. Happiness that day meant standing in front of a heater to warm up, a café meal, despite its marginal food, except for good ice cream. We clambered into bed before 8 PM and slept until 6 AM.

WEDNESDAY, APRIL 10 ORICK TO EUREKA 48 MILES

Our breakfast at the café, prepared and served by women who had worked there for years, tasted better than the evening meal had. We listened to them and caught up on all the local Orick news, enjoying the small town feel like we had grown up with. But by the time we'd finished eating, rain had begun. Despite rain pants, heavy gloves, earmuffs and hoods, the cold wind snapped through us. On the bright side, we had no flat tires.

Many miles to go ...

We biked less hilly but picturesque side roads which helped make up for the raw ride to Trinidad. No surprise, the town had been founded in the 1770s by a Spanish explorer, and I'll bet he and his crew wished there had been a cozy café to warm up in during his adventure. We sipped piping hot soup, gripped steamy tea mugs and cuddled up to the heater to help dry us and our clothes, wet from rain, sweaty from exertion. A nearby fireplace soothed us most.

Back on the road, sharp-eyed Jim spotted a small pod of whales spouting off the coast. How exciting to bike along a vast ocean and detect a tiny spout from a distant whale. Dairy cattle, not whales, populated the pastoral routes to Arcata. We cycled through pastures bisected by the Hammond Bike Trail, reminding us of bike paths in The Netherlands. Neighborly Arcata cyclists helped us find a coffee shop to again warm ourselves.

The timing of our bike ride was not perfect—too late for the Banana Slug Race in Trinidad, too early for Arcata's all-terrain human-powered vehicle race on Memorial weekend. Banana slug races reminded Jim and me of our Oregon ride with Jennifer and Bernd. A favorite photo shows Jennifer's foot next to an impressively large yellow, appropriately named banana slug. Jennifer barely won.

Eureka, yes another Eureka, had played a leading role in the historic West Coast lumber trade and featured hundreds of significant Victorian homes making the entire city a state historical landmark. We gawked at The Carson Mansion, called the grandest Victorian home in America with its incredibly ornate Queen Anne style architecture. Built by lumber baron William Carson, this moss-green trimmed fanciful facade with cream towers and turrets, porches, balconies topped by curlicue what-cha-ma-doodles, has become the home of the exclusively male Ingomar Club. After our senses had been sated by the exuberantly extravagant homes, we pedaled on to see more of the town.

By the time we arrived at our destination, we had come to the edge of town. Oblivious Jim biked right past us and I had to ring my bell three times, our signal to stop, to retrieve him. A bit chagrined but smiling, he shook his head and wondered how he could have missed seeing the four of us standing in the parking lot. Aren't Lead Dogs supposed to look back or sideways?

We had a great motel room with lots of space for our bicycles, a back railing to hang our laundry on, plus an excellent Chinese restaurant next door to feed us. All in all, a very satisfying day.

⚄

THURSDAY, APRIL 10 EUREKA TO REDCREST IN THE REDWOODS

We reluctantly left our warm Eureka motel to venture out into another nippy day. I put on ear-pops (type of small earmuffs), extra foot protection, rain pants to keep out the cold, and heavy gloves. I felt like the Michelin man waddling to my bicycle, this time for a lovely ride through the agrarian setting of Tompkins Hill Road. The sun peeked out and a trickle of mist rose like steam from the backs of pastured horses and cattle, but not from us. We rolled past the College of the Redwoods where the spectacularly idyllic setting made me imagine the simple pleasure of waking up in such a place each day. Rural, with freshly planted fields and emerald meadows enclosed by white fences— not at all what many people would consider California.

I didn't mind missing the hill part of Tompkins, until we turned onto the inclines of Hookton Road when I wondered if it had been a superior change of course or not. The road paralleled the red alder, willow and Douglas fir-lined Eel River. *Do eels still survive there?* We learned that in 1850 Josiah Gregg named the Eel River when he and his exploring party traded a frying pan to a group of Native Americans in exchange for some eels, probably lamprey.

As we crossed Salmon Creek, we discussed the difficulty salmon have surviving what human beings have done to their rivers. In early twentieth century, salmon thrived in this region of Northern California but increased erosion from logging and otherwise changing ecology of the river made it a prime target for salmon-killing runoff, especially when large storms hit.

The worst storm ever to pound this area occurred at Christmastime in 1964. A deadly combination of heavy snowfall in the Salmon Mountains, rain reaching fifty inches in 24 hours, incredible runoff and warmer than usual temperatures created a perfect storm. By the time the flood waters reached thirty-five feet above the sidewalks in Weott, downstream in the Redwoods, several people had perished. Thousands of dairy cattle and other domestic and wild animals had died, and entire towns washed away. The Humboldt County area found itself completely cut off from the rest of the world, and food and supplies had to be helicoptered in.

The battering effect of at least eighteen million board feet of logs created jams that brought down every bridge on the Eel River except one. At Scotia, the river flow generated a maelstrom. Riding along these rural backroads, we could hardly contemplate the devastation of that flood. Now the river looks calm and peaceful, gravel and sand bars reach out into the river inviting us to stay awhile. As with forest fires, nature heals after floods, slowly, slowly, perhaps differently, but resolutely. We are grateful.

Our turn onto Eel River Road led us to the tiny town of Loleta, whose original Wiyot name means *pleasant place at the end of the tide water,* a perfect description. The town has a very relaxed feel about it, maybe because once it had been a hippie enclave. Friendly dogs wandered everywhere. We saw few people but one had amazing dreadlocks, draping all the way to his knees. In the 1970s, Christian commune Lightstone Ranch made Loleta their home. People, particularly in their twenties, had been lured by promises of abounding love, spiritual serenity, and a hardy pioneer existence. Some members hadn't counted on the depressing effects of the fog. Perhaps they hadn't heard the adage, *Where the fog flows, the redwood grows.*

Fog creates an inevitable part of the landscape near the Pacific coast. Information about weather in Loleta notes mild foggy summers, coastal foggy climes, perennial fog. There is even a race called the Foggy Bottoms Milk Run in nearby Ferndale. There is fog early, there is fog late. It reminded me of the late 1960s when our family lived in Fort Ord, California. When we arrived in July, we could see west to Monterey Bay from our home on a hill but couldn't see what lay east of us—because of fog. In September when it lifted, we could see mountains! Fog abounded, even in lovely Loleta.

In the quaint downtown, an unassuming grocery store sat next to a National Historic Register Classical Revival bank building, currently serving as the town's utility office. A sign on the double glass doors said *Slip payments for water and sewer bills under the door, please.* We entered to talk with the manager, a bespectacled woman dressed in beige with matching hair. It must have been a slow day as eager as she seemed to converse with someone, anyone, even five bicyclists. She especially wanted to relate the history of the bank and the building.

Built in 1910 as a Bank of America, it later became the US Bank and finally, Humboldt State Bank. Original beveled glass completed the oak tellers' cages and a latticed mezzanine where the bank president used to stay, not just for work but all night, remained empty. We wondered whether that had anything to do with the status of his marriage or not. An ornate antique pendulum clock hung on the wall, still bonging the time, time that otherwise seemed to have stood still. We thanked our docent and left. We glanced up and saw a cat lolling and sunning itself on a nearby porch roof. I wanted to ask it, *Are we moving too fast?*

A few mellow miles of dairy wonderland led us to Fernbridge. As one would surmise, this tiny village featured a bridge as its centerpiece. Not just any bridge but one on the National Historic Register as the world's longest all-concrete span. We were duly impressed.

Fernbridge prides itself on being the home to several antique shops and the Humboldt Creamery which produces ice cream for various clients including Costco's Kirkland brand. Add that to the list Jim thought did not measure up to his beloved Blue Bunny. Another claim to fame for its sixty residents is being the gateway to the renowned Victorian town of Ferndale. Travelers on nearby US Highway 101 might just zip on by and miss the glory of both Fernbridge and Ferndale. We would do neither, no zipping, no missing.

We angled off on State Road 211 to see if we could find ferns or dales in Ferndale. We didn't. Signs for the Swiss Club and the Danish Club presented more cultural information about the area. Lovely doe-eyed Jersey and Guernsey cattle dotted the flattened landscape. This area is definitely part of the TV ads *From happy cows come good cheese* country. One billboard portrayed a child bottle-feeding a calf and another, a burly farmer hefting a bale of hay. To Retha and me, both farm girls, the whole area smelled like wet manure, referred to by some as the smell of money.

Ferndale's one-square mile town core comprised a National Historic Register Neighborhood. I thought it the most fabulous collection of Victorian buildings I've ever seen, their scroll-work facades aesthetically painted with contrasting colors. We could have spent an entire day there, but cycling and Jim called our names even before we could begin popping into boutique shops and galleries.

As we left, Ray scooted up an incredibly steep driveway into the town cemetery, mausoleums and concrete walls emphasizing the precipitous climb. He said he couldn't bike it all, despite claims of great views of the Pacific from the top. While Ray forayed for fun, the rest of us struggled up rough Grizzly Bluff Road. We flew back down among pastures that would give Wisconsin's *America's Dairyland* a challenge for beauty.

We biked along the Eel River on Blue Slide Road and puzzled over what event could have precipitated its name, particularly the Blue part. Two grinder hills on this route yielded startlingly beautiful scenes of the Eel River Valley but also made level US 101 more tempting. The first hill grew into at least a 10 percent grade by the time we got to the top. Dave stopped momentarily and couldn't restart because of the slope. I watched him struggle and decided I would angle off if I had to stop on the way up. I did but eventually crested it. My breathing recovery time was short but my legs need much more time to revive. We experienced just one more grinder for the day. We all made it.

We glided into Rio Dell, not Del Rio as in Texas, and asked for directions to a park for a picnic and to a grocery store. I asked, "How far is it to the park?" and with his signature shrug Dave responded, "Just over the ridge." My heart dropped. I saw how far and steep the ridge was.

I asked again, "How far is it?" and Jim replied, "Twelve." *Twelve?* Then I learned Jim wasn't talking to me. I tried again, "Did you say, 'Over the ridge' or 'Over the bridge'?"

"Over the bridge." Whew! Just feet away we could ride over a narrow bridge to the store, not twelve miles or minutes plus the challenge of the ridge as I had feared. No wonder Dave had shrugged.

Our picnic in Scotia Park among volumes of multicolored flowers, quiet, and an old railroad engine, created a respite for us. Then we descended on Hoby Grocery in search of food for one and a half days away from such amenities—two dinners, two breakfasts, and one lunch apiece. We didn't know how complete our cooking facilities would be so we bought carefully. Something to heat up in the microwave or oven, cereals, fruits, juice, bread, cookies, peanut butter and tuna. The guys carried most of the food, Retha some, and I, the least powerful, that's positive talk for weakest of the bunch, got the dregs. I didn't mind.

Necessity compelled our return to the highway for five miles of heavy, sometimes scary traffic. When we turned onto the Avenue of the Giants and met astonishing, surreal, filtered sunlight, near euphoria engulfed us. And there was quiet. I thanked God for the serene beauty of this place.

A couple of miles later we saw the first *Road Closed* signs. Uh-oh. Gauging from our past travels, we knew that bicyclists can often make it past road closures. We rode on. The second set of signs had a notice stating a landslide had closed a small section of the road ahead. Why we felt relieved, I don't know, but we forged onward. We came upon two helpful California Department of Transportation workers who said they'd go ahead and guide us through. Yay for them.

We saw a landslide, decided it wasn't so bad and cycled on. Then we saw the real trouble. A huge ditch, fifteen feet deep, fifty to sixty feet across, maybe bigger, loomed ahead of us. The trencher and other equipment operators, kind enough to stop for us, posed for photos as we passed by, then continued. Another little adventure with friendly and accommodating DOT people of yet another state.

We faced one more hill which, in contrast to other hills we'd climbed that day, didn't seem too bad, and arrived at Redcrest Inn, our home for the next two nights. We had two bedrooms, a living room, indoor bathroom, kitchen and porch where our bicycles would stay. Like one of our Alaska cabins, we had to walk through one bedroom to get to the other.

Dave, Jim and I washed our clothes and hung them out in the chilly breeze. We sat outside, sun and shade fighting for dominance, while we waited for our turn to heat our dinners. The oven didn't work so we had to microwave them, slowly, one at a time in an inadequate microwave oven. Sleep overtook us and it was early to bed after an eventful, happy, challenging day.

FRIDAY, APRIL 11 THE REDWOODS

It's college best friend and bridesmaid Judy Conners' sixty-ninth birthday but I can't call her as I usually do because we have no cell service.

We arose early this cloudy morning, watched the schoolkids get on the bus across the road, then sat in bed and caught up on our journal writing. Thoughtful Retha served me a delicious hot chocolate. Ahh, luxury.

By 10 AM, we reveled at a now welcoming azure sky, and left to bike down the Avenue of the Giants, once part of old Highway 101. We stopped to absorb the sight of trillium, wood sorrel, Siberian iris, spring beauties and the unfurling maidenhair and leather ferns. We drifted slowly on, savoring every scent and scene. Ahh…

At the information Center we watched a film about the 1964 flood. We had seen signs marking how high the water had risen, in one location nineteen feet in one hour. No wonder it had devastated the countryside and dairy industry.

As we cycled, we noted the familiar pine fragrance of other evergreens doesn't occur with redwoods. I assumed the somewhat musty smell came from rotting debris around the trees as well as other plants, not the coastal redwoods themselves. Nowhere else are the trees so tall, growing to nearly three hundred eighty feet, with diameters of thirty feet. Although they aren't as old as the oldest bristlecone pine, they are among the oldest living things on Earth. They usually attain eight hundred to nine hundred although some have lived over two thousand years. To our dismay, an estimated 95 percent of the original old-growth redwoods have been cut down. Second growth trees have regenerated from the old growth seeds, naturally or from being planted, but they are less than two hundred years old.

We returned to Founder's Grove and, because there was no place to secure our bikes, walked them on trails among the peace and beauty of the trees. This grove has been called the *quintessential redwood grove* with bountiful huge summer-fog-fed trees, including 346 feet tall Founders Tree and the now fallen Dyerville Giant, 370 feet. The roots of redwoods are shallow but the trees interlock their widespread roots with surrounding trees, using them for added strength. It occurred to me they live like we human beings should, relying on others for added strength, emotional, spiritual, moral and physical, providing those same things for others. A lesson of the Giants.

If the redwoods teach lessons, they also raise questions such as, when a giant tree falls, does it register on the Richter scale? If so, how far away can it be from the seismograph to still register? Our peaceful time amid these amazing trees gave rise to these poems:

SILENT SOLILOQUY

We drifted among the ancients
trespassers all
soft breeze
hushed awestruck humans
Giant Redwoods

Redwoods
undiminished by time
or intruders
keeping watch
nature's sentinels

1994
fallen giants
scar the landscape
did unseen seismographs
mark their demise?

We searched for the Rockefeller Grove and looped down an incredibly pitted, potholed, broken up road, one of the worst we've ever ridden on. We missed the turn-off and eventually turned back after Ray checked out the Grove. The day had flown by at lightning speed.

After showers and laundry, Jim and I prepared spaghetti and tossed salad with apples and mandarin oranges. The manager had left us a note explaining how the gas oven worked so we also baked biscuits. Retha, Ray and Dave cleaned up while Jim and I climbed a nearby hill to the walk-through tree. We'd driven through trees before but had never walked through one, a surreal experience. Weariness convinced us to turn back to prepare our gear for the morrow.

🚲

SATURDAY, APRIL 12 MOM DOWN'S BIRTHDAY, REDCREST TO FORT BRAGG

We left Redcrest on an exquisite day to continue our ride through the redwoods. We paused to listen to the quiet then pursued it on our bicycles.

At ten we stopped for a second breakfast in Miranda at The Avenue Café. My journal notes, "WONDERFUL!" Jim had the most blueberries in and on his pancakes we've ever seen. French toast of thick sourdough bread with cinnamon, vanilla and nutmeg satisfied Retha and me. Ray ate huevos rancheros and Dave chose an omelet. The café owner, a biker, gave us hints about tomorrow's route. We appreciate all the help we can get especially from locals.

We followed along the Eel River which ran fast, slow, quiet, rapid. The temperature rose to 84 degrees. We rode on and off Highway 101 then on and off again, found muted back-roads, lunched along the river, then biked tranquil roads at Benbow. It hadn't always been so hushed; we passed an area where a slide had occurred. I glimpsed two tracks heading up a nearby hill and worried that would be our route. It wasn't. Now the heat started to get to us since we'd started at 39 degrees.

Garberville's grocery, Ray's Market, compelled us to stop there for food and for Ray. I stayed out with the bikes while the others shopped. Two women and a darling two-year old Corgi, Tedwyn, came by. Tedwyn's owner left him with me saying, "I trust you." The other woman, a Tibetan, stayed. We discussed peaceful Tibetan protests in San Francisco which she and her husband had joined. She indicated they would soon move there where more Tibetans live. She vigorously opposed President Bush's attendance at the Beijing Olympics and felt dismayed at all the problems in Lhasa. I told her that Jim and I had been to Tibet and Lhasa three-and-a-half years ago and consider Tibet to be a sovereign country. She said she was pleased to meet someone who had been there. When Tedwyn's owner returned, she asked if I was a practicing Buddhist since I was so interested in Tibet. I responded, "No, I'm a Christian and my husband and I are concerned about what's happening to the Tibetans and their country."

The long, hot way from Garberville to the Redwood River Resort included some road construction but no closures. We checked into our individual apartments then went to the office to choose our frozen dinners. Everyone nuked their own and retreated to our room to eat. The evening was pleasant but we all felt weary and planned to be up and out early the following day.

SUNDAY, APRIL 13 REDWOOD RIVER RESORT TO FORT BRAGG

We ate breakfast in our rooms and met at seven to resume cycling up and down the never-ending hills. We had heard that a large hill, climbing from seven hundred to two thousand feet in two-and-a half miles awaited us. It turned out to be four miles with a grade of 7 to 8 percent. Beautiful weather made the climb not so difficult after all, just long which thrilled and relieved us enough to kind of let our guard down. As a consequence, the next hills took us by surprise with their ferocity: steeper angles with no reprieves, and the great reward of picnicking on cliffs overlooking the Pacific, skies with traces of clouds and fog rolling in. I love biking high above the ocean, then swooping down and up again. Lots of puffers followed by superb downhills made me sing, kinda like the downhill from Redcrest in the Redwoods which had perfectly fitted four verses of *Amazing Grace*. We watched birds, from gulls to turkey vultures soaring overhead, not circling us—yet.

MY MIND SAID, "GIDDY-UP!" BUT MY BODY SAID, "WHOA!"

By now, I had been riding bicycles seriously for thirty-one years. Thirty-one years of delighting in…

…early morning mists of the Flint Hills and Appalachians;

…mid-morning warmth of the East Texas Piney Woods and Great Dismal Swamp;

…high noon baking sun of the Great Plains and Badlands;

…fresh spring flowers of the Mojave and Georgia;

…biting afternoon sleet and snow of the Sand Hills and Talkeetnas;

…sunset shadows of the Rockies and Sierra Nevadas .

Thirty-one years of relying on cycle technology, good nutrition plus a little bad, and training to enable me to ride my bicycle wherever I wanted. Then I met an uphill I couldn't conquer. I knew this would happen sooner or later, but I kept hoping for later. For the past decade I've pondered this dilemma with each long distance bicycle trip we've taken. When would I falter?

Would it be…

…in Maine where the 8 percent grade, heat and humidity forced an iron-legged friend to walk his bike?

…following the trail of emigrants across California's Carson Pass, past lonely pioneer graves?

…in the middle of the bone-jarring, fear-inducing, deafening echo of a tunnel in Arizona's Superstition Mountains?

…emerging from a gulch called Elk Creek Crossing in California's coastal range?

…in the startling beauty of western Iowa's Loess Hills where RAGBRAI riders coming off a curving upgrade ready to savor a swift downhill, instead exclaimed, "Oh damn!" when they spied the next daunting climb?

I'd never walked a hill while bicycling before. It wasn't that I was always in such good shape or used the gearing brilliantly or had such superb technique that I glided up those mountains and heights. There had been times when I ground through the gears, muttering at myself for not having shifted in time or at my bicycle for dropping the chain. But I still made it. I dipped down one ridge and up the next like a bird in flight. I sighed or moaned as I saw an upcoming incline but determined that I would come out on top unscathed.

Sometimes I puffed, choked, pulled and heaved trying to keep the bike steady and not topple over with my feet still clipped to the pedals. I breathed through my nose and out through my mouth just like my indoor cycling instructor told me to do. I sweated. I gave myself fifteen, thirty, or sixty second breaks. I drank water and electrolyte drink. I ate gorp, bananas, oranges and energy bars.

I quoted Scripture, *Get you up to a high mountain.* Prayed, *God please don't let me fall over in front of a car or off a cliff.* Chanted, *I think I can, I think I can….* Sang in my head, *Red and yellow and pink and green, purple and orange and blue, I can sing a rainbow, sing a rainbow, sing a rainbow too....*

I gave myself courage by surveying how far I had come and how stunning the views. I thought of our grandsons, took heart at their young beauty and strived to make them proud of me. I chided myself, *If he can do it, you can do it. You can last for ten more pedal strokes, now ten more, ten more. You can make it to the next road sign.*

So far, I had made it.

April 15, 2008 in my sixty-ninth year of life. The sky was crystalline, sharp wind cooled us as we descended, heat enveloped us as we ascended. Ocean breakers pounded in our ears. Jim informed us The Monster was just ahead. As I peaked the hill before what I assumed would be the Feared One, I glanced over and murmured to myself, *That can't be it. The grade doesn't look that steep. I can do that one. It must be farther on toward the town of Jenner.*

I barreled down the gulch noting the fifteen miles per hour speed limit sign, braked as I approached the hairpin curve and resumed pedaling when I hit the pitched inside curve of the uphill. I clicked into my small chainring and saw *IT* ahead and above me, I could see Retha and Ray with their strength, youth and stamina as they conquered the first aspect of the rise.

Jim and Dave preceded me, cranked their pedals and ultimately stopped, dismounted and pushed their laden bicycles up this 15-20 percent grade. Disheartened but dogged, I agonized until I thought I would tip over.

My mind commanded, *Come on legs! Giddy-up!* but my body said, *Whoa!*

I had expected that having to stop and walk would upset me, but I felt relief. I didn't have to ride this bear. I dismounted, smiled in resignation and commenced to shove my trusty Trek to the next curve, my panniers slapped my backside as I strained. My speedometer indicated I was going 0 miles per hour. *Wait a minute! I am moving!* I managed to get my speed up to an average of one point two miles per hour. Jim and Dave tramped along much faster than I, possibly two point nine, Jim said later. As cars drove down in first gear, I grinned at the occupants, shrugged and waved, "C'est la vie!" They returned the smiles.

When I approached the top of the first section of the upgrade, I heard the growl of an upcoming vehicle and realized there was no safe place to stand on the minuscule shoulder abutting a bluff. *Where could I go?* A pickup flashed its warning lights and passed by as I squeezed against the wall. *Wide load!* It was still far enough back for me to make it up to the next hairpin. I pushed my bike as fast as I could and crossed the road so I would be upside instead of down-side of the hulking yellow bulldozer secured to the back of a semi-trailer. I clutched my bike and pressed against the guardrail.

From his vantage point far above, Ray looked down as the semi's inside wheels on the left side lifted off the pavement just like the tipping truck warning signs we'd seen. I realized I might have taken shelter on the wrong side of the road. The driver stared at me and swung wide across both traffic lanes toward me as the rig crawled and groaned up to the crest. I was terrified. When it passed, my galloping heartbeat slowed and I stopped holding my breath. We were all safe—cars, trucks, 'dozer, cyclists and pedestrian-cyclists.

The line of autos that had been halted at the summit by the escort vehicle slowly snaked down the hill. I scampered as fast as a weary bike pusher can, back across the road and continued the march up. The grade tapered. One more sloping curve brought me to a relatively flat spot. I stopped where Jim, Dave, Retha and Ray waited for me. I needed water. I needed food. I needed a break.

I smiled again. Although I had not conquered Elk Creek Hill, neither had The Hill conquered me.

🚲

Fort Bragg, that Hill day's destination, had its future as a thriving tourist destination determined by San Francisco's devastating 1906 earthquake and ensuing fire, quick reconstruction and completion of a new rail line. Immediately upon entering town, Jim remarked on its wide streets which led us to our cozy B&B and then to a delicious fish dinner at Sharon's by the Sea. I felt grateful to be alive and still able to bike.

🚲

SUNDAY, APRIL 13 FORT BRAGG TO GUALALA

The shivery morning we left Fort Bragg, the wind, well beyond brisk, made riding treacherous. We veered off route to visit the simple but picturesque Point Cabrillo Lighthouse, a welcome reprieve from the noisy highway. Standing on a spectacular headland which extends out into the ocean, the whole station includes a lighthouse, three restored light keepers' houses, a blacksmith and carpentry shop. Nearby redwood forests had been exploited by San Francisco businessmen needing wood, particularly after the 1906 Earthquake. That meant more shipping as well as more shipwrecks in Mendocino Bay, creating a need for the lighthouse, first illuminated in 1909.

The sea continued its spectacular show all along the coastline. We lacked words to describe the cliffs, rocky, sandy beaches, driftwood, dramatic bluffs overlooking the Pacific. I felt both tranquil and exhilarated. Gualala attracted hunters and fishermen who wanted to get away from cities in the 1860s. By the turn of the century this unincorporated town, set in a quintessential rugged California coast area, had become a major commercial hub, complete with a band and an opera house. We stayed south of the village in a cabin with overwhelming sea views which, along with the sound of the sea, captivated us.

🚲

MONDAY, APRIL 14 GUALALA TO BODEGA BAY

Our visit to Fort Ross, a fascinating post on the Sonoma Coast, enlightened us. Although English and Spanish explorers had claimed the coast of northern California more than a century earlier, when the Russians built Fort Ross in 1812, it became the first significant European settlement along this part of the coast. Part of the outreach of the Russian-American Company, an outpost here made perfect sense. Russia meant to colonize Siberia and Alaska bringing their Eastern Orthodox Christianity with them. They established farms, bred cattle, first acquired from the Spanish, and sheep. Something we had not been aware of was how much scientific research the Russians pioneered and contributed in botany, geography, geology, zoology, and other -ologies. By 1839, the fort needed to be sold. After England, France and Mexico refused, it was sold to Captain Sutter, of Sutter's Mill gold-strike fame for thirty-thousand dollars. This abandonment of the fort was the beginning of Russia's withdrawal from North America, culminating in Russia selling Alaska to the United States. Garnering this history from our walkabout at the fort added greatly to our understanding of this part of California's history. Even crossing the flowing water named Russian River made sense now.

We cycled fifty miles farther down the coastal highway, listening to pounding surf, loving the close proximity to the ocean. We traveled along rock outcroppings punctuated by sandy beaches, before we came to Bodega Bay. For many of our generation, Bodega Bay remains only as the place where Alfred Hitchcock set his film *The Birds.* Have any of us really gotten over the horror of the birds attacking? Amid protests, a nuclear power plant had been planned there but was abandoned with the discovery of a fault line across the proposed site. Excavation had already begun so now the locals refer to the site as *The Hole in the Head.* For others, its mudflats are prime territory for clamming. So when low tide hits…look out horseshoe clams!

The Bodega Bay Inn created a visual feast—impressive California gardens with sculptures, a grotto, a fire pit and lots of local art. For years we have received annual messages inviting us to return and attend the art festival. We would have loved to accept the invitation!

TUESDAY, APRIL 15 BODEGA BAY TO MILL VALLEY

We could have spent days seeing everything we wanted to between Bodega Bay and Mill Valley. Unfortunately, we had but one day so we had to skip some entirely, including Point Reyes and Point Arena. We skimmed along narrow Tomales Bay where lots of oyster farming takes place. The grazing dairy cattle we spotted on the hillsides indicated another income source for the area. We turned off Highway 1 to ride inland toward Mill Valley and passed through San Anselmo, a silent film hub in the early days of film, circa 1900s. Arrival in Mill Valley on the slopes of Mount Tamalpais, was the goal for some of us, but Mount Tam itself provided an irresistible invitation to Ray. Even before he saw trails leading up, he had been smitten by the bug which says, "Climb because it is there." The mountain came into being, like many others, by the forces of buckling, folding and lifting of the local geologic plates near the San Andreas fault zone.

He pedaled through the climate zone where scrub bushes, manzanita and other evergreens survive, to the top where he could view San Francisco itself. He returned to the motel a happy but tired man, thrilled to have gone where the rest of us had only dreamed of being.

WEDNESDAY, APRIL 16, MILL VALLEY TO HALF MOON BAY

Biking across the Golden Gate Bridge had long been on Jim's Bucket List and this was the day we would do it. We left Mill Valley and along our way, climbed a steep hill where I thought traffic might immobilize us. When we spotted the Golden Gate Bridge, I felt my heart leap at the cause of so many dreams. We pulled into an overlook to really see the Bridge and had the joy of finding another Lone Sailor Statue like the one in Long Beach, California. I am always moved by seeing one of these statues, depicting a sailor in his blues, cap set jauntily on his head, his rucksack plopped at his feet, and eyes straight ahead to the sea, in this case, San Francisco Bay. Just like my brother Keith would have done.

Jim's long-time dream became a great disappointment for him when the Golden Gate Bridge only poked its head through thick fog. As we rode onto it, we prepared ourselves to stop whenever visibility required, and kind of scooted our bikes along until we could see better. I had walked across the Bridge recently as part of a sixty mile Three-Day Susan G. Komen Breast Cancer walk on a clear day, so I kept that memory but felt sorry for Jim—the fog was not part of his dream.

We arrived in San Francisco quickly and turned to pedal through The Presidio housing complex where we had once hoped we'd live while in the military. Easy stop and go traffic allowed us good access through the acclaimed up and down streets. I loved riding past famed Painted Ladies, colorful, highly decorated Victorian houses. We relished cycling 49-Mile Scenic Drive, continuing past the Cliff House, Golden Gate Park, Dutch windmills and lots of cypress trees. Although sand dunes often blocked our views of the ocean, we were happy to see ice plants and low-growing grasses helped as sand-holders. Despite that, wind had blown sand onto the road so we had to remain alert and bike with caution. But we were open to the ocean where seagulls plied their squawking trade of cleaning up the environment.

Skyline Drive's inclines did not surprise us and connected with Cabrillo Highway, the coastal route. In Daly City, what to our wondering eyes appeared but *Little boxes, little boxes... and they're all made out of ticky-tacky and they all look just the same...* We'd rolled on to the inspiration for the *Little Boxes* song, yellow, blue, pink and green manufactured homes built for suburbia. Rutted, pitted road shoulders led to a smoother bike/walking trail which allowed clearer views of critters and surfers along the route. That scene inspired me to write this poem:

relentlessly pacific

azure navy aquamarine
infinitely crashing foaming sea
ripples in dancing sunlight
briny fragrance of ocean breeze
scudding clouds hopscotch the sun

dolphin fins cut waves
cacophony of harbor seal pups
tumbling dark bodies of surfers
swoosh through troughs
misjudge waves
practice quick dismounts

we pedal amid the glory
smash into spiraling air currents
revel in salt-tanged cheeky wind
spine-tingling downhills lusty climbs

our finite bodies
and the eternally
moon-drawn sea

The lure of biking along the Pacific coast never grew old. We worked hard to get where we had and loved nearly every minute of it, despite narrow shoulders and bumpy roads. High over beaches or riding alongside, we could not get enough of hearing, seeing, feeling and smelling the sea. We clung to hillsides as our route twisted and turned, up and down, along cypress, evergreens, eucalyptus and seagrass. Even echoing mile-long tunnels, fortunately with wide lanes for bikes, did not trammel our spirits.

Pristine Montara State Beach seemed so insulated from San Francisco and its environs. Moss Beach's fog-loving veggie crops—artichokes, broccoli and Brussels sprouts—added to the feeling despite encroaching construction. Quickly we came upon Half Moon Bay, the culmination of the biking part of this trip.

Sandy, Michelle, Will and Griffin greeted us in the parking lot of our motel. Our nieces Tamara and Julie joined the rest of us for dinner at Sam's Chowder House as did Doug and Ellie, Dave's seminary friends, who had been part of our Arizona, Missouri and east to west California rides. We celebrated our families and friends, and our safe, memorable completion of Coasting California's Coast Part 1. Sandy and crew returned to Sacramento. Ray and Retha caught their plane home in Reno. Dave, Jim and I drove through Boulder on our way to Iowa City. Eventually we all arrived home, delighted with our adventure and ready to plan the final episode of Coasting California's Coast Part 2. We could hardly wait.

LESSONS FROM MOLOKAI-MAUI-2009

Riders: Jim/Jan. Drop off: Bill Vogt. Distance: 68 miles

Who knew that a twenty-five-minute flight from Maui could take us from a tropical paradise to a totally different kind of paradise—remarkable beauty, no chain stores, no stoplights. Molokai, like other Hawaiian Islands, had risen out of the sea as the result of volcanic eruptions. Jim and I planned a multi-day bike ride the length of the island and back and visiting friends.

Despite scarce lodging, for our few nights' stay we found a pleasant B&B in the largest town, Kaunakakai. The town consisted of approximately thirty-four hundred people, nearly half the entire island population. We wandered in and out of the few shops where I discovered and had to buy Hawaiian salts: brittle, crunchy, beautiful Red Alaea sea salt, tasting of red iron oxide from added alaea clay, and Black Lava Salt, a blend of sea salt and purified volcanic charcoal.

We reassembled our bicycles for our excursion to the east end of Molokai. Following Kamehameha V Highway, we paralleled Kalohi and Pailolo Channels which isolate Molokai from Lanai and the west end of Maui. To our left rose 4,970 foot volcanic Kamakou. To our right, dozens of fish pond ruins framed the coastline where early residents had fished. They were not accessible to us since private residences backed them. On the mauna (mountain) side, tree-post fence lines separated us from lush grazing land and old orchards at the base of the hackly mountains.

Kamakou's many streams and gulches meant plenty of small bridge and culvert crossings over the twenty-seven miles to Halawa Valley, the end of the road. The closer we came to Halawa, the more the road narrowed to a single choppy lane, and the more the short steep curvy climbs and downhills challenged me. *Did riding a bucking bronco feel like this? Or should I have said bone-shakers, as in early bicycles?*

Traditional Hawaiian way of life had continued in Halawa Valley until well into the twentieth century, and included extensive production of taro, as well as ruins of temples/heiaus, irrigation channels, ancient walls and terraces. Two devastating tsunamis, in 1946 and 1957, washed through the valley, killed residents and demolished the taro ponds.

The fish ponds, whose archaeological remains have been dated at thirteenth century CE, provided a steady protein source for indigenous people. Rounded boulders and coral formed the outline of the ponds and woven branches served as gates which kept fish in, while allowing the tide to wash in and out and provide nutrients for the growing fish. Some ponds have been rebuilt and are still used by local residents.

Leaving Halawa to return to Kaunakakai via the nearly traffic-free road, we experienced the same ups and downs on our bronco bikes, all the way back to our B&B. The scenes changed little except for the playing of the light on them, a gratifying reprise for us. Tangy sea smells gave rise to our memories of other times biking along this vast ocean.

🚲

We rose early to begin our journey to the west coast to finish our cross-island ride and to visit our friends on the west end of the island. We met and worked with Lynn and Bill Vogt on a Habitat Global Village Build in Csurgo, Hungary.

The scenic sixteen mile ride to upcountry town of Maunaloa took us through the central plateau of the island and embraced views of Molokai's south shore. Its turquoise near-shore waters abruptly mutated to deep azure farther out. On the mauna side, open grasslands and mountains dominated. The highway wound up-and-downhill through red and brown arid landscape accentuated by green scrubby growth.

Our favorite part of Maunaloa Town had to be the colorful rainbow-painted Big Wind Kite Factory. With kites, wind socks, whimsical Asian dragons, plus "cool stuff" from all over the world, this family-run factory/workshop/store bulges like a general store gone wild. The owner Jonathan started making kites and selling them on the beach in 1980. Now he creates them, tells tales and teaches kids of all ages how to build their own. He and his wife Daphne had fallen in love with kiting as they followed *The Hippie Trail* in Afghanistan. He proudly explained that the kites in the book *The Kite Runner,* were their kites.

From the road we could see a more subtly painted new Habitat for Humanity house built with a local partner family. As long-time Habitat volunteers, that brought smiles to our faces as we passed by; we didn't stop because no one seemed to be building that day.

Jim biked easily and I struggled on a narrow rural road, seemingly all uphill (it really wasn't) and then along the Molokai Ranch which encompassed just over a third of the island. This working ranch with real paniolos/cowboys raised cattle, horses and mules. Eventually several thousand acres were leased to Libby and Del Monte for pineapple cultivation which became an economic mainstay for Molokai.

As we topped the final hill of our route, we realized we would have a downhill run toward the beach. Then we looked at the road surface—the bumpiest brickiest road we've ever traveled, heading into the housing complex. Tooth rattling? Indeed. Here we were, an orthodontist and his teacher wife going to visit a general dentist and his teacher wife. At least if we needed it after descending, we'd have good dental care. We teachers would consider it a teachable moment.

Lynn and Bill greeted us with typical Aloha warmth and showed us their unique home, its amenities and environs. Even though their property extended to the ocean, their home, consisting of four pods built around a courtyard, had been set back from the beach and elevated because of danger from perilous high tides, waves and tsunamis. Both were tennis aficionados so their tennis court lay between the house and the not-always-pacific ocean.

After lunch Bill announced, "OK everyone, back to your rooms for an hour rest. It's a tradition." Frankly, I rather like what our family calls siestas—reading, relaxing and then napping sounded refreshing and healthful too.

The afternoon sped by as we walked along their lovely white sand beach, each caught up in our own thoughts, and later with each other discussing travels, mutual friends and family. During siesta time my unquiet mind had searched for a word for a poem I'd been working on as an assignment, *Shakespeare's Challenge* for my Writers Group. Knowing our hosts were good problem solvers, I mentioned my poem had to be based on a line from Shakespeare's *The Winter's Tale*. I had already written nine lines about the economic depression but needed help with "The bull market disappeared/___ by the directive:/"Exit, pursued by bear." Lynn quickly offered, "Compelled." Perfect. Assignment completed.

Exquisite filtered Hawaiian twilight enhanced our dinner. Later we shared more thoughts and memories by the warmth of fire and friendship.

Early the next morning after breakfast, we piled our bicycles into the Vogt's van and left their version of Eden to return to Kaunakakai B&B. Grateful alohas to Lynn and Bill were soon followed by aloha greetings to the tourist van driver who picked us up to take us to the beginning of our next adventure on the island.

We joined a cadre of people who had the same idea as we had. Ride mules down a steep path to a remote former leper colony. Kalaupapa National Historical Park, *whose goal is to preserve the cultural and physical settings of the colony*, had a total of 8500 residents between 1866 and 1969.

In 1865 The Hawaiian Kingdom legislature passed a law to try to prevent transmission of leprosy, the incurable disease later known as Hansen's disease, which had been brought to the islands by foreign workers about 1830. By 1865 the population in Kalaupapa had been decimated by epidemics of other Eurasian diseases and only about 140 people survived. The government moved them out to prepare for the development of an isolation settlement for people with the disease. Sadly, those who had been removed lost their cultural ties and connection with the land which had been in their families for centuries. Families were broken up. Research reports that the effects are still felt in the islands to this day.

Jim and I had originally planned to hike down to the colony but rain the previous night had made the trail treacherous. We decided to take the safer way down—by mule. *Think about it, Jan! What makes you think riding a mule will be safer or better?* The guidebook reads: *In the cool Molokai uplands, a pack of mules prepare for the day's ride down to the world's most unique and formerly forbidden village of Kalaupapa. The journey begins from the Mule Barn with a mule guide briefing.* Mule skinners supposedly taught us how to ride and control the beasts, as if we amateurs could possibly control one. I kept thinking *There is a reason for the saying, "Stubborn as a mule."*

As I clutched anything I could get my hands on, we rode down 1700 vertical feet of the most spectacular and highest sea cliffs in the world, according to *The Guinness Book of World Records.* The nearly three-mile trail with twenty-six switchbacks corkscrewed in and out of canyons and ravines. To me, the cliffs appeared to be nearly perpendicular, especially from the back of a mule. Jim remembers the muddy slippery day and feeling apprehension as the mules took off. At least it felt like they took off. He appreciated the sublime views to the sea, but the slick rocks prevented him from ever feeling comfortable. Me too.

Terrified about slipping right off the head of my mule, glimpses of distant ocean were fantastic but I still was scared most of the way down. Afterward I thought about the earlier bucking bronco feeling of the bicycle. I realized I hadn't genuinely experienced this true bone shaker of a mule then. Besides that, I hadn't felt scared on my bike.

Once we reached Kalawao Town, we clambered off our mules and our feet hit ground, wonderfully solid, non-threatening earth. Our next lessons of the leper colony began.

After visiting here, Mark Twain is supposed to have written, *This was a place of stunning beauty, blessed by nature's grandeur and cursed by humanity's ignorance and fear.* The community had remained hidden from the world for many years but within it, incredible tales of struggle and human suffering as well as of courage and love took place. Although few medical persons came there, Belgian missionary priests were among those who cared for people with leprosy on Molokai. The most well-known, Father Damien, served there from 1873 until his death from the disease in 1889. He arrived on a boat carrying cattle and fifty patients bound for Kalawao. The leprosy-afflicted people were dumped into the bay and left to swim or somehow manage to make it to shore if they could. Supplies jettisoned over the sides of the ships relied on currents to carry them ashore or exiles swimming to retrieve them.

Before Father Damien came, the first arrivals lived in rock enclosures, caves, or shacks made of sticks and dried leaves. With the assistance of those exiled there, he built homes, churches and coffins, constructed a water system, planted trees. He spoke the Hawaiian language and organized choirs, schools and bands. Being anything but retiring, he badgered the church and government to arrange for medical services and funds from Honolulu. Eventually other priests and nuns came to carry on his work.

He had been preceded by other caregivers and religious workers—Congregational ministers, Catholic priests, Mormon elders, family and friends of patients. But it was Damien's efforts which attracted worldwide attention and an increased awareness of the disease and its victims. Jim and I were in awe of what he had done and in horror of how the ill had been treated. Fear and ignorance are onerous partners.

Tubercular Robert Louis Stevenson also visited the leper colony. He was moved by Father Damien's care for the patients and described the settlement as a "prison fortified by nature." An accurate description since the rest of the island remained cut off by towering mountains and cliffs.

Since the 1940s, the disease has been curable because of the use of antibiotics. The settlement eventually closed officially but residents of the former colony had permission to stay. They and their descendent families who wished to, continued to live in the neighborhood maintained on the peninsula. Father Damien's gravesite is there as well, next to the white wooden church he helped rebuild, St. Philomena Church.

Damien was beatified by the pope and became Damien the Blessed in 1995, then canonized in 2009 as St. Damien of Molokai. Initially he was buried among his beloved people, then reburied in Belgium. In 1995 a relic of his hand was returned and buried in his original grave in Kalawao. The Hawaiian people rejoiced at his homecoming and celebrated with a Mass, meal, music and a hula dance.

We learned that once a year a barge comes from Honolulu to deliver thousands of pounds of rice, cases of beer, drums of gasoline and supplies to stock the grocery store and hospital. Imagine that grocery list!

Too soon it was time to mount the mules and head back. *It would always be too soon for me.* At rare moments, riding up the cliff felt slightly more comfortable than going down. That is until the mules sensed their closeness to the barns and started to trot, then gallop the last two-hundred yards. Yee-haw!

Before we returned to our B&B, the tour van took us to spots overlooking the sea cliffs and waterfalls, dramatic rock formations and crashing surf. The view below encompassed the church and the bay where the people with leprosy had been dumped by the ships. We had a lot to process after this singular experience.

The following morning we caught a small plane to return us to Maui where we'd vacation and ride bicycles for an additional two weeks. Indelible Molokai memories remain with us.

MYSTERY IN MAUI 2009

Riders: Jim/Jan. Distance: 57 miles

Spending part of winter in Hawaii gave Jim and me snow and ice-free delights. Through our time-share we could stay on Oahu, the Big Island or Maui. After our time in Molokai, we continued our vacation in Maui where we hadn't bicycled since 1993. This time we wouldn't cruise down Haleakala on a mega-brake bike, but instead would pedal our own bikes in the western part of the island. How great to see improvement in the roads plus the addition of biking/walking trails in the area near our condo. *This would be fun.*

Although we biked longer distances on Molokai, on Maui we cycled short ones of up to fifteen miles, exploring the scenery and wayside fresh food stands, especially looking for pineapple. We loved being outdoors in warm breezes and not wearing mittens or parkas. As the days went on we ventured farther and farther exploring sectors of the island we had never seen, but we deliberately chose not to challenge ourselves with the 12-15 percent inclines.

As we bicycled a return route from the sea one morning, I was concerned I couldn't keep going—I couldn't breathe. I stopped abruptly and hung over my handlebars to try to catch my breath. *What's going on?* Jim pulled up beside me to wait.

When I felt better, I got back on my bike, tried to pedal but had to stop within five strokes. *This is absurd! This is just a slight incline not a real hill. What is the matter?* Because I'd had radiation for breast cancer the previous summer, Jim assumed this episode just reflected how tired I had been since then. I wondered. This wasn't just feeling tired. I felt exhausted.

"Do you think you can you keep going?"

"I don't know but I'll try in a few minutes." We waited. The views of the tropical flowers, fresh food stands, subtle warm breezes and lush vegetation didn't soothe me. I just wanted to return to the condo to lie down.

Soon I thought I could possibly pedal or at least push my bike until I could coast down the tiny decline I knew was over the crest of this bump of a hill. I pushed, then climbed on and coasted until I could pedal, however slowly. We made it back, wheeled our bikes onto the elevator and into our condo. I went to bed.

The following day I felt fine and we decided to bike again, this time to the Maui Ocean Center. I felt fatigued once we arrived there but we strolled through a 240 degree view acrylic tunnel within the 750,000 gallon Open Ocean exhibit and other realistically designed natural environments. That totally lifted my spirits and chased away my lassitude. We identified reef fishes we have snorkeled among, including my favorite yellow tangs, Jim's preference the pufferfish, and Hawaii's state fish, humuhumunukunukuapua'a, the reef triggerfish. What a wonderful mellifluous name!

Refreshed, we emerged into our normal non-watery environment and resumed our ride to a nearby park where I needed to rest. I thought *This goes well beyond what our daughters called malaise, ennui, languor.* Despite the pattern of feeling fine then suddenly fatigued during the rest of our vacation, we rode short distances and managed a challenging snorkel trip to Molokini, a small crescent-shaped island off the coast of Maui. We wore wetsuits as guards against the briskly cold waters as we searched for brilliantly colored tropical fish. Another reward—on our return to Maui, we experienced adrenaline-pumping joy as we sailed among a pod of humpback whales breaching within feet of our boat.

Our abbreviated bike rides were supplemented with scenic excursions in our rental car which helped dissipate the disappointment of not being able to bike as far and as long as we'd hoped into hidden corners of Maui. We admired windsurfers scudding across the waves and searched for migrating humpbacks along the coastline. We moseyed through Lahaina, always searching the skies, seas, forests and along beaches for life and color.

Patient Jim believed with time my weariness would dissipate and I'd soon regain my usual energy. I just wanted to know what was going on with my body. We would continue to wonder that very thing for the next six years.

BORTHWICK THE BEAUTIFUL

Christmas of 1987, Jim faced the conundrum of how to disguise an easily recognizable gift. He decided to put it in a humongous unadorned cardboard box and drag it into the living room before the gift opening began. He told me I needed to open that package first.

"Wheels! You bought me wheels!" I clutched one to my chest as Jim beamed. "Yeah. I had them built for you. They have Phil Wood hubs."

I put the wheel down and hugged him. "Thank you. This is super." I knew if Jim had wheels built with Phil Wood hubs, the best kind I knew of, a new custom bike would be the next step. What a spot-on Christmas gift.

Jim and I had been cycling seriously for a decade. We'd biked long distances and truly treasured our bicycles. Both of us plus several of our cycling friends had boosted Fuji's financial status by purchasing their bikes. When we rode together we'd listen to the hum of our wheels on the pavement and croon, "Fujis sing!"

One serious flaw interfered with my riding. I hadn't found a bicycle that truly fit my short legs-long torso body. We spoke with other cyclists, voraciously read every article in biking magazines regarding fitting a bike to a rider. After several years and periodic forays into bike shops to peruse new products, we discussed a custom bike for me. I asked Jim if he wanted one. He grinned, "No. I'm normal. I can buy a bike and it will fit me." Smart aleck.

Thus began the romance of the Borthwick. Jim had researched home-grown Iowa frame builders and found several with excellent reputations. Among them, a retired Lennox engineer-turned-bike-builder from Marshalltown, Gordon Borthwick. We had seen some of his tandems around Iowa City and had spoken with their satisfied owners. Gordon came to a Bicyclists of Iowa City (BIC) meeting and performed complimentary fittings for everyone who wanted to see if their present bikes fit their bodies. He had developed a device to take pertinent body measurements for the best fit: leg, arm and torso lengths and appropriate angles for comfortable and efficient road riding.

What a far cry from buying a bike for a kid and letting her ride it despite its size. No "Oh, she'll grow into it." Maybe, maybe not. In my case, I'd never grow into any of my former bikes and no commercial ones we knew of would work as well as we wanted either. Gordon confirmed Jim's Fuji America fit him perfectly, my bike did not. We made arrangements to see him at his home workshop.

Gordon remeasured me, checked results with those he'd taken at the BIC meeting, and we set about selecting what I needed and wanted. He admitted he had never built such a small bike.

He used chrome-moly steel, a standard frame material, because of its strength, toughness and weldability. We reviewed the various components I wanted including twenty-one gears. Jim had worked out the gear ratios he thought I needed, meaning the distance the wheel would go in one complete revolution. I mm-hmmed my way through the technical stuff we had already studied. I later learned I should have paid more attention to the gear ratio. What worked for Jim did not necessarily work for me since I would never be as strong-legged as he.

Then we turned to my favorite part—frame color. Gordon had a vast number of colors and finishes. I knew I wanted something in a berry color and, after a minimal amount of dithering, I chose a rich mulberry frame. Soon I'd have a bike that fit me plus granny gears for those tough climbs, and it would be gorgeous.

Jim and I hoped the bicycle would be ready for delivery in time for our spring break trip to Louisiana. That didn't happen, so undaunted, I took one last hurrah ride on my singing Fuji. When we ended up riding through hub-deep water as we neared Mississippi, I mentally thanked Gordon for not having my sparkling new Borthwick finished.

A month after we arrived home, Gordon called to say, "Your Borthwick's ready." She needed to come home. She bewitched me with her shining beauty and rode like a dream. A problem arose I hadn't contemplated—I couldn't ride her all the time so where should I store her? Jim gave the obvious answer, "In the garage."

"In the garage? No! I can't stand the idea of her being in the garage where she'll get dusty and possibly nicked." Brainstorm. "I'll keep her in the dining room. She'll be safe and clean there and she won't get bumped."

"In the dining room?"

"I'll put her next to the half-wall. She won't be in the way." Jim relented.

After each ride I'd wipe her off and roll her into the dining room where she spent her nights and eventually, winter seasons, propped against the wall. She looked rather nice there I thought. My family participated in unison eye-rolls.

🚲

Borthwick the Beautiful needed mulberry colored panniers to replace my old yellow-beginning-to-wear-out ones. We found some. They had a variety of pockets to keep gear easily accessible—that can make a difference to biking afflicted people.

Borthwick steadfastly maintained her position in the dining area of our country kitchen for many years. Even after we bought mountain bikes to ride at our Colorado condo, she had adventures from Hawaii to Alaska to Florida and states in between. Then the older I got, the more I needed even lower gears, gears my Trek mountain bike had.

Sadly, Borthwick got her first taste of the garage. She didn't seem to suffer but it didn't seem right. Soon she came back into the house to our family room where she became part of a stationary trainer where I exercised in the winter. When I joined a gym to participate in spin classes, I no longer climbed on her for my indoor riding.

She returned to the garage in an elevated position, hanging upside down from hooks, away from potential damage, but also out of action. I felt a bit guilty each time I looked at her. She looked lonely and unloved. Now that I can no longer ride outside, I think I'll bring her back into the family room where she and I can pedal more happy hours together. We have history, you know.

WOODS, PORTA-POTTIES AND OTHER JOYS

"Never pass up a pit-stop…" Jim's voice echoes in my ears, commanding us to adhere to this bicyclists' rule: *If there is an opportunity to use a restroom, whether you think you need to or not, use it. You will not always have one handy when nature calls.*

On our bicycle trips we welcomed the usual toilets found in campgrounds, picnic areas, fast food places, pubs, restaurants and gas stations. That is, unless they were dirty. Then we preferred using the great outdoors. When we used facilities in commercial establishments, we made sure to buy something to eat or drink. Occasionally that afforded us the by-product of discovering something like Henry Reinhard's Root Beer or rediscovering Cherry Bing candy from our childhoods.

Cyclists recognize the challenge is sometimes more difficult for females than males. Astute Iowa farmers along RAGBRAI routes catered to riders by slipping rolls of toilet paper on fence posts lining their corn fields. RAGBRAI founders insisted the ride be held the last full week in July when the corn would be tall enough for bikers to have privacy. However, there was no defense against the snap-happy photographers who waited to commemorate the occasion when the now-comfortable biker emerged from the green. Not quite the phantom baseball team from *Field of Dreams* but still photo archive-worthy.

Commercial names of portable latrines became familiar to us: KYBO (Keep Your Bowels Open); A King's Throne; Porta-John; Blue Moon Satellite; Call-A-Head; Action Services; and my personal favorite, Johnny On The Spot.

As Sandy, Dave, Jim and I returned home from our east to west California ride, we decided it would be prudent to make a list to help prepare for a future ride across Nevada's Highway 50, the Loneliest Road in the USA. Sandy diligently noted all the possible private-to-OK-if-everyone-else-faces-the-other-way potty possibilities. She mentioned culverts, steep ditches, real toilets, shrubs we dubbed potty bushes, and the rare tree. We kept the information and referred to it each day two years later. Ray, however, chose to disregard it and free-lanced. A voice from above startled him, "Hello down there." The culprit, Charles, our SAG driver, had been hiking in the hills when he spotted Ray and startled him.

During these trips, especially in Southern and Eastern states, we often stopped at tiny churches to rest, eat picnic lunches and use their outhouses. Wherever we cycled, we looked for easy access to woods, then carefully checked for poison ivy or oak, snakes and other critters. During these brief forays into the wild, we frequently raced out of our toilette, flailing wildly, attempting to outrun or shake off mosquitoes or gnats.

An Arizona frontage road ran parallel to the interstate and we excitedly anticipated using the rest area we had spotted. Then we saw the barbed wire fence. Sandy and I were always grateful for our farm kid experience in getting through/over/under barbed wire fences. We propped our bikes against the fence posts and carefully crawled under, moi, or over, the longer-legged folks, the wire separating us from our goal.

Imagine our surprise to find not just regular Porta-Potties, but handicap accessible ones along a highway near Alamagordo, New Mexico. Those for day laborers often sat on a corner of a field or orchard being picked, so we gratefully used them. Gastrointestinal upsets on the road are unhappy experiences. Something I ate in a little store just south of Alamosa, Colorado violently disagreed with me. A deep ditch complete with a culvert became my temporary sanctuary. My long ago Girl Scout leader training plus having had three children made sure I had tissues and Wet Ones.

Towns and businesses along some of our biking route around the Big Island of Hawaii were scarce. I finally reached the point where I'd have to cycle two miles down a hill to a resort or stop at a fire station we saw along the road to ask if I could use their lavatory. I called out, "Hello." An attractive young fireman answered and walked toward me. "I'm sorry to bother you but I am in dire need of a restroom. Would it be possible for me to use one here at your station?" That really wasn't allowed but he made an exception for this desperate woman. I was grateful. I made sure I didn't leave any water spots anywhere.

Ray had a flat as we biked toward San Diego on the PCH, Pacific Coast Highway. Dave decided this would be a propitious time to find a privy. All along Huntington State Beach there are shower and toilet facilities, but when he realized he wanted one, a gateless fence paralleled the highway. What to do? Instead of biking back another mile to an entrance, he decided to burrow…no, to scoop enough sand away to wriggle under the fence. A sequence of photos illustrated his superior technique. His riding companions resisted the temptation to fill in the hole he dug before he returned.

A small slant-roofed brown building in eastern Colorado provided our most fun outhouse experience. A shady patch of gravel, a rainbow hued Prairie Horizon Trail sign welcoming cyclists, plus the latrine proved irresistible. More delights awaited us. Someone had festooned the rustic interior with artificial climbing roses, signs and calendars. A room freshener and clean trash bag, in addition to toilet paper, made this an even more outstanding stop. To top it off, a notebook dangling on twine from a nail, was filled with comments cross-country cyclists had made about their adventures on this Trans-America Bicycling Trail. We added our note about riding across all fifty states.

Who knew a loo in rural Colorado would inspire this tale of hospitality on the High Plains?

COASTING CALIFORNIA'S COAST-PART 2-2011

Riders: Retha/Ray, Dave, Jim/Jan. Drivers: Riders and Jan's uncle, Chuck Adams. Distance: 572 miles minus landslide drive-arounds, plus Point Lobos to Ripplewood turn-off

Dave, Jim and I bundled into the bike-and-gear-packed-van in Iowa City. We drove through clear weather and foul including near white-out conditions in the Sierras. In Half-Moon Bay, after the usual unpacking of the van and cleaning all the road gunk off bikes, we repacked our panniers and put our traveling duds back in the van.

Again at Sam's Chowder House, nephews and niece, Jim Senal, Carl Couchman and Julie shared another scrumptious seafood dinner with us and caught us up on family news. We topped our delightful evening off with a melted chocolate cake dessert. Then back for more pannier readjustment. I discovered my much-loved panniers did not fit on my new back bike rack and scrambled to figure out what to do. With less clothing and other accoutrement, they became lowriders on the front rack. I had never considered that possible snafu.

The next day we did another car-van switch, leaving the van at my uncle and aunt's home; Chuck and Dorothy Adams lived in Pacific Grove where two days later they would host us. On our return to Half Moon Bay, we picked Retha and Ray up from the San Jose Airport, turned the rental car in and made last preparations for taking off in the morning.

HALF MOON BAY TO SANTA CRUZ BY BICYCLE 50 MILES

Gray sky, eucalyptus and cedar fragrances with an occasional barnyard whiff accompanied us today. Farms and ranches lined both sides of our route, we especially noted Sea Horse Ranch with its terrestrial version, not aquatic kind. Near San Gregorio, we rode a bit away from the ocean, protected from blowing sand by cuts in the hills. More precipitous hills than we had imagined faked us out and I felt tired, even though I was entertained by the gamut of colors we saw along the way—yellow, sage, gray, beige, sienna, blue, brown, rust.

We took a side trip to Pigeon Point Beach and anticipated lunch at the Pie Ranch. When we arrived, it was closed but we were allowed to use their picnic tables. We had read about the pies here so felt disappointed not to eat some. The owner and her children came out to talk to us and the children helped us get water as they waited for the school bus. The family began farming in 2004 and have added educational programs for local schools. We didn't have pie but enjoyed a pleasant stop.

A tailwind continued so the ride was infinitely easier than it might have been. Watching the smashing ocean breakers, the vivid scenery, and blue skies, we deemed it wonderful. Upon our arrival in Santa Cruz we went immediately to *Sprockets Bike Shop*. I walked in, a man eyed me and queried, "Rain hood?"

I responded, "Yes. Hi Phil." He smiled and acknowledged I'd remembered his name from our phone conversation. Before we left Iowa I'd called to ask if I could have a rain hood that I had ordered from *Adventure Cycling* delivered to his store. Jim and I bought new tail lights and a sweatband head covering thingie, a successful stop. A man we'd seen on the bike trail overheard our conversations and offered to lead us to our motel. We accepted.

We contacted nephew Carl who said he'd pick us up an hour later. One person climbed into the front seat with him and the other four of us piled, literally, into the back seat and drove off to Sam's, another Sam's but again with excellent food and ambiance on the wharf. Carl loves Santa Cruz and said he hoped that he and Julie could someday both work there. He agrees with the bumper sticker, *Keep Santa Cruz weird*. Neither Jim nor I had ever heard him in such a voluble state—it was fun listening to him discuss his beautiful black and white photography. He dropped us off at the motel and left to drive home to San Jose. A good day of biking, fun and family.

SANTA CRUZ TO PACIFIC GROVE 43 MILES

Rain. On with rain gear, then off when it stopped, leaving us spattered with dirty road water. The clearing day evolved into a pleasurable experience cycling along quiet back roads that edged veggie and strawberry fields. Castroville's large artichoke statue plus acres of the plants convinced us this indeed is the Artichoke Capital of the World. We ate a stand-up lunch at, what else, an artichoke stand. We purchased dried pineapples, juicy mandarins but none of the featured veggie. They would have been eye-catching ornaments for our handlebars, however.

Paved bike paths to Pacific Grove calmed our bodies, minds and souls as we rode beside drifted sand dunes trailing along the ocean. *Had they been designed by a landscape artist?* Tsunami zone signs prompted us to remember nature's dangerous foibles.

Jim and I reminisced about living in Fort Ord where he spent a year's internship in the US Army. We did not look for our former home high up on a hill or George Marshall School Mara had attended. The ice plant-covered hillsides made us remember Mara being dragged through such plants by Keith's dog Tiki. The stains never did come out.

While tootling through Monterey, we passed familiar sights of Old Monterey's historic buildings plus the lion water fountain at Dennis the Menace Park where our children loved to play. Next stop—a bike shop. The cassette on Jim's bike had worn out so he could not shift gears properly. He found a shop, bought and had the cassette installed while the rest of us wandered through the cascades of flowers among the golden adobe buildings constructed with rustic timber porticos.

We decided to take the longer, scenic and less hilly route to Chuck and Dorothy's home in Pacific Grove. We pedaled to Point Pinos Lighthouse, the longest continuously operating one on the West Coast. We all wondered how far the light could be seen since the tower seemed really short. Glorious seascapes and sounds thrilled us—Jim and I were finally bicycling along the Monterey coast we had once lived near, seen in photos and postcards for years. Reality check? We loved it.

Pacific Grove, established in 1875 by a group of Methodists, later boasted a Chautauqua, then became an artist's haven. Many streets are lined with ornate Victorian homes, but best of all, Monarch butterflies migrate two thousand miles from Canada to their breeding habitat within Pacific Grove neighborhoods, ergo the Butterfly Capital of the US. We've seen them other times when we visited here. In spring, they have gone but we got to see colorful gardens planted specifically to attract them.

On the way up yet another hill toward that day's destination, we met a young cyclist, a Topeak Cycling Gear representative. He had come to the area for the Sea Otter Classic Celebration of Cycling at Laguna Seca, which kicks off the road bike and mountain bike season. Jim and I showed him our well-used and much appreciated Topeak handlebar bags—that pleased him. Over the forty years since we lived in the area, when I thought of Laguna Seca race track, I didn't think of bicycle races. I thought of James Dean being killed as he drove toward the track where he planned to race his Porsche Spyder.

One last hill to our home for the night just about did me in. Exhaustion overwhelmed me and I thought I might not make it up the final rising curve to the house. Why? I asked myself.

As always with Chuck and Dorothy, we shared lots of laughter. Chuck, in character, regaled us with his yarns and Dorothy did an excellent straight woman routine, much to his and our delight.

Chuck decided Retha needed to be a member of his version of The Liars Club, saying she had all the qualifications. That consisted of laughing at his rambling narration, intently listening to his tales and poking fun at some of them. She became a proud member.

PACIFIC GROVE TO BIG SUR ABOUT 25 MILES FOR DAVE, JIM/JAN, 47 FOR RETHA/RAY

Dorothy prepared a perfect biker breakfast—delicious scrambled eggs, fruit and oatmeal. Later in the morning, Chuck joined in our ride by driving the van to Point Lobos to pick us up.

What a treat to cycle legendary 17-Mile Drive's exquisite shoreline. Spanish Beach, named for the explorers who camped there while looking for Monterey Bay, exposed us to a broad expanse of the sea, in contrast to the ancient-looking trees that cropped up along the route. Jim fondly recollected his memories of golfing through stormy fifty-five miles per hour winds at Pebble Beach. Despite being a perfect golfing day when he played Spyglass Hill, he deemed it to be the more difficult of the two. He never did get to play Cypress Point.

Harbor seal pups' sounds lured us but we could not see them. Their protected pupping area sported a high cloth fence which blocked everyone from peeking into their birthing grounds. Seal Rock gave us distant but full views of other marine mammals and the cacophony of barking seals and sea lions entertained us. So did great lumbersome elephant seals. Offshore, beguiling, sweet-faced sea otters back-floated, tethered to kelp, rocks at the ready on their chests to break open the shells of their favorite food, abalone.

The iconic 250-year-old Lone Cypress always evokes a sense of the place in us as do the coastal cliffs, beaches and bare sun-bleached ghost cypress trees. Someone said this tree is as representative of the Monterey Peninsula as the Eiffel Tower is to Paris or the Pyramids are to Egypt.

Bicycles? Where are your golf clubs?

We loved Carmel's whimsical, sometimes peculiar, houses juxtaposed to the otherwise beach-town atmosphere. They created a fairyland with their curved rooflines, round windows, and large shake roofs. Perfect blue sky and biking temperatures made the day even better. How we loved breathing fresh sea air.

We arrived at the many-fingered promontory of Point Lobos Reserve and went to Whaler's Beach where more harbor seal pups amused us. Small but mighty Whaler's Museum surprised me with all the information describing abalone fishing, whaling and processing. An unexpected exhibit included one of the first cheese presses for, what else? Monterey Jack cheese.

We pedaled to the area our family loved when we lived in Fort Ord: the walk past the witch's tree, around the peninsula to a solitary rock and the hollow tree. Jim and I shared memories of also being there eleven years earlier with our whole family after Julie and Carl's wedding. Grandsons Ryan and Cameron loved crawling into the hollow tree as much as our daughters had. We spotted sea otters at a distance but sadly couldn't spend the time to go down the rocky incline to our favorite tide pools. Our family thinks the Pacific coastal tide pools here are the best.

Jim, Dave and I biked to the entrance of Point Lobos to meet Chuck who brought our van, while Retha and Ray continued cycling to Big Sur. We loaded the bikes and drove Chuck back to Pacific Grove, told him and Dorothy our goodbyes and thank yous for a memorable and fun time. We did not know that would be the last time we would see him. To our great sadness, he died two years later.

Before we left home, we had heard about the landslides/landslips along coastal Highway 1 where we planned to ride. Chuck and niece Tamara provided more details and phone numbers for the California DOT, Highway Patrol and Sheriffs' departments. Using those we tried to keep apprised of conditions that might affect us as we progressed down the coast.

Plan A, simply using the van/rental car switch all the way, had to be scrapped because of another snafu. Landslips had occurred at the Bixby Bridge north of Big Sur, with a landslide at Limekiln south of Big Sur. So on to Plan B: Bike where we could, then drive the van the long way round on inland roads then back to Highway 1. One of the choices, which CHIPS, the California Highway Patrol, recommended included taking winding, unknown condition Nacimiento-Ferguson Road across Hunter-Liggett Military Reservation and past Father Sierra's Mission San Antonio.

Jim, Dave and I decided to take that more scenic route so asked a local how to get to the Nacimiento-Ferguson Road. He offered to guide us to it, another Good Neighbor Sam move. Veggie farming dominated the area until we entered the military base. An extraordinarily precipitous and narrow serpentine road delivered us to the Pacific. Jim navigated the hour and a half drive expertly, despite some other less than thoughtful drivers.

When we reached Highway 1, we turned north, back toward Carmel and Pacific Grove, through the Limekiln construction area, and oohed and aahed at the views we'd relish the next day on our bicycles. We arrived at our Ripplewood cottage just after Retha and Ray.

We listened raptly as they related their story: They arrived at the Bixby Bridge slip site about 2 PM but authorities only allowed people to cross at 7 AM and 4 PM to accommodate workers, school children, resorts buying food, etc. Hundreds of people had lined up to cross the one-half mile. Older or disabled people were ferried across on golf carts while others walked, pushed cartloads of groceries and goods or their bicycles. They described a scene that must have looked like refugees, this time from landslides. Retha and Ray reported biking steep climbs but speedy downhills away from the ocean and into the woods. They relished doing the ride at their pace.

Our accommodations, a lovely woodsy cabin with indoor facilities, had the important positive features of good beds and no bed-bugs. We ate locally and felt sympathy for business owners who suffer during times like this when tourists cannot easily get to their establishments.

🚲

BIG SUR TO SAN SIMEON, ABOUT 60 MILES, TRADE-OFF DRIVING VAN

Morning quickly plunked us at the bottom of a long arduous climb, fortunately the toughest of the twenty-five miles of hills that day. The vistas, one side roiling ocean and the other ancient forest, compelled us to repeatedly stop to absorb mouth-dropping sights and drink in our fill of nature's splendor. Fresh salty smell of the sea, sound of thumping rough surf, rocks carved into small caves and arches, spectacular waterfalls—what could possibly surpass Big Sur's consuming beauty?

The previous night we had learned of another landslide at appropriately named Ragged Point, between us and San Simeon. We kept asking people if they'd heard anything about road conditions—even CHIPS and the sheriff's office didn't, but said they'd find out and let us know. They did. The one hundred yards wide, several feet deep slide had been deemed impassible since it obliterated portions of the highway. We hoped we would be out of the slide area and that more torrential rains would not fall. We were grateful to not be stranded between two slide areas with no way to get the van out. That meant another trip over Nacimiento-Ferguson Road, this time being a first for Retha and Ray.

We were able to bike a while, then stopped in Lucia to load our bikes back on the rack after our considerably shorter ride, bought sandwiches and prepared for yet another trip over the coastal mountains. The store proprietor there told us, "Be careful going over the mountains. There's a big cattle truck coming over. Be careful for your safety and for the cattle—three of them are mine." We were careful and safe, thanks to Jim's driving skills. Back on inland Highway 101, we continued to Paso Robles, returned to the coast and Highway 1 and turned north to San Simeon and our seaside motel. Walking the beach placated our souls since we lacked much riding that day. None of us felt tempted by a tour of the glories of Hearst Castle whose owner had originally thought he'd build a comfortable bungalow on the hill at San Simeon.

⚲

SATURDAY, APRIL 16TH—RED LETTER DAY: DAVE'S 75TH BIRTHDAY 58 MILES, TRADE-OFF DRIVING VAN

Dave celebrated by not having to drive! As is common, we experienced early morning coastal marine layer, fog. Ray drove in the morning and I in the afternoon so I could go to a grocery store to get cakes for Dave's birthday and for Retha and Ray's eighteenth anniversary on Sunday. I chose a couple of cute little ones with a big 75 for Dave's special celebration.

A picnic lunch with a view of Morro Bay's iconic rock reminded me of family members who loved to go there to camp. The rock is a volcanic dome that towers more than 550 feet over the harbor and named by Juan Cabrillo during his voyage along the coast midway through the 1500s. While waiting for the others to arrive, I had fun people-watching on the pier, especially kids on the beach dancing in the cold water and gasping when a wave hit them.

Until this bike trip, I had hated being a SAG driver, I always wanted to be on my bike. Increasing feelings of exhaustion had plagued me repeatedly over the past few months and my energy had been zapped as we cycled the demanding ups of Highway 1. I always recovered to cycle on, but the *What is causing this?* question nagged me.

When I stopped for the cyclists at a corner fruit-veggie stand, we ate strawberries— enormous, succulent, flavorful organic strawberries purchased by the Birthday Boy and shared with the rest of us. And after we ate dinner that evening, a personality plus server brought Dave, Retha and Ray a strawberry whipped cream dessert. Then we returned to our room for the birthday cake surprise—dessert after dessert is a bit much, even on one's seventy-fifth birthday. Did we toddle to our bikes in the morning?

⚲

PISMO BEACH TO LOMPOC ANOTHER RED LETTER DAY-RETHA AND RAY'S 18TH ANNIVERSARY 47 MILES TRADE OFF DRIVING VAN

Beautiful corduroy fields and straight evenly-spaced furrows of rich dark soil limned our early morning route. All stages of prepping soil, planting and harvesting took place concurrently. From a distance, plastic-covered fields resembled snow-blanketed hills, close up we found those same fields with green poking out leaf lettuce, kale, and cauliflower. Despite the pleasant eucalyptus and cedar lined roads, farms and small towns looked dusty and tired. Guadalupe, however, had spruced up its downtown, store fronts and churches with paint and flowers to make it look inviting.

I loved the long whiz-bang downhill as we careened past flowering fields into Lompoc where we stayed for the night.

⚲

LOMPOC TO SANTA BARBARA 58 MILES, TRADE OFF DRIVING VAN

Brown and green rolling hills formed the background for vineyards in the Lompoc-Vandenberg Air Force Base area. Our route flowed from quiet-away-from-traffic to paralleling the roaring ocean and a railroad track. Tall cliffs lined the highway along Refugio and El Capitan Beaches and names like Gaviota and Goleta became familiar to us.

We arrived in Santa Barbara where two climates and various currents converge. The southern-coursing Pacific currents push away from land making rougher seas, while higher winds and fogs come from the north. Milder weather with warmer currents prevailed as we traveled south. Rockier earth suited ranging livestock; chaparral and pines evolved into more fertile, rich soil perfect for avocados, citrus and palm trees in the more temperate climate.

We registered into our motel and walked to Stearns Wharf to check out this once longest deep-water pier in California. Mostly restaurants and shops, the pier has its share of people fishing, strolling, and enjoying the pleasant ocean and Santa Ynez Mountain views. We biked to red-tile roofed Spanish architecture Santa Barbara Mission, the Queen of the Missions. Adjacent to it, Mission Historical Park is graced by a Memorial Rose Garden with 1500 rose plants. It also includes a thoughtful addition of a fragrance garden for the blind. What I guess is called southern California coastal architecture combines Spanish, Moorish, Mediterranean features, such as the red-tile roofs and light stucco walls, similar to my mother's simpler southern California home.

One highlight of our visit—friend Nellie Weber's delightful daughter Sabra and energetic grandson Trystan joined us for dinner. Sabra, a long-time friend of Sandy and Dave also had been Jim's patient. The following day, Jim and Dave did the van-car switch and drove to Imperial Beach on the Mexican Border. While Ray explored Santa Barbara by bicycle. Retha and I had long conversations. The time spent sharing our faith, personal histories, and whatever came into our minds became a pivotal point in our friendship, going far beyond simply bicycling together.

When the guys returned all five of us had the joy of biking the rest of the way together.

SANTA BARBARA TO MALIBU 66 MILES, ALL RIDE!

Cycling along the winding roads provided more ocean-viewing pleasures. We thought biking into Malibu was fun, especially on the bike lanes, and seeing the striking hillside Pepperdine University campus with its fantastic view of the Pacific.

MALIBU VIA LOS ANGELES TO LONG BEACH AND GLENDA'S HOUSE ABOUT 50 MILES

We had planned carefully for this day. Jim had meticulously selected the bicycle routes that would keep us away from heavily trafficked areas as much as possible. Nearly the whole way to Long Beach would be on paved recreational trails and we wanted to make sure we did not have to bike extra miles by missing a turn.

Immediately, we encountered the hallmarks of Malibu's garbage pickup day. Plopped in the middle of the bike lanes were dozens and dozens of filled trashcans. Where they were not, cars had parked straddling the bike lanes. So much for safely cycling through this extended stretched-along-the-highway burg. But bougainvilleas galore brought sparks of beauty and helped quash the sour odor of garbage in the sun.

Happiness was getting out of town. Added happiness? In Pacific Palisades, we easily connected with The Strand, a paved shoreline path that begins at Will Rogers State Beach, with its south end at Torrance County Beach. We arrived in Santa Monica where glistening sand enticed us to roll our bikes off the path, sink our toes into warm sand and watch some beach volleyball. This huge area of open beach, pocked with tall palm trees, led to the fabled Santa Monica pier. One of the popular activities is to walk to the end of the pier to watch the waves roll in from the Pacific. We joined in.

Of great interest to us, this environmentally active community has developed an urban runoff facility that catches and treats millions of gallons of water every week and then sells it to grey water users. They have set a goal of attaining 100 percent water independence and encourage bicycles as transportation. We helped with that last part.

Retha and Ray with the Queen Mary

388

As we passed Venice's Muscle Beach, I related a story about friend Jim Fredrickson whose legs had been paralyzed by polio in his teenage years. As a patient at a nearby rehabilitation center, he had to have special treatments. One day he and his aide arrived in Muscle Beach just as some testosterone-driven arrogant young males exhibited their rope climbing prowess. Helped out of his wheelchair by his aide, Jim, paralyzed legs dangling, quickly shinnied up the rope and back down again, was assisted to his wheelchair and pushed through the sand to the car. The young men stood there, mouths agape.

Unlike other piers we've seen, on Venice's Fishing Pier we saw mostly fishermen and seagulls. The rest of the way to Glenda's, we encountered more people walking, running, rollerblading, skateboarding, a wonderful atmosphere on these well-used paths.

Once we left Santa Monica we began to feel more and more secure in how well the day could go. The trail with its bike friendly signs turned inland and maneuvered around thousands of boats docked in Marina del Rey, the world's biggest man-made small craft harbor—the world's largest boat garage. We biked a narrow jetty toward the ocean, admired the wetlands and followed the beach through seaside towns. As we wound our way into Palos Verdes, the route gave way to designated bike lanes along streets, followed the road around the peninsula, climbed, rolled and eventually descended into San Pedro. We pedaled the Los Angeles River Bike Trail too, going around the Port of Los Angeles into Long Beach's port area.

We rode on the levees along the Los Angeles River, skirted parks and playgrounds and schools. As we pedaled through the Los Cerritos Wetlands, part of many marshes, lagoons, sloughs and estuaries in the area, we had to remind ourselves we were cycling through an enormous metropolitan area. It didn't seem like it. Eventually we reached Terminal Island in Long Beach. From that point on, Jim thought it took us forever to get to Glenda's house. We rode through parks along Queen's Way near the docked Queen Mary, a floating museum and hotel and a fun place to stay with a family. We discovered that one Christmas when our grandsons played swashbuckling pirates on every deck they were allowed on.

In Bluff Park, another Lone Sailor statue, identical to the one we saw near the Golden Gate Bridge, looks out to the Astronaut Islands. Each of the four islands is named after a space explorer killed on a mission; they are actually oil platforms cleverly camouflaged with tall buildings covering drilling platforms. A few feet away from this Lone Sailor is Keith's memorial bench. His death left Glenda a widow and Julie and Tamara fatherless, but with incredible loving memories of him and the adventures they shared. Glenda, Jim and I make a little pilgrimage to his bench whenever we visit her. We sat on it, contemplated his life and ours, the view of the Pacific Ocean he loved so much, miss his physical presence and often have a picnic. We bikers shared a few moments there before continuing on.

Glenda greeted us with hugs and a warm welcome. We congregated in her backyard, unwinding in comfortable lawn chairs, admiring her aged but still bearing fruit Meyer lemon tree. After we refreshed ourselves with showers, Puppy Rosie, Glenda's rescue treasure, entertained all of us with her kisses and lap-cuddles. Lady Rosie, Glenda's friend who had chanced upon lost Puppy Rosie and brought her to Glenda's loving home, was a caterer so prepared a marvelous picnic for us. We ate until we could barely move, relishing the smells, colors and flavors of fresh food prepared with love and shared with people we love.

After an evening of delightful conversation and Glenda's hospitality, our yawns convinced us we needed sleep. Jim and I stayed with Glenda while the other bikers slept in Lady Rosie's RV.

LONG BEACH TO OCEANSIDE ABOUT 60 MILES

Glenda, with Puppy Rosie's assistance as official hostess, served an early morning breakfast. Being with Glenda is always special and leaving after such a short time was teary for me. But off we rode toward San Diego. Fortunately, Jim and I had driven the initial stages of this route frequently so managed to get us through the traffic, across a marina and to the PCH, the Pacific Coast Highway. Long Beach, like other Pacific coastal villages and cities, faces the phenomenon of morning fog, called May Gray or June Gloom. No foggy term rhymed with April so we just had a modicum of April fog.

We scooted past Seal Beach Naval Weapons Station and came to Bolsa Chica Ecological Reserve which we've always called the wildlife sanctuary. It is among the many marshes, bogs, lagoons, sloughs and estuaries in the area that serve as spawning ground plus nursery for ocean and shellfish. Migratory birds abound, and importantly, the plants here produce enormous quantities of oxygen.

Across from it, Ray's bike had another unwelcome flat, the only kind there is. Dave decided while it was being fixed, he would find a privy, which engendered the story of his escapade in "Woods, Porta-potties and Other Joys."

Riotously painted houses and apartments sometimes separated us from the ocean beach view we preferred, but wetlands and marinas on the other side kept nature in our focus. Cycling through commercial areas tested our riding and reaction skills dodging traffic, but we relaxed at flower-be-decked entrances to private communities and crunched the munchies we'd packed.

The watery world of Newport Beach, Corona Del Mar and Laguna Beach accompanied us all the way to the border. Although we couldn't always see the ocean, we could feel its presence—sand, beach, fog, roar, salty air, beach-goers, surfboards, pelicans. The pelicans amazed us by flying in undeviating lines instead of the usual hodge-podge, plummeting together yet staying in their straight-line formation. Better than we did as cyclists.

We could only hear the traffic on PCH so the mostly parallel bicycle path made an incredible difference in our feelings of safety, and we were closer to the sea. Dana Point sported an artificial breakwater and a manmade island while San Onofre Beach featured domed nuclear reactors which were subsequently shut down four years later due to safety issues.

Oceanside with its picturesque palm-lined pier that charms photographers, became our overnight stop .

⚲

OCEANSIDE TO TRAIL'S END 63 MILES

Carlsbad is known for its beaches and LEGOLAND, Encinitas for surfing, think Beach Boys and *Surfin' USA* and its beach culture. We didn't participate in any of them. We just kept pedaling to our own internal beach songs.

When we arrived in Del Mar, I gave a sigh of relief. This was an area I knew fairly well because of being a Route Safety crew member on my bicycle for several Susan G. Koman 3-Day Breast Cancer Walks in San Diego. But this time I was carrying more than sunscreen, rain jacket and water so it felt different even as we sailed down the same hills and puffed up some more.

The area named for the rare Torrey pine that grows in the wild along this coastline was super-familiar. The climb from the beach to the Torrey Pines Golf Course did not present the same challenge this time because we stayed on Carmel Valley Road instead of following on a dirt path up precipitous Torrey Pines Hill within the State Reserve. What a relief. During the 3-Day events, I had always been afraid I'd have to give up. I didn't want to do that—I wanted to inspire the walkers by showing that a nearly 70 year-old woman could pedal that killer of a hill. I was encouraged by hearing them root for me.

There were no cheering crowds on the road except for our group. We all made it. The rest of our time in San Diego would be downhill or flat, except of course, for the odd hill that got in the way. What I looked forward to next was the boardwalk on two-mile Mission Beach, another part of the 3-Day Walk. The route along the ocean with homes and businesses on the other side brought back many memories to me. I had loved patrolling there, greeting and cheering for the walkers, making sure their spirits were up, watching the skaters, boogie boarders, beach volleyball games and children playing in the sand. The boardwalk was also where a 3-Day photo of me was taken for the San Diego paper after a rainstorm. My bike was decorated with flowers and I wore a flower bedecked helmet, ribbons trailing, bright yellow rain cape flowing in the breeze. Great memories.

Biking through this picturesque city was a delightful experience, especially the time spent next to the sea. We stopped to snack and see where we had come from, where we would go and the surrounding seascape of boats, harbors and seaside parks and condos. We edged along the airport, the Naval Base and through Chula Vista where we turned toward Imperial Beach and the Silver Strand Boulevard a couple of miles from the Mexican border.

We spotted the Imperial Beach United Methodist Church where our van waited for us. We thanked the pastor and church personnel for van-sitting and went by van to San Diego for our overnight.

Was it possible this adventure was over? As with many bicycle trips, this one seemed anticlimactic. Jim and I had pedaled a continuous route from Canada through Washington, Oregon and California in four different sections from 1983 to 2011. Of course, there were slight interruptions such as the mudslides in California which compelled us to not pedal some miles. We had done it in high spirits and felt good about it. But as with so many really wonderful experiences, we wanted more.

Early in the morning, Retha and Ray left from San Diego Airport, Dave, Jim and I headed for Iowa City by van.

We didn't know it then but that would be our group's last long-distance ride together. Jim and I were happy with what we had accomplished and hoped I would eventually write about it. Although it was not by bicycle we did not stop moving and traveling. With Habitat for Humanity we helped build houses in twenty countries and other hiking and travel adventures took us to over fifty others. Life was good and bicycling had made it even better.

⚲

But things happen, unexpected and sometimes tragic. Years later, on a bright spring day in early May Sandy called us. Dave had been struck from behind while riding his bicycle and died immediately. Sandy's and many other hearts broke that day but memories of him sustain us. We will remember.

In memory of our much-loved friend, Dave Schuldt
April 16, 1936-May 6, 2019
We miss his companionship, his joy in God's creation,
his sense of justice, his gift of singing, and his willingness
to always be ready for a bike ride.

⚲

IN RETROSPECT...

When I reflect on our years of cycling across the fifty states and in other countries, the continuum amazes me. From the first throes of *Should we?* and *How do we do this?* I am filled with wonder at the fact we did it. Opportunities arose and we seized them. Once Jim and I had rid ourselves of malaise and plunged into the active, a different focus stimulated and altered the direction and parameters of the rest of our lives. New doors opened and inspired us to more fully understand this basic fact: our time on earth is limited, and if we are really going to participate in life, we'd better get at it.

We knew how to ride bicycles but had so much more to learn. We winged it, absorbed lessons from others and forged on, as little biking ventures morphed into adventures. With hope and determination we challenged ourselves to attempt more than I had ever expected, bit off huge chunks of excitement and managed to survive and thrive.

I learned biking extended well beyond the physical act of pushing pedals and moving forward. Complex spiritual and emotional aspects of it took root and deepened. Cycling became times of discovery, remembrance, introspection and growth, totally interconnected with my journey of life, real off-the-road life.

Decades after our original foray across Iowa, I've been off my bike for several years. Health issues have taken the forefront and at times stymied me and the doctors. Fatigue and breathlessness pounced on me whenever I biked or even walked.* I miss riding, but not as much as I thought I would—writing this book inspired me as I remembered our pedaling times. Memories burbled to the surface, some poignant, others joy-filled, waiting to be captured. For those of us fortunate and healthy enough to have been there, these are treasured memories.

From the dreams of a little farm girl who always wanted to see what was on the other side of the hill, to a little girl in a grown up body trying to capture that same dream, I continue to grow and wonder. In the years left of my life on earth, what else is on the other side of the next hill? I plan and hope to find out.

*Good news: In 2015 Mayo Clinic doctors diagnosed me with a heart condition called cardiac amyloidosis. At last, the unknown had a name. In 2018 I participated in a clinical trial for a drug now approved by the Federal Drug Administration. It won't cure me, but I feel joy to have been part of the study which will not only help other people, but has given me the positive results of less fatigue and more energy too. Now in 2021, I'm happy to be in another clinical drug trial. This drug too, may help future patients and maybe me too, to be more fully in the life we once knew. Blessings and hope abound.

MORE ROADSIDE ATTRACTIONS

RAGBRAI Ritual: Our gang dips their wheels in the Mississippi

We're doing what? Mara, Jan, Tania, Jennifer at Battle of Saratoga site

394

Mara, Tania, Jennifer and Jan weathering the New York rain in their new rain jackets

Jan, Betty, Cara and Connie drift along a Wisconsin backroad

Does this sign apply to us?

Apparently not

396

Corn fields and oat shocks in Ohio remind Jan of her childhood.

Alongside another mountain lake

Northern Michigan downhill

Colorado Cooperation

Jan, Sandy and Dave are enveloped in Alaska's glory

Lunchtime!

On the Oregon Coast

Jan Going to the Sun

Jan and Jim on the Katy Trail alongside the Missouri River

Jim and lonely windmill in Western Nebraska

Jim and Jan among Arizona saguaros

Dave memorializes The Loneliest Road in America

Looking to the next pass

Jan, Retha, Dave and Ray along the California coast

405

Jennifer, Bernd and Jan eat their *sandwiches* on the Oregon coast

Ray, Jan, Retha, Dave and Jim on their last long-distance ride together

IN GRATITUDE

A big thank you to all those who heard our biking tales and said, "You should write a book." Those words echoed in my brain for many years, encouraging me to keep writing no matter how long it took.

A special thank you for our fellow riders and forever friends: the intrepid Sandy and Dave Schuldt, who bicycled thousands of miles with us through trying times and good, remaining our dear friends; Connie and John Carlson whose biking adventures prompted us to plan to ride long distances, and then happily joined us; Retha and Ray Haas who lent their youthful verve, spiritual maturity and friendship; Betty Oglesby who rode many of our early trips with us and whose positive spirit enlivened ours; Vicki Burketta whose challenges and zest, including knee surgery, became part of the life of the rides.

My thanks to the wonderfully supportive members of University Club Writers whose motto is Ruthlessly Kind. They live that phrase which has been instrumental in my ability to keep writing and sharing what I wrote with others. Their wisdom, encouragement, joy and laughter not only made me a better writer but a better person. Thank you as well to my Tree House Writers friends Maxine Carlson and Donna Behlke who listen carefully, support and help me grow.

I am grateful for my dear friend and editor Jan Abramowitz, for her patience, perseverance and her promises that we would survive this book.

A special thanks to our daughter Tania, who with her kind but unerring eye, kept me on a clearer and better writing path. However, neither she nor anyone else is responsible for any errors you may find. I created them all by myself.

To my publisher Steve Semken who unblinkingly took a chance on me. Thank you for your patience and guidance.

To map-maker extraordinaire Russell Frazier, the maps you designed helped make our rides more vivid. Thank you.

I appreciate and thank all the Readers who helped put different eyes on what I had written and asked questions I hadn't considered: Jan Abramowitz, Ethel Barker, Suzee Branch, Tania Down, Retha Haas, Ray Haas, Mary Humston, Dan Nidey and Sandra Schuldt.

To my loving family, you have all blessed me more than you know. Tania, Mara, Doug, Jennifer and Bernd, you have always encouraged and inspired me, I thank you for being who you are. Your love and words make me wiser and braver. Grandsons Ryan and Cameron, you have no idea how you emboldened me to do more in my life because I wanted you to be proud of me. To Pri, our new granddaughter, thank you for cheering me on. I love you all so much.

Reaffirming the fact that "Jim's dreams became my own," I owe him extra thanks. He always thought I could do this—both bike and write. He helped remember our bicycle excursions, sometimes differently than I did, but after some coaching, he began to say, "This is your book. Say it the way you remember it." Thank you for all you bring to our lives, dear amazing Love of my Life.

ABOUT THE AUTHOR

Jan Down is an Iowa native who began her formal education in a one-room school house. A retired teacher, she still loves learning and helping others learn through sharing experiences. As an avid volunteer for Habitat for Humanity, Jan has helped people in twenty foreign countries build their homes, with the wonderful benefit of gaining so much more than she could ever give.

She lives with her husband in Iowa City, Iowa where she continues her volunteer work at her church and in her community. This book chronicles their extraordinary adventure of bicycling across every state in our nation. Her descriptive narration delivers a vicarious and enjoyable vacation to the reader. Enjoy the ride!